T5-DIJ-667

Prentice-Hall, Inc.
Englewood Cliffs, NJ 07632

Holley Ulbrich

Clemson University

International
Trade
and
Finance

Theory and Policy

Library of Congress Cataloging in Publication Data

ULBRICH, HOLLEY H.
  International trade and finance.

  Includes bibliographies and index.
  1. Commerce.   2. International finance.   I. Title.
HF1411.U42 1983   382   82-16605
ISBN 0-13-473959-0

Editorial/production supervision
  and interior design: *Steve Young*
Cover design: Ben Santora
Manufacturing buyer: *Ed O'Dougherty*

Printed in the United States of America

10 9 8 7 6 5 4 3 2 1

ISBN 0-13-473959-0

Prentice-Hall International, Inc., *London*
Prentice-Hall of Australia Pty. Limited, *Sydney*
Editora Prentice-Hall do Brasil, Ltda., *Rio de Janeiro*
Prentice-Hall Canada Inc., *Toronto*
Prentice-Hall of India Private Limited, *New Delhi*
Prentice-Hall of Japan, Inc., *Tokyo*
Prentice-Hall of Southeast Asia Pte. Ltd., *Singapore*
Whitehall Books Limited, *Wellington, New Zealand*

To my students

Contents

PART 1
The Setting

1   Introduction

Why Study International Economics?, 3   How International Trade Differs from Domestic Trade, 5 How Trade Theory Developed, 8   Economics and Politics: Interactions, 9   Key Terms, 10   Review Questions, 11   Suggested Readings, 11

2   Trade and the Domestic Economy

The Volume, Composition, and Direction of Trade, 12 Trade and the Macroeconomy, 15   Trade and the Microeconomy, 26   Summary, 30   Key Terms, 30 Review Questions, 31   Suggested Readings, 31 Appendix: Review of Indifference Analysis, 32

PART 2
The Microeconomics of Trade   35

List of Tables

List of Figures

Preface

This book grows out of 13 years of teaching international economics, mostly to undergraduate economics and business majors at Clemson University. This is an effort to provide a text that they can read, understand, enjoy, and apply to the international events around them. The theory is presented in graphic and intuitive form as much as possible with minimal use of mathematics, and there is emphasis on history, institutions, and policy. Appendices offer either extensions that some instructors may choose to omit or background that some students may not have, for example, the derivation of the *IS-LM* curves. Most of the students in the course I have taught have had intermediate macroeconomic theory, and all have taken intermediate microeconomic theory, but the book allows for the possibility of only the two-semester principles sequence as background. Every effort is made to integrate the as yet incompletely synthesized monetarist and traditional approaches in the international finance area.

Those to whom I am indebted are countless, and most are former students whose questions, problems, and term projects were the inspiration for a text that reflects their needs and concerns. I am grateful to Ralph Byrns, Stephen Reynolds, and Myles Wallace for numerous helpful comments and suggestions; to Immanuel Wexler, who first sparked my interest in international economics; to Dianne Haselton and Jolene Walker for meticulous typing through many corrections; to my colleagues at Clemson University who were sounding boards on my questions and uncertainties; and most of all, to my family, who put up with many hours of my working on the book when they would have preferred that I be otherwise occupied.

Holley Ulbrich
Clemson University

PART 1

The

Setting

The first two chapters of this book establish the framework in which we examine the microeconomics of international trade and the macroeconomics of international finance. This framework is a mixture of theoretical, historical, institutional, and political considerations. Since the two "pieces" of international economics are extremely interdependent, it is necessary to establish some overview of both parts of the international picture at the outset, before we consider them separately in Parts 2 and 3.

International trade determines the composition of the flow of exports and imports, the relative prices, the international investment decisions, and the choice of a commercial policy mix. The sum total of these decisions determines the balance of payments, or the supply and demand for foreign exchange, which in turn determines an equilibrium exchange rate. Changes in that exchange rate in turn affect all those microeconomic decisions with which we began.

Thus, teaching trade first leaves out the necessary monetary context, while teaching international finance first omits the underlying purpose of international financial arrangements, which is to facilitate efficient international resource allocation through trade and resource movements. A general framework that presents the interrelatedness of the two topics is an uneasy compromise with the circular nature of the subject at hand.

Chapter 1 considers the general statistical picture of trade, the historical development of trade theory, and the relationship between international economics and international politics. Chapter 2 establishes a theoretical context by looking at how trade fits into the microeconomy (comparative advantage) and the macroeconomy (macroeconomic models with a foreign sector).

CHAPTER 1

Introduction

WHY STUDY INTERNATIONAL ECONOMICS?

Most Americans perceive international trade as a remote and esoteric subject, but it touches each of us every day. Imagine a breakfast without international trade! No coffee, no tea, no hot chocolate, no bananas. As you drive to work in your Japanese compact car on French tires or pedal your Japanese or French ten-speed, chances are good that you will pass one or more multinational firms. IBM, Ford, General Electric, and most other major U.S. corporations (including the fast-food outlet where you may eat lunch) have affiliates all over the world. Phillips Petroleum, Norelco, Nestlé, Shell, and Michelin are just a few of the well-known foreign corporations with American operations. Most students encounter a few foreign-born professors and have foreign classmates. Chances are that someone in your own family was born abroad within the last few generations. Your Bic pen is French, your television set is likely to be Japanese, and the gasoline in your car is probably from an OPEC nation. If you are a fan of the Public Broadcasting System, you probably watch a lot of programs produced in Great Britain. Your overseas counterparts are using American calculators, eating American wheat, and watching American movies.

How important is trade to us? In relative terms, it is more important than it used to be, but it is still relatively modest. Only about 13 percent of our GNP consists of exports; a similar percentage of our total spending was

TABLE 1-1 Selected Imports and Exports as a Percentage of the U.S. Market in 1976

Industry	Exports as a Percentage of Output	Industry	Imports as a Percentage of New Supply
Wheat	66%	Crude rubber	100%
Oilfield machinery	63	Diamonds	100
Missiles, space vehicles	62	Bauxite	94
Milled rice	58	Crude petroleum	53
Medicinals, botanicals	47	Motorcycles, bicycles, and parts	51
Construction machinery	43	Finfish, shellfish	47
Aircraft	41	Potash	47
Corn	39	Raincoats	47
Soybeans	38	Zinc	47
Tobacco	37	Radios and TVs	43
Pulpmill products[1]	35	Iron ore	39
Solid-state semiconductor devices	34	Pulpmill products[1]	33
		Watches and clocks	32
Turbines	32		
Cotton farm products	29	Textile machinery[1]	30
Textile machinery[1]	28	Sugar	29
Electronic computing machinery	26	Women's shoes	27
		Passenger cars	20
Industrial trucks, tractors	20		

[1] Note that textile machinery and pulpmill products are significant on both sides of the international market.

Source: U.S. Department of Commerce, Bureau of the Census, *U.S. Commodity Exports and Imports as Related to Output, 1976 and 1975* (Washington, D.C.: Government Printing Office, 1980), pp. 1–4.

on imported goods in 1980. But that number masks its importance in particular products and industries. Exports were an important market (more than 20 percent of sales) for 32 four-digit industries[1] in 1976, while imports were a significant source of new supply (and often competition!) in 30 such industries that year. Some of the industries for which trade is significant are listed in Table 1-1. And, of course, trade is significant in absolute amounts. Thirteen percent of 1980 GNP may not sound impressive until you consider that this meant $345 billion of exports and $334 billion of imports that year—sums larger than the GNPs of all but a few nations.

Finally, trade is of critical importance in certain products, particularly tropical foodstuffs, oil, and various minerals and other raw materials for which most of what we consume is imported. Some of these also appear in Table 1-1.

Even if trade is important in absolute amounts to certain industries and

[1] "Four digit industry" refers to the 400 identifiable industries in the U.S. Department of Commerce's Standard Industrial Classification.

4

in particular products, you might still wonder why there is a separate course in international trade. Is not international trade, like domestic trade, governed by the laws of supply and demand, by the hope of profits and the fear of losses, by calculations at the margin, and, in general, by all the principles that one learns in microeconomics? How is international trade different?

There are two answers to this question. The first is found in the special institutions surrounding international trade and the political issues that emerge when individuals trade across national boundaries. The second lies in some special analytical tools of trade that developed to deal with the general equilibrium problems so important in this field.

HOW INTERNATIONAL TRADE DIFFERS FROM DOMESTIC TRADE

Trade between an American and a Mexican is different from trade between a New Yorker and a Floridian because nationals of different countries confront differences in legal, cultural, and economic frameworks. Policies of national governments influence many aspects of economic life up to the country's borders (and from 3 to 200 nautical miles beyond, depending on whose definition of coastal boundaries is used). The most obvious differences between domestic and foreign trade lie in differences in *currencies* and languages and in the existence of *tariffs*. But a firm or individual considering a foreign location for a plant or a job (which is also part of international trade) would also be interested in considering such country-to-country variations as differences in income taxes, unemployment compensation, social welfare programs, investment regulations, environmental restrictions, and safety standards, all of which also are expressions of *national sovereignty*.

Institutional Differences

Currency is the most visible difference between domestic and foreign trade. If all countries used a single currency, international trade would be greatly simplified. Why is there no single multinational currency? The main reason is that one of the most fundamental powers of a national government is the authority to issue its own money. If, for example, the United States provided all the world's money, Americans could use inflationary policies to transfer real resources from the rest of the world to themselves. Naturally, the leaders and citizens of other countries would resent this privilege. When the dollar served as the key international currency from 1950 to 1971, this was exactly what happened. How and why this occurred is described in Part 3 of this book.

An alternative solution to the problem of different currencies is to have them exchanged at fixed ratios; for example, one American dollar might always be equal to five French francs. This has also been tried and found unacceptable, for reasons that are also explained in Part 3. When exchange rates are not fixed, as has been true since 1973, and an American signs a contract to buy something from France or Mexico, someone bears an exchange risk. For example, if the contract is established in dollars, the foreign firm does not know how many pesos or francs it will receive at the time of payment. Ways of using the market system to deal with this risk are discussed in Chapter 13, but the point here is that the existence of exchange rate risk complicates foreign trade and makes it less certain than domestic trade. Other things being equal, traders will give preference to domestic suppliers and customers who create no currency trading problems.

Language is part of a broader problem of information and communication. While economists often assume perfect competition for analytical purposes, no markets—domestic or foreign—function perfectly. *Transactions costs*, defined broadly to include transport costs and information costs, keep the same product from selling at the same price in all markets. Sometimes markets within countries are separated more effectively from each other than are markets in different countries. For example, there is probably more trade between Quebec and New York than between New York and Oregon. But, in general, national borders segment markets because of the special barriers imposed by higher transport and transactions costs and by a significantly weaker transmission of market information, partly because of language but also for other reasons. This, too, makes international trade different from domestic trade.

Tariffs, quotas, and other intentional barriers to trade are another source of difference. Most countries allow goods and services to flow freely from one section of the country to another. The U.S. Constitution specifically forbids states to impose restrictions on interstate trade. But every country imposes such restrictions on trade from abroad, not only on goods and services but also on labor and capital. The arguments for and against these restrictions and the effects of tariffs and quotas are central concerns of the microeconomics of trade, which is the subject matter of Part 2.

Another respect in which international trade differs from domestic trade is in the ways different domestic laws and institutions that were designed for internal policy purposes have unintended effects on the volume and composition of trade. Differing welfare programs, employment regulations, and educational or training facilities influence the demand and supply of labor and the relative prices of the goods labor produces. Environmental restrictions, investment laws, capital market regulations, and tax laws affect the inflow and outflow of capital, while health and safety standards, systems of weights and measures, labeling requirements, and other product specifications influence the flow of goods and services across national boundaries.

These types of interference, deliberate and otherwise, are discussed in Chapters 6 through 8.

Finally, domestic monetary and fiscal policies affect international trade through their impact on prices, interest rates, and income. Income is an important determinant of imports, whereas prices affect both exports and imports, and interest rate differentials are important in determining capital flows. The influence of macroeconomic policy on trade introduced in Chapter 2 is examined in greater detail in Chapters 14 and 15.

In summary, trade between countries is subject to special problems and limitations because of different currencies, transaction and information costs (including language), tariffs and quotas, domestic laws and institutions, and independent monetary and fiscal policies.

Analytical Differences

International trade and finance use many of the traditional tools of microeconomics and macroeconomics. Tariffs, quotas, and exchange rates are normally discussed within a supply and demand framework. *Comparative advantage* can be illustrated with production possibilities curves, familiar to most people from the principles course, and consumption indifference maps, which are usually taught in intermediate microeconomics and which are explained briefly in the appendix to Chapter 2. The effects of trade on the level of economic activity are usually analyzed with such traditional macroeconomic models as *IS-LM* (presented in an appendix to Chapter 14 for those unfamiliar with this technique). However, there are a few additional analytical concepts and tools used mainly in international economics. In general, these concepts and tools stem from the fact that international trade focuses more heavily on exchange than on production and consumption and also that there is more emphasis on *general equilibrium* than in other courses that apply microeconomic and macroeconomic theory to special topics. General equilibrium in microeconomics means that we consider aggregates of suppliers and demanders simultaneously to determine the prices and quantities of everything being traded. If that sounds complicated, it is; but usually we simplify the problem to consider only two countries and two commodities. Nevertheless, you can see that is very different from looking at just the price and quantity of one good considered in isolation.

The price encountered most often is the *terms of trade*, which is the price of exports divided by the price of imports (or often, the quantity of imports divided by the quantity of exports). Terms of trade are introduced in Chapters 3 and 4.

Another special concept to be introduced in Chapter 4 is the *offer curve*, which reflects a country's supply of exports and demand for imports simultaneously. The intersection of a pair of offer curves for two countries describes general equilibrium and the terms of trade.

Another tool especially useful in trade theory is the *excess supply and demand* diagram, used to measure the effects of trade and of tariffs on prices, output, and consumption in both the exporting and importing countries. This technique is explained in Chapter 8.

All these tools and concepts have applications outside of trade theory, but they are used more often in international trade and were developed by economists in the context of international trade questions.

HOW TRADE THEORY DEVELOPED

Interest in questions of international trade and protection emerged at about the same time as the rise of nationalism in roughly 1400 A.D. The dominant school of thought on the subject of international trade and payments in the period from 1400 to the late 1700s was *mercantilism*. Mercantilism was an imperial approach to trade that stressed colonization, the development of domestic industry by restricting exports of raw materials, and, most of all, acquiring wealth in the form of gold and silver by consistently running a surplus of exports over imports. It was a highly nationalistic policy, which ran into intense criticism in the eighteenth and nineteenth centuries from the new laissez-faire (classical) school of economists.

In fairness to the mercantilists, it should be pointed out that there were elements of shrewd management and even development theory in this policy. Kings and other leaders had to raise money to support armies for the many wars that took place as well as threats of domestic insurrection, and the foreign sector was the most highly monetized and therefore the easiest to tax. The gold and silver inflow could enrich the royal treasury more easily than could wresting produce from the peasants or alienating the domestic landed gentry with more visible taxes. Restrictions on exports of machinery and raw materials was a form of infant industry development policy. And the nationalism that was a central focus of mercantilism might increase international hostility and sacrifice the consumption gains of trade, but it could also unite a nation emerging from feudalism into a single entity capable of defense and economic development.

The classical school, however, spotted two major weaknesses in mercantilist reasoning that became the cornerstone of not only theory but also public policy in the nineteenth century, especially in England where these criticisms were developed. The English philosopher David Hume (1711–1776) identified one such fallacy. Since the money supply of the time was based on gold and/or silver, the inflow of precious metal would expand the money supply and raise domestic prices. This would make exports less competitive abroad and imports cheaper relative to domestic substitutes. Exports would fall and imports would rise. Thus, a policy of trying to maintain an export surplus indefinitely would be self-defeating. This automatic correction process is called the *specie flow mechanism.*

Furthermore, as Hume's friend and the father of modern economics, Adam Smith, pointed out in his 1776 classic, *The Wealth of Nations*, a country's wealth consists not in its stock of precious metals but in the quantity and variety of goods and services, domestic and foreign, that its citizens are able to consume. This wealth is promoted not by an inflow of precious metals but rather by an inflow of goods and services.

The two strands of this argument—that an export surplus cannot be maintained indefinitely and that consumers gain from trade—remain at the heart of the discussion of free trade versus protectionism today. Hume and Smith together raised doubts about the wisdom of mercantilism as a commercial policy. David Ricardo (1772–1823) and John Stuart Mill (1806–1873) dealt more telling blows to mercantilism by demonstrating the gains to both parties from trade on the basis of comparative advantage, a concept to be developed in Chapters 2 and 3. Ricardo was the first to demonstrate that, even if one country is absolutely more efficient than the other in the production of both of two commodities, trade will nevertheless benefit both countries if the one specializes in that product in which its relative efficiency is greater while the other produces that product in which its relative inefficiency is less.

John Stuart Mill refined, clarified, and extended this analysis to demonstrate the superiority of free trade over mercantilism from the standpoint of the consumer. The arguments of Ricardo and Mill influenced England's movement to virtually free trade in the midnineteenth century. While their contributions may appear theoretical, they were in fact very policy oriented. From the time of Hume to the present, this preoccupation with policy has been a hallmark of much of the international economics literature. This raises the question of the relationship between economic theory and analysis and practical policy, a question important to all areas of economics but particularly pervasive in international economics.

ECONOMICS AND POLITICS: INTERACTIONS

Economics is supposedly a positive science. That is, faced with an identifiable problem, economists will apply their "kit" of analytical tools to identify potential solutions. These solutions are then scrutinized carefully in terms of such criteria as efficiency, impact on income distribution and economic growth, and compatibility with monetary and fiscal policy. This analysis is then available to the policymaker, who, after weighing other social and political considerations, renders a final choice of policy to be pursued. Thus, "positive" economists supposedly do not make final policy recommendations or decisions. But in practice it is difficult to separate clearly policy analysis from policy recommendations. And very often the recommendations that appear to flow quite naturally from the economist's analysis are not those actually implemented. Even if economists' recommendations are adopted, they usually are modified substantially. Two ready examples are the widespread preferences of economists for free trade and floating exchange rates, which have been only very slowly and never completely incorporated into actual policy.

In most cases, the gap between economic analysis and actual policy can be explained by political considerations. Examples are not hard to find. In the middle 1970s, liberalized trade with the Soviet Union, justified on economic grounds, became inextricably linked with the emigration of Soviet Jews, a politically sensitive issue. In the late 1960s, national pride as well as reluctance to impose economic losses on political allies who had held dollars as reserves delayed the inevitable and economically sensible devaluation of the dollar. Political alliances of strategically placed members of Congress with particular industries and interest groups clearly shape trade legislation and influence trade negotiations, especially in protecting inefficient or declining industries from foreign competition.

The gap between what is desirable economically from a national standpoint and what is feasible politically in a particular time and place may be very wide indeed. There is a good reason for this. Few, if any, policy changes will have only gainers and no losers. When economists try to bridge the gap between analysis and recommendation, they usually do so with the interests of the majority in mind. It is easy to overlook the political clout of the threatened minority who stand to lose. Keep this in mind as you consider free trade and protectionism, policy toward cartels and multinationals, the costs and benefits of economic integration, and the choice of international monetary arrangements. Identifying the potential losers often explains the compromises you observe between economically "best" policies and the realities you observe in commercial policy, cartel policy, immigration laws, international monetary policy, and restrictions on capital flows.

KEY TERMS

barriers to trade
comparative advantage
exchange rates (fixed, floating)
exchange risk
excess supply and demand
gains from trade
general equilibrium
mercantilism

national sovereignty
offer curve
policy analysis
specie flow mechanism
terms of trade
transactions cost

REVIEW QUESTIONS

1. How is international trade different from trade between regions of a single country? In what respects do you think it might be similar?
2. It has been argued that economic analysis is not developed in a vacuum but, rather, in response to policy questions facing a particular society at a particular time. One example is the development of Keynesian macroeconomics in response to the Great Depression. In what respect is this true of the theory of international trade? Can you think of other examples from other branches of economics?
3. Economic analysis often leads to policy recommendations that are not adopted at all, are adopted in part, or are modified. The reason usually lies with the political influence of those who stand to lose if the new policy were adopted. Try to identify all the gainers and losers from
    a. taxing oil imports.
    b. eliminating tariffs on shoes.
    c. lowering the international price of our currency.
    d. subsidizing the export of raw cotton.
    e. restricting foreign investment in the United States.

SUGGESTED READINGS

EKELUND, ROBERT B., JR., and ROBERT F. HEBERT, *A History of Economic Theory and Method*, pp. 28–41. New York: McGraw-Hill, 1975.
HELLER, H. ROBERT, *International Trade: Theory and Empirical Evidence*, 2nd ed., chap. 1. Englewood Cliffs, N.J.: Prentice-Hall, 1973.
KINDLEBERGER, CHARLES P., *Power and Money*, chaps. 1 and 2. New York: Basic Books, 1970.

CHAPTER 2

Trade and the Domestic Economy

How does international trade affect what goes on in our domestic economy? How does it affect the price level, the level of output, the rate of growth, and the level of employment? At the microeconomic level, how does it affect individual workers and consumers, firms and industries? How does it affect competition, efficiency, and the distribution of income? We address these broad questions in Chapter 2 as a general framework for the more specific topics treated in the remainder of this book.

THE VOLUME, COMPOSITION, AND DIRECTION OF TRADE

Trade is a significant component of GNP for many countries. Generally, the share of trade in GNP varies inversely with country size (measured by either population or GNP). For the United States, for example, only about 13 percent of GNP is exported and approximately the same fraction is imported. For a small country such as Denmark, imports account for about one-third of total spending. Distance also affects trade. Australia and the Netherlands have close to the same GNP, but only 13.3 percent of Australia's GNP is exported, whereas exports account for 46.1 percent of the Netherland's output. Table 2-1 summarizes exports relative to GNP for a selected group of countries of various sizes and levels of development. Note the particularly high export ratios for the oil exporting countries—Libya, Saudi Arabia, and Venezuela.

The reasons for differences in the relative importance of trade are not hard to find. Most large countries contain a diversity of climates, natural resources, and industries and can provide wide ranges of consumer goods; small countries only gain access to such diverse goods and resources through trade. Countries with a broad north-south geographic span, such as the United States, China, and the Soviet Union, can produce a greater variety of foodstuffs than can a country contained wholly within a narrow span of climates, such as Guyana or Switzerland. Large countries spread broadly from east to west enjoy access to a great variety of natural resources, which makes them less dependent on imported raw materials. Finally, producing for a large (and preferably affluent) domestic market permits a great array of industries to achieve the economies of scale that are necessary if they are to be competitive with foreign producers. At the same time, the existence of an ample home market means that producers have less incentive to seek out foreign markets, so that exports tend to languish in large developed countries. All these conditions are particularly true in the United States.

TABLE 2-1   Export Trade as a Share of GNP, Selected Countries

Country (year)	Exports as a Percentage of GNP
Australia (1973)	13.3%
Austria (1977)	20.5
Belgium/Luxembourg (1977)	45.8
Brazil (1977)	7.2
Canada (1973)	20.4
Finland (1977)	25.8
France (1977)	16.7
Germany (West) (1977)	22.9
Guyana (1976)	61.4
Japan (1973)	9.0
Libya (1976)	56.2
Netherlands (1977)	41.1
New Zealand (1973)	21.7
Norway (1977)	24.3
Saudi Arabia (1976)	73.4
South Africa (1973)	12.1
Switzerland (1977)	28.8
Venezuela (1976)	30.1

Source: *U.N. Statistical Yearbook* (New York: United Nations, 1978), pp. 476 ff.

TABLE 2-2 Composition of Trade by Country Groups, 1977

	Country Group					
	Exports			Imports		
Commodity Class	*Developed Market Economies*	*Developing Market Economies*	*Centrally Planned Economies*	*Developed Market Economies*	*Developing Market Economies*	*Centrally Planned Economies*
Food and beverages	11.3%	15.0%	8.8%	11.4%	9.9%	13.4%
Raw materials (excluding fuel)	7.6	8.6	8.7	8.2	5.1	8.6
Fuel	19.7	57.1[a]	19.1	22.1	15.1	10.1
Chemicals	6.9	1.5	4.7	6.8	7.3	6.8
Machinery and transport equipment	28.3	4.1	29.2	24.8	36.1	34.6
Other manufactures	24.5	13.5	22.1	24.8	22.6	24.2

[a] This category includes the OPEC nations.

Source: *U.N. Statistical Yearbook, 1978* (New York: United Nations, 1978), pp. 482–486.

With whom does a nation trade? As you might expect, geographic proximity is an important determinant. The United States, for example, conducts about 20 percent of its trade with Canada, and over one-third in the Western Hemisphere. Nearly half the trade of the European Economic Community is with other members of the EEC. Among other countries in the Western Hemisphere (excluding Canada and the United States), 15 percent of trade is with one another and over 50 percent of their exports and 43 percent of their imports lie within the hemisphere. Almost 20 percent of New Zealand's imports are from Australia. Trading blocs (such as the European Economic Community or the Central American Common Market) strengthen this tendency to trade with neighbors.

There is the widely held belief that trade consists primarily of food and raw materials flowing from underdeveloped countries to industrial nations with a reverse flow of manufactures. This is not entirely true. The 14 non-communist nations classed as industrial (the United States, Canada, Japan, and 11 nations of Western Europe) account for over 65 percent of world trade, and over 60 percent of that trade is with one another. Excluding petroleum, raw materials and food account for only about 20 percent of world trade, and the developed market economies export about as much as they import in these categories. A breakdown of the shares of broad categories of products by country groups is given in Table 2-2. The largest single group in dollar volume is machinery and transport equipment, followed by other manufacturing and then mineral fuels. Food and beverages are fourth in total dollar value.

Finally, the importance of the United States to world trade is much greater than one might assume from the low ratio of U.S. trade to GNP. The United States accounts for over 13 percent of world imports and nearly 11 percent of world exports and ranks first as a supplier of imports for 33 of the 100 U.N. member countries and first as an export market for 37 of the 100. American foreign trade has a significant impact on output, employment, prices, competition, and composition of output not only at home, but abroad as well.

TRADE AND THE MACROECONOMY

Trade as a Source of Growth

One of the enduring arguments for foreign trade is that it has the potential to increase real output (GNP) and the standard of living (consumption). The value of output is increased by specializing in those products in which the country is relatively more efficient, a topic considered later in this chapter and in greater detail in Chapter 3. The standard of living is enhanced by exchanging those products for imported goods that can be produced abroad more cheaply than at home. This idea can be illustrated graphically on a production possibilities curve such as that shown in Figure 2-1.

Most readers will be familiar with the concept of the production possibilities curve (or frontier) from introductory economics. It is simply a locus of all the possible combinations of two goods that can be produced with a given stock of resources or inputs. If it is drawn curved, this implies that both commodities are subject to increasing marginal costs as the producer becomes specialized more and more completely in one product or the other. The cost ratio (and also the price ratio in perfect competition, where the two are equal) can be found by drawing a tangent line to the production possibilities curve and measuring its slope at that point. For example, at B in the diagram, where OX_2 of X and OY_2 of Y is being produced, the cost of X in terms of Y forgone is given by the slope of the tangent line TT'. This line is also the price ratio for that particular output combination.

The situation in Figure 2-1 makes a great many simplifying assumptions that will be identified and examined in Chapter 3. For now, it is sufficient to note that this is a world of only two commodities, both subject to increasing marginal cost and produced under conditions of perfect competition. If this country is initially producing at A, where the production possibilities curve is tangent to the highest attainable indifference curve, then its citizens are enjoying the highest standard of living available without trade

FIGURE 2-1   A Diagrammatic View of Trade and Growth

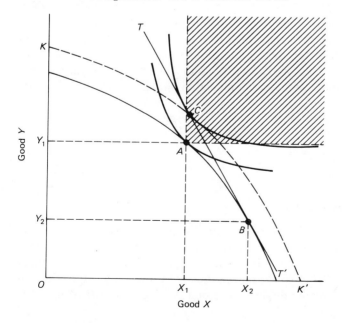

and/or additional resources (OX_1 of X and OY_1 of Y). Any point northeast of A (in the shaded area) would lie on a higher indifference curve and would therefore represent a higher standard of living.

How might a country improve its standard of living? Clearly, the answer is not to move along the production possibilities curve, because it is already touching the highest attainable indifference curve. Any other point on the production possibilities curve is on a lower indifference curve and must therefore represent a lower standard of living. Improvement to a point such as C can be achieved in either of two ways. One way is to increase resources and/or improve technology so as to shift the entire production possibilities curve outward until it is tangent to a higher indifference curve passing through C. This is represented by the second production possibilities curve in the diagram labeled KK'.

An alternative possibility is trade. If the international price ratio is given by line TT', this country can change its output mix from A to B and trade some of the additional output of X for Y. This makes it possible to produce at B and consume at C by exporting X for Y at a ratio more favorable than the domestic cost-price ratio. Thus, trade enables us to separate production from consumption, moving outside the limits set by the production possibilities curve.

This is, of course, a narrow view of the matter, for we have really identified three sources of growth—increased resources, improved technology, and exchange based on comparative advantage—and have implied that only the last of these three is a result of being part of the international economy. In fact, the other two sources of growth are also frequently of foreign origin. The spread of technology from country to country has a long history and has probably accelerated in recent decades as a result of improved communication as well as the rapid growth of multinational corporations. Immigration of labor has been an important source of early growth in many countries, particularly in Canada, the United States, and Israel. An inflow of foreign capital has been a significant contributor to economic growth in many developed and developing nations.[1] Imported raw materials and energy sources have been crucial to such resource-poor industrial nations as Britain and Japan. We return to these other international influences on growth in Chapters 6 and 7.

Effects of Growth on Trade

As a country grows in output and standard of living, its patterns of trade tend to change. The ratio of imports and exports to gross national product is likely first to rise and then to fall, although this may be modified by the nature of growth.

[1] Factor movements complicate the issue of gains from trade; they may be a source of expanded output, but they also consume some of that additional output. This question recurs in Chapter 6.

In the early stages of growth and development, the relative importance of trade (and particularly the ratio of imports to gross national product) tends to rise as consumers with larger incomes expand the range of their consumption choices to include goods not yet available domestically. Imported capital goods, energy, and raw materials are often required to keep the process of development moving. The establishment of local plants of multinational corporations in growing countries often brings with it an influx of capital equipment, parts and semifinished goods, and foreign consumer goods to suit the preferences of foreign nationals employed by the multinational.

As a country approaches maturity, however, the growth of trade and particularly imports tends to slow down. A number of reasons have been suggested for this:

1. The relative growth of service industries in developed economies. Services do not lend themselves as readily to trade as do goods, with some obvious exceptions, namely, shipping, tourism, and banking.
2. The increased demand for "social overhead capital"—schools, hospitals, highways, airports, power plants—which is generally a matter of on-site construction with a minimal import component.
3. The developing country eventually developing its own capacity to produce many products that once were imported.
4. Developed countries tending to protect (with tariffs and quotas) those industries in which they had a comparative advantage initially, even when they have subsequently developed other export industries in which their relative efficiency is even greater. Textiles and shoes in the United States are cases in point.

These arguments for the rise and fall of imports relative to GNP are generalizations that may or may not hold true for particular countries. Several other factors also influence whether trade in both imports and exports rises (1) more rapidly than (protrade-biased growth), (2) more slowly than (antitrade-biased growth), or (3) at about the same rate as (neutral growth) gross national product. A bias toward or against trade during growth can arise from either the production side or the consumption side.

During economic growth, the production possibilities curve shifts outward due to an increase in the resource base or an improvement in technology or a combination of the two. This shift in the production possibilities curve could be a radial expansion, or it could represent an increase in the productive capacity for one good relative to the other. In a two-good model, one good is the exportable good (the one in which this country has a comparative advantage) and one is importable. The three possibilities are illustrated in Figure 2-2. (Note that the indifference curves are radial expansions of each other; that is, tastes remain unchanged as income rises.)

In panel (a), the capacity to produce exportable goods has expanded relative to the capacity to produce importable goods. This may be due to

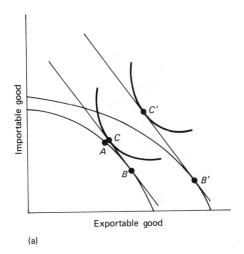

(a)

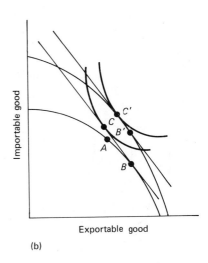

(b)

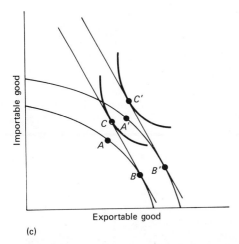

(c)

FIGURE 2-2
Production Biases in Trade

technological improvements specific to the exportables industry or because of an increase in the resource base that consists mainly of those resources used more intensively in the exportables industry. In either case, the share of exportables in total production (at a constant international price ratio) increases. (Constant proportions in production would mean that B and B' would lie on the same line radiating from the origin, whereas constant proportions in consumption would mean that C and C' would be on a single line radiating from the origin.) Production of exportables relative to total output would rise, and the ratio of trade to GNP would rise. If the improvement in technology or the increase in the resource base favored the import-competing industry, the opposite would occur, and trade would fall relative to GNP, as in panel (b). If the improvement in technology or the increase

19

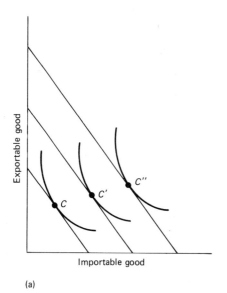

(a)

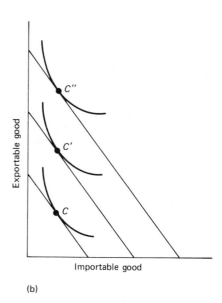

(b)

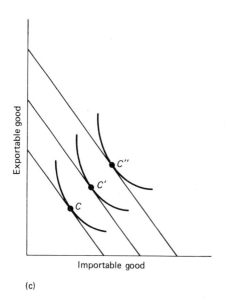

(c)

FIGURE 2-3
Consumption Biases in Growth

in resources affected both industries equally, neutral growth would occur as in panel (c), and the ratio of trade to GNP would remain constant.

The second source of change in the trade-GNP ratio as a country grows lies in what happens to the population's consumption preference as output, income, and standard of living grow. Do people want more exportables relative to importables, or vice versa? Or do their desires for both grow in equal proportions? These three possibilities are illustrated in Figure 2-3.

At constant prices (indicated by the parallel straight lines), the consumption combination preferred contains a higher proportion of the importable good relative to the exportable good as total consumption (or standard of living, or utility, indicated by higher indifference curves) is increased in panel (a). This means an expansion of trade relative to GNP, or a protrade bias in consumption.

In panel (b), as total consumption increases, the relative proportion of exportables in total consumption rises. This represents an antitrade bias in consumption. Panel (c) represents neutrality; that is, as consumption increases, the proportions of the two products consumed remain constant and so does the ratio of trade to GNP.

This discussion should give you some idea of how difficult it is to predict what will happen to the volume of trade relative to total production or consumption as an economy grows. The arguments for trade first rising and later falling relative to GNP suggest that consumption bias toward exportables is dominant initially but that, as an economy grows and develops, both production and consumption biases are antitrade. This argument is complicated, however, by the existence of many goods, including predominantly nontraded services and social overhead capital (infrastructure), and by the existence of protection (tariffs and other trade barriers). In fact, in the period since World War II and particularly in the 1970s, the ratio of trade to GNP has risen for both developed and less developed countries.

Trade, GNP, and Stability

The other important macroeconomic impact of trade is on fluctuations in the level of output, employment, and prices. We are also interested in the reverse relationship—the effect of changes in the level of economic activity on trade. These effects may be viewed in either a Keynesian framework or a monetarist framework. We consider both approaches, but the conclusions about the impact of the foreign sector on the domestic economy are essentially the same, namely that an increase in exports relative to imports will stimulate the level of domestic economic activity in output (and employment), or prices, or some of each. A rise in imports relative to exports will have the opposite effect. An increase in the level of economic activity will tend to increase imports relative to exports, whereas a decline in economic activity will raise exports relative to imports. (For present purposes, we ignore capital flows and concentrate on imports and exports. Capital flows are taken up in Chapter 14.)

You should recall from the introductory course that, in a Keynesian (closed economy) framework, equilibrium occurs where aggregate demand equals aggregate supply. Aggregate supply or GNP is usually symbolized by Y. The components of aggregate demand are consumption, C, gross private domestic investment, I, and government purchases of goods and services, G, so that in equilibrium

$$Y = C + I + G \tag{2.1}$$

(All variables are in real terms; for the moment we are ignoring prices.)

But Y is also income received by the factors of production, which can be used in any of three ways; it can be consumed, C, saved, S, or paid to the government in taxes, T. Thus, Y is also

$$Y = C + S + T \tag{2.2}$$

and equilibrium occurs where what we earn is equal to what we choose to spend:

$$C + I + G = C + S + T \tag{2.3}$$

If we assume that government balances its budget ($G = T$), this reduces to

$$S = I \tag{2.4}$$

as the conditions of equilibrium; that is, leakages out of the income stream in the form of saving (income not spent on consumption) are offset exactly by injections back into the income stream in the form of investment. In an open economy, however, we must include imports, M, as a use of income and exports, X, as another use of GNP. Thus equation 2.1 becomes

$$Y = C + I + G + X \tag{2.5}$$

and equation 2.2 is now

$$Y = C + S + T + M \tag{2.6}$$

If we once again let $G = T$, this reduces to

$$I + (X - M) = S \tag{2.7}$$

If net exports, $X - M$, are positive, then the level of injections is greater than leakages (saving) and income must rise to bring saving up to a level equal to $I + (X - M)$, since the level of saving is determined by the level of income. Thus, an export surplus is associated with a higher equilibrium level of output (and employment, which depends on output) than would occur in a closed economy. Conversely, an import surplus ($X < M$) would lead to a lower equilibrium level of income than would occur in a closed economy. As we see later, this simple argument is the basis for the employment argument for tariff protection; if we reduce imports and create an export surplus, we raise the level of output and employment.

A slightly more complex version of this model uses the Keynesian multiplier analysis, modified to incorporate the foreign sector. The principal change is that there is now a function relating consumption to the level of income, whereas investment and government spending are treated as independent of the level of income. The consumption function is

$$C = C_o + bY \qquad (2.8)$$

where C_o is a constant (that part of consumption independent of the level of income) and b is the marginal propensity to consume, or the fraction of an additional dollar of income that will be spent on consumption. I (investment) and G (government purchases) are written as I_o and G_o, respectively, indicating some constant unspecified numerical value. Substituting in $Y = C + I + G$,

$$Y = C_o + bY + I_o + G_o \qquad (2.9)$$

which can be solved for Y:

$$Y = \frac{1}{1 - b} (C_o + I_o + G_o) \qquad (2.10)$$

This expression means that any change in autonomous spending (C_o, I_o, or G_o, which can be lumped together as autonomous spending A_o) will lead to a change in Y that is equal to $1/(1 - b)$ times the shift in the consumption, investment, or government demand schedule, or

$$\Delta Y = \frac{1}{1 - b} \left\{ \begin{matrix} \Delta C_o \\ \Delta I_o \\ \Delta G_o \end{matrix} \right\} \qquad (2.11)$$

The expression $1/(1 - b)$ is the familiar Keynesian multiplier. What we are interested in is seeing how this is affected by adding exports and imports, where

$$X = X_o \qquad (2.12)$$

and

$$M = mY \qquad (2.13)$$

Exports are autonomous because they are determined by income in the rest of the world and other influences but are independent of the domestic level of income. Imports, like consumption, rise and fall with the level of income and output. The coefficient m is called the marginal propensity to import.

If we substitute 2.12 and 2.13 in the expression

$$Y = C + I + G + (X - M) \qquad (2.14)$$

we obtain

$$Y = C_o + bY + I_o + G_o + X_o - mY$$

Solving for Y, the result is

$$Y = \frac{1}{1 - b + m}(C_o + I_o + G_o + X_o) \qquad (2.15)$$

There are two obvious differences between the open economy equilibrium equation 2.15 and the closed economy expression 2.10. One is that the multiplier now includes the marginal propensity to import, m. The other is that there is an additional source of disturbances; X_o is added to C_o, I_o, and G_o as a source of demand shifts leading to multiplied changes in national income, Y.

The new multiplier $1/(1 - b + m)$ is smaller than $1/(1 - b)$. (Try some representative values, e.g., $b = 0.75$, $m = 0.05$, to verify this.) A smaller proportion of any increase in income is spent on the purchase of domestically produced goods and services because some of it "leaks" out of the economy in the form of increased demand for imports. In Figure 2-4, this is illustrated in terms of a business cycle; the solid line represents cyclical fluctuations in output in a closed economy and the dashed line represents an open economy.

FIGURE 2-4   Cyclical Fluctuations: Closed Versus Open Economy

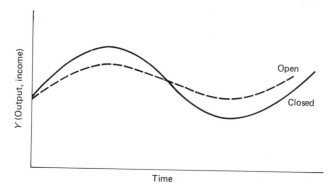

Thus, the foreign sector reduces the impact of shifts in aggregate demand on output in both directions. However, the foreign sector can also be a source of shifts via X_o; changes in export demand upward or downward can set off multiple expansion of output in the same direction. Whether or not the addition of the foreign sector is, on balance, a stabilizing or destabilizing influence depends on whether the fluctuation originates internally (shifts in C_o, I_o, or G_o) or externally (X_o). Cyclical fluctuations are believed to originate most often within the developed or industrialized countries and to be transmitted through their import demand to the less developed countries. To the extent that this is true, foreign trade would tend to stabilize developed countries and destabilize underdeveloped countries.

There is one final qualification to the Keynesian model. In this model, C_o, I_o, G_o, and X_o are all assumed to be independent of one another. This may or may not be valid for developed countries, but in underdeveloped countries, there is a strong possibility that one or two export industries may be the area in which investment is concentrated and may also provide the major revenue source to a government whose expenditures are heavily revenue-determined. A rise in export sales due to an upswing in economic activity in the industrial world is likely to stimulate both investment (in the export industry) and government spending, whereas a fall in export sales is likely to drag both investment and government spending down with it. This effect would lead to a "boom or bust" situation, greatly magnifying the impact of changes in export sales.

The increase (decrease) in national income may be entirely in output, entirely in prices, or (more likely) in both, with the mix depending on how close to full employment the economy was initially. Any increase in prices will tend to reduce exports and stimulate imports, reducing the export surplus. This is a point made more strongly in the monetarist approach. A rise (fall) in the level of output in one country will tend to increase (decrease) the level of imports but will have no significant effect on exports. Thus, during expansionary periods of rising income and prices, imports rise relative to exports, whereas during recessions, imports tend to fall relative to exports.

In the monetarist view, going back at least to David Hume (1732), the net inflow of money from an export surplus will expand the money supply and through the money supply increase output and/or prices, according to the familiar equation

$$M = \frac{1}{V}(PQ) \qquad (2.16)$$

where M is the money supply, V is the velocity of money, P is the price level, and Q is the level of real output.

While early monetarists observed this relationship as a simple cause and effect phenomenon, modern monetarists give it a behavioral explanation. Equation 2.16 represents the demand for money as a fraction of total spending. When money balances increase, individuals find themselves with excess money balances and increase spending, raising P (the price level) and/or Q (the level of real output). Excess supply of money in an open economy translates into excess demand for goods and services, reflected in an excess of imports over exports until the excess supply has either gone abroad or has been absorbed into the larger cash balances needed to support a larger GNP ($= P \times Q$). This result is not significantly different from that of the Keynesian model, except that monetarists tend to emphasize the increase in prices rather than output in an economy that gravitates naturally toward full employment. The resulting rise in prices, again, will dampen export sales and will stimulate imports so that, over time, exports and imports tend to be in balance. The opposite chain of events would occur in response to an excess demand for money.

More general models that consider capital flows and allow for changes in exchange rates between currencies are treated in Chapter 14.

TRADE AND THE MICROECONOMY

Specialization and Comparative Advantage: Efficiency Gains

The benefits of trade at the microeconomic level lie primarily in the improved efficiency of resource allocation. We explore this in greater detail in Chapter 3, but at this point some simple illustrations may illuminate the concept of comparative advantage.

Suppose that there are two individuals, Robinson Crusoe and Friday, and two goods, fish and coconuts. Friday, being a native, is more efficient at both catching fish and gathering coconuts. The amount they can catch or gather per day is as follows:

	Friday	Crusoe
Coconuts/day	12	6
Fish/day	9	6

Each of them works a six-hour day. Before they discovered the joys of specialization based on comparative advantage, each was spending one-third of his time catching fish and two-thirds gathering coconuts. Their prespecialization production and consumption was as follows:

	Friday	Crusoe	Total
Coconuts	8	4	12
Fish	3	2	5

Friday is absolutely more efficient at both activities. If he worked a twelve-hour day, while Crusoe watched, they could both enjoy just as many coconuts and more fish. Friday, however, is unlikely to agree, so Crusoe must do something to make himself useful. Since he is less efficient at producing both goods than is Friday, he should specialize in that product in which his margin of inefficiency is less, which is fish. (A more thorough explanation of the choice of fish as Crusoe's product is given in Chapter 3, but the reader can verify this choice by seeing what happens to total output if Crusoe specializes in coconuts and Friday in fish.)

After specialization, the output is as follows:

	Friday	Crusoe	Total
Coconuts	12	0	12
Fish	0	6	6

This represents a net gain of one fish with no increase in effort. Each still works six hours a day. The total gain results from specialization. When they sit down to their evening meal, there are just as many coconuts as previously and one extra fish to be shared as a result of specialization. Each is reallocating resources along his production possibilities frontier and is then trading to a better consumption mix than he was able to obtain out of his own efforts, as is illustrated in Figure 2-5. In each panel, *A* is the initial consumption-production mix, *B* is production after specialization, and *C* is final consumption. Since *C* in each case involves one-half more fish and the same amount of coconuts, both Crusoe and Friday have gained from specialization and sharing the resulting gains.

FIGURE 2-5   The Gains from Trade

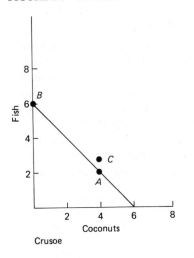

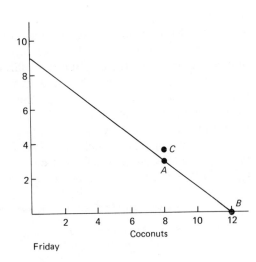

Trade and Competition

A second microeconomic gain from trade lies in increased competition, especially when the domestic industry is so highly concentrated that each firm has some degree of monopoly power. This may be the result of limited market size, artificial barriers to entry, or other factors. The results of monopoly power are likely to be higher prices, less output, less innovation, and more persistent profits than would be the case if there were more competition. Competition from imports can help to remedy these defects.

A classic case in point is the American automobile industry, which was producing large and fuel-inefficient cars in the late 1950s while ignoring a small but significant share of the market interested in more economical, reduced-sized vehicles. When these buyers turned to imports and foreign producers began to capture a significant share of the market, Detroit was forced to respond with compact cars of its own, such as the Ford Falcon and the Chevrolet Corvair.

Jean Jacques Servan-Schreiber, a French journalist, made a similar point in his 1963 classic *The American Challenge*, arguing that American competition would force improvement among French firms that had grown lethargic in the comfortable safety of a protected domestic market.[2] The challenge to which he referred in this case was not as much from imports as from local plants of American-based multinational corporations. As we see in later chapters, the movement of capital, skilled labor, and technology provides an alternative to direct exchange of goods and has many of the same effects, especially on efficiency of resource allocation and on competition.

Trade and Economies of Scale

The third microeconomic gain from trade lies in attaining a scale of operations that permits economies of scale, lowering costs for producers and prices for consumers. Adam Smith recognized this advantage of trade in his 1776 classic *The Wealth of Nations* when he stated that "the division of labor is limited by the extent of the market."[3] There is a minimum market size needed to support one, two, a dozen, or a hundred firms in a particular industry or market at levels that permit firms to operate reasonably close to their minimum average cost. The minimum market size varies with the nature of the industry. A market that can support 40 textile plants may be too small to support a single automobile firm. Economies of scale are measured by the long-run average cost curve, two examples of which are illustrated in Figure 2-6. Sales of M_1 units per year would bring a firm in industry

[2] Jean Jacques Servan-Schreiber, *The American Challenge* (New York: Athanaeum, 1968).

[3] Adam Smith, *An Inquiry into the Nature and Causes of the Wealth of Nations*, 1776 (New York: Modern Library, 1937), p. 17.

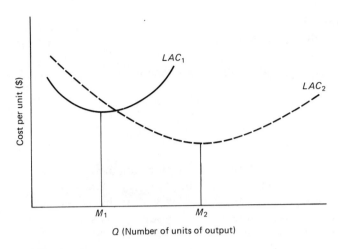

FIGURE 2-6 Economies of Scale

1 with cost curve LAC_1 to the lowest unit cost, whereas M_2 would be needed in an industry in which the typical firm faced LAC_2. Obviously, for the same sales volume, there is room in the marketplace for more firms in industry 1 than in industry 2. Similarly, if industry 2 had a potential market share for a firm of less than M_2, but it became possible to expand the size of the total market to M_2 through trade, it might be feasible to establish industry 2 in this particular country, or for industry 2 to have enough firms for domestic competition. Scale economies are generally most important in heavy industries and least significant in consumer nondurables such as canned food, shoes, and flowers.

Economies of scale and competition are closely interrelated. Industries with substantial scale economies are likely to be highly concentrated, so that foreign competition would benefit consumers. Conversely, the existence of substantial economies of scale would mean that a new entrant would need access to a broad market to be competitive (i.e., to produce at or near the minimum point of the long-run average cost curve). Access to world rather than merely to home markets allows additional firms to be established even in some relatively small countries, increasing worldwide competition. Through international trade, consumers are more likely to be able to enjoy both the benefits of large-scale production and the gains from competition simultaneously.

Finally, there are some benefits to trade (and some costs) that are difficult to identify with precision. Trade widens the options available to consumers, improves communications between nations, and creates interdependence, which lessens the possibility of international hostilities. The sharing of cultures, technology, and ideas has historically been one of the significant side benefits to trade. But the major economic benefits to trade are those noted in this chapter; trade is a source of enhanced consumption and growth, a contributor to stability (or, occasionally, instability), an opportunity to increase output through specialization and to lower costs through economies of scale, and a source of competition to keep domestic oligopolies in line.

SUMMARY

This chapter addresses some general questions about the interaction between the foreign sector and the domestic economy. Trade promotes economic growth directly through specialization and exchange as well as indirectly through transfer of technology and productive resources. As a country grows, the relative share of trade in GNP tends first to rise (consumption effect) and then to fall. The exact pattern depends on whether the growth in output is antitrade biased, protrade biased, or neutral and whether consumption preferences become skewed more toward importables or exportables as the economy grows.

Trade reduces the size of the spending multiplier (a stabilizing effect) but adds exports as a potential source of instability. Thus, trade will be primarily stabilizing only for those fluctuations originating within the country. In addition, if X, G, and I are interdependent, trade can be highly destabilizing.

Imports tend to rise relative to exports during inflations, creating an import surplus. The opposite is true in recessions.

The major source of microeconomic gains from trade results from more efficient resource allocation based on comparative advantage. Other gains arise from increased competition and economies of scale.

KEY TERMS

antitrade-biased growth
closed economy
competition
economies of scale
efficiency gains
equilibrium output
foreign trade multiplier
gross national product
indifference curve (map)
long-run average cost curve
marginal propensity to import
market size

net foreign investment
neutral growth
oligopoly
open economy
production possibilities curve
protrade-biased growth
social overhead capital (infrastructure)
specialization
standard of living

REVIEW QUESTIONS

1. In what way does trade promote growth? How does growth in turn tend to affect the share of trade in total production and consumption?
2. Let $b = 0.7$ and $m = 0.04$. If investment rises by $15 billion, by how much would output, Y, increase in a closed economy? In an open economy?
3. Using the data in Table 2-1, suggest some reasons for the variations in the ratio of trade to GNP among the countries listed.
4. Why do imports rise during expansions and fall during recessions?
5. Under what circumstances would trade tend to fall (or rise) relative to total output as an economy grows and develops?
6. Suppose that a pair of students goes into business washing windows and mowing lawns. Each works a four-hour day and charges $1 per window and $3 per lawn. Their output per hour is as follows:

	Lawns	Windows
Jones	2	10
Smith	4	12

Compare the earnings after specialization with the combined amount they would earn if they each divided their time equally between lawns and windows.

SUGGESTED READINGS

ALLEN, WILLIAM R., ed., *International Trade Theory: Hume to Ohlin.* New York: Random House, 1965.
DORNBUSCH, RUDIGER, *Open Economy Macroeconomics*, chap. 1. New York: Basic Books, 1980.
HELLER, H. ROBERT, *International Trade: Theory and Empirical Evidence*, 2nd ed., chaps. 2 and 5. Englewood Cliffs, N.J.: Prentice-Hall, 1973. The appendix has a useful review of relevant microeconomic concepts.
HIRSCHLEIFER, JACK, *Price Theory and Applications*, 2nd ed., pp. 66–78 and 203–206. Englewood Cliffs, N.J.: Prentice-Hall, 1980.

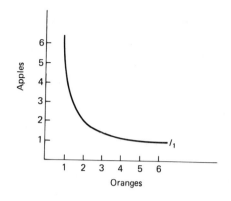

FIGURE 2A-1
An Indifference Curve

APPENDIX

Review of Indifference Analysis

An *indifference curve* is a useful analytical device that shows all the various combinations of two goods between which the consumer is indifferent, that is, which give him or her equal satisfaction. In Figure 2A-1, our consumer is equally happy with five oranges and one apple, two oranges and two apples, or one orange and five apples.

Indifference curves are normally convex to the origin because of the principle of diminishing marginal utility, which states that the more of a commodity one has, the less satisfaction will be derived from an additional (marginal) unit. To give up one apple out of five, our consumer is willing to be compensated with only one orange, because he has so many apples and but a single orange. But to give up a second apple (leaving only three) for more oranges (of which he already has two), our consumer must be convinced by a more generous price. If he is offered three more oranges for the next apple, our consumer will be indifferent between trading or keeping

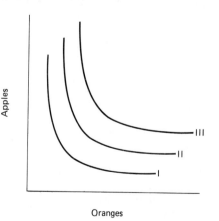

FIGURE 2A-2
An Indifference Map

what he has. All the combinations on I_1 represent equally satisfying combinations of apples and oranges.

Figure 2A-2 shows an indifference map, or a set of indifference curves. Each indifference curve represents a given level of satisfaction and shows the various apple-orange combinations that will create that level of satisfaction. An indifference curve above and to the right of another represents a higher level of satisfaction because it always contains one or more combinations that include more of at least one commodity and no less of the other.

Social indifference curves can be constructed for societies (groups of individuals) showing the consumption combinations between which a society is indifferent, but the theoretical difficulties in doing so are substantial because of the problem of making interpersonal comparisons of utility. The indifference curves and maps that we use in the next two chapters ignore this distinction between individual and social indifference curves. This is an analytical convenience that will enable us to make some useful and valid observations about the gains from trade.

The student might wish to refer to any good intermediate microeconomics textbook for a more detailed discussion of indifference curves and indifference maps.

PART 2

The Micro-economics of Trade

Part 2 of this text concerns the microeconomic theory of international trade, a variety of topics related to the questions of prices and quantities, flows of final goods and flows of resources, imperfect competition, political arrangements, and public policy toward trade.

The first three chapters (Chapters 3, 4, and 5) consider what is traditionally called the "pure theory" of international trade, a label intended to distinguish this body of thought from the theory of commercial policy, which deals with the effects of tariffs, quotas, and (largely since World War II) customs unions. The topics usually considered under this heading are the theory of comparative advantage, with all the refinements thereto (Chapter 3), the role of demand (Chapter 4), and the modern emphasis on supply determinants in the Heckscher–Ohlin model and other explanations of the basis of trade (Chapter 5). Chapter 6 is a somewhat less traditional extension of the pure theory to consider factor movements. Chapter 7 is a logical follow-up to Chapter 6 to look specifically at the result of particular types of capital flows in the context of the multinational corporation as well as its close relative, the international cartel.

Chapters 8, 9, and 10 deal with commercial policy—the barriers that nations deliberately place in the way of free movements of goods, services, and/or productive resources. The theory is established in Chapter 8; arguments for protection (on welfare and other traditional economic grounds) are evaluated in Chapter 9; and a brief history of experience with commercial policy, mainly in the United States, is given in Chapter 10. The microeconomics of trade concludes with a discussion of the theory and real world experience with economic integration, generally referred to as customs unions in Chapter 11.

CHAPTER 3

The Classical Model of Specialization and Trade

**CLASSICAL COMPARATIVE
ADVANTAGE: SMITH
AND RICARDO**

The simple numerical example of the gains from specialization and trade in Chapter 2 traces its history back to David Ricardo, an early-nineteenth-century British economist who first developed the theory of comparative advantage in his 1817 classic, *Principles of Political Economy and Taxation*. Prior to Ricardo, the economist's case for free trade rested rather shakily on the foundation of absolute advantage, as enunciated by Adam Smith in *The Wealth of Nations* (1776):

> If a foreign country can supply us with a commodity cheaper than we ourselves can make it, better buy it of them with some part of the produce of our own industry, employed in a way in which we have an advantage.[1]

Absolute advantage refers to some kind of clear superiority of one producer over another in the production of a particular product in terms of resource inputs per unit of output or output per unit of resource input. This concept has its clearest interpretation in the context of the *labor theory of value* (which was the framework for both Smith and Ricardo). The labor theory of value held that the prices of products were proportional to their

---

[1] Adam Smith, *An Inquiry into the Nature and Causes of the Wealth of Nations*, 1976 (New York: Modern Library, 1937), p. 424.

labor inputs. Thus, if product A uses twice as much labor as product B, A will be twice as expensive as B. When Smith used the word "cheaper," he implied (as is made clear elsewhere in *The Wealth of Nations*) that the foreign good uses less labor input; in modern terms, we would say that fewer resources are used in its production. Few would quarrel with the benefits of trade in cases where absolute advantage in physical efficiency can be demonstrated. The problem with absolute advantages arises when one country is physically more efficient (i.e., has an absolute advantage) in everything with respect to some unfortunate would-be trading partner. What is the less efficient country to do? Unemployment for its "inefficient" resources is not an acceptable answer.

Ricardo dealt with this question in a classic example in which there are two commodities, wine and cloth, and Portugal has an absolute advantage over England in both. His example was as follows:

	Labor-hours/Cloth	Labor-hours/Wine
England	100	120
Portugal	90	80

He points out that by trade (at an arbitrary ratio of one wine to one cloth) both parties could gain. England could exchange one cloth, costing her 100 labor-hours, for one wine, which would have cost her 120 labor-hours had she produced it herself—a clear saving of 20 labor-hours. Portugal can exchange one wine (cost: 80 labor-hours) for one cloth (domestic cost: 90 labor-hours), saving 10 labor-hours.

There are two important messages here. The first is that both parties can gain from specialization and trade. Specialization and exchange is not a zero-sum game.[2] The second is that there is a basis for specialization even when one of the two parties has an absolute advantage in both of the two products. In this case, Portugal is more efficient in both. Each country can gain if it specializes in that product in which its relative efficiency is greater or its relative inefficiency is less. This is the product in which it has a *comparative advantage*.

ASSUMPTIONS OF THE CLASSICAL MODEL

Before proceeding further, we need to pause and identify the implicit assumptions behind Ricardo's example (also known as classical comparative

---

[2] A zero-sum game is one in which the gains to the winners are just offset by the losses to the losers.

advantage or the classical model of international trade). Some are obvious:

1. The labor theory of value.
2. Two countries, two commodities.

A careful reading of Chapter VII of Ricardo's *Principles* will uncover many of the others. It is assumed implicitly that

3. Factors of production are completely immobile between countries but readily mobile within countries.
4. Resources are fully employed.
5. Specialization occurs at constant average costs (rather than at increasing or decreasing costs).
6. There are no transport or other transactions costs (including trade barriers).
7. Exports and imports are equal in value (or balance-of-payments equilibrium, an approximate but not perfect equivalent).
8. Perfect competition prevails.

Each of these assumptions will be dropped in turn to examine whether the classical case for free trade (gains to both parties) continues to be valid under less restrictive conditions.

LABOR THEORY OF VALUE

The first of the classical assumptions to be dispensed with, and indeed the most expendable, was the labor theory of value. Value in exchange, or price, is determined not only by production costs (including but not limited to labor) but also by demand. This insight comes to us by way of John Stuart Mill, and it represents a significant clarification of microeconomic theory in general and trade theory in particular. To put what Mill was saying in more contemporary language, the value or real price of one good is the alternative production forgone or the next best use of the resources devoted to its production—its opportunity cost. If the resources used to produce one unit of cloth in England could have been used instead to produce five-sixths of a unit of wine, as in Ricardo's example, then five-sixths of a unit of wine is the cost of a unit of cloth in England, while cloth in Portugal (by similar reasoning) costs one-and-one-eighth units of wine. Cloth is cheaper in England in terms of wine forgone, whereas wine is cheaper in Portugal in terms of cloth forgone. (Wine costs one-and-one-sixth units of cloth in England and only eight-ninths of a unit of cloth in Portugal.)

The shift from a labor theory of value to an opportunity cost theory also gives us a simpler definition of comparative advantage. A country has a comparative advantage in that product in which its opportunity cost of production is lower.

Mill made another improvement over Ricardo by identifying the range within which the terms of trade must fall. The range, under constant costs, is set by domestic opportunity costs in each country. (In Ricardo's example, these limits are from eight-ninths to one-and-one-sixth units of cloth per unit of wine.) Within those limits, the precise terms of trade will depend on demand conditions, a topic explored further in Chapter 4.

We can summarize all these considerations in a numerical example based on Mill's analysis. Suppose that we had the following information:

	Can Produce		And Before Trade Is Producing	
	Wine or Cloth		Wine and Cloth	
England	20	60	10	30
Portugal	60	80	45	20
Total			55	50

Can each party gain from trade? That is, can each obtain at least as much of both commodities and more of one of them after trade compared with their pretrade consumption?

Let us begin to answer this question by determining who should specialize in which product. England's opportunity cost for one unit of wine is three units of cloth. (Under constant costs, producing 20 wine costs 60 cloth forgone, which means 1 wine costs 3 cloth forgone.) Portugal's wine costs one-and-one-third cloth per unit. Thus, Portugal's wine is cheaper in cloth forgone, while England's cloth is cheaper in terms of wine sacrificed. After specialization they will have

	Wine	Cloth
England	0	60
Portugal	60	0
Total	60	60

Are they better off? Not yet! World output has risen by 5 cloth plus 10 wine, but England now has no wine and Portugal no cloth. We can only be sure that both parties are better off if each has at least as much of both commodities as before trade and more of at least one.

How are the gains to be divided? First, the two parties must settle on terms of trade, which can fall anywhere from $1\frac{1}{3}$ cloth to 3 cloth per unit of wine. Suppose that the terms of trade settle at one cloth to two wine. There are a number of possible combinations of wine and cloth for each country that make both better off. One is

	Wine	Cloth
England	15	30
Portugal	45	30
Total	60	60

In this case England took all her gains in wine, trading her extra 30 units of cloth production for 15 wine, which gave her a net gain of 5 wine over her pretrade position. Portugal took all her gains in cloth for a gain of 10 cloth. Other combinations are also possible.

Putting the sequence of *autarky*[3] → specialization → trade together, the process looks like this:

	Before Trade (Autarky)		After Specialization		After Trade	
	Wine	*Cloth*	*Wine*	*Cloth*	*Wine*	*Cloth*
England	10	30	0	60	15	30
Portugal	45	20	60	0	45	30
Total	55	50	60	60	60	60

Thus, the gains from trade consist of the increase in output made possible by specialization and the sharing of those gains through trade. What trade has done for both countries is to enable them to separate production from consumption.

It is possible to put the same information in graphic form, using production possibilities curves. This is done in Figure 3-1.

Each country moves from its initial consumption-production combination *A* to total specialization at *B* and then trades at the ratio 1 wine = 2 cloth to a new consumption combination *C*. Note that *C* is not the only possible superior consumption position attainable through trade at these terms of 1 wine = 2 cloth. England, for example, could also arrive at point *D* through trade, taking all her gains in cloth. In this case, England would be consuming 10 wine and 40 cloth after trade, a gain of 10 cloth, whereas Portugal would have 50 wine and 20 cloth, a gain of 5 wine over her pretrade position. Alternatively, each country might take part of its gains in extra cloth and part in extra wine. This would correspond to points between *C* and *D* for each country on the terms of trade line. Any point from *C* to *D* contains at least as much of one commodity and more of one or both than the pretrade combination *A* and, therefore, represents a gain in welfare. These points are only attainable through specialization and trade.

---

[3] Autarky is a policy of national self-sufficiency, with no imports or capital inflows.

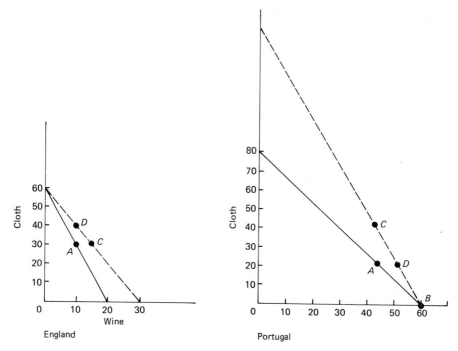

FIGURE 3-1   A Graphic Representation of the Gains from Trade

Dropping the labor theory of value in favor of an opportunity cost theory has actually improved the classical model. This change makes it possible to measure the size of the gains from trade and the various ways of dividing those gains between the two trading partners.

BALANCE-OF-PAYMENTS EQUILIBRIUM: A MONETARY EXAMPLE

In the examples from Smith, Ricardo, and Mill, the implicit assumption was one of barter; in a world of barter, exports and imports would be equal in value. In the real world, however, exchanges are not made this way; an American automobile exporter does not negotiate an "equal value" swap arrangement with a Brazilian shoe producer. Transactions are made independently of one another, based on prices and rates of exchange, and it is very likely that the value of exports will be greater than or less than the value of imports. Is it possible to demonstrate the gains from trade in a world where we are not given quantities and production possibilities curves, but only own-currency prices? A numerical example should shed some light on both the question and the answer.

	Bicycles (each)	Beer (bbl)
United States ($)	100	25
Germany (DM)	400	50

How can the consumer identify which country has the cheaper bicycles and which the cheaper beer? To begin, we can measure the opportunity cost of bicycles in both countries. Under constant costs, to produce a bicycle in the United States requires taking resources out of beer production that would have produced four barrels of beer, that in Germany the resources needed to produce one bicycle (400 DM) would have produced eight barrels of beer. The opportunity costs are

United States	1 bicycle = 4 beer
Germany	1 bicycle = 8 beer

Clearly the United States has a comparative advantage in bicycles and Germany in beer. But an exchange rate is necessary to convert German prices into dollars so that the consumer can make the correct decision, that is, to buy American bicycles and German beer.

Suppose that the exchange rate were set arbitrarily at 5 DM = $1. Then, German bicycles would cost $80 and German beer $10. American consumers would want to buy both products in Germany, and so would German consumers. The United States would be running a balance-of-payments deficit. This would put downward pressure on the price of the dollar and upward pressure on the price of the Deutsche mark. The cost of both German goods would rise to American, and the price of both American goods would fall to German. Suppose that the price of dollars fell to 3 DM. Then, German bicycles would cost $133.33, and German beer would cost $16.67. Everyone would choose to buy American bicycles and German beer, and trade would take place on the basis of comparative advantage. But to ensure that this will occur, it is necessary to have an exchange rate that correctly reflects patterns of comparative advantage. Thus, the assumption that exports pay for imports or of balance-of-payments equilibrium is equivalent to assuming that the exchange rate correctly reflects comparative advantage. In this particular case, any exchange rate from 2 DM = $1 to 4 DM = $1 will correctly reflect comparative advantage;[4] the exact rate of

[4] These limits were computed by setting the price of bicycles in Germany equal to the price of bicycles in the United States and the price of beer in each country equal to each other, which occurs at $1 = 4 DM and $1 = 2 DM, respectively. Any lower price for dollars than 4 DM will make American bicycles cheaper than German, and any exchange rate higher than 2 DM = $1 will make German beer cheaper than American beer.

exchange will depend on the relative strengths of demand, a topic considered in Chapter 4.

While the topics of exchange rates and balance-of-payments equilibrium will not be taken up until Part 3, it is clear that trade and balance-of-payments questions are closely interconnected. The assumption of an appropriate exchange rate is essential to ensuring that trade will, in fact, take place on the basis of comparative advantage.

CONSTANT VERSUS INCREASING COSTS

The classical assumption of constant costs was a great convenience for developing numerical examples, but it is not very consistent with real world experience. Constant costs imply that the opportunity cost of one good in terms of the other forgone does not change as we specialize more and more in one good and produce less and less of the other. The alternatives to constant costs are increasing costs or decreasing costs, as is shown in Figure 3-2.

In the case of either increasing costs or decreasing costs, the opportunity cost of steel in terms of cloth forgone changes as we specialize more and more in one commodity or the other. (Opportunity cost is measured as the slope of the production possibilities curve at any given point.) This creates a problem in determining comparative advantage. Under constant costs, it was possible to compare the slopes of the two countries' production possibilities curves to determine which should specialize in which product. Now there is no single pair of numbers to compare. We can, however, determine which should specialize in what in a slightly different manner.

In the case of decreasing costs, it is readily apparent that in most cases both countries will specialize totally. In Figure 3-3, if country I is initially producing at A, then opportunity costs at the margin are given by the absolute value of the slope of a tangent line at A; in this case, the marginal opportunity

FIGURE 3-2   Production Possibilities Curves with Constant, Increasing, and Decreasing Costs

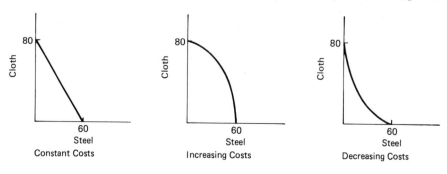

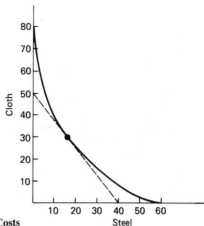

FIGURE 3-3
Specialization with Decreasing Costs

cost of cloth is 40 steel/50 cloth, or four-fifths of a steel. If cloth is available from the other country at a price of less than four-fifths of a steel, country I will specialize in steel and trade for cheaper foreign cloth. At a higher price for cloth, it will specialize in cloth. Assume that the international terms of trade facing this country are 1 cloth for 1 steel. As country I moves toward cloth specialization, the cost of cloth in terms of steel forgone becomes progressively lower—three-fifths of a steel, two-fifths of a steel, and so forth. Thus, the gains from trade increase as it becomes more and more specialized. As long as the other country's production is large enough to meet its needs for steel,[5] country I will not stop short of total specialization. The resulting posttrade production (B) and attainable superior consumption points (C to D) at terms of trade (BT) are shown in Figure 3-4. Decreasing costs are likely to occur when both industries have substantial economies of scale.

A far more likely prospect is that at some point both commodities will be subject to increasing marginal opportunity costs. That is, as we move closer to specialization in steel (or cloth), we are taking resources out of cloth (or steel) production that are more and more specialized in or suitable for cloth production and less and less productive in steel. This gives us the familiar production possibilities curve that is concave to the origin, as in Figure 3-5.

The main result of replacing the constant cost assumption with increasing costs is to explain the real world phenomenon of partial specialization. Suppose that this country is initially (before trade) consuming and producing at A in Figure 3-5. Opportunity costs of steel in terms of cloth

[5] The "small-country problem," which occurs when one of the two partners is too small to produce enough of the product in which it has a comparative advantage to meet the needs of both countries, will lead to incomplete specialization under either constant or increasing costs. This situation is discussed later in this chapter.

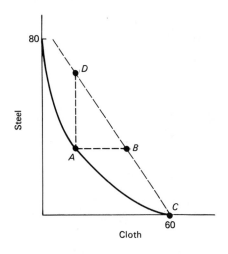

FIGURE 3-4
Pre- and Posttrade Production and Consumption
with Decreasing Costs

are measured by the slope of the tangent line *RR* to the production possibilities curve at *A*. (The small triangle *AXY* is an approximation of the slope at *A* and indicates that at this point approximately one unit of steel must be given up to produce one more unit of cloth, or vice versa.) If this country is facing the international terms of trade given by the slope of line *TT*, or approximately one steel to two cloth, it will move to producing at *B* and consuming at some point along *TT*, most likely between *C* and *D*. Why? One unit of cloth production given up enables this country's residents to produce one additional unit of steel that can then be traded internationally for two

FIGURE 3-5   Pre- and Posttrade Production and Consumption with Increasing Costs

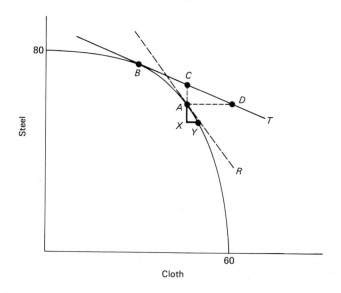

units of cloth, a net gain in consumption of one cloth. However, as it moves toward steel specialization, increasing costs are encountered. The next unit of steel production may cost 1.2 units of cloth, leaving a net gain of only 0.8 units of cloth. Specialization in steel will continue until the economy arrives at *B*, at which the marginal cost of steel in terms of cloth forgone (measured by a tangent line to the production possibilities curve at *B*) is equal to the cloth cost of steel internationally. Further specialization in steel would mean that additional units of domestic steel would be more expensive than would international steel, so specialization stops short of being complete. It can then trade back along the terms of trade line to points such as *C* (more steel, same amount of cloth) or *D* (more cloth, same amount of steel) or in between (more or both), all of which are clearly superior to their pretrade consumption-production point *A*. Thus, even under conditions of increasing costs, the classical demonstration of consumption gains from trade remains valid. Comparative advantage in a particular country is determined by comparing domestic marginal opportunity costs to the terms of trade offered by the rest of the world. Had the offer been one-half unit of cloth per unit of steel, specialization would have moved in the opposite direction.

We can also measure the volume of trade conveniently on this diagram. In Figure 3-6, we have the same situation in which this country moves from its pretrade consumption-production combination *A* to production at *B* and consumption at *E* (a point on the terms of trade line between *C* and *D*). Measuring production at *B* and consumption at *E*, we find that the residents of this country are exporting *BF* of steel (10 units) and importing *FE* of cloth (20 units) at terms of trade *BE* (1 steel to 2 cloth). All this information is

FIGURE 3-6   Volume of Trade with Increasing Costs

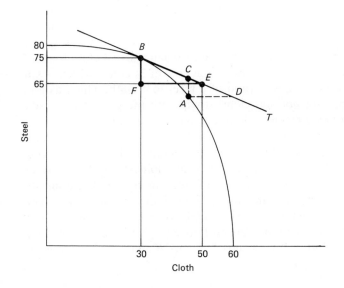

contained in the *trade triangle BEF*, a right triangle the hypotenuse of which goes from the production combination at *B* to the consumption combination at *E*. The slope of this hypotenuse reflects the terms of trade.

ADDING TRANSPORT COSTS

In all the previous examples, it was assumed that the process of getting goods back and forth between the two countries was costless, or at least no more costly than moving them around within the country. That is, shipping costs were built into the domestic opportunity costs or dollar prices used to determine comparative advantage. But, in fact, the transactions costs of moving goods between countries are usually higher than within countries; as we observed in Chapter 1, this is one factor that makes international trade different from domestic trade. Distances are usually greater; information is harder to obtain; currency exchange problems create risks and delays; and health and safety and labeling requirements are different, adding to the cost of international sales compared with domestic sales. If we allow for these transactions costs, which we lump together under the name of transport costs, can we still demonstrate the existence of mutual gain based on comparative advantage? The answer is yes, and it can be shown to be true under either constant or increasing costs. Consider the following situation.

Assume that in the United States 1 steel costs 2 cloth and in England that 1 steel costs 4 cloth. In the absence of transport costs, each would trade at some intermediate ratio such as 1 steel = 3 cloth. Suppose that transport costs for either one steel or 3 cloth amount to half a unit of cloth (and there are no internal transport costs). Then, for the United States, 1 steel sells for 3 cloth internationally less $\frac{1}{2}$ cloth transport costs, or $2\frac{1}{2}$ cloth net, which is still better than the domestic price of 2 cloth. There is still a gain of $\frac{1}{2}$ cloth on each unit traded internationally. Similarly, England pays 3 cloth for each steel plus $\frac{1}{2}$ cloth in transport costs for a total cost of $3\frac{1}{2}$ cloth, which is still more favorable than the domestic ratio of 1 steel to 4 cloth. Thus, as long as the transport costs are not sufficient to wipe out the gains from trade, trade will still take place on the basis of comparative advantage.

If, however, transport costs were $1\frac{1}{2}$ cloth per 1 steel or 3 cloth, trade would not occur because it would no longer be beneficial. The United States could now net $1\frac{1}{2}$ cloth per 1 steel, less than the domestic price for steel, and England would have to pay $4\frac{1}{2}$ cloth per steel, more than the domestic price. Trade between England and the United States would cease. This argument is illustrated diagrammatically in Figure 3-7, where line T_1 represents the terms of trade without transport costs, T_2 with $\frac{1}{2}$ cloth transport costs, and T_3 with $1\frac{1}{2}$ cloth transport costs. Points *B* and *C* are examples of

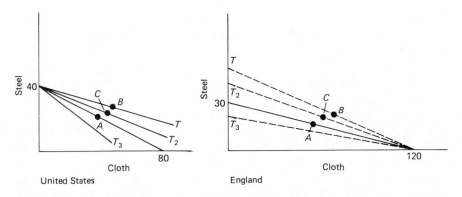

FIGURE 3-7   Transport Costs with Constant Production Costs

potentially superior consumption points attainable at terms of trade T_1 and T_2, respectively.

What about increasing costs? This situation is represented for one country in Figure 3-8, where A is the pretrade production and consumption point. At international terms of trade TT, this country would normally produce at B and consume at some point such as C. But the terms of trade including transport costs will be at some less favorable angle such as $T'T'$, which is tangent to the production possibilities curve at B' and leads to consumption at a point such as C', clearly inferior to C but better than the original combination A. Transport costs have reduced the extent of spe-

FIGURE 3-8   Transport Costs with Increasing Production Costs

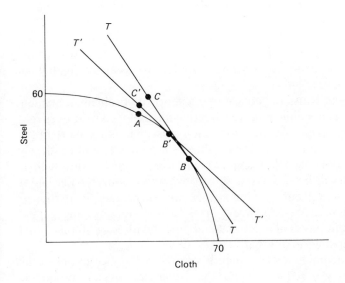

cialization and the volume of trade. Nevertheless, as long as transport costs are not so high as to completely wipe out the gains from trade, the case for free trade remains intact.

Historically, changes in transport costs have been important in determining the volume and composition of trade. The expansion of trade under the Roman Empire is a classic example. Prior to the advent of the "Pax Romana," trade around the Mediterranean was risky—roads were poor, robbers were everywhere, and journeys were long and arduous. Consequently, trade took place only in goods with a high value-to-weight or value-to-volume ratio and usually could not be produced locally—spices, dyes, precious metals, and jewels. But Roman roads patrolled by Roman legions drastically reduced the cost of transport. Travel was made faster, safer, and easier, in a word, cheaper. The result was a great increase in the volume of trade and also a change in composition to include basic foodstuffs and fabrics for the masses, motivated by relatively small place-to-place price differentials that were no longer offset by substantial transport costs.

FULL EMPLOYMENT

The assumption of full employment implies that the country is operating on, rather than inside, the production possibilities frontier. When there are idle resources, the opportunity cost of producing another unit of cloth or steel is zero: no alternative production need be forgone. It is possible to have more cloth with no sacrifice of steel, more steel with no sacrifice of cloth, or even more of both. No foreign offer can be cheaper than that!

Clearly, more may be gained by utilizing resources more fully than by trade. No foreign country can compete with zero opportunity costs. This assumption appears to be critical and nonexpendable. It is, in fact, an assumption that underlies most of microeconomic theory, which investigates the most efficient utilization of resources under the assumption that all resources are fully employed.

Full employment is usually considered a short-run problem, amenable to appropriate macroeconomic policy. Directing unemployed resources into import substitution, to get to the production possibilities frontier, might make sense if those resources could be shifted subsequently and costlessly into export production once full employment were attained. But such is rarely the case, as will be discussed shortly when we consider the factor mobility assumption. Resources tend to become specialized in particular products. Workers relocate and invest in skills and training, and capital becomes embodied in physical plant and equipment with long lifetimes that are not readily adaptable to alternative uses.

In addition, unemployment frequently occurs in many countries at the same time. If country A reduces imports to create employment-producing import substitutes, country B is likely to do the same, to solve the same kind of unemployment problem, or retaliate, or both. (This was the kind of reasoning that led to the Smoot–Hawley Tariff of 1930.) Under these circumstances, neither country would attain the production possibilities frontier, but both would be directing resources away from their more efficient (export) industries and into those industries in which each has a comparative disadvantage (import substitutes). Compounding the welfare loss from unemployed resources is an additional welfare loss from redirecting resources into less efficient uses. This situation is represented diagrammatically in Figure 3-9.

Suppose that this economy (country A) were initially producing at X and consuming at Z, exporting XY of cloth and importing YZ of steel at terms of trade TT. If country A chooses to move toward the production possibilities frontier by import substitution, the initial result would be consumption at Z and production at Y. Employment is improved but consumption is unchanged. However, if retaliation by country B created a reduction in A's cloth exports equal in value (at terms of trade TT) to the reduction in steel imports XY, this would drive country A to produce and consume at X. Point X lies on a lower indifference curve than does the initial consumption point Z.

Thus, while the full-employment assumption is essential to the classical model of comparative advantage, dropping this assumption does not justify

FIGURE 3-9   Unemployment and Import Substitution

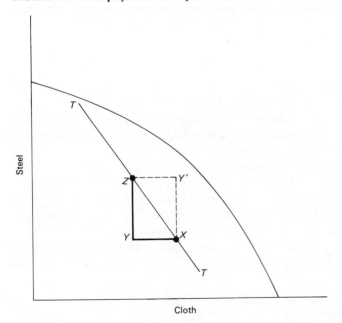

a policy of interference with free trade. We examine the employment question more fully in Chapter 9, where the employment argument for protection is discussed.

MORE THAN A TWO-BY-TWO WORLD

The preceding examples of comparative advantage were cast in a two-country, two-commodity framework. The mathematics required to deal with an m-country, n-commodity situation is beyond the scope of this book. However, it is possible to discuss the situations of two countries trading many commodities and that of many countries trading two commodities to show in a qualitative fashion that trade will continue to take place on the basis of differences in opportunity costs. For simplicity, we consider only the constant cost case.

Consider the situation of two commodities, wine and cloth, and five countries, A, B, C, D, and E. Costs for each commodity in terms of the other forgone are given for each country in Table 3-1. International terms of trade are assumed to fall in the middle, at 3 cloth to 1 wine.

The greatest gains from trade occur between A and E, but in a five-country world, it is likely that total specialization by A in cloth and E in wine will not produce sufficient quantities to supply the needs of A, D, and E for cloth and A, B, and E for wine, so B and D become secondary (next-lowest-cost) suppliers of cloth and wine, respectively. Country B has less to gain and offer than does A, but it can still gain by purchasing wine from D and E at the international price of 3 cloth per wine rather than at the domestic price of 4 cloth per wine. Thus, four of the five countries can still gain from trade based on different opportunity costs. If world demand for wine pushed the price (terms of trade) above 3 cloth per wine,[6] country C would also become a wine supplier and a cloth importer; below a 3:1 ratio, C would export cloth and import wine. Countries with similar patterns of comparative advantage (A and B, as well as D and E) would not trade with each other or would trade very little.

The other possibility is that there are only two countries but many commodities. Commodities can be ranked in comparative advantage for each country by taking the ratio of their respective costs. For example, suppose that the United States and Canada produce cars, steel, cloth, wheat, and lumber and that their costs are as given in Table 3-2.

Clearly, the United States will export cars and import lumber; depending on where the terms of trade (reflected in exchange rates) happen

---

[6] The role of differences in demand in determining the precise international terms of trade is examined in Chapter 4.

TABLE 3-1 Comparative Advantage in a Multicountry Model

Country	Cloth per Unit of Wine	Primary Supplier Of	Primary Supplier To	Secondary Supplier Of	Secondary Supplier To	Primary Source Of	Primary Source Is	Secondary Source Of	Secondary Source Is
A	5:1	Cloth	E, D	—	—	Wine	E	Wine	D
B	4:1	—	—	Cloth	D, E	Wine	E	Wine	D
C	3:1	Does not trade; domestic opportunity costs = international terms of trade[1]							
D	2:1	—	—	Wine	A, B	Cloth	A	Cloth	B
E	1:1	Wine	A, B	—	—	Cloth	A	Cloth	B

[1] This is unlikely to occur under increasing costs.

to fall, the United States may or may not export steel and import wheat. Cloth will probably be produced domestically in both countries (classifying it as a *nontraded good*). Trade is most likely in those products in which the cost spread is greatest. This example raises another interesting possibility. Suppose that the United States and Canada are initially trading cars and steel for wheat and lumber and that there is a shift in U.S. preferences toward houses in preference to cars. The United States will try to buy more Canadian lumber. In a two-commodity model, as we shall see in Chapter 4, the terms of trade will shift. In a multicommodity model, there can also be a change in the composition of trade.

If exchange rates are fixed, demand will drive prices up in Canada and down in the United States (because of the shift away from cars). As the total price levels change, U.S. cloth will become cheaper relative to Canadian cloth and may be added to our list of exports. The extra lumber will be purchased by shifting cloth from a nontraded good to an export good. (A similar result would occur under floating rates, except that the adjustment would show up in the exchange rate rather than in the price level, as is explained in Chapter 13.)

Not only does comparative advantage survive in a multicommodity world; this more realistic model also explains a major source of demand for protection. Wheat in our hypothetical example might at one time have been high on the rankings in comparative advantage for the United States, followed by furs, whale oil, and wooden ships. But as new industries such as cars and steel arose, having an even higher rank in comparative advantage, wheat would have dropped in relative position from export to nontraded to importable with no change in physical efficiency! The ranks of protectionism are filled with firms and industries to whom this has happened, shoes and textiles being the most conspicuous examples. They forget that if we are to export our new, high-technology, sophisticated manufactures, we have to be able to import something else, often from those lines in which our comparative advantage was once substantial.

TABLE 3-2   Ranking Comparative Advantage in a Multicommodity World

Commodity	U.S. Cost (U.S. $)	Canadian Cost (Can $)	U.S. Cost/ Canadian Cost[1]	U.S. Rank in Comparative Advantage
Cars (ea)	4,000	6,000	0.667	1
Steel (ton)	100	110	0.91	2
Cloth (bolt)	240	250	0.96	3
Wheat (ton)	300	250	1.20	4
Lumber (1,000 bd ft)	2,000	1,200	1.667	5

[1] Exchange rates are ignored since only relative costs matter.

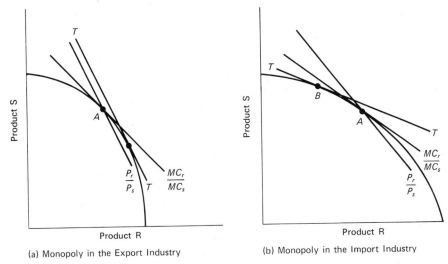

(a) Monopoly in the Export Industry   (b) Monopoly in the Import Industry

FIGURE 3-10 **Patterns of Specialization with Monopolistic Conditions in One Industry**

IMPERFECT COMPETITION

The assumption of perfect competition, like the full-employment assumption, is a common premise not only in trade theory but also in microeconomic theory in general. This assumption implies that prices reflect marginal costs, so that we can use domestic price ratios and domestic opportunity cost ratios interchangeably in determining comparative advantage. In perfect competition, of course, in the long run $P_r = MC_r$, so the assumption that $P_r/P_s = MC_r/MC_s$ (= the slope of the production possibilities frontier), is actually a weaker form of the perfect competition assumption. What happens if $P_r/P_s \neq MC_r/MC_s$, or specifically, if $P_r/P_s > MC_r/MC_s$, reflecting monopoly in industry R?

The result depends (back in a two-by-two world) on whether R, the monopolized industry, is the export industry or the import industry.[7] These two cases are depicted in panels (a) and (b), respectively, of Figure 3-10, where A is the initial production point, B is the posttrade production point in the absence of monopoly, and TT is the international terms of trade ratio. The price signals to which consumers and producers respond, however, are not domestic marginal cost ratios relative to international terms of trade but rather domestic *price* ratios compared with the international terms of trade. As we move toward specialization in R in panel (a), the domestic price ratio

---

[7] The terms export industry and import industry refer to those industries that have comparative advantages and/or disadvantages, respectively, when the marginal cost ratio at A is compared with the international terms of trade in each case.

will rotate into equality with *TT* long before the marginal cost ratio does so. Consequently, specialization will stop short of *B*. While this country will gain from trade, the extent of specialization and thus the gains from trade are reduced by the presence of monopoly in the export industry. This is a corollary to the familiar problem posed by domestic monopolies, which restrict output below and raise prices above competitive levels.

In panel (b), monopoly exists in the import-competing industry. Product R is now defined as import competing because the international terms of trade *TT* have been shifted so that R is now cheaper internationally than domestically, measured either (correctly) by comparison with the marginal cost ratio at *A* or (incorrectly) by comparison with the domestic price ratio at *A*. Production should move to *B*, at which the international terms of trade *TT* are equal to the slope of the production possibilities frontier. In fact, specialization will move beyond *B* to a point at which the price ratio (which rotates upward along with the marginal cost ratio) is equal to the international terms of trade. This country will overspecialize in product S, the competitively produced product. This country will still gain from specialization and trade, attaining a consumption point above *A* on the terms of trade line, but resources will be allocated less efficiently than they would be in the absence of monopoly.

Monopoly distortions can be corrected with appropriate tariffs, a subject considered in Chapter 9. It is sufficient to note here only that the existence of monopoly does not eliminate the gains from specialization and trade on the basis of comparative advantage. In addition, the monopoly power that gave rise to the distortion will be reduced by foreign competition.

FACTOR MOBILITY

The factor mobility assumption is really two assumptions rolled into one:

1. Factors of production are completely mobile within countries.
2. Factors of production are completely immobile between countries.

This pair is sometimes referred to as the "strong" factor mobility assumption. A weaker form, closer to real world experience, is that factors of production are more mobile within countries than between countries. This is another of the characteristics noted in Chapter 1 as differentiating international from domestic trade.

Internal factor immobility creates some real problems for the theory of comparative advantage and the resulting argument for free trade. The problem is illustrated in Figure 3-11. The movement from *A* to *B* along the production possibilities frontier is neither costless nor instantaneous. Resources must be taken out of cloth (moving from *A* to *D*) and then transferred

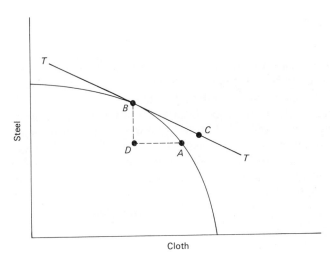

FIGURE 3-11   Free Trade and Factor Immobility Within a Country

into steel (moving from D to B), creating some short-run structural and frictional unemployment. There is a cost of relocation and retraining that must be borne by either the owners of the resources or by the entire society, although it is generally believed (and seems to be supported empirically) that these short-run losses are more than outweighed by the long-run gains from free trade in efficiency, competition, and economies of size and scale. It can be argued, however, that these gains accrue to society as a whole and that society should therefore absorb some of the short-run losses through retraining and relocation assistance. This argument was incorporated into law in the adjustment assistance provisions of the Trade Expansion Act of 1962, which are discussed in Chapter 10.

The other half of the assumption does not allow for factors of production to move from one country to another. Relaxing this assumption also does not negate the case for free trade based on comparative advantage but, rather, offers an alternative route to the same end.[8] Now there is a choice between moving outputs and moving inputs, based on the relative costs of transportation. The gains from free trade with Japan are still there whether we acquire Japanese inputs directly (movement of Japanese labor and/or capital to the United States) or indirectly (movement of Japanese labor and capital embodied in Japanese goods to the United States). If the final product is fragile, heavy, or perishable, moving the inputs closer to the final market might be more cost-effective than moving the final product. Product movements and input movements are substitutes for each other.

[8] Moving factors of production from country to country raises problems of the *distribution* of the gains from trade, however. Country A may gain total GNP from factor mobility, but the gains are shared among more resource owners and consumers, some of whom may lose individually.

SMALL COUNTRIES AND
LARGE COUNTRIES

There is one final qualification to the classical theory of comparative advantage that needs to be raised at this point. Suppose that one of the two countries, Upland, is so small relative to the other that, even if it specialized totally (under constant costs) in the product in which it has a comparative advantage (cloth), the total output of cloth would not be sufficient to meet the pretrade consumption levels of both countries. This situation is illustrated in Figure 3-12. Initial cloth consumption is 10 (Upland) plus 25 (Downland), or 35 cloth. Upland's total production is not sufficient to meet that demand, let alone provide additional cloth.

The solution is for Upland to specialize, while Downland produces at *b*—more steel, less cloth, but incomplete specialization. Numerically, this leads to the following solution:

| Country | Pretrade | | After Specialization | |
	Steel	Cloth	Steel	Cloth
Upland	10	10	0	20
Downland	50	25	70	15
Total	60	35	70	35

Downland is producing just enough cloth to keep world production at

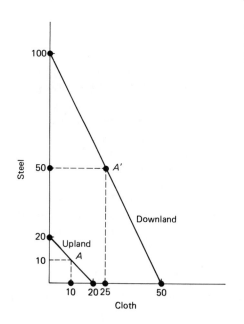

FIGURE 3-12
Small Countries and Incomplete Specialization

its original level and is expanding its steel production, so that there is a world output gain of 10 steel. On what terms will they trade? Remember that this is a world of perfect competition and no transport costs. Under those circumstances, the Upland steel buyers are indistinguishable from the Downland steel buyers in the Downland market. They are so small in number relative to the total market that they can buy as much as they want at the Downland going rate (internal terms of trade) of 1 cloth to 2 steel. Thus, the final allocation will be

	Steel	Cloth
Upland	20	10
Downland	50	25
Total	70	35

Upland has traded 10 cloth for 25 steel. Notice that in this case *all* the gains from trade go to the small country, Upland. Since Downland can only have one price for steel in terms of cloth and one is already established under incomplete specialization, the international price will be the same as Downland's domestic price ratio. Any time a trading country is so small relative to world trade that it cannot affect the terms of trade, it reaps all the gains from trade.

In the absence of monopoly-monopsony power, small countries usually have more to gain from trade than do large countries. Large countries already have many of the gains from trade within their bigger domestic markets.

DYNAMIC GAINS
FROM TRADE

The arguments for free trade presented in this chapter are static; that is, they only consider the immediate gains from allocating resources more efficiently. The greater gains from trade may actually be dynamic, as was suggested in Chapter 2 when we examined the relationship between trade and growth and in this chapter when we considered the benefits of international factor mobility.

Countries that have little margin over subsistence for saving and investment can use some of the gains from trade for that purpose, leading to further outward shifts in the production possibilities curve. Trade in intermediate goods and basic inputs can have a synergistic effect on output and productivity. Accompanying the flow of inputs and final product is a flow of information, ideas, techniques, and values that have the potential to speed up the growth process in industrialized and less developed countries alike.

Finally, the benefits of competition are dynamic as well as static.

Competition, as Servan-Schreiber[9] suggested, calls forth a response from previously sheltered firms that increases output and improves allocation of existing industrial resources.

While the dynamic gains from trade are far more difficult to measure than are the static gains, they are likely to be much more significant in the long run in enhancing output and economic well-being.

SUMMARY

The classical model is the economic case for specialization and trade based on the principle of comparative advantage, which in contemporary language means that each country should specialize in that product in which its opportunity costs of production are lowest.

This model is based on a long list of simplifying assumptions, each of which was examined to see whether the classical conclusion about efficiency gains from specialization and trade remained valid as we move closer to the real world. Dropping the labor theory of value actually improves the classical model by introducing the production possibilities approach. The assumption of balance-of-payments equilibrium is necessary to ensure that prices will correctly reflect comparative advantage. Replacing constant costs with increasing costs enables us to understand the real world phenomenon of incomplete specialization. Incorporating transport costs explains why the volume of trade is less than one might expect, or why trade sometimes does not occur at all. Relaxing the full-employment assumption helps us to understand the demand for protection. Examining a multicountry or multicommodity world enables us to explain who trades with whom and also the existence of nontraded goods. Imperfect competition leads to over- or underspecialization but does not eliminate the gains from trade. Factor immobility internally can complicate the process of adjusting to free trade, whereas factor mobility externally allows the option of moving inputs as an alternative to moving outputs. Finally, the existence of trading countries of disparate size helps us to understand why small countries are more specialized than are large countries and also have more to gain from trade.

KEY TERMS

absolute advantage
autarky
comparative advantage
constant costs

[9] Jean Jacques Servan-Schreiber, *The American Challenge* (New York: Athanaeum, 1968).

decreasing costs
exchange rate
factor mobility
full employment
gains from trade
imperfect competition
increasing costs
labor theory of value
marginal opportunity costs
nontraded goods
opportunity cost
production possibilities curve
partial specialization
specialization
terms of trade
trade triangle
transport costs

REVIEW QUESTIONS

1. Consider the following example:

	Initial Production		Can Produce	
			Either	*Or*
	Wheat	*Oil*	*Wheat*	*Oil*
Canada	100	50	200	100
Mexico	80	80	160	160

Which country has a comparative advantage in which product? Why? Determine their postspecialization production. Assuming that they trade at a ratio of 1½ wheat per oil, find one potentially superior posttrade consumption combination for each country. Then, graph all this information on a production possibilities curve.

2. Suppose that the information were given in prices instead of quantities; that is,

	Price Per Unit	
	Wheat	*Oil*
Canada ($)	5	10
Mexico (pesos)	30	30

Can you still determine comparative advantage? Within what limits must the exchange rate fall?

3. Explain what happens when you drop each of the following assumptions:

labor theory of value	factor immobility (externally)
constant costs	balance-of-payments equilibrium
perfect competition	full employment
factor mobility (internally)	no transport costs
two countries	two commodities

4. Why might small countries gain more from trade than large countries? Do they also risk more?
5. Explain what the term comparative advantage means and how it leads to the theoretical case for specialization and trade.

SUGGESTED READINGS

BHAGWATI, JAGDISH, and V.K. RAMASWAMI, "Domestic Distortions, Tariffs, and the Theory of Optimum Subsidy," *Journal of Political Economy*, 71, no. 1 (February 1963), 44–50.

CHACHOLIADES, MILTIADES, *Principles of International Economics*, pp. 34–53. New York: McGraw-Hill, 1981.

HABERLER, GOTTFRIED, "Some Problems in the Pure Theory of International Trade," *Economic Journal*, 60, no. 238 (June 1950), 223–240.

HARROD, ROY, *International Economics*, chap. 1. Chicago: University of Chicago Press, 1958.

HELLER, H. ROBERT, *International Trade: Theory and Empirical Evidence*, 2nd ed., pp. 40–42. Englewood Cliffs, N.J.: Prentice-Hall, 1973.

KREININ, MORDECHAI, *International Economics: A Policy Approach*, chap. 11. New York: Harcourt Brace, 1979.

MILNER, CHRIS, and DAVID GREENAWAY, *An Introduction to International Economics*, pp. 5–7. New York: Longman, 1979.

MUNDELL, ROBERT, "International Trade and Factor Mobility," *American Economic Review*, 48, no. 3 (June 1957), 321–335.

CHAPTER 4

Modern Theory:
Demand and the Terms of Trade

In Chapter 3, we determined the limits within which the terms of trade must lie in a two-country, two-commodity world. These limits are set by the domestic opportunity costs of production in each country or by supply conditions. But what about demand? As we shall see, people's tastes and preferences and responses to relative prices will determine where within those limits the precise terms of trade will settle. In extreme cases, demand patterns might even reverse the pattern of trade that we would predict on the basis of comparative advantage.

THE RANGE OF THE TERMS
OF TRADE AND THE GAINS
FROM TRADE

The constant costs analysis of Chapter 3 led to the fairly self-evident conclusion that the international terms of trade must fall between the limits set by domestic opportunity costs. If, for example, the United States has an opportunity cost ratio of 1 cloth = 2 wheat and Canada's is 1 cloth = 4 wheat, and the United States is totally specialized in cloth at 100 units, then the range of the potential terms of trade as well as the possible trading combinations are given by the

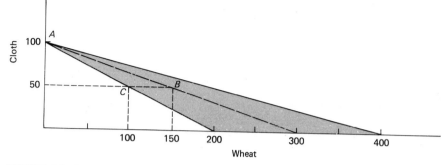

FIGURE 4-1   The Range of the Terms of Trade

shaded area in Figure 4-1. Any point in the shaded area is a potentially superior consumption combination for the United States and is associated with a particular terms of trade ratio that can be measured as the slope of a line passing through that point and point A, the U.S. initial cloth-wheat endowment (100, 0). For example, point B is a consumption combination of 50 cloth and 150 wheat obtained from Canada at a cost of 50 cloth—a trading ratio of 1 cloth = 3 wheat. If the United States had been producing and consuming originally at C (50 cloth, 100 wheat), this represents a gain from trade of 50 wheat. Terms of trade that are closer to Canada's opportunity costs will permit even larger gains from trade. Clearly, the choice of the terms of trade is important in allocating the gains from trade (the increase in total consumption) between the two partners. It is equally clear that demand must play some role in determining exactly where within those limits the terms of trade will fall. Exactly how demand enters in will be explored shortly, when we develop the *offer curve*. First, however, we need to consider the increasing cost case.

The range of the terms of trade is more difficult to determine in the

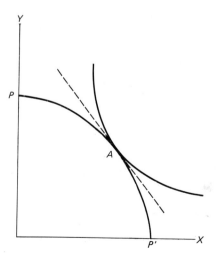

FIGURE 4-2
Pretrade Opportunity Costs

increasing cost case because domestic opportunity costs (technology) no longer set the limits. Demand enters from the beginning, since the pretrade opportunity costs (slope of the production possibilities curve in Figure 4-2, also called the marginal rate of transformation of X into Y, are determined by the equality between that slope and the marginal rate of substitution of Y for X in consumption, which is the slope of the highest attainable indifference curve tangent to PP').[1] Trade will occur as long as the other country's MRT_{xy} ($= MRS_{xy}$) is different from this country's, and the direction of difference will dictate the direction of specialization. The international terms of trade will lie between the two countries' initial opportunity costs, as before. Since the posttrade terms of trade will be equal (ignoring transport costs), there is no gain from trade *at the margin* (i.e., on the last unit), but there is an increase in total welfare in either one country or both. This is readily verified by the analysis of Chapter 3, which demonstrates the gains from trade to either or both countries in the increasing cost case.

RECIPROCAL DEMAND
AND THE OFFER CURVE

The graphical tool used to determine the terms of trade in a two-country, two-commodity model is the offer curve, sometimes known as the reciprocal demand curve. Offer curves show the total quantity of exports offered for imports at various terms of trade. If the exportable commodity is on the horizontal axis and the importable commodity is on the vertical axis, the offer curve will curve upward from the origin, as indicated in Figure 4-3.

The shape of the curve is the result of the fact that both commodities are subject to diminishing marginal utility. The simple offer curve of Figure 4-3 is drawn on the assumption that country A has a fixed stock of cloth (total specialization under constant costs). As cloth is traded away, A's inhabitants move up the utility schedule for cloth, and each remaining unit is more valuable than the one just traded because fewer units of cloth exist. At the same time, as the consumers acquire more wheat, additional units are subject to diminished utility. Therefore, country A can only be induced to part with more cloth in trade for wheat if it receives a better price for the cloth i.e., if the terms of trade become successively more favorable. "Favorable" terms of trade is a relative term that goes far back in the history of commercial policy. Terms of trade become more favorable when the ratio of quantity of imports to quantity of exports Q_m/Q_x, increases, or when the price ratio P_x/P_m increases.

Note that (in the diagram) country A will only trade 10 cloth for 5 wheat at the relatively unfavorable ratio of 1 wheat = 2 cloth but that, as the price

[1] Marginal rate of transformation (MRT_{xy}) is the amount of Y that must be sacrificed to produce one more unit of X. Marginal rate of substitution of X for $Y(MRS_{xy})$ is the additional amount of Y required to compensate for the loss of consumption of one more unit of X.

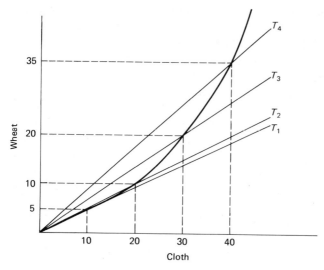

FIGURE 4-3 Offer Curve of Cloth for Wheat

or terms of trade becomes more favorable, it is willing to export more cloth. At T_4 (35 wheat for 40 cloth or 1 wheat = $1\frac{1}{7}$ cloth), country A is willing to trade more of its valuable cloth than at less favorable terms because it is receiving a higher wheat price for cloth.

This rationalization can be formalized by using indifference analysis, illustrated in Figure 4-4. In panel (a), we are given an indifference map for cloth and wheat. Line PP represents a constant cost production possibilities curve. This country is totally specialized in cloth at B. Point A_1 represents the optimal combination for production and consumption in the absence of trade. The dashed lines emanating from B represent alternative possible international terms of trade, and the points $A_2, A_3, \ldots , A_i$ represent the consumption combinations (C_i, W_i) of cloth and wheat that they would choose at each price ratio.

The points W_1, W_2, W_3, W_4 represent both imports and consumption of wheat at various alternative terms of trade, since all wheat consumed is imported. Exports of cloth are the difference between production (B) and consumption (C_1, C_2, C_3, C_4) and can be found by measuring that horizontal distance in panel (a). For example, X_1 (exports of cloth for W_1 of wheat) = C_1B, $X_2 = C_2B$, and so on. Plotting these points in panel (b) of Figure 4-4 traces out an offer curve of the expected shape.

An offer curve for the other country can be developed in similar fashion. Since the other country's exportable commodity is on the vertical axis, its offer curve will bend in the other direction, and the two should intersect as shown in Figure 4-5.

The offer curve of the cloth exporter is O_1, the offer curve of the wheat exporter is O_2, and equilibrium occurs where country 1's offer of cloth for wheat is exactly matched by country 2's offer of wheat for cloth. This occurs where OW of wheat is traded for OC of cloth at terms of trade OT, a line with a slope of OW/OC.

Under constant costs, the offer curve will be bounded by the domestic opportunity costs in the two countries, since neither country would trade at terms less favorable than its own domestic ratio. Thus, supply (or costs) sets the limits to the offer curve whereas demand determines the precise terms of trade between those limits. This situation is sketched in Figure 4-6, where the domestic terms of trade are 1 cloth = 2 wheat and 1 cloth = 4 wheat. It is possible for the offer curve to lie along the domestic terms of trade up to a

FIGURE 4-4 A Simple Derivation of the Offer Curve

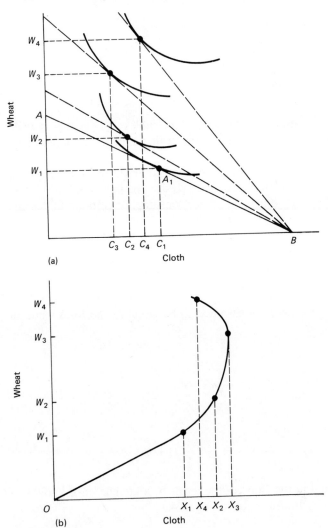

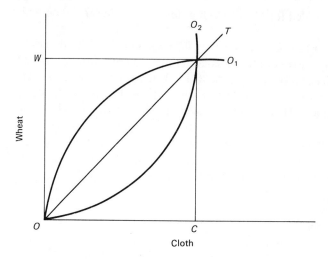

FIGURE 4-5   Equilibrium with Two Offer Curves

point at which the increased consumption of importables and decreased availability of exportables leads to a refusal to trade further except on (increasingly) more favorable terms.

The process of adjustment by which the terms of trade are reached should be familiar from traditional microeconomic analysis. The individual (*i*th) buyer or seller is a price taker and adjusts his or her consumption of importables and exportables so that

$$\left(\frac{MU_x}{MU_y}\right)_i = \frac{P_x}{P_y} \tag{4.1}$$

Since the total value of exports is assumed to be equal to the total value of imports,

$$P_x Q_x = P_y Q_y \tag{4.2}$$

and thus

$$\frac{P_x}{P_y} = \frac{Q_y}{Q_x} \tag{4.3}$$

The term Q_y/Q_x is equal to the slope of the terms of trade line (also known as the *gross barter terms of trade*). Substituting in 4.1,

$$\left(\frac{MU_x}{MU_y}\right)_i = \frac{Q_y}{Q_x} \qquad\qquad (4.4)$$

As the total purchases are adjusted, the aggregate purchases change Q_y/Q_x until finally the ratios are equal across all consumers and are equal to Q_y/Q_x. Thus, the consumption mix for each individual and the international terms of trade are determined simultaneously.

The increasing cost case is somewhat more complex. The diagrammatic exposition of the derivation of an offer curve under increasing cost is left to the appendix to this chapter, but the rationale for the shape of the offer curve is clearly strengthened by increasing costs. Let us assume that country A is initially producing some of both cloth and wheat at a cost ratio of 1 cloth = 2 wheat (which also equals the marginal rate of substitution in consumption for each consumer). If the initial offer from abroad is anything in excess of 2 wheat to 1 cloth, country A will expand its cloth production, reduce its wheat production, and export cloth for wheat. Country A's inhabitants encounter a fall in the marginal utility of cloth relative to wheat as well as increasing costs of production for cloth and decreasing costs of production for wheat. Because country A encounters increasing costs of production for exportables, increased volume of trade will be acceptable only at successively more favorable terms of trade. This reinforces the curved shape of the offer curve from the cost side.

The offer curve, especially under increasing costs, combines a supply curve (for exportables) and a demand curve (for importables). A pair of offer curves thus characterizes general equilibrium and the simultaneous determination of quantities and relative prices in a two-country, two-commodity world.

FIGURE 4-6   Opportunity Costs and Offer Curves

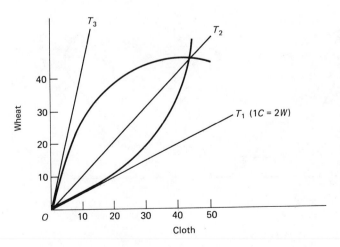

This tool has many useful analytical applications, especially in understanding commercial policy.

SHIFTS IN THE OFFER CURVE

Shifts in the offer curve can originate from changes in either demand or supply conditions. On the demand side, a change in tastes and preferences can shift the indifference map either horizontally or vertically and shift the offer curve. Figure 4-7 illustrates a change in tastes and preferences in favor of the importable good and the resulting shift in country A's offer curve, determining a new equilibrium volume of trade and terms of trade.

The offer curve for A has shifted upward, reflecting a larger amount of imports demanded for every possible volume of exports. This is because country A now values exportables more highly relative to importables and can be induced to part with the same amount of exportables only at more favorable terms of trade. The terms of trade have shifted in A's favor because of an improved bargaining position. A is both less anxious to import and less willing to export. A shift in tastes and preferences toward importables would have the opposite effect.

Tastes and preferences could shift for a number of reasons—changed age distribution of the population, social or institutional changes, or new uses for

FIGURE 4-7   Shifts in the Offer Curve

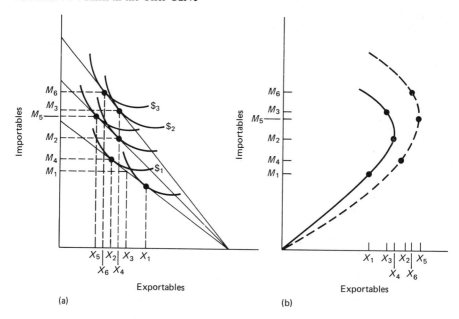

(a)

(b)

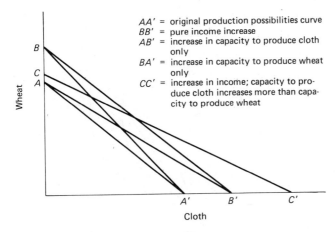

FIGURE 4-8   Shifts in Supply Conditions

one of the products, for example. Note that we have not considered two of the traditional sources of changes in demand—changes in the price of substitutes and changes in income. These are relevant only in a partial equilibrium model. In our general equilibrium two-commodity model, importables are the only substitute for exportables, and relative price can change only in response to changes in supply conditions (a shift in the production possibilities curve) or a change in tastes and preferences. Income is also represented by both the production possibilities curve (since income equals total production) and the indifference map (income equals consumption) and will, therefore, show up as both a supply and a demand variable.

On the supply side, either country's production possibilities curve can shift and will result in a shift in the offer curve. If we limit our analysis, for graphic simplicity, to the constant cost case, the production possibilities curve can shift outward in parallel fashion (a pure income increase), or it can shift outward in nonparallel fashion, reflecting both an income increase and a relative price change. (We ignore the possibility of an inward shift.) Some of the possibilities are illustrated in Figure 4-8.

An outward shift in the production possibilities curve can result from the availability of additional resources or from improvements in technology. If the technological improvement benefits both industries equally the shift will be radially outward (BB').[2] If it benefits only one industry, the shift will leave one of the end points unchanged (AB' or BA'). If it benefits one industry more than the other, the shift will be of the CC' variety.

Similar possibilities exist for resource growth, since (as we explore further in Chapter 5) different products use different resource combinations. If the resource growth is in the same proportion as the original resource base, the

[2] This case is referred to in the literature as neutral growth. All others are variants of biased growth.

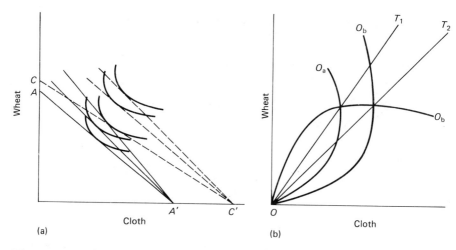

FIGURE 4-9 Shifts in the Offer Curve: Neutral Growth

production possibilities curve will shift outward in radial fashion. But if the additional resources are weighted more heavily toward cloth-producing resources, the shift will be of the AB' or CC' variety. (If, for example, cloth uses a higher ratio of labor to capital than does wheat, and the increase in resources is mostly labor, we would expect a shift to CC' rather than to BB'.)

Let us examine the effects of two such shifts on the offer curve, the neutral growth case (BB') and the growth-favoring-exportables case (CC'). These are illustrated in Figures 4-9 and 4-10.

In both cases, when the cloth exporter's offer curve shifts outward relative to the partner's, there is a worsening of the terms of trade; that is, they move closer to A's opportunity costs as represented by the slope of the production

FIGURE 4-10 Shifts in the Offer Curve: Biased Growth

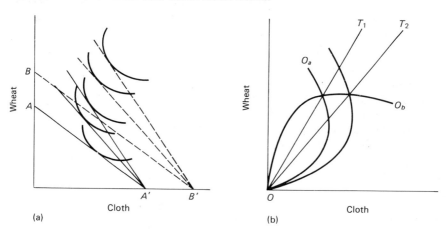

possibilities curve. Because A now has more of cloth (exportables), she is more willing to part with it. A can now consume more of both goods than before; some of the benefits of A's growth spill over to B in the form of an improvement in A's terms of trade. Note, however, that the relative shift in the terms of trade in B's favor is greater in the second case than in the first. An increase in the capacity to produce cloth (exportables) relative to wheat (importables) changes A's domestic opportunity costs. Wheat is now more expensive in terms of cloth forgone than before, and A will be more anxious to buy wheat abroad, worsening A's bargaining position and shifting A's offer curve so as to benefit B. You might want to try some of the other cases as an exercise.

ELASTICITY OF THE OFFER CURVE

The shape of the offer curve depends on the shapes of the underlying production possibilities curve and indifference maps, as is made clearer in the appendix to this chapter. If it is fairly simple to transfer resources from one commodity to another, the production possibilities curve will be less convex, or closer to linear, and the offer curve will be less bowed, or more elastic. If it is more difficult to convert resources between uses (sharply increasing marginal costs in both commodities), the offer curve will be more curved and will bend back more sharply. Similarly, if the two commodities are relatively close substitutes in consumption, the indifference curves will show less curvature—more nearly negatively sloped lines—and the offer curve will again be less bowed or more elastic. If they are poor substitutes, the indifference map will be more curved and so will the offer curve.

The elasticity of the offer curve reflects both supply elasticities (incorporated in the production possibilities curve) and demand elasticities (reflected in the indifference map). Its elasticity, like any elasticity, is the percentage change in quantity divided by the percentage change in price, but in this case the price is measured by the amount of domestic output forgone per unit imported.

You may recall from earlier courses that the price elasticity of either supply or demand can be written as

$$\frac{\Delta Q/Q}{\Delta P/P}$$

which can be rewritten as

$$\frac{\Delta Q}{\Delta P} \cdot \frac{P}{Q}$$

The first term, $\Delta Q/\Delta P$, is the marginal terms of trade, which is the slope of the offer curve at the point of intersection—the additional amount of imports received for one more unit of exports sacrificed. The second term, P/Q, is the reciprocal of the average terms of trade, which is measured by the ray from the origin AB. Thus, $P/Q = 1/(BD/AD)$, or AD/BD, as illustrated in Figure 4-11. The elasticity of the offer curve for cloth at the point of intersection of the two curves is thus $BD/CD \times AD/BD$, or the slope of BC divided by the slope of BA. This can be simplified somewhat, since $CD = AD - AC$, to $1/(1 - AC/AD)$. Because elasticity depends on both the average and the marginal terms of trade, it will vary along the offer curve, which will have an elastic, unitary, and inelastic range.

The elasticity of the offer curve is important for commercial policy, as we shall see in later chapters. Imposing a tariff or quota can be represented as a shift in the offer curve, and the effect on price (terms of trade) and quantity (volume of imports) is crucially dependent on the benefits that the tariff-imposing country wishes to receive. Figure 4-12 illustrates two possible outcomes of a shift in one country's offer curve. In panel (a), it intersects the other country's offer curve in a fairly elastic range. The terms of trade worsen slightly, but the volume of both imports and exports rises. In panel (b), the cloth offer curve intersects the other offer curve in its inelastic range. Not only do the terms of trade deteriorate sharply, but the volume of imports falls while the volume of exports rises.

FIGURE 4-11   Measuring the Elasticity of the Offer Curve

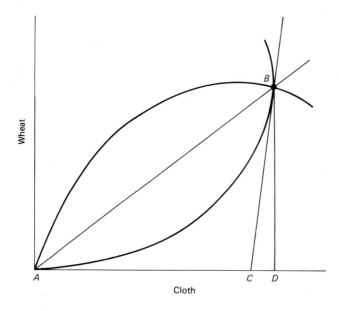

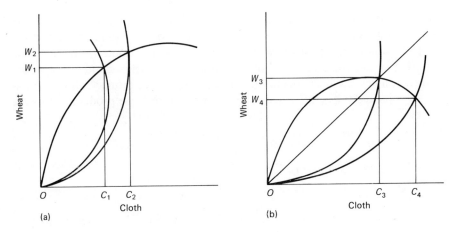

FIGURE 4-12 **Effect of Elasticity of the Terms of Trade**

IMMISERIZING GROWTH

In extreme cases, the fall in the Q_x/Q_m ratio may more than offset any growth in the capacity to produce exportables so that economic growth actually makes a country worse off. This unusual situation is illustrated in Figure 4-13. Note that the other country must have an offer curve that reflects a strong preference for its own exportable commodity. The fact that B's offer curve is flat and bends back sharply at relatively low levels of trade indicates that B's demand for cloth is relatively inelastic, that is, insensitive to changes in the terms of trade.

Before growth, A is trading OC of cloth for OW of wheat. After growth,

FIGURE 4-13 **Immiserizing Growth**

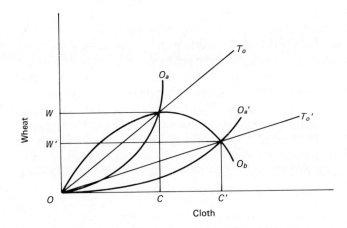

A is trading OC' (substantially *more* cloth) for OW' (less wheat). Note that two conditions are necessary; the growth must be export biased, and the other country's offer curve must be relatively insensitive to changes in the terms of trade. It has been argued that both conditions have held for many underdeveloped countries, whose increased capacity to produce primary products (especially foodstuffs) has met price-inelastic demand for those products on world markets.[3]

MEASURING THE TERMS OF TRADE

The theoretical concept of the terms of trade—what you get for what you give—has such far-reaching policy implications that it becomes very important to measure changes in the terms of trade from one period to the next. The case of immiserizing growth is only one instance of the use of this concept, which has important international economic policy implications. Terms of trade have also come up in discussions about OPEC—changes in what the petroleum exporters are receiving in the form of real goods and services per barrel of oil. In Chapters 8 and 9, we encounter the terms of trade argument for protection— the deliberate use of a tariff to exercise monetary power and lower the price paid to a foreign producer, thus improving one's own terms of trade at another's expense. In Chapter 11, we encounter a similar argument for customs unions— the combined effect of enhanced bargaining power and a judiciously designed common external tariff can be an improvement in the union's terms of trade.

The concept also appears elsewhere in different form. Parity for farmers is a terms of trade concept. Measures of well-being such as the number of hours a laborer must work to buy a shirt are another variant of terms of trade. This concept is an attempt to penetrate the veil of money prices to view the relative prices of goods and services in barter terms.

There are several approaches to measuring the terms of trade. One is to construct price indexes for imports and exports in much the same fashion as we construct the consumer price index and the producer price index. If imports have risen in price relative to exports, this means that one physical unit of our exports will buy fewer physical units of imports than before—a deterioration in our terms of trade. The price measure of the terms of trade is P_x/P_m (called the *net barter terms of trade*); a fall in its value means less favorable terms of trade. For example, in the United States the 1976 import price index (base 1970) was 224 and the export price index was 183. The net barter terms of trade rose from a base of 1.00 in 1970 to 1.22 in 1976, a 22 percent decline in our terms of trade.

---

[3] A similar fate befell American agriculture in the 1950s and 1960s as rapid increases in food output drove down prices and farm income.

The second widely used measure is the *gross barter terms of trade*, or Q_x/Q_m. This is the measure that corresponds to the terms of trade line on the offer curves in this chapter. If the value of exports were indeed equal to the value of imports, this figure could be arrived at fairly easily. Since

$$P_x Q_x = P_m Q_m \qquad (4.5)$$

then

$$\frac{P_x}{P_m} = \frac{Q_m}{Q_x}$$

so that the gross barter would be merely the reciprocal of the net barter terms of trade. In the real world, however, it is possible to export more or less than is imported, so a more indirect approach must be used.

Let the subscript 0 denote the base year and the subscript 1 denote the year for which we are trying to compute the gross barter terms of trade. Then, the gross barter terms of trade are given by

$$\frac{Q_{x_1}/Q_{x_0}}{Q_{m_1}/Q_{m_0}} \qquad (4.6)$$

The top half is an import quantity index and the lower half is an export quantity index. We cannot measure quantities directly; there is no way to add cars, bottles of wine, or tons of soybeans except with prices. But we do have the dollar volume and the price index. For imports, the index would be constructed as follows:

$$\frac{Q_{m_1}}{Q_{m_0}} = \frac{P_{m_1} Q_{m_1}}{P_{m_0} Q_{m_0}} \times \frac{1}{P_{m_1}/P_{m_0}} \qquad (4.7)$$

where $P_{m_0} Q_{m_0}$ = dollar value of base year imports and $P_{m_1} Q_{m_1}$ = dollar value of current year imports.

If P_{m_0} is the base year prices, it is equal to 1.00 and P_{m_1}/P_{m_0} is then equal to the current year import price index.[4] Thus, for 1976, dollar value of U.S. imports was \$123.9 billion. Imports in 1970 were \$39.9 billion. The import price index (base 1970) was 224. Thus,

$$\frac{Q_{m_1}}{Q_{m_0}} = \frac{123.9}{39.9} \times \frac{1}{2.24} = 1.39$$

[4] The index is generally given in the form P_{m_1}/P_{m_0} = 158 (a 58 percent increase in prices), but when it is used to deflate, it should be written as 1.58.

Similarly,

$$\frac{Q_{x_1}}{Q_{x_0}} = \frac{114.7}{42.5} \times \frac{1}{1.83} = 1.47$$

The gross barter terms of trade are

$$\frac{Q_{x_1}/Q_{x_0}}{Q_{m_1}/Q_{m_0}} = \frac{1.47}{1.39} = 1.058$$

Since the base period index is 1, the rise in this ratio indicates a deterioration in the gross barter terms of trade. The net barter terms of trade equal .817. The net and gross barter terms of trade should normally give the same indication; a rise in one should be accompanied by a fall in the other, both indicating improvement or deterioration in the terms of trade.

Other types of terms of trade indexes have been constructed, but these two are the most widely used and are satisfactory for most purposes.

DEMAND REVERSALS AND THE PATTERN OF SPECIALIZATION AND TRADE

The importance of demand in determining the volume and terms of trade is demonstrated in the offer curve. Opportunity costs determine the pattern of specialization and the limits to the terms of trade, whereas demand plays an important role in the precise outcome. But it can be demonstrated that in extreme cases a country will import the product in which it would be predicted to have a cost advantage and export the product in which it has a cost disadvantage. This peculiar case is known as *demand reversal*, and it occurs under increasing costs where comparative advantage is more difficult to identify with precision.

In Chapter 3, we assumed the existence of both pretrade and posttrade price ratios to determine comparative advantage and the terms of trade. In the real world, all we have is the posttrade prices. We might, however, infer which country should have a comparative cost advantage by superimposing one country's production possibilities curve on the other's, as in Figure 4-14.

Country A is represented by production possibilities curve AA' and country B by BB', with their pretrade positions at P_a and P_b, both representing more or less equal preference for the two commodities X and Y. At any terms of trade intermediate between their respective present (marginal) opportunity costs, A will move toward specializing in Y and B in X, as we would expect

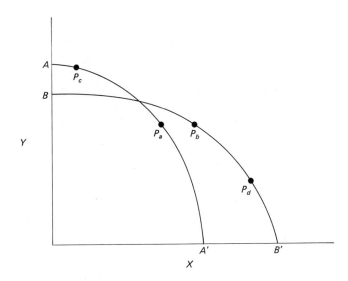

FIGURE 4-14 Demand Reversal

from the relative shapes of their production possibilities curves. But suppose instead that the pretrade positions were P_c and P_d—each has a strong preference for the commodity they would be expected to export. In this case, terms of trade intermediate between their present opportunity costs would lead each country to specialize *less*, move toward the center, and trade back to a combination weighted more heavily with the preferred commodity. This is illustrated for country A in Figure 4-15.

FIGURE 4-15 Specializing in the "Wrong" Commodity

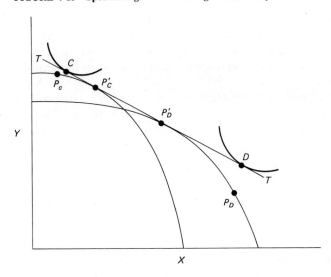

In nontechnical terms, demand reversals occur when a country has a strong preference for its own "export" good and is already so heavily specialized in that good before trade that it has already encountered sharply increased marginal costs. Trade enables it to move toward a more balanced output combination. Normally, we think of trade as requiring more specialization in production to provide a higher level of "balanced" consumption. In this case, trade permits specialization in consumption out of a more efficiently "balanced" production in each country.

SUMMARY

Demand determines exactly where the terms of trade will fall between the limits set by domestic opportunity costs in the constant cost case.

In the increasing cost case, the interaction of diminishing marginal utility (demand) and increasing marginal cost (supply) jointly determines the terms of trade (price) and the volume of trade (quantity).

This can be represented graphically by a pair of offer curves, each of which depicts the various quantities of exports offered for imports at alternative terms of trade. The intersection of the offer curves determines the terms and volume of trade.

The offer curve can shift in response to changes in tastes and preferences (demand), resource availability, or technology (supply). If the demand shift is toward exportables, the terms will shift in the exporter's favor. If the supply increases the capacity to produce exportables more than importables, the terms of trade will shift in the other country's favor.

It is possible for changes in the terms of trade to more than offset the gains of economic growth so that a country is consuming less instead of more after experiencing economic growth (immiserizing growth).

The terms of trade can be measured either as P_m/P_x (net barter terms of trade) or as Q_m/Q_x (gross barter terms of trade). A rise in the net barter terms or a fall in the gross barter terms represents a deterioration in the terms of trade.

Demand reversals refer to the phenomenon of importing a commodity in which a country would appear to have a comparative advantage. Demand reversals result from a strong preference for one's own exportable commodity.

KEY TERMS

demand reversal
diminishing marginal utility
exportables
gross barter terms of trade

immiserizing growth
importables
net barter terms of trade
offer curve
reciprocal demand
terms of trade

REVIEW QUESTIONS

1. Compute the change in the U.S. gross and net barter terms of trade from 1976 to 1981 and try to explain the change.
2. Suggest some reasons why demand reversals might occur.
3. Under what circumstances might we expect immiserizing growth? What policies can you devise to deal with this problem?
4. Sketch a pair of offer curves (be sure that you can derive them from a linear production possibilities curve and an indifference map). Experiment with shifting them and observing the resulting effects on the terms of trade and the volume of trade. Try the following:
    a. a primarily horizontal shift outward (inward) in the lower curve.
    b. a primarily vertical shift outward (inward) in the lower curve.
    c. a proportional outward shift in both curves.
    d. both shift out, but one more than the other.
5. Speculate on what the relative shapes of different offer curves tell you about demand elasticity and/or supply conditions.

SUGGESTED READINGS

CHACHOLIADES, MILTIADES, *Principles of International Economics*, pp. 146–159. New York: McGraw-Hill, 1980.
HELLER, H. ROBERT, *International Trade: Theory and Empirical Evidence*, 2nd ed., chap. 5. Englewood Cliffs, N.J.: Prentice-Hall, 1973.
MILNER, CHRIS, and DAVID GREENAWAY, *An Introduction to International Economics*, chap. 4. London and New York: Longman, 1979.

APPENDIX

Deriving the Offer Curve

In this chapter, the offer curve was derived under constant cost conditions. Offer curves of a more general nature can be derived from an indifference map and an increasing cost production possibilities curve. In Figure 4A-1, the domestic indifference map and production possibilities curve are drawn in the

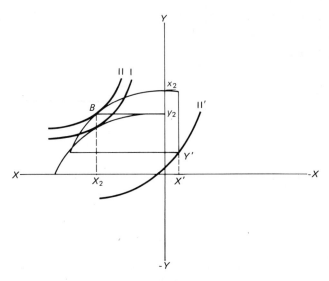

FIGURE 4A-1 Derivation of a Trade Indifference Curve

FIGURE 4A-2 Deriving an Offer Curve

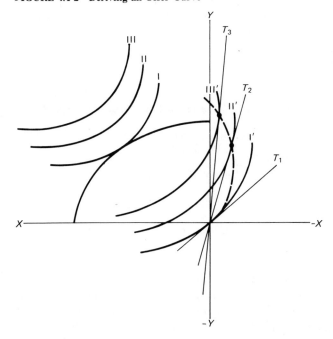

second quadrant to leave the other three quadrants available for exports and imports. (The X axis is thus reversed from its usual direction.) A point in the fourth quadrant would represent exports of both X and Y; first quadrant, exports of X and imports of Y; third quadrant, imports of X and exports of Y. Point A is the pretrade optimum, producing and consuming at X_1, Y_1.

If we introduce the possibility of trade, this country may be able to attain a higher indifference curve through trade. For example, suppose that this country were to trade X' for Y'; its citizens would be consuming at $B(X_2, Y_2)$, which is on a higher indifference curve. Notice that we displaced the production possibilities curve from the origin to make it tangent to indifference curve II. The origin was displaced into the first $(-X, Y)$ quadrant. This country is now producing $\overline{X_2X'}$ of X and $\overline{Y'Y_2}$ of Y. (The — indicates measurement from one point to the other on the axis.) They are consuming X_2, Y_2. The displaced origin is due to the separation of production from consumption. We can now slide the production possibilities curve along indifference curve II and trace out a whole series of X', Y' trading combinations that will give the same level of consumption satisfactions as X', Y' with consumption at B. Those trading combinations lie on the curve II$'$, which is called a trade indifference curve. A trade indifference curve shows the various exchanges of quantities of X for Y (Y for X when extended into the third quadrant) that will leave the inhabitants of this country on the same indifference curve (II, in this instance). A whole family of such trade indifference curves, each corresponding to a particular domestic indifference curve, can be traced out as are represented in Figure 4A-2.

If we draw an arbitrary terms of trade line from the origin, this country will seek out its highest available trade indifference curve (corresponding to its highest attainable indifference curve) at those terms of trade, which will occur at a tangency point. A series of these tangency points at other terms of trade trace out an offer curve. Note that, as the terms of trade become flatter, this country may shift from an X exporter to a Y exporter, tracing out another offer curve of Y for X in the third quadrant.

CHAPTER 5

Modern Theory:
Heckscher–Ohlin and the Supply Side

In the preceding chapters, we assumed a difference in pretrade domestic opportunity costs that gave each country a comparative advantage in the production of one of the two commodities. The direction and size of these differences determine the pattern of specialization and play a major role in establishing the terms of trade, the volume of trade, and the gains from trade. Even in the increasing cost case, it was assumed that in most instances there would be differences in the shapes of the production possibilities curves, so that with reasonably similar demand conditions there would still be a cost-determined basis for specialization and trade.

In this chapter, we go behind the production possibilities curves to investigate where differences in comparative costs originate. Some cases are obvious. Petroleum exporters require an endowment of crude oil; cocoa and banana can be expected to come from tropical climates, furs from colder areas of the world, and so forth. But much of what is traded is not determined that strongly by climate or natural resources. Why, for example, do Italy and Brazil export shoes while Japan and the United States dominate exports of electronic equipment? The answer may be partly in the other factors of production, labor, and capital.

In addition to making our theoretical model more complete, an explanation of the origin of comparative advantage should have useful predictive and policy implications in a world in which comparative advantage can change rapidly. We shall also find that this addition to the model helps to explain relative factor earnings within and between countries and offers some useful insights into which groups will favor free trade and which will prefer protection.

FACTOR INTENSITIES
AND FACTOR ENDOWMENTS

Eli Heckscher and Bertil Ohlin separately developed an explanation for the source of comparative advantage based on differences in *factor intensities* between commodities and *factor endowments* between nations. Factor intensity refers to the relative proportion of capital to labor required to produce a particular commodity. Factor endowment is the relative amounts of the factors of production that a country has.

The simplest approach to factor intensity is to assume that there is one and only one ratio of capital to labor to be used in the productive process for each commodity. If, for example, steel used capital and labor in a ratio of $4K:1L$ and cloth had a ratio of $1K:2L$, then we could classify steel as capital intensive and cloth as labor intensive. Even if the ratios were $4K:1L$ and $2K:1L$, respectively, steel would be relatively capital intensive and cloth would be relatively labor intensive. Heckscher and Ohlin assumed that factor intensity was technologically determined and would not vary significantly from one country to another.

At this point we need to pause and identify some implicit assumptions that have been made in the definition of factor intensity. We are still in a two-country, two-commodity world, and we have added another dimension to "twoness"—two factors of production, labor and capital. The ratio in which they are used is fixed and does not change with either changing factor prices or changes in the composition of output. Capital and labor are clearly defined, separable, and measurable inputs. Other assumptions will surface as we proceed, but these—two inputs, fixed proportions in production, and definable, measurable, and distinct inputs—are the most important.

Factor endowments are even more difficult to measure than are factor intensities. Fortunately, we are only interested in relative rather than absolute factor endowments. Relative pretrade prices of factors should give us an approximate measure of endowments. The price of labor is the wage rate, and the price of capital is the real interest rate (which may be expressed as $\$X$ per \$100 of capital, e.g., 6 percent interest is \$6 per \$100 worth of capital). Thus, if labor receives \$20 per day and capital is \$10 per \$100 unit (10 percent interest) in country A price to trade, while the prices are \$40 per day and \$12 per unit in country B, then country A is relatively better endowed with labor and B with capital. (The price ratios of labor to capital are 2:1 and 3⅓:1 in A and B, respectively, so labor is relatively cheaper in A.)

Once again, we can identify some simplifying assumptions. We seem to have assumed that relative prices reflect only relative supplies, not demand. When we talk about "endowments," we also appear to assume that factors are neither mobile between countries nor capable of increasing over time. And, again, we are dealing with only a two-factor world.

With all these qualifications, the basic *Heckscher–Ohlin proposition* is as follows:

> A country will export that commodity whose production is relatively more intensive in its abundant factor of production and import that commodity which is relatively more intensive in its scarce factor of production.

It is fairly easy to demonstrate that the former will be relatively cheaper than the latter and that this country will, therefore, have a comparative advantage in the commodity that uses relatively more of its abundant factor of production. Table 5-1 presents a simple numerical illustration in a common currency; Table 5-2 does the same in own-country currencies.

Cloth, the labor-intensive commodity, is cheaper in country II, the labor-abundant country. Notice that, if *either* the relative factor abundance is the same (the same capital to labor price ratio) *or* the relative factor intensities are the same (same capital to labor use ratio), then the relative prices of cloth and steel (P_c/P_s) will be the same. You can test this by substituting different sets of numbers in Table 5-1. For example, try $6 and $10 for the prices of capital and labor, respectively, in country II.

Notice that in Table 5-2 we have also made labor more expensive than capital in both countries but that we have kept a difference in *relative* price. Labor is 2½ times as costly as capital in country I, and only 1½ times as expensive in country II, making the latter *relatively* more labor abundant. We would, therefore, predict that II would export cloth and import steel. In country I, one unit of cloth costs $31/$22 = 1.41 steel forgone. In country II, one unit of cloth costs 950 DM/700 DM = 1.36 steel forgone. Country

TABLE 5-1   A Simple Demonstration of the Heckscher–Ohlin Proposition: Common Currency

(1) Country	(2) Commodity	(3) Capital/Unit	(4) Labor/Unit	(5) Price of Capital	(6) Price of Labor	(7) Cost/Unit (3) × (5) + (4) × (6)
I	Cloth	2	5	$3	$5	$31
	Steel	4	2			22
II	Cloth	2	5	$6	$2	22
	Steel	4	2			28

TABLE 5-2 A Simple Demonstration of the Heckscher–Ohlin Proposition: Own Currencies

(1) Country	(2) Commodity	(3) Capital/Unit	(4) Labor/Unit	(5) Price of Capital	(6) Price of Labor	(7) Cost/Unit (3) × (5) + (4) × (6)
I	Cloth	2	5	$3	$5	$31
	Steel	4	2			$22
II	Cloth	2	5	DM100	DM150	DM950
	Steel	4	2			DM700

II does indeed have a comparative advantage in cloth, as the Heckscher–Ohlin proposition would predict.

A more general proof of the Heckscher–Ohlin proposition under a less stringent factor intensity assumption is given in the appendix to this chapter.

CONSEQUENCES: FACTOR PRICE EQUALIZATION

One of the most interesting extensions of the Heckscher–Ohlin proposition was its implications for relative factor prices under protection and under free trade. If a country reduces its level of protection (i.e., moves toward free trade), it will expand its production of the good that is intensive in its abundant factor and contract production of the good that is intensive in its scarce factor. Demand for the abundant factor will increase and demand for the scarce factor will decrease, raising the price of the abundant factor (previously the "cheap" input) and lowering the price of the scarce factor (originally the "expensive" input). Thus, the return to the two factors of production will tend to converge. Since the opposite is happening in the other country (B's scarce factor being A's abundant factor), the ratio w/r (price of labor over price of capital) will tend to be equalized between countries. These two convergences as a result of trade are known as the *factor-price equalization theorem*.

This development in country A, where labor is abundant and capital is scarce, is depicted in Figure 5-1, where D_1 and S_1 are the original demand and supply curves in each panel. D_2 in each panel represents the increased demand for labor and capital, respectively, as a result of expanding the production of the labor intensive commodity. Note that demand for labor (D_l) expands a great deal while demand for capital (D_k) increases very little. Finally, D_3 represents demand for each factor after contracting the production of the capital intensive commodity, which is now being supplied more heavily from abroad. Note again that D_k falls proportionally more than does D_l when we reduce production of the capital intensive good. The result is that w_3 and r_3 are much more nearly equal than are the original w_1 and r_1.

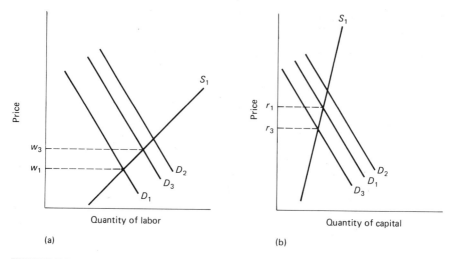

FIGURE 5-1 Factor-Price Equalization in One Country

The other country is experiencing equalization in the opposite direction (*r* rising, *w* falling). Thus, the *w*/*r* ratios, originally highly divergent because of differing factor endowments, move closer together.

Another way of looking at the factor-price equalization theorem is to view commodity movements between countries as a substitute for factor movments. Country A could acquire a more balanced resource base by exporting labor and/or importing capital to produce a "balanced" combination of the two commodities. Instead, a balanced resource base is achieved indirectly by importing the scarce factor—capital—embodied in capital-intensive goods, and exporting the abundant factor, labor, embodied in labor-intensive goods. The resulting equalization of relative factor prices between countries reduces the incentive to relocate factors of production.

The factor-price equalization theorem has some interesting implications for tariff policy. The scarce factor of production benefits from protection, since protection will expand the production of scarce-factor-intensive import substitutes relative to exportables and thus increase the demand for (and price of) the scarce factor. The abundant factor will prefer free trade, which increases its relative return. This helps to explain why the South, as an exporter of agricultural products in a land-abundant country, was originally the strongly free trade section of the United States. As relative factor abundance changes, so do preferences of regions and interest groups. Capital was originally scarce and its owners were protectionist in this country, but they have moved toward free trade as capital became relatively more abundant. We return to these questions in Chapter 10, when we look at the history of commercial policy.

EMPIRICAL TESTING:
THE LEONTIEF PARADOX
AND OTHER RESULTS

Wassily Leontief, a Harvard economist, tested the Heckscher-Ohlin proposition for the United States using data gathered in a massive input-output analysis of the American economy. He measured the direct and indirect capital and labor input requirements for a number of industries and used these data to compute the capital and labor requirements per million dollars of U.S. exports and U.S. import substitutes. Assuming, as he did, that the United States was capital abundant and labor scarce relative to the rest of the world, one would expect our exports to be capital intensive and our imports to be labor intensive. Leontief found exactly the opposite to be the case: capital-intensive imports (actually import substitutes) and labor-intensive exports. Needless to say, Leontief's results spurred a great deal of further empirical work and also numerous attempts to explain his paradoxical findings in theoretical terms. Subsequent empirical studies did not support the Heckscher–Ohlin proposition consistently either.[1]

However, more recent efforts have questioned both Leontief's methods and results. Edward Leamer, in a 1980 article, suggests that Leontief's data are not, in fact, inconsistent with the Heckscher–Ohlin proposition. He argues that, for Heckscher–Ohlin to be verified, all that is needed is that production be more capital intensive than consumption, which was valid for the United States with Leontief's 1947 data. Leamer also suggested that a test in a year in which the value of exports greatly exceeded the value of imports is invalid, since the assumption that $X = M$ is fundamental to both the classical and the Heckscher–Ohlin models.

Leontief's study, valid or not, did stimulate considerable additional theoretical and empirical work as economists searched more vigorously for a workable explanation of the basis of trade. Some researchers focused on reexamining the assumptions of the Heckscher–Ohlin model; others attempted to develop alternative or supplementary explanations of the basis for trade.

EXPLANATIONS:
EXAMINING
THE ASSUMPTIONS

Since the logic of the Heckscher–Ohlin proposition is flawless, the explanation for the Leontief paradox must lie in some invalid assumptions. Most

---

[1] For a brief summary of some of the earlier studies, see H. Robert Heller, *International Trade: Theory and Empirical Evidence*, 2nd ed. (Englewood Cliffs, N.J.: Prentice-Hall, 1973), pp. 68–70.

of the assumptions were implied rather than stated explicitly, but the relevant ones can be identified as follows:

1. Capital and labor are the sole factors of production (only two factors).
2. The factors of production are homogeneous.
3. Relative factor abundance is reflected in relative factor prices; that is, the abundant factor is the relatively cheaper factor of production.
4. A commodity that is relatively more labor intensive in one country will be relatively more labor intensive everywhere.
5. Trade patterns are market determined and are not distorted by tariffs and other barriers.

This does not exhaust the list of assumptions, but these five provide fertile grounds for explaining the Leontief paradox.

1.   A third factor of production could in fact dominate the pattern of trade in commodities in which that factor is significant. Suppose that there are two commodities, A and B, whose two-factor intensities are $(3K, 2L)$ and $(1K, 3L)$, respectively, so that A would be classed as capital intensive and B as labor intensive. But, if their three factor intensities, incorporating land or natural resources (R), are given by $(6R, 3K, 2L)$ and $(1R, 1K, 3L)$, respectively, then the even greater difference in land-natural resource intensity could be the decisive factor in determining comparative costs. Land as the third factor is believed to be a particularly relevant explanation for the U.S. case, 25 percent of whose exports are agricultural.

2.   Leontief himself raised the question of whether the factors were homogeneous, labor in particular. As the argument was developed by others, it became known as the human capital explanation. Capital can take not only the obvious forms of factories, machinery, tools, and roads, for example, but can also be embodied in the knowledge, skills, and training of skilled workers. Since consumption and/or current earnings must be deferred to acquire skills, and since these skills enhance labor productivity in the same way as additional physical capital, this intangible accumulated investment in human beings should be considered part of our capital stock. Consider two commodities whose factor intensities are $A(4K, 3L)$ and $B(3K, 4L)$. On a simple two-factor scale, A is capital intensive and B is labor intensive. But if A uses unskilled labor while B uses engineers and skilled technicians, the breakdown might be $A(4K, 1HK, 3L)$ and $B(2K, 4HK, 3L)$, and when we add human to physical capital, the intensities become $A(5K, 3L)$ and $B(6K, 3L)$. Thus B is really more capital intensive than A when human capital is separated out from "raw labor" and regrouped with physical capital. Again, this explanation is particularly relevant for the United States as well as Japan, both of which have made considerable investment in human capital and export the kind of technologically sophisticated products that tend to be of the human-capital-intensive form.

3.   The relatively more abundant factor may not be cheaper if there

are market imperfections or if there are demand reversals (discussed in Chapter 4). This latter possibility is particularly relevant to trade between countries whose resource endowments are more nearly similar than their tastes and preferences. Figure 5-2 illustrates this possibility.

Since $w_1 > r_1$ and $w_2 < r_2$, clearly $w_1/r_1 > w_2/r_2$; that is, the abundant factor (indicated by the position and slope of the supply curve) is relatively more expensive in each country. This would occur if each country had a strong preference for that product in which it had a comparative advantage. If relative factor prices rather than relative physical endowments of factors were used to predict the pattern of trade, the Heckscher–Ohlin proposition would predict trade patterns correctly, but it would add little, if anything, to the original explanation of comparative advantage.

Monopoly conditions—strong unions, for example, or barriers to entry

FIGURE 5-2   Demand Reversals and Factor Prices

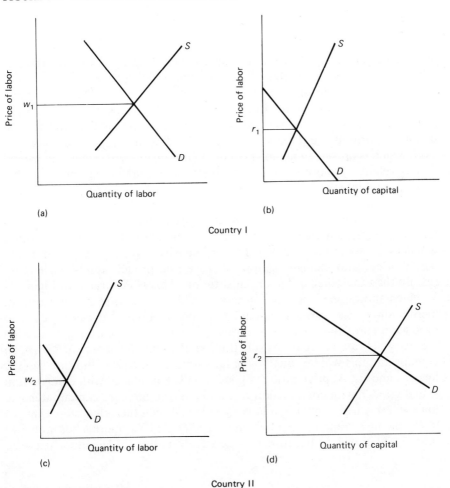

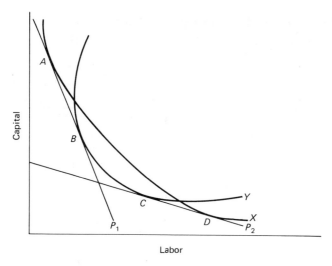

FIGURE 5-3   Factor Intensity Reversal

in industries that should have a comparative advantage—can also distort relative factor prices and thus distort normal trade patterns.

    4.   Factor intensity reversals between countries is one of the most appealing explanations of the Leontief paradox. The Heckscher–Ohlin proposition assumes, in the strong version, that technology is uniform; that is, factor proportions are fixed and the same in all countries. The weaker version, which is presented in the appendix to this chapter, assumes that a good that is relatively more capital intensive in one country will be relatively more capital intensive everywhere, although the precise ratio may vary.

    It is easy to conjure up contradictory images, such as labor-intensive agriculture among the Southeast Asian peasant farmers versus capital-intensive American agriculture with tractors and harvesters and all the other wonders of modern technology. Factor intensity reversals can occur as the factor price ratio changes simply because one product lends itself more readily than the other to factor substitution. This is illustrated in Figure 5-3, which shows one isoquant for good X and one for good Y. (An isoquant merely shows the various capital-labor combinations that can be used to produce a particular quantity of output.) The slope of the isoquant is called the marginal rate of technical substitution of capital for labor ($MRTS_{kl}$). In equilibrium, this will be equal to the factor price ratio; two ratios are shown, lines P_1 and P_2. At price ratio P_1, good X will be produced with combination A and good Y with combination B; that is, X will be more capital intensive than will Y when capital is relatively cheap. When the price ratio changes to P_2, the new combinations become C and D, and X is more labor intensive than Y. This occurs because it is relatively easier to substitute between

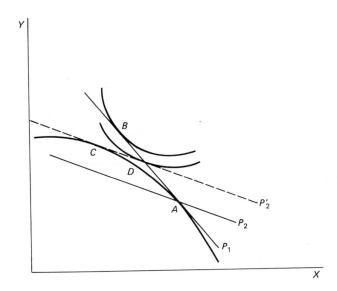

FIGURE 5-4 Tariff-Distorted Trade

capital and labor in industry X (as shown by the flatter isoquant) than in
industry Y. Thus, good X could be capital intensive in one country and labor
intensive in another, providing no basis for predicting the pattern of trade.
Empirical evidence, however (in particular a 1961 study by Arrow, Chenery,
Minhas, and Solow),[2] indicates that such strong factor intensity reversals
are not very common.

    5. Trade barriers are the final explanation. If the United States
chooses to erect barriers to trade in those goods in which she has a comparative disadvantage, then relative prices are distorted and the resulting
trade will not follow the pattern that the Heckscher–Ohlin proposition would
predict. Tariffs distort relative prices as is shown in Figure 5-4. If P_1 is the
international price ratio, this country should produce at A and consume at
B. But if P_2 is the tariff-distorted price ratio, production will be at C and
consumption at D. Instead of specializing more in X, this country has specialized more in the "wrong" product, Y.

    These findings leave the Heckscher–Ohlin explanation for the basis
of trade considerably weakened. Nevertheless, it remains the principal explanation of the source of comparative advantage. More recent attempts to
devise alternative explanations for the basis of trade have tended to complement rather than to supplant the Heckscher–Ohlin proposition.

---

  [2] K.J. Arrow, H.B. Chenery, B.S. Minhas, and R.M. Solow, "Capital-Labor Substitution and Economic Efficiency," *Review of Economics and Statistics*, vol. 43 (August, 1961),
pp. 225–51.

OTHER EXPLANATIONS
OF THE BASIS OF TRADE

There are several supplementary approaches to explaining the basis of trade: economies of scale, technological progress, the product cycle, and demand similarities.

Economies of scale refers to the declining portion of the U-shaped long-run average cost curve, as shown in Figure 5-5. Product X, whose long-run average cost curve is shaped like LAC_x, would require a much higher volume of output to attain the minimum average cost than would product Y, whose cost curve is described by LAC_y. Only a large home market (population plus income) would give a country the cost advantage to export product X. A smaller country could quickly become competitive in product Y. In this case, scale economies would "assign" products by home market size at least as much as by relative resource endowment.

Technological progress is much more rapid in those countries in which substantial outlays are made for research and development. These countries will initially enjoy a monopoly in new or greatly modified products until the technology becomes widely available. At that point the product will "migrate" to that country (or those countries) with the resource mix most suited to its production.

The *product cycle* hypothesis is closely related to the technological explanation. At the early stages of development, both the production process and the product itself are nonstandardized. The initially producing country serves as the test market in which the product and the process are refined and standardized, and also as the original exporter. Once again, as the product becomes widely consumed and standardized, productions will migrate to those locations with the resource endowment advantage, and the

FIGURE 5-5   Economies of Scale

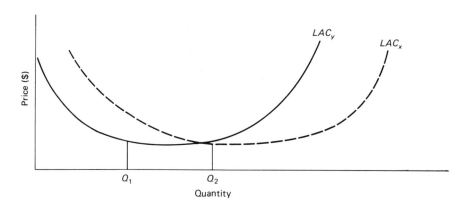

country where the product originated may become an importer. Hand-held calculators, television sets, and bicycles are among the products for which all three of these explanations are helpful. The latter also emphasize the dynamic nature of comparative advantage. A comparative advantage in product X today says nothing about tomorrow.

Demand similarities, according to Stassen Linder, derive from the fact that the nature of trade in manufactures is not based on resource endowments as much as it is on the nature of domestic demand.[3] Products are developed and refined for the home market first and then (later) are exported. Thus, he would expect that sophisticated, costly, or luxury goods would originate in high-income countries and would also be exported primarily to other high-income countries, while simple, lower-quality, or basic manufactures would be primarily produced in and traded among less developed countries. This does not, of course, preclude exports from poorer countries to the low-income segment of the population in developed countries or exports from the industrial countries to the more affluent minority in less developed countries. But he does suggest that the bulk of trade in manufactures will be between countries with similar income levels, which is closely associated with patterns of demand. The resource explanation remains valid for primary and resource-intensive products. Linder's model appears to be consistent with observed patterns of trade in manufactured goods.

SUMMARY

The differences in comparative costs that were just assumed to exist in previous chapters were explained in this chapter as the result of differences in factor intensities between goods and factor endowments between countries. A country should have a cost advantage in that product that is relatively more intensive in her more abundant factor of production.

Specialization on this basis will lead to a reduction in the difference between factor earnings within countries and factor price ratios between countries (*factor-price equalization theorem*).

Empirical testing by Leontief and others failed to verify the pattern of trade predicted by the Heckscher–Ohlin proposition (*Leontief paradox*). Efforts to explain the Leontief paradox included a third factor of production, nonhomogeneous factors, distortion of relative factor prices by monopoly or demand differences, factor intensity reversals, and trade barriers.

Economies of scale, technological progress, the product cycle, and demand similarities offer complementary explanations of the basis of trade.

[3] Linder, Stassen, *Trade and Trade Policy for Development* (New York: Praeger, 1968).

KEY TERMS

demand similarities
economies of scale
factor endowment
factor intensity
factor intensity reversal
factor-price equalization
Heckscher–Ohlin proposition
human capital
Leontief paradox
product cycle
technological progress

REVIEW QUESTIONS

1. Using the explanations suggested in this chapter, try to give reasons for the composition of exports for the United States, Canada, Japan, or Denmark.
2. Using Table 5-1 or 5-2, change the capital-labor ratio for steel so that it is the same as for cloth (e.g., 2:5 and 4:10). Verify that the price ratios will be the same in both countries. Repeat the exercise with different factor intensities but identical factor price ratios. Why is there no difference in comparative costs unless *both* Heckscher–Ohlin conditions are fulfilled?
3. Which lobbying groups are most protectionist in the United States? Why do you think this is true, in the light of the factor-price equalization theorem?
4. Identify some of the major new consumer products of the last 20 years. Trace their pattern of production and export. See if you can identify examples of economies of scale, technological progress, product cycle, and/or demand similarities.

SUGGESTED READINGS

BALDWIN, ROBERT E., and J. DAVID RICHARDSON, *International Trade and Finance: Readings*, chaps. 1–4. Boston: Little, Brown, 1974.

CHACHOLIADES, MILTIADES, *Principles of International Economics*, chaps. 5–6. New York: McGraw-Hill, 1981.

HELLER, H. ROBERT, *International Trade: Theory and Empirical Evidence*, 2nd ed., chaps. 5 and 7. Englewood Cliffs, N.J.: Prentice-Hall, 1973.

LEAMER, EDWARD B., "The Leontief Paradox Revisited," *Journal of Political Economy*, 88, no. 3 (June 1980), 495–503.

ROOT, FRANKLIN R., *International Trade and Investment*, 4th ed., chap. 4. Cincinnati, Ohio: Southwestern, 1978.

APPENDIX

The Heckscher–Ohlin Proposition Revisited

A more general version of the Heckscher–Ohlin proposition can be developed with the aid of a geometric device called an Edgeworth–Bowley box, as is shown in Figure 5A-1.

The sides of the box represent initial endowments of labor and capital. The box is filled with isoquants such as those shown in Figure 5-3. Each solid isoquant represents the various combinations of capital and labor to produce a given amount of steel. Higher isoquants represent greater amounts of steel, using more of both capital and labor. The dashed isoquants are for cloth and are drawn with reference to origin O_c, showing various combinations of capital and labor that can be used to produce various amounts of cloth. The numbers on each isoquant are the outputs of steel or cloth that each isoquant represents. If, for example, we were producing at A, we would be using O_sL_1 of labor and O_sK_1 of capital to produce 23 units of steel and O_cL_1 of labor and O_cK_1 of capital to produce 22 units of cloth. All our resources are being used. Note also that we would only produce at the tangency point of two isoquants. At any other point, such as B, we would be producing the same amount of steel (23) but less cloth (20). Note that steel always uses a higher ratio of capital to labor than does cloth. Steel is the capital-intensive commodity.

FIGURE 5A-1   An Edgeworth–Bowley Box

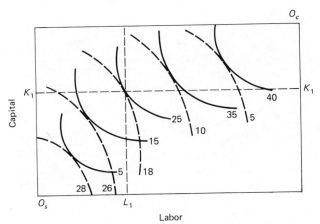

The Edgeworth–Bowley box will give us a production possibilities curve as shown in Figure 5A-2. Each tangency point gives us a possible steel-cloth output combination that is the most we can get of one for a given amount of the other with our available resources. The steel-cloth combinations shown are (5, 28), (15, 26), (23, 22), (29, 18), and (32, 12).

Suppose we were to keep the isoquants the same (uniform technology) but changed the shape of the box to reflect more capital relative to labor (different factor endowments). Since the cloth isoquants are now drawn with respect to a relocated O_c, they get shifted upward. The new Edgeworth–Bowley box is given in Figure 5A-3, and the new resulting production possibilities curve is illustrated in Figure 5A-4.

Thus, we have a difference in production possibilities curves that, with similar demand conditions, will lead to greater specialization in the direction Heckscher–Ohlin would predict. The country reflected in Figures 5A-1 and 5A-2 has a greater relative endowment of labor and, therefore, a greater productive capacity in the labor-intensive commodity, cloth, whereas the country of Figures 5A-3 and 5A-4 is better endowed with capital and can, therefore, be expected to export steel.

This more general approach does not require rigid factor proportions, but it does preserve different factor endowments and a weaker interpretation of different factor intensities to demonstrate the resulting difference in comparative costs in the form of differently shaped production possibilities curves.

The Edgeworth–Bowley box can also be used to point out an interesting curiosity that results from specialization and trade. In the labor-abundant country, both commodities will become more capital intensive as a result of trade! The opposite will occur in the capital-intensive country. This pe-

FIGURE 5A-2   A Production Possibilities Curve

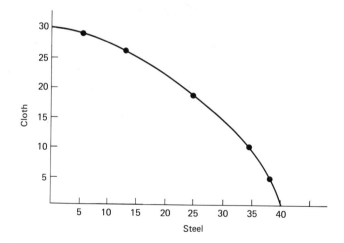

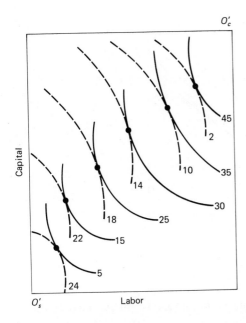

Capital

45

2

10

35

14

30

18 25

22 15

5

24

O'_s Labor

FIGURE 5A-3
Edgeworth–Bowley Box with Different Factor Endowment

culiar conclusion is illustrated in Figure 5A-5. The Edgeworth-Bowley box is drawn for the labor-abundant country, with only the contract curve and the initial and final allocation of labor between cloth and steel shown. Initially, $\overline{OK_1}$ of capital and $\overline{OL_1}$ of labor are devoted to cloth, while $\overline{K_1K}$ of capital and $\overline{L_1L}$ of labor is devoted to capital. The capital-labor ratio can then be measured as the slope of a line from the relevant origin (O_c for

FIGURE 5A-4 Production Possibilities Curve with Different Factor Endowment

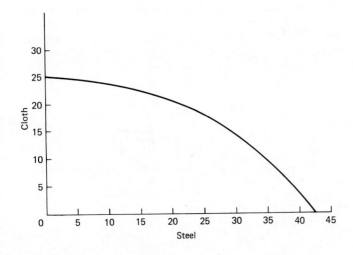

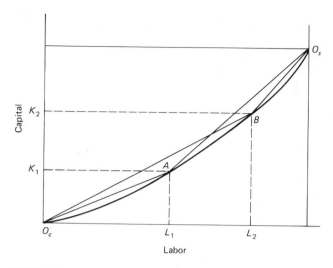

FIGURE 5A-5   Capital-Labor Substitution Under Trade

cloth, O_s for steel) to the point on the contract curve, in this case point A. Now suppose that as a result of trade it expands production of cloth and reduces production of steel. This is equivalent to point B on the contract curve, with $\overline{OK_2}$ of capital and $\overline{OL_2}$ of labor in cloth and $\overline{K_2K}$ of capital and $\overline{L_2L}$ of labor in steel. Notice that both commodities have become more capital intensive, as the slopes of O_cB and O_sB relative to O_cA and O_sA indicate.

What is the commonsense explanation of this peculiar result? The contraction of the steel industry releases relatively large amounts of capital and relatively little labor, whereas the expansion of cloth absorbs much labor and little capital. This will tend to drive up the price of labor relative to capital; but the w/r ratio cannot long diverge from the world w/r ratio

FIGURE 5A-6   Expansion of One Input

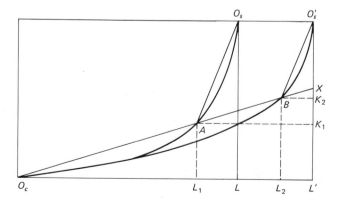

because of the factor price equalization theorem. The temporary cheapness of capital (or costliness of labor) induces the substitution of capital for labor in both industries until their marginal products and their prices are once again brought into line with world ratios.

The Rybczynski Theorem

The Edgeworth–Bowley box combined with factor-price equalization can be used to show what happens to the output mix when only one factor grows. If the stock of labor grows while the stock of capital is unchanged, the output of the labor-intensive commodity will expand while that of the capital-intensive commodity will contract. This is illustrated in Figure 5A-6.

Since the capital-labor ratio is determined by the w/r ratio prevailing worldwide, output of cloth must expand along ray O_cX, which represents the prevailing capital-labor ratio for cloth. This will require a contraction of steel production to remain on the new contract curve.

ADDITIONAL KEY TERMS

Edgeworth-Bowley box
production possibilities curve
Rybczynski theorem

CHAPTER 6

Factor Movements in International Trade

THE VOLUME AND DIRECTION
OF FACTOR MOVEMENTS

One assumption underlying the classical theory of comparative advantage is that factors of production are immobile between countries. This enabled us to focus on the welfare gains from the free movement of commodities in international trade. In Chapter 5, for the most part, we treated the supply of inputs as "endowments"—given and immutable, much less mobile between countries than commodities are. Later in the chapter, however, it was indicated that the resource base can change as a result of internal accumulation (or sometimes loss) of capital, population growth, or discovery and depletion of natural resources. The result of an increase in the resource endowment is an outward movement of the production possibilities curve that will change the volume, the terms, and, perhaps, even the direction of trade.

Factor movements between countries can also change the production possibilities curves of both the country of emigration and the country of immigration. This possibility is illustrated in Figure 6-1, which shows two alternative ways for a country to attain a higher level of welfare.

Good Y is capital intensive; a flow of capital from country II in panel

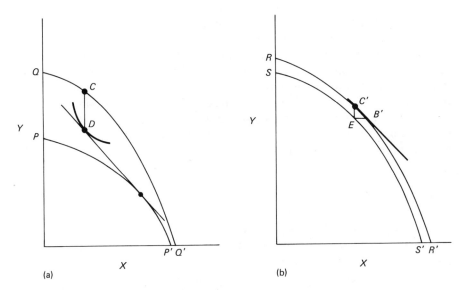

FIGURE 6-1 Welfare Gains from a Capital Flow

(b) to country I in panel (a) leads to a substantial increase in I's capacity to produce Y (production possibilities shifts from PP' to QQ') and only a modest decrease in II's (from RR' to SS'). Country I can attain point C by trade or by importing capital to shift the production possibilities curve outward. Up to CD can be exported in principal and interest payments and still leave country I better off. Country II can attain C' either by trading $B'E$ of Y for EC' of X *or* by a capital flow that shifts its production possibilities curve inward slightly but generates an import flow of interest and/or principal payments sufficient to put them at C'. It is even possible that the flow of capital (or labor) may produce an aggregate welfare increase that is greater than that which can be achieved through commodity trade.

Figure 6-1 illustrates clearly the substitutability between commodity trade and factor movements as ways of increasing economic welfare. At different periods in history and in different areas of the world, commodity movements, capital flows, or labor migration have dominated. The United States, Australia, and Canada all were developed by inflows of labor, followed by flows of capital and then return flows of primary products to the "mother" country. Capital flows have played a major role in providing a more balanced resource base to the less industrialized sectors of the modern world, especially since 1960. Capital flows from the United States, for example (both public and private), increased by 124 percent from 1960 to 1976, and the share in those capital flows that went to areas other than Canada and Western Europe rose substantially during the same period. Israel has relied heavily on imports of both human and financial capital to bring about a rapid transformation of her production capabilities. "Guest" workers have played an important role in the last two decades at the bottom end of the wage-skill scale in England, Northern Europe, and the United States, where wages are high and labor, especially unskilled labor, is scarce. Flows of raw materials, particularly petroleum, are classed as commodity trade but are, in fact, more akin to factor movements in their effect on the total resource base and thus the production possibilities of the importing countries.

In this chapter, we examine the movement of capital, labor, technology, and natural resources separately, considering the motives, the effects, and the policy questions raised in each instance.

CAPITAL FLOWS

Capital is probably the most mobile of the three broad classes of inputs. Capital is transferred from one country to another in financial form, but the financial transfer permits a real flow of physical capital either directly or indirectly. A direct transfer would be a shipment of machinery and other productive equipment. An indirect transfer could be in the form of imported consumer goods, especially food, which would free domestic resources to produce capital by building roads, factories, power plants, and so on. Japan and England are the only countries that became highly industrialized without substantial initial inflows of foreign capital. Table 6-1 summarizes the pattern of total OECD/DAC[1] and U.S. capital flows for recent years.

Note that private capital has grown much more rapidly than has official development assistance, especially in the United States where official aid has been at a virtual standstill in nominal terms since the early 1960s and has declined sharply in real terms.

Capital flows from the public sector (economic and military aid in both grants and loans) are motivated primarily by political and strategic considerations rather than by direct economic benefits. Private capital flows, however, are generally in response to opportunities for profit.

A firm invests capital abroad in response to profit opportunities that are greater than the profit that could be earned by investing at home. There are three possible responses to an opportunity to sell abroad: export, buy into (or buy out) an existing local firm, or build a plant in the foreign country. What might influence the decision—especially the choice between exporting and foreign production?

Products may be either input-oriented or market-oriented, depending on transport costs. If the inputs are relatively easy and inexpensive to move to the production location, while the product is fragile, heavy, bulky, perishable, or risky to ship, the producer will locate near the market. Glassware, fresh produce, and construction are all examples of market-oriented pro-

[1] Organization for Economic Cooperation and Development and Development Assistance Committee. These include all major noncommunist developed countries.

TABLE 6-1 Capital Flows to Less Developed Countries, Selected Years, 1961–1978 (millions of dollars)

	1961	1966	1971	1974	1978[a]
From all OECD/DAC countries					
Official development assistance	$5,197	$5,984	$7,660	$11,305	$19,900
Private capital	3,106	3,959	8,063	12,034	44,600
From the United States					
Official development assistance	2,943	3,349	3,324	3,439 }	16,200
Private capital	1,102	1,506	3,384	5,669 }	

Sources: *International Economic Report of the President, 1976* (Washington, D.C.: Government Printing Office, 1976), pp. 167–169; U.S. Department of Commerce, Bureau of the Census, *Statistical Abstract of the United States, 1980* (Washington, D.C.: U.S. Government Printing Office, 1980), p. 930.

[a] Data are rounded to nearest $100 million.

duction. If, on the other hand, the inputs (labor with specialized skills, heavy raw materials, etc.) are difficult or costly to move, then the industry will locate near these immobile resources, shipping the final product longer distances. Steel industries tend to locate close to iron and coal supplies. Fishermen and fishing-related industries locate on the coast for obvious reasons. The American electronics industry has tended to cluster around the ample supply of technically skilled labor in California's "Silicone Valley" and in the Northeast; the textile industry has migrated to the less costly labor, cheaper power, and abundant water supplies of the Southeast. Similar location patterns can be observed between nations. Some industries are not tied to either inputs or markets and are relatively footloose in locational orientation. But certainly a market-oriented industry is much more likely to establish a local firm abroad, shipping what specialized resources it needs to permit local production. (This is especially true if the inputs represent "one-shot" shipments of capital and/or infrequent relocation of skilled labor and management rather than regular flows of raw materials and intermediate goods.) A resource-oriented industry is much more inclined to export, whether that industry is developed with local or foreign capital and management.

The relative cost of relocating inputs versus transporting final goods is one of several elements in the decision to export or to produce abroad. A second consideration would be the relative cost of local substitute (or complementary) resources, since some inputs will be shipped in, whereas others can be acquired on the local market. The availability of cheap foreign labor as an argument for building a plant abroad is the best known example. Capital could also be more available and/or cheaper; the cost of complementary government services (taxes relative to roads, airports, education, etc.) could be lower; electric power, good soil, water, and other natural resources may be cheaper and/or more readily available.

A third consideration would be political risk in those numerous Third World countries whose governments are of doubtful stability. Expropriation is always possible. An American government agency, OPIC (Overseas Private Investment Corporation), offers insurance against political risks, but historically U.S. firms have preferred investing in those countries (mostly developed) with greater political stability.

Finally, barriers to trade—tariffs and nontariff barriers—may disrupt flows of commodities sufficiently so that moving some of the inputs inside the tariff wall may be the only feasible alternative. This is generally believed to be a major reason for heavy American investment in Europe at the time of the formation of the European Economic Community. A common external tariff was to go into effect that would make it difficult for American exporters to preserve their market shares in other ways. Many underdeveloped countries have also attempted to use tariffs, not only to protect existing domestic industries but also to encourage further investment, both foreign and domestic, in those industries.

Capital flows have a number of economic effects besides those already identified—namely, the realignment of the relative resource base in both parent (capital-exporting) and host (capital-importing) countries and the displacement of exports (imports) by local production. Among the other economic effects are (1) the balance-of-payments impact and (2) changes in relative factor earnings, as adjustments occur in the marginal productivities of complementary or substitute factors. Political questions of sovereignty and competing jurisdictions are deferred until Chapter 7, when they can be discussed in the context of cartels and multinational enterprise.

The balance-of-payments effect will be considered in more detail in Chapter 13, but it is important to take note of it here because balance-of-payments considerations play an important role in policy toward capital flows. When exchange rates are fixed, the initial capital transfer *may* (and usually does) create a deficit in the parent country and a surplus in the host country. (If the transfer is entirely in the form of export of capital goods, inventories, semifinished goods, and so on, then there may be no net balance-of-payments impact.) Under floating rates, the capital transfer will put downward pressure on the parent country's currency price and upward pressure on the host country's currency.

The subsequent flow is just the opposite. The parent country receives a return flow of profits or interest and principal repayments that create a surplus in the parent country and deficit in the host country. The parent country is also likely to see an increased flow of exports of parts, capital equipment, and intermediate goods and some possible displacement of exports to both the host country and, possibly, to third countries if the host country becomes an exporter. The U.S. Department of Commerce estimates that it takes about nine years to "break even"—that is, for the positive effects of profits, interest, principal, and exports to offset the initial capital outflow. Thus, countries with balance-of-payments problems often impose controls on the outflow of capital for that reason.

A capital outflow will have two effects on the return to labor that labor will find undesirable. First, a substantial capital outflow will increase the scarcity of capital relative to labor and thus will raise its relative return. Second, capital and labor are complements as well as substitutes in production. When labor has more capital with which to work, the productivity of labor is increased and wages will rise also. A capital outflow represents a slower accumulation of capital domestically, limiting increases in productivity and thus in wages. In addition, the bargaining power of organized labor will be weakened by competition from abroad. If owners of capital have alternatives elsewhere, they will be in a stronger position to resist union wage demands.

For all these reasons, organized labor has an understandable interest in imposing restrictions on the outflow of capital. If this powerful force is linked to balance-of-payments problems, the likelihood of restrictions on capital outflows becomes very high. The United States has periodically imposed restrictions on capital outflows, but such controls have been temporary and for balance-of-payments reasons only. Most underdeveloped countries severely restrict capital outflow because of their own internal capital needs for development purposes.

Controls on capital outflows can range from outright prohibition, through limitations on amounts, regions, or industries, to tying the outflow to purchases in the parent country, to a discriminatory tax on foreign earnings.

Host countries impose controls also, but generally of a different nature. Often, the concern relates to the preservation of national sovereignty (especially in the case of a small country dealing with a large corporation). This topic is discussed further in Chapter 7. A country may also attempt to control the direction of development or to obtain concessions from the investor (royalties, labor training, building ancillary facilities) by exploiting a quasi-monopoly position with respect to location or valuable natural resources. Investment review boards are frequently used for one or all of these purposes. In the United States, the Committee on Foreign Investment monitors the impact of foreign investment in the United States, and certain industries are restricted for national defense reasons, but little if any other control is exercised over capital inflow.

LABOR MIGRATION

Labor tends to be less mobile internationally than capital. The institutional barriers of language, culture, social insurance, and tax systems loom greater for labor. However mobile labor may become nationally, crossing the border

constitutes a far bigger step. Mobility is greatest between countries with a
common bond of language or history or a shared border. Much of the movement of labor in history has been due to natural disasters, revolutions, or
wars. The United States still has identifiable ethnic regions formed by inflows
from such diverse events as the English Restoration, the Franco–Prussian
War, the Irish potato blight, World Wars I and II, the Hungarian and Cuban
revolutions, the fall of Vietnam, and the genocide in Cambodia. Some immigrants came involuntarily, as convicts or slaves. Between disasters, workers were attracted to the United States by fables of gold-paved streets. Great
waves of immigrants to North America from the midnineteenth century until
World War I finally provoked immigration restrictions. Table 6-2 describes
the pattern of immigration since 1820.

The successful lobbying for immigration restrictions can be understood
in economic terms as a scarce resource (labor) protesting an inflow that
would make labor more abundant and lower its relative return. There were,
of course, other reasons as well. Ethnic prejudice certainly accounted for
some of the hostility. Immigrants incur costs of relocation and adjustment
that tend to be subsidized by the taxpayer in a welfare state. Finally, not
all American labor was opposed to immigration. Even in a mobile society,

TABLE 6-2   Immigration into the United States, 1820–1978

	Total Immigration (000)				
	1820–1978	1820–1860	1861–1900	1901–1940	1941–1978
Total	48,664	5,062	14,062	19,166	10,339
			Origin of Immigrants (%)		
	1820–1978		1961–1970	1971–1978	
Europe		74.4%		33.8%	19.0%
Hungary/Austria	8.9%		0.8%	0.4%	
Germany	14.3		5.7	1.7	
Great Britain	10.1		6.3	3.0	
Ireland	9.7		1.1	0.3	
Italy	10.9		6.4	3.4	
U.S.S.R.	6.9		0.1	0.8	
Asia		5.0		12.9	33.4
Korea	0.5		1.0	5.9	
America		18.6		51.7	45.1
Canada	8.4		12.4	3.9	
Cuba	1.1		6.3	6.7	
Mexico	4.4		13.7	15.2	
West Indies	1.5		4.0	5.8	
Rest of world		1.1		1.7	2.5

Source: *Statistical Abstract of the United States, 1980*, U.S. Department of Commerce, Bureau
of the Census (Washington, D.C.: Government Printing Office, 1980), p. 93. Individual countries
are only listed if they accounted for 5 percent or more of total immigration in any of the periods
indicated.

labor consists of overlapping and partially noncompeting groups. The more skilled labor saw immigrants as a source of cheap labor who would lower the cost of consumer products without competing directly with them for jobs and wages. It was mainly the group already at the bottom of the income ladder that opposed further immigration, and it was not until the voting franchise was broadened considerably that this group was able to gain some protection for its precarious position on the economic ladder.

From a national viewpoint there is probably some optimum population at any given time, which, with available capital, technology, and natural resources, will maximize per capita output. This idea is sketched in Figure 6-2. In this diagram the optimum population lies between X and Y. Up to X, the ratio of labor to capital and natural resources is too low to utilize these complementary resources efficiently. Beyond Y, there is more labor than can be efficiently equipped with capital and natural resources. An improvement in technology, an accumulation of capital, or a discovery of natural resources can shift the GNP per person curve to the right so that optimum population now lies between X' and Y'. Optimum population is also a function of the percentage of the population that is able and willing to engage in productive work.

Even if two countries are both beyond the optimum population, a reallocation of population from a country with greatly excess population to one with only moderate excess population can raise world welfare under appropriate assumptions. This possibility is illustrated in Figure 6-3, which assumes equal capital and natural resource endowment and uniform population. The diagram depicts a definite increase in per capita output in the overpopulated country as population falls from P_3 to P_4. Total output has risen from OG_4FP_3 to OG_3DP_4. The larger shaded area (G_4G_3DE) represents

FIGURE 6-2   Optimum Population

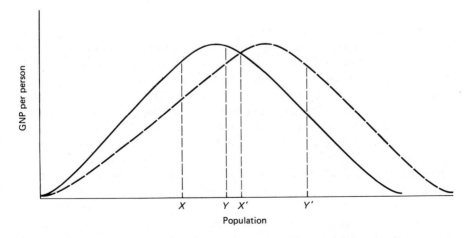

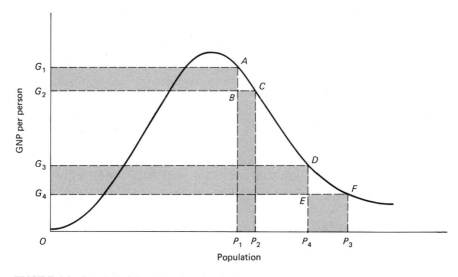

FIGURE 6-3 Population Transfers and World Welfare

the gain in output per person to increased average productivity and the smaller shaded area the lost output due to fewer workers (P_4EFP_3). The outcome in the less populated country is potentially positive, also, even though its population is beyond the optimum. If the increased output of the additional workers (P_1BCP_2) more than offsets the output loss from falling average productivity (G_1ABG_2), this country will also have a greater GNP. However, there is a distributional problem. The increased GNP in the second (less populated) country is associated with a lower GNP per capita, whereas in the first country both total and per capita GNP have risen. Nevertheless, if the distributional problem can be resolved, total world welfare will have increased.

   This diagram sheds some light on the fact that there are far more constraints on immigration than on emigration in a world that appears to have exceeded optimum population on a global and, therefore, also on an average basis. Few countries can be described as underpopulated relative to their endowments of capital and natural resources and to available technology.

   One exception to the lack of emigration restrictions has been an attempt by less developed countries to deal with the so-called "brain drain." The brain drain refers to the tendency of skilled professionals and technicians—doctors, engineers, business managers, professors—to emigrate to the more developed, industrialized countries that offer more in the way of complementary resources for skilled labor, thereby raising their productivity and thus their earnings. Effective demand for their services is also greater in developed countries. While underdeveloped countries "need" these professionals, market signals send them elsewhere. Doctors, for example, prefer to work in modern, well-equipped hospitals among a population that is willing and able to pay for quality medical care. Students from underdeveloped countries, whose basic education may have been subsidized by their home countries, go abroad to complete their education and often choose not to return.

From the viewpoint of world welfare, the brain drain reallocates resources so as to increase their productivity and is therefore desirable. But the distribution of those benefits is decidedly one-sided, and when the country of emigration can claim an investment in the emigré on which it wishes to earn a return, the question of the right to emigrate becomes very complex indeed.[2] The long-run solution lies in providing complementary facilities and adequate effective demand in the home countries to discourage emigration of skilled human capital.

Other effects of labor movements are similar to the impact of capital flows. Labor movements substitute for flows of labor-intensive goods in the same direction or movements of capital or natural resources in the opposite direction. Labor migration can also have some limited effect on the balance of payments if the worker is temporary or if he or she makes remittances to relatives in the home country or continues to purchase goods and services from home. Migration raises the relative return to labor in the country of origin and lowers it in the country of destination. Traditionally, labor unions have advocated strict immigration laws for this reason.

TECHNOLOGY

The process of technology transfer and restrictions on the flow of technology have been among the most widely debated issues of the 1970s. In earlier chapters, we assumed that fixed technologies were equally available to all participants in the international marketplace. This assumption is inaccurate for several reasons. First, technology is not a given endowment but rather a scarce resource much like capital. Resources must be devoted to the development of technology and the resulting inventions, processes, or innovations are often of a proprietary nature. Efforts are made to keep technological innovations secret to create a competitive advantage for the innovator, from which he or she reaps a return on investment in discovering or creating the technology. Where possible, patents or copyrights are secured so that would-be users are obliged to secure a license and perhaps pay royalties to use the process or produce the product. Patents, copyrights, brand names, and trade secrets severely restrict flows of technology within countries and even more so between countries.

[2] This issue is part of the complex question of restrictions on the emigration of Soviet Jews.

Technology is, at least for the lifetime of the patent or copyright, private property. It can sometimes be leased or licensed; if it is embodied in capital goods, it can be acquired by purchasing the appropriate capital goods. Often, the technology is useless without skilled support personnel (engineers, managers, etc.) and components. If the patent or process is licensed, there is fertile ground for developing a cartel. If the firm wishes to retain control but sees advantages in foreign production for marketing reasons or, because of the availability of low-cost complementary local resources, then it is likely that the firm will build or acquire a foreign operaton; a multinational enterprise is the result. Both these ways of transferring technology are discussed in Chapter 7.

There are not only obstacles to technology transfer on the part of those who hold the property rights but also problems of adaptation of technology to a different resource mix. Small-scale, more labor-intensive methods that are less dependent on skilled and sophisticated human and physical capital are often more suited to the inputs available in underdeveloped countries. The idea of a different technology[3] in response to different input mixes has received much attention, but private investors have not yet sensed sufficient profit opportunities in developing "appropriate" (small-scale and/or labor-intensive) methods to make the necessary commitments to expenditures on research and development.

Technology rarely travels alone. It is usually embodied at least partly in human and/or physical capital or in intermediate goods. Thus, many of the comments made earlier about the movement of capital and labor apply also to technology transfer. There are, however, a few economic effects tied specifically to technology transfer.

Free movement of technology between countries speeds up the process of locating production of a good in the most economically efficient place from a combined input and transport cost standpoint. From a world standpoint, this is beneficial. From the viewpoint of a country such as the United States, which makes a heavy investment in research and development, rapid transfer of technology reduces its share of the return on research and development. If the new technology is under the control of a multinational, that firm will continue to earn its expected return in profits, license fees, and/or royalties, but some of the factor rents from the technological monopoly will accrue to foreign rather than to domestic resources. If steps were taken to accelerate the flow of technology between countries, the firm would have less or briefer control, reducing the return on research and development expenditures, and thereby discouraging further investment in technological progress.

---

[3] Best known is E.F. Schumacher's *Small Is Beautiful* (New York: Harper & Row, 1973). See also Karl Hess, *Community Technology* (New York: Harper & Row, 1979).

NATURAL RESOURCES

Natural resources are for the most part not mobile—land, water, and climate not at all, heavy resources such as coal and timber very little. These resources tend to be embodied in goods and services for export; because of their own immobility, they often constitute the major determinant of comparative advantage. However, energy sources and minerals represent significant transfers of natural resources between countries. The United States, Japan, and the European Economic Community are heavily dependent on imported energy sources, relying on foreign suppliers for 19 percent, 90 percent, and 61 percent,[4] respectively, of all their energy needs. These three are also dependent on imports for a wide range of industrial raw materials, importing virtually all their chromium, cobalt, manganese, natural rubber, nickel, tin, and tungsten. Japan also imports over 90 percent of her aluminum, copper, and iron.[5] The United States has shifted her role over time from an exporter of primary products and an importer of manufactures to the reverse. Japan, a resource-poor country, has been dependent on imported materials and energy sources for industrialization from the beginning.

Many resource-rich countries have begun to recognize the strength of their bargaining position as monopolistic or oligopolistic sellers and have used this leverage to raise prices, restrict output, or try to develop processing, refining, and manufacturing industries at home on this raw materials base. Oil countries in particular recognize the inevitability of depletion and the need to use the revenues and the leverage from these natural resources to develop a broader industrial base for the postmineral era of their economy. Cartels have been a natural by-product of this discovery of market power, as we discuss further in Chapter 7.

SUMMARY

In this chapter, we examined the movement of inputs between countries that completes the model of commodity trade and lays the groundwork for the discussion of cartels and multinational enterprise in the next chapter. Factor movements can substitute for commodity flows and they are equally capable of increasing total welfare.

Capital is the most mobile input. It flows in response to profit opportunities and is most likely to be chosen in preference to exporting when the product is market oriented, when complementary resources are cheaper or

---

[4] *International Economic Report of the President*, 1976, (Washington, D.C.: Government Printing Office, 1976), p. 171.
[5] Ibid., p. 184.

more readily available abroad, where political risks are not perceived as high, or where barriers to trade make exporting more difficult.

Capital flows create balance-of-payments deficits initially in parent countries and surpluses in host countries, but after an average of about nine years, this is offset by the return flow of profits, interest, and principal as well as by exports of intermediate products.

Capital flows will raise the relative return to capital and slow down the growth of labor productivity in the parent country. For this reason, organized labor tends to oppose capital outflows.

Host countries impose controls to protect their sovereignty, to attempt to control development, or to exert leverage if they are in a strong bargaining position.

Labor movements can bring a country to or beyond optimum population. Migration can potentially increase welfare in both countries. The "brain drain," or emigration of skilled labor from developing countries, has been a response to the availability of complementary resources and greater effective demand for skilled labor services in developed countries, but it has made developing countries worse off. Labor migration changes relative earnings in both countries and has some limited impact on the balance of payments.

Technology transfers usually take place under licensing arrangements or through multinational enterprises. Those who create a technological innovation wish to maintain control to earn a return on the expenditures for its development. Even if technology is available, it may be necessary to adapt it to local resources and conditions.

Natural resources are generally less mobile, except for energy sources and minerals. Resource-rich countries are beginning to recognize the power of their monopoly situations and the danger of ultimate depletion and have responded with attempts to cartelize many basic raw materials industries.

KEY TERMS

brain drain
direct transfer
emigration
factor movements
host country
immigration
indirect transfer
input-oriented product
market-oriented product
OPIC
optimum population

parent country
technology transfer

REVIEW QUESTIONS

1. Using Figure 6-3, convince yourself that a small population transfer from a country above optimum population to one below optimum will always increase welfare in both countries.
2. Suppose you were a member of a foreign investment review board in a resource-rich underdeveloped country. What would you demand from would-be investors? Why?
3. Explain how tariffs on commodities stimulate movements of factors of production between countries.
4. What can be done to accelerate the flow of technology between countries while protecting the property rights of those who developed the new technology? Who benefits from the flow of technology?

SUGGESTED READINGS

BALDWIN, ROBERT E.,   "International Trade in Inputs and Outputs," *American Economic Review Papers and Proceedings*, 60, no. 2 (May 1970), 435–440.
BARANSON, JACK, "Technology Transfer Through the International Firm," *American Economic Review Papers and Proceedings*, 60, no. 2 (May 1970), 430–434.
CHACHOLIADES, MILTIADES, *Principles of International Economics*, pp. 132–137. New York: McGraw-Hill, 1981.
CHISWICK, BARRY, "The Economic Progress of Immigrants: Some Apparently Universal Patterns," in *Contemporary Economic Problems, 1979*, William Fellner, ed., pp. 357–399. Washington, D.C.: American Enterprise Institute, 1979.
FINDLAY, RONALD, "Some Aspects of Technology Transfer and Direct Foreign Investment," *American Economic Review Papers and Proceedings*, 68, no. 2 (May 1978), 275–279.
HELLER, H. ROBERT, *International Trade: Theory and Empirical Evidence*, 2nd ed., chap. 8. Englewood Cliffs, N.J.: Prentice-Hall, 1973.
KINDLEBERGER, CHARLES, *Power and Money*, chaps. 9–11. New York: Basic Books, 1970.
LAFFER, ARTHUR B., and MARC A. MILES, *International Economics in an Integrated World*, chap. 7. Glenview, Ill.: Scott, Foresman, 1982.
MEIER, GERALD M., *The International Economics of Development*, chaps. 5 and 6. New York: Harper & Row, 1968.
MUNDELL, R.A., "International Trade and Factor Mobility," *American Economic Review*, 47, no. 3 (June 1957), 321–335.

CHAPTER 7

Imperfect Competition
in International Trade:
Cartels and Multinationals

One of the assumptions underlying the classical model of trade is perfect competition. This assumption is violated by the existence of cartels, which are collusive oligopolies on a global scale. Both perfect competition and factor immobility, as well as the broader assumption of the existence and relevance of national boundaries, are shaken by the proliferation of multinational enterprises. The economic effects of cartels and multinational firms and policies to deal with them have been high on the list of concerns at official international economic gatherings in the 1970s. OPEC (Organization of Petroleum Exporting Countries) is only the most famous in a history of cartels dating back to medieval times and beyond and is also the most successful of numerous cartelization efforts of the last decade. Multinationals also have a long history, but they have experienced their most rapid growth and diversification in the period since World War II.

CARTELS

A cartel is an international association of separate producers of a particular product or group of products who join together to set prices, control output, and allocate markets. Such actions within the United States would violate our antitrust laws, but, because cartels are legal in other countries, American producers are granted an antitrust exemption to participate in cartels under the Webb–Pomerene Act of 1921. The primary purpose of the cartel is exactly the same as the purpose of creating a domestic monopoly: raising prices by restricting output and generating greater profits. Before World War II, cartels were generally controlled from Europe and were based either on control over raw materials or on technological monopoly over certain patents and processes. In recent years, newly formed cartels have been based in less developed countries and concentrated in raw materials and other primary products. Prewar cartels were formed by private firms; present-day cartels usually have substantial government involvement. The new cartels, however, have a more complex array of goals than just the simple one of joint profit maximization. We look at these goals after we have a general view of cartel theory.

Economic Effects

The models that explain cartel behavior are drawn from oligopoly theory and are equally relevant to both the prewar and the more recent type of cartel and to both domestic and international oligopolies. A cartel that is based on raw materials or on primary products rather than on patents and processes must have control over most of the supply in the hands of a small number of participating firms or countries to be effective.[1] For a patents and processes cartel, control over technology is sufficient. A second necessary condition is inelastic industry demand; that is, the product should have few good substitutes. These two conditions make it possible to raise the price substantially, cut output slightly, and reap greater profits without a threat of being undercut by outside competition. Increased industry profits from restricting output are illustrated in Figure 7-1. Note that total revenue has increased from OP_1AQ_1 (the rectangle outlined in boldface) to OP_2BQ_2 (the shaded area). We cannot determine the profit-maximizing output without some reference to costs, but it is obvious that total revenue has increased substantially with the production cutback from Q_1 to Q_2.

If we add hypothetical marginal and average costs for the industry, treating the cartel as if it were a monopoly, we can identify the industry's profit-maximizing price-output combination. This is done in Figure 7-2. The joint profit-maximizing combination is P_1, Q_1, with industry profits measured by the shaded area. If this industry were competitive, price and quantity would tend toward P_2 (lower) and Q_2 (higher) at which price equals minimum average cost. A cartel, therefore, poses the same problems for society as does a monopoly: high prices, deliberately restricted output, persistent prof-

---

[1] A different statement of this condition is inelasticity of supply. However, small numbers of firms is also an essential condition for purposes of cartel management and control.

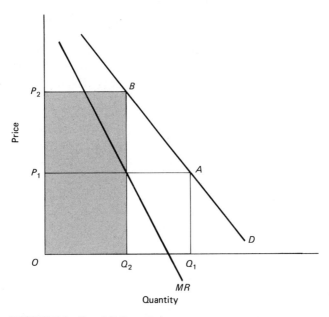

FIGURE 7-1   Cartel Policy: Higher Prices, Lower Output

FIGURE 7-2   Monopoly Versus Competition

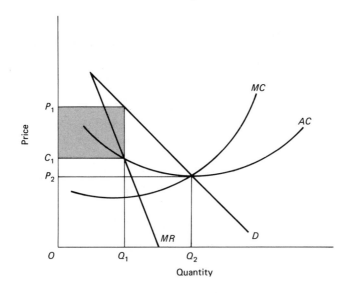

its, and average cost greater than the minimum. (Note that the monopolist-cartel determines output by setting marginal revenue equal to marginal cost.)

No monopoly, collusive oligopoly, or cartel can be expected to persist indefinitely. There are always forces that ultimately weaken their hold over the market. Competition will eventually appear either from other firms—new or not originally part of the cartel—or from substitutes, or even from both. Even a monopoly such as the local electric company is aware that at high enough rates it will induce a substantial shift to gas, oil, wood, energy conservation, home power generators, or other alternatives. In the case of a cartel (or a collusive oligopoly), there is a second destructive force in addition to the shift to existing substitutes or the emergence of new substitutes. Conflict within the group or competition from nonparticipants has cut off the life of most cartels at under five years. Figure 7-3 should help us to see why.

Let us assume that Figure 7-3 depicts the situation facing one of the members of the international helium cartel, with (for simplicity) four participating firms of equal size. Demand curve *A* represents the typical firm's one-fourth share of the industry's demand curve. This represents the quantities the firm can sell at various prices if everyone in the helium cartel raises and lowers prices together. Demand curve *B* represents the amounts that this firm can sell if it raises and lowers the price and other firms do not follow. This curve is much more elastic; the industry's product has no good

FIGURE 7-3   Cartel Disintegration

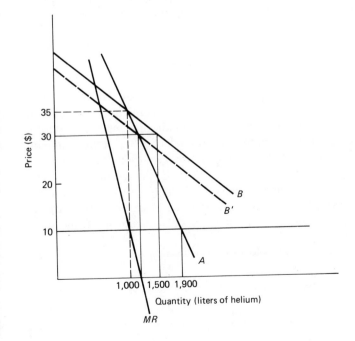

substitutes, but the product of this firm is easily substituted for the products of other firms in the same industry. Finally, $MC = \$10$ represents a constant marginal cost of producing helium of $10 per liter. Figure 7-3 shows us total revenue and total profits for three situations: the joint profit-maximizing price of $35 (for which $MC = MR = \$10$), the unilateral price cut to $30, and an industrywide price cut to $30. These results are summarized in Table 7-1.

If this firm cuts the price unilaterally and the others do not follow, its sales increase dramatically and so do its total revenues and profits. This is the temptation to "cheat" on the agreed-on price that has always plagued cartels and usually leads to their downfall. The cheating is usually more covert: smaller price cuts, discounts to favored customers or others, concealed price shaving, and provoking a responding price cut from other cartel members.

If the other members follow the price cut, the market price falls to $30 and each firm is now faced with a new set of choices: stay on the "share-of-industry" demand curve A or change the price unilaterally, moving along the new demand curve B' that intersects the share-of-industry demand curve A at the going market price of $30. Again, there is a potential for increasing profits by cutting prices if the rest of the industry does not follow the price cut. Once a cartel finds itself in a price cutting sequence such as this, it is likely to degenerate toward the competitive solution—in this case, 1,900 liters per firm at $P = MC = \$10$, with no profits.

How do cartels persist in the face of this temptation to cheat? Part of the answer is that few of them do survive for very long. One approach that will increase the probability of cartel survival—and part of the explanation for the persistence of OPEC—is the willingness of a leading firm to absorb most or all of the production cutbacks required to sustain the higher price. This situation is shown in Figure 7-4.

If A is the demand curve facing the industry and MC is the marginal cost curve, then P_1 and Q_1 is the industry's profit-maximizing combination. If the cartel were formed under competitive conditions, precartel output would have been Q_2, requiring a production cutback of $\overline{Q_2Q_1}$. If the dominant firm is willing to absorb all needed production cutbacks, then smaller firms— a sample is in panel (b)—can sell all they want at the posted price P_1. They are facing a perfectly elastic demand curve B at P_1. Note that this firm will choose to expand output from Q_c to Q_f by setting price equal to marginal cost. (Even though the industry's marginal cost curve is constant, the small

TABLE 7-1   Total Revenue and Profit at Alternative Prices

	$P = 35$	$P_b = 30$	$P_a = 30$
Total revenue ($P \times Q$)	35,000	45,000	33,000
Profit [$Q_1(P - MC)$]	25,000	30,000	22,000

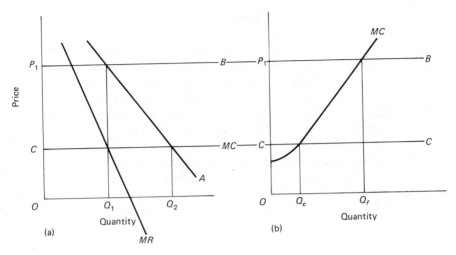

FIGURE 7-4 Dominant Firms Cartel

firm can be expected to have a conventional upward-sloping marginal cost curve, especially in the short run.) Thus, the dominant firm (or firms) may have to absorb not only the initial production cutback $\overline{Q_1 Q_2}$ but also compensate for the expanded output of small firms. This is only likely to be feasible where small firms are relatively few in number and/or are subject to steeply sloped short-run marginal cost curves. This latter is likely to be true of mining and tropical agriculture, where long time periods are needed to expand the scale of operations.

Cartels tend to be unstable unless there are very few firms and very high barriers to entry or unless they are held together by the pursuit of other goals in addition to maximizing combined profits in the short run. The Arab members of OPEC have some clearly defined political goals, but it has been necessary to establish and retain cooperation from non-Arab members of OPEC with more direct economic benefits. Other goals could include conservation (or optimizing the rate of depletion) of a nonrenewable resource, stabilizing prices, or using economic leverage to improve the terms of trade, attract industrial development, or win other desired concessions from importing countries. A cartel with a long-run perspective will be aware that a price high enough to maximize short-run profits will also be high enough to encourage a search for substitutes, making the long-run demand curve not only more elastic but possibly also lower. This will reduce long-run profit potential. OPEC, for example, has stimulated conservation efforts (fuel-efficient cars and appliances, insulation, car pools, public transportation, reduced heating and cooling) as well as both private investment and public subsidies to the search for more oil and for research and development in alternative energy sources. The development of substitutes explains why cartels are most likely to develop in raw materials and foodstuffs and less likely to develop manufactures where the cartel has to rely on a closely guarded patent on the product or process.

Cartels are also more likely to persist where the barriers to entry are sufficiently discouraging. Development of new raw materials sources requires considerable investment in capital and search costs. Raw materials industries are vulnerable to cyclical fluctuations in demand and tropical crops to weather conditions, and both are often only feasible to establish in underdeveloped countries where the political risks are high. Even in developed countries, there are risks in investing in raw materials development because of increased environmental and safety restrictions. Often, the lag between the investment, whether in planting coffee trees or in drilling for oil, and the final return in sales revenue is so long and the various risks in the interim so high that even a substantial price increase will not call forth an increase in extra-cartel supply.

The greatest short-run threats to a cartel are not external (competition from substitutes or nonmembers) but internal. A cartel must find some system of allocating and monitoring market shares so that profits are allocated in a way that all members find acceptable. Continuous renegotiation of prices and market shares by members with different goals and different preferences for short-run versus long-run benefits is necessary to keep a cartel from disintegrating.

Recent Cartel Experience

The OPEC cartel was organized in 1960, but found itself in a buyers' market—a glut of oil—and did not engage in cartellike behavior until 1973. The 1973 price hike came out of the conflict with Israel but found a response in a sellers' market, as demand had expanded much more rapidly than had supply in the intervening 13 years. Much of what has happened since then would have been predictable from our model. Armed with incomplete information about the shape of the demand curve, the response of outside suppliers (especially the Alaskan North slope and Britain's North Sea field), and the cross elasticity of demand between oil and other energy sources, OPEC went on a price-searching expedition that ultimately led to a more than tenfold increase in the average price of a barrel of oil. The long-run consequences are gradually appearing; demand is moving into a more elastic range where further price increases provoke greater quantity declines. The difficulties of absorbing and allocating production cutbacks have continued to plague the OPEC cartel despite its impressive success in increasing the profits of its members. If widespread conservation or shifts to substitutes occur, the temptation to cheat will increase. Early predictions that OPEC would not last have failed to be fulfilled, but the cartel model described in this chapter is certainly descriptive of the oil cartel.

Other efforts to organize cartels have been less successful. A copper cartel ran afoul of plentiful supplies of recoverable scrap; proposed coffee and banana cartels have met with little success. The bauxite cartel, whose three members control 75 percent of known supplies, has had considerable success. The OPEC model has a powerful appeal to resource-rich under-developed countries, but its accomplishments may be hard to duplicate in other primary products.

MULTINATIONAL ENTERPRISES

What Is a Multinational?

A multinational enterprise is defined loosely as a corporation with headquarters in one country and plants in one or more other countries. This leaves a number of questions unanswered. What percentage of ownership is required to make the foreign plant truly a subsidiary rather than a joint venture or a portfolio investment? What about nonmanufacturing overseas operations, such as service and distribution facilities? There is a vast gray area between the totally domestic company and the true multinational firm with a global reach and a global perspective.

The essential elements of a multinational enterprise have been defined as direct (rather than as portfolio) investment abroad, collective transfer of resources including knowledge and entrepreneurship, and location of income-generating assets in several countries.[2] There are several lower stages of internationalization at which a firm could stop or through which it could pass, including exporting, licensing portfolio investment, and joint ventures. The difficulty in drawing a distinction lies in the last two categories. The direct investment and resource transfer requirements eliminate portfolio investment. Joint ventures are closely related to multinationals; generally an ownership requirement of 50 percent plus will make the distinction between joint ventures (less than 50 percent) and a multinational enterprise.

Theory

Why would a firm go abroad in preference to exporting or investing in an existing foreign local firm? Capital theory suggests that the rate of return on investment overseas must be greater than the rate of return on further domestic investment and greater by enough to compensate for the additional risks and uncertainties involved.

---

[2] Neil Hood and Stephen Young, *The Economics of Multinational Enterprise*. (London: Longman, 1979), pp. 2–3.

In fact, if capital markets functioned worldwide as efficiently as they do domestically and if product markets were highly competitive as well, there would be no rationale for the multinational corporation. Exporting would be one alternative; portfolio investment, which transfers capital to foreign local entrepreneurs whose knowledge of local conditions gives them a decided advantage, would be the second option. Direct foreign ownership and control, therefore, must result from imperfections in capital markets, or product markets, or both. The most obvious imperfections are trade barriers, imperfect knowledge, and so on, discussed in Chapter 6, which make capital transfer preferable to exporting. But this does not explain the preference for direct over portfolio investment.

In capital markets, corporations that are based in the United States, Canada, Western Europe, or Japan have better access to their well-developed home capital markets than do foreign corporations either in internal capital or by issuing debt (bond) or equity (stock). This gives the firm based in these countries an advantage over foreign entrepreneurs, especially in less developed countries. Not only financial but human capital markets in the developed countries as well offer more breadth, depth, and ready access to established domestic firms. This, however, does not explain why the multinational enterprise chooses to invest directly in preference to transferring the capital to a local firm and sharing in its rate of return.

To explain direct investment, we must turn to imperfections in the product market, where the similarity between cartels and multinational corporations becomes more apparent. Some of the forms that imperfect competition may take include the following:

1. The investing corporation may have patents and technology that it is unwilling to allow to be used without the degree of control that only ownership provides.
2. The investing corporation may produce a highly differentiated product, such as Coca-Cola, which the foreign local producer cannot duplicate or even imitate successfully. If export is not a lower-cost solution, then direct ownership allows the multinational to take advantage of this limited degree of monopoly.
3. The investing corporation may have control over a supply of raw materials or other inputs, which again creates a limited degree of monopoly.

In all three cases, direct ownership will provide the degree of central control necessary to exploit the element of monopoly in the same way as a cartel tries to do and to reap greater profits by restricting output and raising prices. The fact that cartels have been unstable historically, short-run coalitions of independent firms indicates that the prospects for long-run profits are greater for a multinational to make a direct investment rather than a portfolio investment in a somewhat independent local firm. The explanation of imperfect product markets, in conjunction with the discussion in Chapter 6 of market-oriented versus resource-oriented location, also helps to explain why so much multinational investment is in other developed countries and, in particular, why there is so much foreign investment in the United States, one of the most capital-rich countries in the world.

Policy Issues

The public policy problems posed by multinationals cover a broad array of political as well as economic questions, mostly for the host but sometimes for the parent country too. These range from bribery in Japan, to fishing rights in Peru, to expropriation of private assets in Iran, to accusations of private business plotting, to overthrowing the government in Chile. Some of the issues were raised in Chapter 6. The major economic issues that have been raised are the following:

1. Do multinationals improve or worsen the efficient international allocation of productive resources? And if they do make resource allocation more efficient, are the gains shared or does one country (host or parent) lose even though there is a net gain? These questions include the possible effects on employment in the parent country.
2. Do multinationals increase or decrease competition in the host country? In world markets?
3. Do multinationals accelerate the spread of technology from developed countries to less developed countries? If they do so, is it beneficial, or does it preclude or discourage the development of alternative technologies more appropriate to the resource endowment and/or the culture of the host country?
4. How high are the costs to host governments in terms of diminished sovereignty and autonomy resulting from the presence of large foreign corporations that may be able to exert greater economic influence in some areas than the government?

These questions do not exhaust the list, but they do identify the major concerns of host governments. The impact of capital transfers on the balance of payments was considered in Chapter 6 and will be raised again in Chapter 13, so it will not be addressed here. Let us examine each issue in turn.

Resource Allocation

Certainly multinationals reallocate resources—physical capital, human capital, intermediate goods, raw materials, entrepreneurship, and technology—from parent to host countries. In most cases, it would be safe to assume, as we argued in Chapter 6, that this transfer represented an improvement in economic efficiency, especially if it leads to some "equalization" of the resource proportions in the two countries. Raw materials are transferred from where they are abundant to where they are scarce. Capital—physical and human—is transferred from the developed to the developing countries. This resource reallocation has precisely the same effects on potential world output as do specialization and trade. What is uncertain in both cases is the division of the gains, both between host and parent

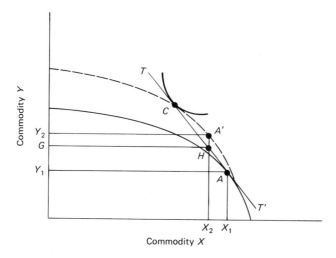

FIGURE 7-5　Immiserizing Growth from a Capital Transfer

countries and among groups within the host country. The first question parallels the possibility of immiserizing growth in trade. The net increase in output in the host country could conceivably be more than absorbed by payment of interest and dividends abroad, particularly if the resources required by the multinationals in the host country were already employed and had to be diverted from other uses, so that the gross change in output is considerably more than the net change. This possibility is illustrated in Figure 7-5.

In Figure 7-5, capital is transferred (through establishing a subsidiary of a multinational corporation) to an underdeveloped country that had been specialized heavily in the production of a labor-intensive commodity X, producing at A and consuming at C along the international terms of trade line TT. After the capital transfer it will produce at A', where the $MRTS$ again equals TT. The net increase in output is GY_2, because output of X has fallen from X_1 to X_2 while output of Y has risen from Y_1 to Y_2. At the international terms of trade TT, $\overline{X_1X_2}$ of X is equivalent to $\overline{Y_1G}$ of Y, so the excess $\overline{GY_2}$ is the net output increase. If interest and dividends exceed $\overline{GY_2}$ ($= \overline{HA'}$), this host country will be on a lower consumption indifference curve and will therefore be worse off.

A similar result could befall the parent country, whose loss of output could exceed the interest and dividend repatriation. Both these results could occur only under conditions of less than perfect competition in resource markets.[3] But imperfectly competitive resource markets are, in fact, a con-

---

[3] Under perfect competition, to attract the necessary resources out of X production, the multinational will have to pay all those resources the value of their marginal product, $\overline{X_1X_2}$ $= \overline{Y_1G}$. Therefore, only $\overline{GY_2}$ will remain as a return on the capital transferred. Under imperfect competition it is possible that resources will receive less than the value of marginal product.

dition under which multinationals are most likely to emerge, develop, and prosper. The possibility of a net loss to one country (never both), even with a world efficiency gain, goes far to explain the mixture of hostility and caution with which most governments in underdeveloped nations approach a prospective multinational subsidiary in their countries. This also explains why so many of the disputes between multinationals and host governments center around the taxation and repatriation of earnings.

We encounter similar arguments against the removal of tariffs, which increases world output but also redistributes income within the country. In general, a change that increases output should be considered desirable, but if the distributional changes are ignored, we may find powerful opposition to the change from those who expect to lose.

In the parent country, the question of employment effects is usually raised also—as it has been by labor unions in the United States. Multinationals are accused of "exporting jobs." Exports from the parent country may be displaced in the host country by local production, and even in third countries by host country exports. The parent country may even become an importer, further displacing home production.

There are several ways of approaching this problem. From the theoretical standpoint, the unemployment displacement is temporary and transitional. If there are problems of internal factor mobility, they should be resolved by making resource markets operate more efficiently rather than by sacrificing productive efficiency. We explore this argument more fully in Chapter 9 when we consider the employment argument for protection. However, there are a few qualifications that need to be added to this argument.

Multinationals argue that they leave the comfortable home environment only to defend export markets that would otherwise be lost because of tariffs, local self-sufficiency policies, and/or third country competition.[4] Thus, the domestic jobs would have been lost in any case. Also, there are jobs created in the home office, in support services (legal, financial, etc.), in intermediate products, in parts and machinery, and in complementary goods. All these would mitigate the expected unemployment impact of foreign investment. Empirical studies give a broad range of measured employment effects depending on the assumptions made.[5]

Competition

The effects of multinationals on competition in the home country and worldwide have been hotly debated for 20 years, ever since the publication of Jean Jacques Servan-Schreiber's *The American Challenge,* referred to

---

[4] U.S. Department of Commerce, *The Multinational Corporation: Studies on U.S. Foreign Investment* (Washington, D.C.: U.S. Government Printing Office, March, 1972), pp. 75–78.

[5] A summary of some of the major studies is given in Hood and Young, *The Economics of Multinational Enterprise,* Chap. 2.

earlier. He expected an invasion of the newly formed European Economic Community by efficient, well-managed American firms. This, he argued, would force many sleepy, inefficient French firms that had been resting cozily inside the French tariff wall to shape up or go out of business, improving price, quality, and array of choices for French consumers and thereby increasing competition. Alternatively, the multinational could buy out or forestall the development of local competition, thereby reducing actual or potential competition. The interesting questions are which of these two tendencies dominates and where, and in what industries. In general, multinational firms tend to be in oligopolistic industries and are likely to be large firms in the industry, which predisposes one to think that the growth of multinationals would tend to reduce competition. This possibility is greater in less developed countries, where there is less likely to be preexisting local competition and where market size is too small to support more than one, or at most two, multinational affiliates in any particular industry. Procompetitive effects are more likely to occur in developed countries that are already producing in that industry and that can support several firms. As for industries, what little evidence exists[6] tends to indicate that multinationals arise within already oligopolistic industries rather than making industries less competitive and more nearly oligopolistic. Thus, on a worldwide basis, the existence of multinationals probably makes little difference for the overall level of competition.

Technology

Indisputably, multinational firms accelerate the transfer of technology between countries, although the technology may not have much of a spillover effect on the local economy. It is not uncommon for a technologically sophisticated multinational affiliate to constitute an "enclave," existing alongside a relatively primitive economy with which it interacts very little. On the other hand, underdeveloped countries do not have the resources to devote to research and development, so a transfer of existing technology from the industrial countries offers some promise of a short cut in this aspect of development. Certainly, the multinational will make available to the less developed host country processes and technologies that would not be available if it were not possible to establish wholly owned foreign operations.

Host countries, especially those that are less developed, have two complaints. One has to do with the terms or prices at which foreign technology is made available. The other has to do with the appropriateness of the technology being transferred.

The price is determined by the international patent system, which makes possible the restrictive terms and conditions, such as restrictions on output or exports or requirements to buy machinery, parts, or intermediate

---

[6] Ibid., pp. 215 ff.

products. These conditions would exist whether the technology transfer were through a multinational or by license to an otherwise independent local firm, so the use (or abuse) of monopoly power resulting from patents is really a criticism of patents rather than of multinationals.

Multinationals have also been criticized for transferring technology without adapting it to the local resource base. Hood and Young[7] point out that, while underdeveloped countries would prefer technologies that utilize their abundance of unskilled labor and economize on their scarce resources of capital and skilled labor, this may not be as simple as it sounds. Technology is developed in the industrial countries on the basis of existing resource availability and prices, and the technologies that underdeveloped countries want may simply not be economical to develop. It may not be reasonable for less developed countries to expect multinationals to invest in the development of more flexible technology where the return is highly uncertain and the resulting technology is usable only in limited markets. If the multinational can obtain capital as cheaply (or more so) in international markets as at home, relative factor price signals will probably be too weak to encourage a search for unskilled-labor-intensive technology. A possible resolution lies in trying to attract those industries to underdeveloped countries that are generally more labor intensive, such as shoes and textiles.

E. F. Schumacher's *Small Is Beautiful*[8] makes an appealing case for small-scale, labor-intensive technologies. The social value of the development of such technologies probably exceeds their private value to the developers. While it may be appropriate for a developing country to bargain with a multinational to develop such methods in return for other concessions, there is no reason to expect the private marketplace to lead to development of a more labor-intensive technology that does not provide an adequate return to the developer.

Sovereignty and Autonomy

The most volatile and least purely economic issue is the question of the power relationship between the multinational firm and the government of the host country. The multinational is likely to be a major landowner, taxpayer, and employer, with more potential impact on output, employment, and prices than the government in many small countries. The strongest bargaining position for the government is before the fact, especially if there are natural resources involved, although the powers to tax and to expropriate are always present in the face of established multinationals. These are, however, one-shot weapons, and the risk of losing the multinational may be too high to make them useful tools. Once again, no easy answers exist. The multinational enterprise arose, in part, to circumvent the straightjacket of

[7] Ibid., pp. 186–189.

[8] E. F. Schumacher, *Small Is Beautiful* (New York: Harper & Row, 1973).

national boundaries—tariffs, taxes, minimum wage laws, environmental regulations, and restrictions on migration and capital flows, among others. If multinationals build plants abroad in an effort to minimize such constraints rather than in response to genuine market signals, world efficiency may not be served best in the process. Efforts to coordinate some of these policies through GATT (General Agreement on Trade and Tariffs) and other negotiations have had some limited success in the late 1970s in curbing these artificial incentives to direct investment abroad.

SUMMARY

A cartel is a multinational oligopoly that sets prices, allocates markets, and attempts to allocate markets among its member producers. Some cartels are also concerned with supplementary goals such as economic development, conservation of a depleting natural resource, or greater price stability.

Cartels are most likely to succeed if the control over most of the supply of raw materials is in the hands of a few producers and if demand is inelastic. High barriers to entry will allow it to persist. Because the firm's demand curve is much more elastic than the industry's, each firm will be tempted to share the price and increase profits. This temptation to cheat is a major threat to cartel stability in the short run. This is why prior agreements among cartel members on the allocation of output and markets are so important. The development of outside competition and/or good substitutes threatens the cartel in the long run.

A multinational enterprise is a firm with plants in several countries. Firms are attracted into direct foreign investment by higher rates of return abroad. The alternatives to direct investment are exporting or portfolio investment, which would be the logical choices under competitive conditions. Some type of imperfect competition, therefore, must explain the preference for direct investment. Better access to capital markets and specialized resources, patents, technical secrets, and highly differentiated products are some of the forms that this imperfect competition takes.

A number of questions have been raised about the economic impact of the multinational corporation. The major questions revolve around effects on resource allocation, distribution of gains, competition, technology transfers, and the sovereignty and autonomy of host governments.

KEY TERMS

alternative technologies
autonomy and sovereignty (host governments)
barriers to entry

cartel
cartel disintegration
cheating
competition
dominant firm cartel
host country
joint venture
market imperfections
multinational corporation
oligopoly
OPEC
parent country
portfolio investment
production cutbacks
transfer of technology

REVIEW QUESTIONS

1. Many countries have a foreign investment review board of some kind that decides whether to permit a multinational firm to locate in its country. Put yourself in the place of a review board for a country that is (a) large and industrialized, (b) small and industrialized, (c) large and underdeveloped, and (d) small and underdeveloped. Develop some criteria for deciding whether a particular multinational should be admitted or not.

2. Take another look at Figure 7-5 and see if you can figure out a comparable parent country diagram that shows all the gains "plus" going to the host country and a net welfare loss to the parent country.

3. Check the necessity of the conditions of cartel success as follows:
   a. Redraw Figures 7-1 and 7-2 with elastic demand curves.
   b. Figure out what would happen in Figure 7-4 if there were freedom of entry and no significant control over supply.

4. Long-run demand curves are always more elastic than are short-run demand curves. Why? What does this imply about cartel survival?

5. Why are labor unions so opposed to firms building plants abroad? Are they justified?

6. Why have technologies more suitable to the resource endowment of less developed countries failed to develop? How could this be changed?

SUGGESTED READINGS

BALASSA, BELA, ed., *Changing Patterns in Foreign Trade and Payments,* 3rd ed. New York: W.W. Norton, 1978. Essays by Raymond Vernon, Thomas

Horst, George Hildebrand, John Culver, and John Dunning on various facets of the economics of multinationals.

BLOUGH, ROY, *International Business: Environment and Adaptation*. New York: McGraw-Hill, 1966.

DANIELSON, ALBERT, "The Theory and Measurement of OPEC Stability," *Southern Economic Journal*, 47, no. 1 (January 1980), pp. 51–64.

EPSTEIN, EDWARD J., *Cartel*. New York: Putnam, 1978.

GUISINGER, STEPHEN, ed., *Private Enterprise and the New Global Economic Challenge*. Indianapolis, Ind.: Bobbs-Merrill, 1979. A collection of lectures; see especially those by Raymond Vernon, Moeen Qureshi, and Paul Volker.

PINDYCK, ROBERT S., "The Cartellization of World Commodity Markets," *American Economic Review Papers and Proceedings*, 69, no. 2 (May 1979), pp. 154–58.

SAMETZ, ARNOLD W., "The Foreign Multinational Company in the United States," in *Multinational Corporations, Trade, and the Dollar*, eds. Jules Bachman and Ernest Bloch, pp. 87–105. New York: New York University Press, 1974.

VERNON, RAYMOND, *Sovereignty at Bay: The Multinational Spread of U.S. Enterprises*. New York: Basic Books, 1971.

———, "Multinational Enterprises: Performance and Accountability," in *Multinational Corporations, Trade, and the Dollar*, eds. Jules Bachman and Ernest Bloch, pp. 65–80. New York: New York University Press, 1974.

———, ed., *The Oil Crisis*. New York: W.W. Norton, 1976.

VERNON, RAYMOND, and LOUIS T. WELLS, JR., *Manager in the International Economy*, 4th ed. Englewood Cliffs, N.J.: Prentice-Hall, 1981.

CHAPTER 8

Tariffs and Other Instruments of Commercial Policy

THE TOOLS OF COMMERCIAL POLICY

In Chapters 3 through 5, we developed an elaborate model that demonstrated the gains from free trade under a variety of possible conditions. Yet, despite the demonstrable efficiency benefits from free trade, most countries use tariffs, quotas, and/or nontariff barriers (as well as export taxes) to limit the flow of goods from one country to another.

These represent the major tools of what is known as commercial policy. Some writers would add capital controls, immigration restrictions, and limitations on the transfer of technology to the list. Since these were discussed in Chapter 6, we confine ourselves in this chapter to restrictions on the flow of goods and services. We reserve the "why" of commercial policy for Chapter 9 and concentrate in this chapter on the nature and effects of deliberate barriers to free trade in goods and services.

TARIFFS

The most familiar barrier is a tariff, which is an import tax. Tariffs may be used to raise general revenue for the government—the tariff was, in fact, the mainstay of federal revenues in the United States up until the Civil War. They may be used to complement domestic excise taxes on certain goods or to discourage the consumption of certain foreign goods for which there are no close domestic substitutes. But the primary purpose of the tariff has usually been to reduce the ability of the foreign producer to compete effectively with the domestic counterpart, that is, protection.

A tariff is an excise tax. It can be *specific* (e.g., 50 cents a dozen, a dollar a ton), or *ad valorem* (10 percent of price at entry), or even *compound* (a specific component plus an ad valorem component). The official tariff schedule of the United States was always drawn up by the U.S. Congress. The last such schedule, developed in 1930, is called the Smoot–Hawley Tariff, after its authors. Since 1934, tariff reductions have been negotiated with other countries as adjustments to the Smoot–Hawley Tariff. The process by which tariffs are established and modified is discussed in Chapter 10.

Tariffs have a complex array of economic effects. They reduce the efficiency of resource allocation, raise revenue for the government, and redistribute income both among countries and within countries between producers and consumers. Figure 8-1 identifies some of these effects in the country imposing the tariff.

Before the tariff, this country was producing OA on the domestic supply curve S_d and was selling it at a price P_f, the world price. (Note that we are assuming no transport costs and perfect competition.) Consumers are purchasing a quantity OD, of which OA is from domestic sources and AD is from imports.

What happens when a tariff is imposed? If this is a small country that cannot influence world price (an assumption we relax shortly), the price will rise by the full amount of the tariff to P_t. Domestic production will expand to OB, consumption will fall to OC, and imports will fall to BC. The gov-

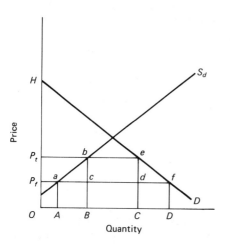

FIGURE 8-1
Economic Effects of a Tariff: One Country

ernment receives revenue of $BC(P_{f+t} - P_f)$, or rectangle $bcde$. These results are summarized in Table 8-1.

Another way of looking at the effects of a tariff is to examine the loss of consumers' surplus. The concept of consumers' surplus is really very simple. Suppose that my demand curve for bread is as follows:

Price per Loaf	Quantity of Loaves
$1.00	1
0.75	2
0.50	3

If bread is $0.50 a loaf, I will buy three loaves at a cost of $1.50. The first loaf was worth $1.00 to me, the second $0.75 cents, and the third $0.50, so they were worth $2.25; but since I got all three loaves at the price of the third loaf, I received more utility than I sacrificed in the amount of $0.75. Consumers' surplus has a similar interpretation when we aggregate demand curves. In this case, the loaf of bread is worth $1.00 to the first buyer, $0.75 to the second, and $0.50 to the third. Once again, at a price of $0.50, there is an aggregate consumers' surplus of $0.75 (an approximate measure of the excess utility gained over utility sacrificed in buying bread). When price falls, consumers' surplus increases; when price rises, consumers' surplus falls.

In Figure 8-1, the value of consumers' surplus is measured by the triangle $P_f Hf$. When the tariff is imposed, price rises to P_t and consumers' surplus falls to the smaller triangle $P_t He$. The total reduction in consumers' surplus is, therefore, the quadrilateral $P_f P_t ef$.

Where did it go? We can separate it into four components. Some of it went to the government as tariff revenue $bcde$, which could be redistributed to consumers as lower taxes or more public goods. There may be some redistribution among consumers, but this does not really represent a loss. Some of it is used up in increased marginal costs as we move up the domestic supply curve—triangle abc. Since the supply curve is the sum of the firms' marginal cost curves, this is called the *efficiency effect*. This is a net loss to society.

Some of it goes to the factors of production in the protected industry.

TABLE 8-1 Economic Effects of a Tariff: One Country

	Before Tariff	After Tariff
Domestic production	OA	OB (up)
Domestic consumption	OD	OC (down)
Price	P_f	P_t (up)
Imports	AD	BC (down)
Tariff revenue	—	$bcde$ (up)

Since revenues have risen by $P_f P_t bc$, while costs have only increased by abc, the quadrilateral $P_f P_t ba$ represents "rents" to the protected industry resulting from the tariff privilege. Again, this is not lost, but it is redistributed from consumers to producers. This is called the *protective effect*.

Finally, there is triangle *def*, which represents the loss to consumers from reduced consumption and which is not transferred to anyone. This plus triangle *abc* is sometimes referred to as *deadweight loss*.

These effects are summarized in Table 8-2. The deadweight loss represents a reduction in welfare; the revenue effect and protective effect represent redistribution of income.

Even in this very simple model it is easy to see how forces for protection develop. Even though there is a loss to the country as a whole—abc + def—there are some net gainers in the protected industry who will see lobbying for tariffs as a way of advancing their own interests. Their case becomes even stronger in the context of a two-country model, which is illustrated in Figures 8-2 and 8-3. Panel (a) in Figure 8-2 represents the home country (the one imposing the tariff), and panel (c) represents the exporting country. Panel (b) represents excess supply and demand that determines world equilibrium price and imports and exports. Panel (b) is derived from the other two panels. Before we can add a tariff, we need to digress to explain panel (b) of this diagram.

In the absence of trade, equilibrium would be (P_{e_1}, Q_{e_1}) in the first country and $P_{e_2}, Q_{e_2})$ in the second country. But, at a lower price in country 1, such as P_3, quantity demanded would exceed quantity supplied by an amount AB. At a world price of P_3, this country would produce OA, consume OB, and import AB. The quantity AB represents excess demand in this country at a world price P_3. If we take AB and plot it in panel (b) as OA', then (P_3, OA') represents one point on this country's excess demand curve for this commodity. By taking a whole series of prices, we can trace out an excess demand curve ED (or a demand for imports) at various possible prices. (Needless to say, excess demand is zero at P_{e_1} and negative at prices above P_{e_1}.) Similarly, we can trace out an excess supply curve ES for country 2 by taking prices above P_{e_2}. Where ED intersects ES, we have found a

TABLE 8-2   Separating the Effects of a Tariff into Its
             Components

Component	Measurement (Figure 8-1)
Reduction in consumer's surplus	$P_f P_t ef$
Revenue effect	$bcde$
Efficiency effect	abc
Protective effect	$P_f P_t ba$
Deadweight loss	def
Total efficiency plus welfare loss	$abc + def$

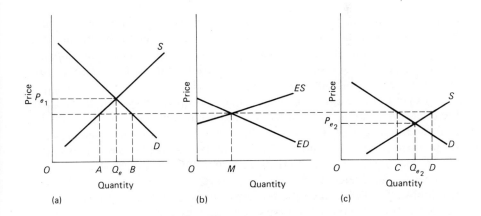

FIGURE 8-2   World Equilibrium with Excess Supply and Demand

world price at which the first country's import demand equals the second country's export supply (P_w and OM). You can take P_w back to each country's supply and demand panel and determine production, consumption, and imports or exports in each country.

Now we impose a tariff. The tariff can be represented as a second excess supply curve. Country 2's excess supply curve has not changed, but country 1's consumers have to add the tariff to arrive at a foreign supply price. A specific tariff will give a parallel excess supply curve, while an ad valorem tariff will lead to a divergent ES' such as the one shown in Figure 8-3.

What happens? The new excess supply curve ES' intersects the excess demand curve at (P_t, OM'). Price paid in the importing country has risen and volume has fallen to OM'. But OM' in the exporting country is available

FIGURE 8-3   A Tariff in a Two-Country Model

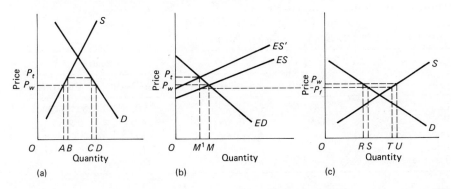

at a lower pretariff price of P_f. Thus, price rises in the importing country, but by less than the amount of the tariff. The rest of the tariff has been shifted backward in the form of a lower price received by the foreign supplier. Table 8-3 summarizes the other effects—consumption, production, trade, and tariff revenue—in the two-country model.

Several interesting conclusions may be drawn. First, the tariff serves the interests of domestic producers and foreign consumers (note the change in foreign consumers' surplus) at the expense of domestic consumers and foreign producers. The most articulate lobbyists will be the domestic producers, but sometimes there arises a counteralliance of domestic consumers (as voters) and foreign producers. While foreign producers do not vote, they can lobby. They also have the powerful threat of retaliatory tariffs against the protecting country's exports, so that they can find allies against protection in the ranks of domestic producers of exportable goods. These constitute the pro-free-trade forces in the tug-of-war between protection and trade liberalization.

Second, in this model the domestic price in the importing country rises by less than the amount of the tariff; that is, some of the tariff ($P_w - P_f$) is shifted backward to the foreign producer. While there will still be losses to consumers in the importing country, the loss will be mitigated by the backward shifting of the tariff to the foreign producer. The protective effect is reduced also. Since the rise in import price is smaller, the reduction in import quantity will be less.

Figure 8-4 compares the small country (price taker) outcome with the situation depicted in Figure 8-3. Initial price is P_w; a tariff of $P_t - P_f$ ($= P'_t - P_w$) is imposed on imports. If this country is a price taker, price will rise from P_w to P'_t, and imports will fall from BG to DE. (The reader should be able to determine revenue effects, efficiency loss, etc., from the diagram.) If, however, part of the tariff is shifted backward to the foreign supplier, the final price is P_t rather than P'_t (the amount $P_w - P_f$ is shifted backward to the foreign supplier). Imports fall from BG to CF, and the combined efficiency and deadweight losses are represented by the two small shaded triangles in the diagram. Furthermore, there is a possibility of net gain for the home country here.

TABLE 8-3   Tariff Effects in a Two-Country Model

	Country 1		Country 2	
	Before Tariff	After Tariff	Before Tariff	After Tariff
Consumption	OD	OC (lower)	OR	OS (higher)
Production	OA	OB (higher)	OU	OT (lower)
Imports/exports	AD	BC (lower)	RU	ST (lower)
Price	P_w	P_t (higher)	P_w	P_f (lower)
Tariff revenue	—	$abcd$	—	—

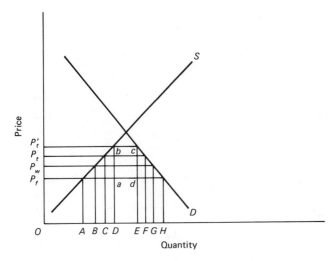

FIGURE 8-4   Effects of a Tariff with and without Foreign Price Effects

Note that tariff revenue is given by rectangle *abcd*, which consists of two smaller rectangles: the upper part represents a transfer from home country consumers, and the lower part represents a transfer from foreign producers. If the lower rectangle, representing in effect a tax on foreign suppliers, exceeds the sum of the efficiency and deadweight losses, the residents of this country may benefit from a tariff even though there is a reduction in world welfare. While a gain will not always result (as we shall see shortly, it depends on elasticities of supply and demand), it is possible for one country to gain from a tariff at the other's expense in some cases if there is no retaliation. In game theory language, even a negative-sum game can produce some winners, but we need to bear in mind that in a negative sum game the total of the gains to the winners is always less than the sum of the losses of the losers. In that case, all parties could gain (through appropriate transfers) by not playing the game at all.

Elasticities and Tariffs

The effects of a tariff on prices and quantities depends on the elasticity or responsiveness of supply and demand. For a small country, only domestic supply and demand matter, but for a large country, both domestic and foreign elasticities affect the size and distribution of gains and losses. Figure 8-5 depicts a small country with elastic and inelastic supply and demand. The reader should sketch out the other two cases (supply elastic and demand inelastic and supply inelastic and demand elastic).

Panel (a) represents the more elastic case. Both are drawn with the same initial world price and quantity of imports and in both cases a tariff

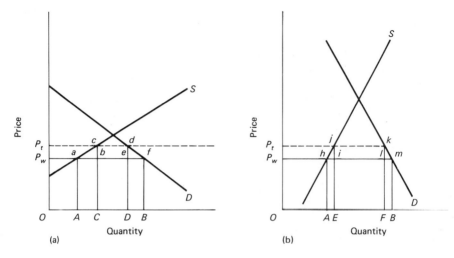

FIGURE 8-5   Effect of Elasticities on a Tariff: The Small-Country Case

of $P_t - P_w$ is imposed. In the elastic case, imports and consumption fall more and domestic production increases more than in the inelastic panel (b) case. Less revenue is raised by the government (same tariff on fewer imports), and the combined deadweight and efficiency loss is greater. While the more elastic case is likely to be more appealing to the domestic producer,[1] it has considerably less appeal to the government, domestic consumers, and foreign producers.

If we can come up with four elastic-inelastic cases for the small-country (i.e., single-country) model, the possibilities are greatly multiplied when we get to the large-country case with two sets of supply and demand curves. For simplicity, we consider only one case and make both curves elastic domestically and inelastic abroad. Readers should consider other combinations to enhance their own understanding.

In Figure 8-6, the general impact can be read off the middle panel. Relatively elastic supply and demand in the home country creates a very elastic excess demand curve, whereas inelastic conditions abroad make excess supply relatively inelastic. As a result, the price rises only slightly in the importing country and falls substantially in the exporting country. The slight price rise provokes a surge in production and dramatic decline in consumption in the home country, whereas a much larger price drop is needed to bring about the same quantity result in the exporting country. Most of the tariff is shifted back to the foreign supplier. Nothing conclusive can be said about efficiency effects relative to elasticities because the effi-

---

[1] Since the domestic producer is probably more interested in rectangle $P_w P_t ca$ than in anything else, the gain in that region depends not only on elasticities but on the initial distance of the supply curve from the vertical axis. For equal distance, the gain would be greater in the more elastic case.

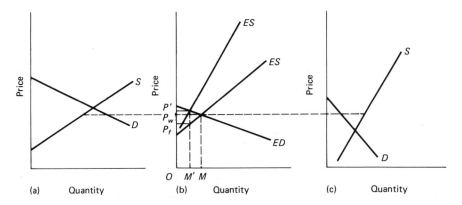

FIGURE 8-6 Effects of Elasticities on a Tariff: A Two-Country Case

ciency and deadweight loss triangles on linear supply and demand curves are each equal to $\frac{1}{2} \times \Delta P \times \Delta Q$ (Q produced for the efficiency loss and Q consumed for deadweight loss). The more elastic case will give larger ΔQ's and smaller ΔP's, whereas the less elastic case will do the opposite.

The Optimal Tariff

The previous section gave some indication that it was possible for a country to design a tariff to improve its own welfare at the expense of the other country by imposing a tariff on a good for which the foreign excess supply curve was highly inelastic. This gain is a result of excess tariff revenue[2] more than compensating for the deadweight loss as is illustrated in Figure 8-7. For simplicity, we have shown only the supply and demand in the importing country.

Inelastic foreign excess supply is implied by the sharp drop in the price (P_f) received by the foreign supplier. Total tariff revenue is *bdgh*, of which *bdce* is "paid" by the domestic consumer and *cegh* is "paid" by the foreign supplier. As long as *cegh* exceeds the loss *abc* + *def*, the tariff revenue can be redistributed to compensate the losses with some left over. But, if the tariff were to go much higher, imports would shrink to the point where very little tariff revenue would be raised from either consumers or foreign producers. That is, eventually the fall in import quantity would more than offset the gain in improved terms of trade (= lower foreign supply price). This raises the question of how high the tariff should be to maximize the welfare gains to the home country. The easiest way to see this is with the offer curves developed in Chapter 4.

Since an offer curve is also a total revenue curve, inelastic foreign supply and demand are represented in Figure 8-8 with an offer curve that

---

[2] Excess tariff revenue is that part of the tariff that comes from a reduction in price received by a foreign supplier rather than an increase in the price paid by the domestic consumer.

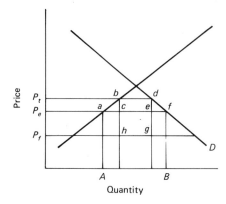

FIGURE 8-7
Welfare Gains from a Tariff

bends back rather sharply (O_m). At the equilibrium point, this country is on indifference curve I,[3] which is tangent to terms of trade line OT at the intersection of the two offer curves. The object of the tariff is to redraw our offer curve (by adding an appropriate tariff) so that it will intersect *its* offer curve at a point where the new terms of trade line is tangent to our highest attainable indifference curve. For example, at A, the terms of trade reflect tariff revenue of AB (measured in the imported good), and the home country is on higher indifference curve II. However, increasing the tariff to CD would clearly put us on a lower indifference curve than II. Around point E (precisely where depending on the shape of the indifference curve) would call for an optimal tariff EF, where the other country's offer curve is tangent to our highest attainable indifference curve.

All of this, of course, assumes that the other country does not retaliate with a tariff of its own, which could make us worse off than before either tariff. A cycle of retaliatory tariffs with successive offer curves and trade at A, B, C, and D is shown in Figure 8-9. It is highly probable that C and D would be on lower indifference curves for both countries than would A. This likely outcome is a powerful deterrent to widespread use of tariffs to improve the terms of trade.

Measuring the Effective Rate
of Protection

Often, it would be helpful to measure some aggregate or average level of tariff protection so that we could make comparisons between countries or between different time periods for the same country. This task presents

---

[3] Is the indifference map facing the wrong way? No, because the horizontal axis represents exports, not consumption. (The vertical axis represents both imports and consumption since in this simplified illustration all consumption is imported.) If our output is X_1, then consumption of X is $X_1 - X_2$ and the indifference map is drawn with reference to an origin at X_1.

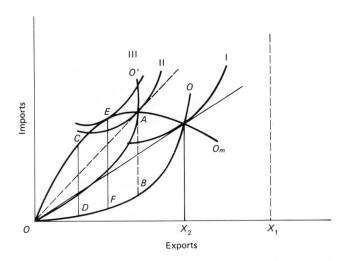

FIGURE 8-8   The Optimal Tariff

some very difficult problems. For instance, in the early 1930s when American protectionism was at its peak, the weighted average of tariffs paid was 53 percent. By 1962, it had fallen to 37 percent. But this understates the fall in the level of protection, because many U.S. tariffs were so high in 1930 that the goods subject to the tariff were not imported at all. The average tariff is computed as

$$\bar{T} = \sum_{i=1}^{n} T_i Q_i$$

where $\bar{T}$ is the average tariff, T_i is the tariff on the ith good, and Q_i is the

FIGURE 8-9   Optimal Tariffs and the Cycle of Retaliation

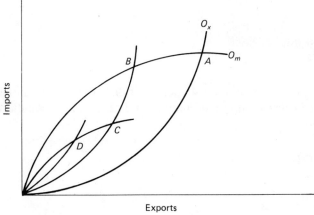

amount of the ith good imported. The Q_i reflects how important a component of total trade the ith good represents. But a good subject to a prohibitively high tariff would have a $Q_i = 0$, so its tariff would not be reflected in $\bar{T}$. The weighted average is still the only widely used measure of the height of a tariff wall, but it must be viewed in the light of supplementary information such as changes in the volume of imports relative to GNP and the percentage entering duty free. For example, a high percentage of duty-free imports coupled with a low ratio of imports to GNP would indicate that most tariffs are so high that most of what manages to surmount the tariff wall consists of those noncompeting goods with no tariffs.

Even for specific goods, there are difficulties in measuring the effective rate of protection, which can be much higher or lower than the nominal tariff. This is due to the fact that many goods are produced with imported raw materials or intermediate products. For example, a pair of shoes produced in the United States may cost $25, of which $10 is imported raw materials and the other $15 is value added in this country. Suppose that the tariff on shoes is 30 percent and that the tariff on imported materials is 5 percent. But we are protecting, not the entire production process, but only the 60 percent of the process carried on in this country (the value added). If we let

$$erp = \text{effective rate of protection}$$
$$T = \text{nominal tariff rate}$$
$$a_m = \text{percentage of the final product that is imported}$$
$$1 - a_m = \text{percentage value added in this country}$$
$$T_m = \text{tariff on imported component of production}$$

then

$$erp = \frac{T - a_m T_m}{1 - a_m} \tag{8.1}$$

In the shoe example,

$$erp = \frac{.30 - .05(.40)}{.60} = \frac{.28}{.60} = .46$$

that is, the effective rate of protection is 46 percent rather than the nominal 25 percent. If there are several imported inputs, $i = 1, 2, \ldots, m$, equation 8.1 can be generalized to

$$erp = \frac{T - \sum_{i=1}^{m} a_i T_i}{1 - \sum_{i=1}^{m} a_i}$$

Very low or zero tariffs (or even subsidies) on imported raw materials and intermediate products coupled with a high nominal tariff and a very low percentage value added at home can lead to extremely high effective rates of protection.

For both individual products and overall levels of protection, the nominal tariff is a very inadequate measure of the actual height of the tariff wall.

QUOTAS

Next to tariffs, the second most common form of protection is a quota, which is a physical or dollar value limitation on the volume of imports of a particular commodity. A quota can even be combined with a tariff in a *tariff quota*; a certain amount can enter duty free, after which a tariff is imposed. Quotas are usually set on an annual basis. Once the quota is filled, no more can be imported until the next year.

As tariffs were reduced among industrial countries from 1934 onward (see Chapter 10), quotas became a favorite alternate protective device. They offer more certainty to the competing domestic producer because, unlike a tariff, the result is not dependent on the elasticity of foreign excess supply. Figures 8-10 and 8-11 show the effects of a quota.

Figure 8-10 represents international equilibrium before imposition of a quota in a slightly different fashion from earlier versions. S_d is domestic supply, ES_f is foreign excess supply, and S_t is the sum of quantities available to this country at various alternative prices, obtained by summing S_d and ES_f horizontally. Equilibrium is at P_{e_1}, Q_e, with domestic production OA and imports from abroad $OB = AQ_e$.

FIGURE 8-10   International Equilibrium Before Quota

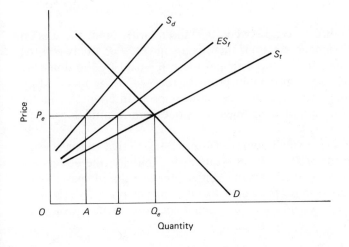

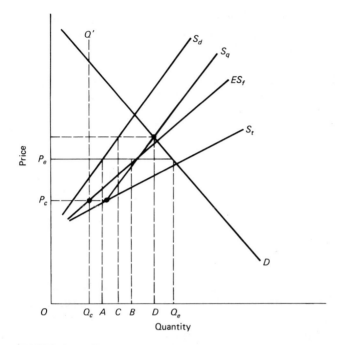

FIGURE 8-11   Economic Effects of a Quota

In Figure 8-11, we impose a quota QQ' on this situation. (Note that the quota must be less than OB if it is to be effective.) The foreign excess supply curve is the same up to P_c, at which price the quota is filled. Above P_c, foreign suppliers are willing to offer more than OQ, but they cannot, so the foreign excess supply curve becomes vertical at that price and the combined supply curve becomes parallel to S_d. Price rises to P_f, consumption falls from OQ_e to OD, and domestic production rises to OC. Imports are $OQ = CD$.

There are two differences between this and a tariff. First, there is no revenue to the government. Second, there is a gap $(P_f - P_c)$ between the price received by the foreign supplier and the price paid by the domestic consumer. This represents monopoly profit of $(P_f - P_c) \cdot OQ$ received by those fortunate enough to have the license to import. In addition, quotas throw more of the burden of adjustment on price than a tariff does. This can be seen in Figure 8-12.

Figure 8-12 shows a small country (= price taker) that is considering imposing either a tariff of $P_2 - P_1$ or a quota BC. Initially, the effects are the same, but not if supply or demand shifts. Suppose that demand shifts to PD'. Under a tariff, imports rise to BE at constant price P_2. Under a quota, constant imports of $BC = GF$ are maintained only by allowing price

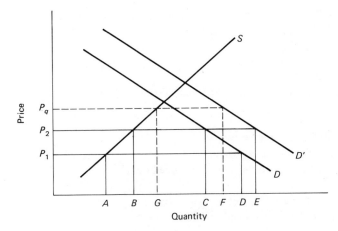

FIGURE 8-12   Equivalence of a Tariff and a Quota

to rise from P_2 to P_q. Price must bear the entire burden of adjustment, and monopoly profits to holders of import licenses increase.

Because price and quantity share the adjustment burden under a tariff, economists find a tariff preferable to a quota under most conditions.[4] Except for the revenue effect, the usual efficiency and redistributional effects of a tariff are also present under a quota, as the reader can verify with ease. The revenue effect takes the form of monopoly profits to those who are able to obtain import licenses. A perceptive government might consider auctioning quota import licenses to the highest bidder, thereby obtaining most of those monopoly profits as government revenue.

OTHER NONTARIFF BARRIERS

The catch-all category of nontariff barriers includes not only quotas but a whole array of other government practices and regulations that interfere with the free flow of goods between countries. Some are designed intentionally to interfere with trade; others serve primarily domestic objectives and only interfere incidentally with trade. The sum total of these nontariff barriers has only in the last 20 years been recognized as a major trade impediment as a consequence of some 40 years of progressive lowering of trade barriers under the Reciprocal Trade Agreements Act of 1934, the General Agreement on Trade and Tariffs (GATT) of 1947, and the Trade

[4] Quotas create political problems of allocation, an invitation to graft, corruption, black markets, and other politically undesirable side effects. This is an additional reason for preferring tariffs.

Expansion Act of 1962. The following is a general listing of some major categories of nontariff barriers (NTBs), which is by no means exhaustive:

1. State trading
2. Export taxes and subsidies
3. Differences in labeling requirements, performance standards, electrical codes, and so on
4. Border tax adjustments
5. Discriminatory public procurement policies
6. Selective domestic subsidies and aids
7. Dumping regulations and customs valuation procedures.

Each of these is discussed in greater detail. Note that inappropriate exchange rates, discussed in Part 3 of this book, could also constitute a nontariff barrier to trade.

State Trading

State trading refers to the government acting as the buyer or seller of a particular commodity internationally. As a seller, the government is the agent of domestic producers, although its goals and the goals of particular sellers or even all sellers taken together need not coincide. As a buyer, governments in state trading are acting as purchasing agents for domestic consumers, again subject to the same qualification.

Why do governments engage in state trading? There are a number of reasons. The state may operate a monopoly in that product (for example, state-run liquor stores, tobacco, matches in some European countries). In communist countries, of course, state trading is a logical extension of state ownership and control of all enterprises. In the case of agricultural products, some countries raise the domestic price artificially through price supports and sell the surplus abroad at a lower world price through the government. Resource-rich countries often act as monopolists in the export of resources to obtain a more favorable price and sometimes to obtain some optimal rate of depletion. As a monopoly buyer of goods deemed socially desirable (capital equipment, food, medicine), the state may be able to exert some monopsony power to obtain more favorable terms of trade. The primary effect of state trading is to reduce competition in international trade, which is likely to result in distortions of the kind described in Chapter 3 and thereby worsen the efficient international allocation of resources.

Export Taxes and Subsidies

Many countries tax or subsidize exports. Export taxes can be used to discourage the export of a particular good. For example, a country that wishes to develop refining and manufacturing of domestic raw materials may tax exports of those raw materials to create an advantage for actual or potential domestic users. An export tax may also be used to take advantage of a monopoly or near-monopoly position in particular goods (usually raw materials) whose foreign demand is highly inelastic. As Figure 8-13 indicates, total revenue increases from OP_1AB to OP_2CD when price is raised from P_1 to P_2. This may be successful only as a short-run strategy, since the higher price will encourage both a shift to substitutes and a search for other sources of supply. Government-sponsored cartels often use export taxes as part of the overall cartel strategy, as was discussed in Chapter 7. An export tax creates a gap between the international price ratio and the domestic price ratio in the exporting country and will, therefore, worsen the efficient international allocation of resources. (Reread the discussion of distortions in Chapter 3.)

Export subsidies are used for different reasons, although they create a similar distortion in resource allocation and the pattern of production. (Such subsidies are strongly condemned by Article XVI of the General Agreement on Trade and Tariffs.) Agricultural subsidies to compensate for domestic price supports are the most common subsidies and may be used temporarily to help develop a broader marker for a new industry. Indirect subsidies take the form of subsidized shipping and insurance as well as trade fairs and export promotion.

Differences in Product Standards

Regulation of safety, health, and performance characteristics of consumer products has proved to be a particularly intractable barrier to trade liberalization. Separate labels or product lines may have to be produced for each of several different markets, and unless the foreign market is substan-

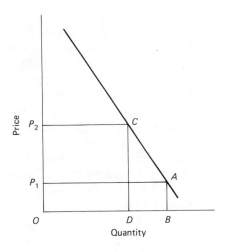

FIGURE 8-13
Monopoly Gains from Export Taxes

tial, it may not be worth the additional cost. Generally, these regulations are designed for domestic purposes and are not intended to interfere with international trade. The effect, however, is similar to a tariff or higher transport costs. Some progress was made during the 1974–1979 Tokyo Round of tariff negotiations, but it is far more difficult to reach agreement on standardizing product codes and labels than it is to negotiate reciprocal reductions in tariffs.

Border Tax Adjustments

When goods are taxed as they pass through the various stages of production, they have accumulated some taxes in the price by the time of export. The same good in a foreign country may have accumulated more tax, less tax, or even no tax at all. The tax difference, therefore, constitutes a relative price distortion that interferes with the efficient allocation of resources and patterns of trade.

This problem came to the forefront in the early years of the European Economic Community, when tariffs among the six countries were eliminated but tax differences remained. The solution adopted (later replaced by a uniform value added tax) was the *destination principle*; a good should bear the tax of the country in which it is sold rather than that in which it is produced. This calls for a rebate of indirect taxes on exports and the imposition of taxes on imports equivalent to what would have been paid on the same good at the same stage of production in the importing country.

The primary distortion in trade arises from the fact that neither accumulated taxes on exports nor equivalent taxes on imports can be determined with any degree of precision. It is very likely that border tax adjustments could contain hidden export subsidies (overrebating) or import tariffs. A second source of controversy lies in differences in relative reliance on indirect versus direct (roughly, sales and excise versus income) taxes. Sales and excise taxes are rebated; corporate income taxes are not because they are generally believed to be paid by the owners rather than shifted forward to the consumer in higher prices. This creates a competitive disadvantage in raising capital for firms in countries that rely primarily on direct taxes.

As with the preceding category, border tax adjustments create difficulties in arriving at a satisfactory resolution through negotiation. A tax system represents some sort of domestic consensus about the allocation of the tax burden among citizens, and the impact of that choice on international trade patterns is very much a secondary consideration. Both consumer product regulations and tax-induced price distortions are barriers to trade that were not even noticed until the last 20 years as some of the more traditional barriers—especially tariffs—were lowered enough to make these other obstructions more visible.

Discriminatory Public Procurement Policies

Governments are major purchasers of goods and services, and they tend to spend a far larger share at home than do other buyers. Requests for bids from prospective suppliers—the most usual procedure—are often made in a manner that favors domestic producers. Often, public agencies are required to give preference to domestic suppliers, sometimes up to a certain price differential. In the United States, the law is the Buy American Act of 1933, which gives preference to domestic suppliers. State and local governments frequently follow a similar pattern. Clearly, this procedure has the same kind of economic effects as a quota or a tariff. As with the preceding two categories, this has been a very difficult problem for trade negotiators to resolve.

Selective Domestic Subsidies and Aids

Any public policy that favors one industry over another distorts relative prices relative to actual costs and can thus distort the pattern of production and trade from what would be expected on the basis of comparative advantage. Special investment incentives favor capital-intensive over labor-intensive firms. Government subsidies for natural resource exploration and development favor those resource-producing and resource-using industries. Government-sponsored research and development aids some industries and not others. Negative examples can be found also; the minimum wage hurts industries using more unskilled labor than others, whereas environmental regulations impose far more costs on some firms than on others. If all governments offered the same aid or imposed the same burdens, no international distortion would result, but obviously the size and nature of these interventions varies greatly from one government to another. Once again, negotiations to eliminate these distortions pose a formidable challenge to national sovereignty.

Dumping Regulations and Customs Valuations Procedures

Unlike most of the preceding types of nontariff barriers, which arose from conflicting domestic policies, this last category deals directly with traded (imported) goods and services. "Dumping" refers to selling goods more cheaply abroad than at home (after allowing for shipping costs, tariffs, etc.). Dumping is equivalent to an export subsidy except that it is done by the seller rather than by the government. *Sporadic dumping* is periodic disposal of accumulated surpluses abroad so as not to disrupt the home market. *Predatory dumping* is intended to drive out foreign competitors while enjoying a higher price under a tariff-protected monopoly at home. *Persistent dumping* is undertaken to take advantage of different elasticities of demand—more elastic abroad where there is competition, less elastic at home where tariffs or quotas keep competing goods off the market. *Reverse dumping*, which receives less attention, is charging a higher price abroad than at home.

Complaints usually arise from competing domestic producers in response to persistent or predatory dumping (which are difficult to distinguish in practice). They argue that their inability to compete is not based on differences in comparative costs but on distorted prices arising from the dumper's protected monopoly position in the home country. If the complaint can be validated, the government can, under the General Agreement on Trade and Tariffs, impose compensatory tariffs (known as countervailing duties). Dumping regulations become nontariff barriers when relief is granted in dubious cases or in amounts that are excessive as compared with the price difference. The long delay in settling dumping cases is an additional source of difficulty, especially in the United States.

Customs valuations procedures are primarily but not exclusively an American problem. One area of dispute lies in the fact that the United States and Canada are the only major trading nations that do not use the Brussels Tariff Nomenclature system of valuation. Uncertainty about tariff classification, especially when U.S. customs officials are instructed to class doubtful items so as to collect the highest tariff, does not encourage foreign producers to sell in this country. The United States is also one of the few which values imports f.o.b. (free on board); most others value imports c.i.f. (cost, insurance, and freight), which makes nominally identical tariffs vary by an average of 10 percent, with a wide range above and below for particular products. Finally, there are a few products for which the United States calculates the tariff on the basis of the price of the American-produced equivalent rather than on the actual import price (American selling price, or ASP), which makes the nominal tariff appear low relative to the actual tariff.

Finally, in all countries, the cost, delay, and inconvenience of complying with customs procedures is itself a deterrent to international trade.

SUMMARY

The major tools of commercial policy to discourage imports are tariffs, quotas, and other nontariff barriers (NTBs). A tariff is a tax and can be specific, ad valorem, or compound. Tariffs reduce consumers' surplus; some of the loss is redistributed to the competing industry and some to the government as tariff revenue, while the rest is accounted for by increasing marginal costs (efficiency effect) and deadweight loss. If the country is large enough to affect world price, there may also be effects in the exporting country—lower prices, lower output, and increased consumption. The efficiency of world resource allocation is reduced in either case.

The ability to shift some of the burden of the tariff to the foreign supplier depends on the relative elasticities of excess supply and excess demand. It is possible to have the importing country gain from tariffs at the other country's expense even if there is a reduction in combined (world) welfare. The optimal tariff is the one that maximizes home country welfare and can be determined from offer curves and an indifference map. The effort to impose an optimal tariff is likely to lead to retaliation leaving both partners worse off than under free trade.

The effective rate of protection is the net tariff as a percentage of domestic value added and can be much higher or lower than the nominal tariff.

A quota is a physical or dollar limit on imports of a particular good. Quotas raise domestic prices, increase domestic production, and reduce domestic consumption. The welfare effects are similar to tariffs except that monopoly profits to licensed importers replace tariff revenue and lead to license allocation problems. Also, a tariff permits increased imports in response to increased demand, whereas a quota just raises prices farther.

Other nontariff barriers include state trading, export taxes and subsidies, differences in labeling requirements and health and safety standards, border tax adjustments, discriminatory public procurement policies, selective domestic subsidies and aids, dumping regulations, and customs valuation procedures.

KEY TERMS

ad valorem tariff
American selling price
border tax adjustment
Buy American Act
commercial policy
compound tariff
consumers' surplus
countervailing duties
deadweight loss
destination principle
dumping
effective rate of protection
efficiency effect
excess demand
excess supply

export subsidy
export tax
nontariff barrier
optimal tariff
persistent dumping
predatory dumping
quota
revenue effect
reverse dumping
specific tariff
sporadic dumping
state trading
tariff

REVIEW QUESTIONS

1. Measure the change in consumers' surplus and "producers' surplus" in the exporting country when a tariff is imposed on its export. You can use Figure 8-3.

2. Try some different elasticity combinations from Figures 8-3 and 8-6 and describe the difference in the economic effects of a tariff. If you use an ad valorem tariff, under what conditions will the dollar amount of the tariff per unit be lower or higher?

3. Why do competing domestic producers prefer quotas to tariffs?

4. If tariffs reduce world welfare, how do you explain why tariffs are used so widely?

5. Using Figure 8-9, measure the loss of consumers' surplus under a quota and separate it into four identified components.

6. Suppose that Slobbovia produces pewter vases with imported tin, lead, and copper. The tariff on vases is 40 percent; the tariffs on tin, lead, and copper are 5 percent, 2 percent, and 7 percent, respectively; and the imported materials represent 10 percent, 5 percent, and 15 percent, respectively, of the value of the final product. Calculate the effective rate of protection.

7. Identify the nontariff barriers that arise primarily from differences in domestic policies; those that are legitimate trade interventions with potential for abuse for protective purposes; and those whose purpose it is to intentionally change the pattern of trade.

SUGGESTED READINGS

BALDWIN, ROBERT E., *Non-Tariff Distortions of International Trade*. Washington, D.C.: Brookings Institution, 1970.

BALDWIN, ROBERT E., and J. DAVID RICHARDSON, *International Trade and Finance: Readings*, chaps. 5, 9–11. Boston: Little, Brown, 1974.

BHAGWATI, JAGDISH N., *International Trade: Selected Readings*, chaps. 8 and 9. Cambridge, Mass.: M.I.T. Press, 1981.

CHACHOLIADES, MILTIADES, *Principles of International Economics*, chaps. 8–10. New York: McGraw-Hill, 1981. See especially his discussion of the theory of tariffs.

HELLER, H. ROBERT, *International Trade: Theory and Empirical Evidence*, 2nd ed., chap. 9. Englewood Cliffs, N.J.: Prentice-Hall, 1973.

CHAPTER 9

Arguments for Protection

Thus far, the arguments we have considered for tariffs have been of a re-distributive nature. In general, gains accrue to protected producers (or, more generally, to protected factors of production) at the expense of consumers, foreign producers, and world efficiency. The secondary argument for protection in the previous chapter was the optimal tariff, under which the improved terms of trade led to a redistribution of the gains from trade in favor of the tariff-imposing country in the absence of retaliation.

In fact, most of the arguments for protection (or against removal of protection) are based on redistribution. There are, however, arguments for protection that contend that the welfare of society as a whole will be improved by a tariff. These general arguments for protection that have theoretical validity rely on the existence of market imperfections in the forms of externalities and/or monopoly power. Other arguments for protection use tariffs to deal with domestic problems for which other types of policies might accomplish the same goal more directly. A third group of arguments can be demonstrated to involve incorrect economic reasoning. We deal with each of these groups of arguments (valid, partially valid, and invalid) separately. Before we identify and evaluate arguments for protection, however, it will be helpful to review the case for free trade.

THE CASE FOR FREE TRADE

The presumption in favor of free trade rests primarily on the argument of Chapters 3 and 4 that specialization increases output and that the gains can be shared (and usually will be) so as to make both trading partners better off. In a world of scarce resources, there are only three ways in which an economy can consume beyond its present production possibilities frontier.[1] It can discover or acquire additional resources (raw materials, imported labor, or capital), or it can create additional resources (human and physical capital) by diverting resources from present consumption to enhance future consumption. The country can seek out or invest in a search for improved technology to obtain more output from existing resources. Or, finally, it can trade. Trade is usually the least painful of these three options. In addition, trade may facilitate the other two types of growth.

In addition to the direct efficiency benefits of trade, there are at least two and possibly three other sources of benefits. Trade increases competition. If the producer of import substitutes is a monopolist (or a sluggish oligopoly), foreign competition will expand quantity available and reduce prices and profits to the benefit of consumers. Second, and closely related, is an expanded array of consumer choice. Both these benefits became evident in the late 1950s and early 1960s when the major American automobile manufacturers persisted in producing large, fuel-inefficient cars. Only loss of market share to small foreign cars finally convinced them to add a line of compact cars.

Finally, there are economies of scale. There are some industries that can attain minimal average costs only by selling to a global market and many more that need at least a broader market than their home country supplies. Airplane manufacturing and shipbuilding are among the more notable examples. The lower costs of production represent improved resource utilization and usually lead to lower prices for consumers.

All these benefits of trade need to be kept in mind as we consider arguments for protection. The case for free trade has probably been presented no more effectively anywhere than in the nineteenth-century satirical essay by Frederick Bastiat called "The Petition of the Candlemakers," which is reproduced in the appendix to this chapter.

---

[1] If, of course, the economy is inside the production possibilities curve, then a higher level of output can be obtained by utilizing unemployed or underemployed resources without resorting to trade. This is the situation that John Maynard Keynes had in mind when he observed "there is nothing a tariff can do that an earthquake can't do better."

ECONOMICALLY VALID
ARGUMENTS

All economically defensible arguments for protection rest on externalities or relative price distortions. The two best known examples of externality arguments are the *infant industry* and *national defense* justifications for protection.

The infant industry argument is that an industry that does not presently have a comparative advantage may be able to acquire a comparative advantage if given a sheltered period during which to train labor, adapt technology, and develop a home market adequate to provide an economical scale of operation. Comparative advantage is not static: a country's resource endowment is not necessarily suited to a single commodity or even to its present group of commodities in a dynamic, multicommodity world. But the industry may never have an opportunity to get started in the face of foreign competition. The essence of infant industry protection is that it is *temporary* and that the protected industry will eventually become competitive. Protection compensates for the high start-up costs of being the first firm in virgin territory.

This argument is both appealing and plausible, but it rests on either imperfections in capital markets or on externalities. In the former case, it would appear that well-functioning capital markets could see past the initial losses to the long-run profits if the industry will indeed become profitable within a reasonable period of time. Only those industries whose ultimate profits would not be adequate over some reasonable time period to compensate for the initial losses would be unable to secure the necessary capital. If the industry is not profitable within a reasonable length of time, then it is a misallocation of scarce resources to establish that industry in preference to expanding existing industries or establishing other industries. If, of course, capital markets are not functioning well, so that the opportunities are not perceived, or if there are barriers to capital flows, industries that should be established in a particular country may not be. This aspect of the infant industry argument was probably more relevant when the argument was developed 200 years ago than in an era of multinational corporations with a global perspective and considerable freedom in raising and transferring capital between countries.

A stronger case can be made for an externality-based infant industry argument, specifically in the presence of production externalities—benefits to other industries that the new industry creates and that it cannot recoup in any way. The industry may develop roads, power supplies, and a trained labor force that are then available for other industries to use without incurring the development and training cost. Or the first industry may be providing an input or a market to other industries. Such externalities benefit the society as a whole, but they are not incorporated into the profit and loss calculations of the proposed industries. If

PR = private revenues

PC = private costs

SR = social revenues (positive externalities)

all measured over some reasonable time period, then there are three possibilities:

$$PR > PC \quad \text{and} \quad PR + SR > PC \tag{1}$$

$$PR < PC \quad \text{and} \quad PR + SR < PC \tag{2}$$

$$PR < PC \quad \text{but} \quad PR + SR > PC \tag{3}$$

Case (1) is profitable on private grounds and the social revenues are a "bonus." Although one might argue that the industry will underproduce, it will be established without tariff protection. Case (2) is not profitable on either private or social grounds. To establish such an industry would represent a misallocation of resources. This leaves case (3) as the infant industry in need of protection—desirable from a social standpoint but not profitable on private grounds. But even in case (3) there is a qualification; the industry must eventually become self-sustaining, because most of the social benefits are generated in the early years. To continue to protect an industry that is never competitive would involve an inefficient allocation of resources, once the social benefits have diminished to a very modest annual level or even disappeared entirely.

There are some practical objections even to this theoretically justified but restrictively defined class of deserving industries. It is difficult to identify the industries that qualify and to quantify the social benefits involved. There is a tendency, especially on the part of the "candidate" industry, to overestimate the magnitude of the social benefits and on the part of governments to use this argument somewhat indiscriminately to support protection that is really based on other motives.

The problems involved in applying the infant industry externalities (social benefit) argument are typical of the transition from complex theoretical economic arguments to concrete real world situations. Because of the difficulty in quantifying social benefits, it is almost impossible to identify precisely which—if any—of the industries qualify by the criterion established.

Finally, a tariff is not the only possible approach. A subsidy is a workable alternative that will not only make the cost more explicit but will also come up for a regular budget review, which makes it more likely to be eliminated when no longer needed.

A recent twist on the infant industry argument has surfaced in the United States in the automobile industry, where a rapid shift in the composition of demand to small, fuel-efficient cars caught the domestic industry unprepared and gave a temporary advantage to foreign producers whose domestic demand already favored small cars. Automakers argued for temporary protection to help them convert and reestablish their competitive position. The request was denied by the International Trade Commission, which held that existing adjustment assistance (see Chapter 10) was an adequate remedy.

The national defense argument for tariff protection, like the infant industry argument, relies on externalities in the form of social benefits. In this case, the benefits consist of availability of particular goods during wartime when foreign supplies might be cut off. In the United States, the most painful experience of wartime supply problems occurred during the War of 1812 when the British blockade cut off supplies of virtually all imported commodities. World War II also interfered with our supplies of rubber from the Far East and magnesium, whose supply was under the control of a powerful German cartel.

For each item whose availability in wartime is ensured by a protective tariff, the same test must be applied as in the infant industry case. If the industry is profitable on private grounds, there is no need to subsidize it to guarantee its existence in case of war. If it is unprofitable on private grounds, then some assessment must be made of the value of the social benefits to see whether they are sufficient to justify subsidizing an unprofitable industry. It is even more difficult to quantify these benefits for national defense than for infant industry because the social benefits must be multiplied by the probability of a war that will interfere with the supply and discounted for the time period before the hypothetical war might occur. Even if the product or service is of sufficient strategic importance to justify some sort of "guarantee," a tariff is not the only option. Stockpiling (as is done for some raw materials), government production, development of alternative sources of supply, and direct subsidies are all viable options that would focus more narrowly on the level of production we would need to maintain.

PARTIALLY VALID ARGUMENTS

There are two groups of partially valid arguments: those based on domestic distortions and those based on redistributive effects of imposing or eliminating tariffs. Domestic distortions were discussed in Chapter 3; the major types of distortions are illustrated in Figure 9-1. Assume that X is the export commodity in each case. In panel (a), $P_x/P_y(PP)$ is lower than $MC_x/MC_y(CC)$, indicating either monopoly in Y or some kind of subsidy to X.

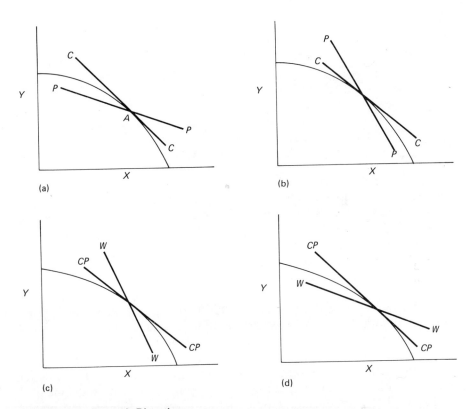

FIGURE 9-1   Domestic Distortions

The *PP* line could be rotated into equality by either an export tax on *X* or an import subsidy on *Y* (negative tariff). In panel (b), the opposite is true; the relative price of the exportable commodity is too high ($P_x/P_y > MC_x/MC_y$), which is due to monopoly in *X* or some kind of subsidy in *Y*. The price line could be rotated into equality with *CC* by an export subsidy on *X* or a tariff on *Y*.

Panels (c) and (d) represent deviations between the domestic and the international price ratio rather than domestic distortions. In panel (c), the world price of *X* relative to *Y* is higher than it is domestically after trade, because of foreign tariffs on *X*, foreign export subsidies on *Y*, or monopoly power in international trade. Panel (d) represents foreign export subsidies on *X*, tariffs on *Y*, or monopoly power. A tariff could be an appropriate remedy in either case. In panels (b), (c), and (d), a tariff is only one remedy and not necessarily the best choice; it might be more appropriate to work for removal of the domestic or foreign distortion than to create an additional offsetting distortion.

These distortions arise from numerous sources: subsidies to raw materials suppliers, border tax adjustments on exports and imports, government

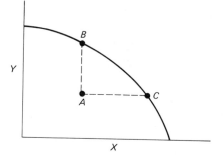

FIGURE 9-2
Unemployed Resources

research and development benefiting some industries more than others, and all the nontariff barriers mentioned in Chapter 8. Using tariffs to correct for these would be theoretically valid, but because of the problem of measuring the size of distortions and because tariffs are uniform with respect to source while distortions vary from country to country, the practical application would be even more difficult than in the infant industry and national defense cases.

A group of related arguments for tariffs (or against their removal) are concerned with the *employment effects* of trade and tariffs. One strand of the employment argument is somewhat related to the distortions argument because the domestic opportunity cost of either commodity is zero when there are unemployed resources. We do not need trade to make us better off; we can increase our well-being simply by moving from producing at *A* in Figure 9-2 to producing at *B*, *C*, or in between. Once we are on the production possibilities frontier, trade will still make it possible to get beyond it.

How do tariffs solve unemployment problems? People are employed (relatively inefficiently, but employed) in producing substitutes for goods formerly imported. If the import substitutes are more labor intensive than average, labor demand will increase even more. (Recall the discussion of the full-employment assumption in Chapter 3.) However, there are some drawbacks to this approach to creating full employment.

First, substantial reductions in imports would be needed to have much impact on employment. Approximately 86,000 jobs are associated with each $1 billion change in imports.[2] Of our $206 billion of imports in 1979, $75 billion were raw materials and noncompeting agricultural products. Thus a one-percentage-point reduction in unemployment (just over 1 million jobs) would require a reduction in imports of $11.6 billion, which represents 9 percent of competing imports for which substitution might be possible. Import substitution of that magnitude would almost certainly provoke retal-

[2] Robert Baldwin, "Trade and Employment Effects in the United States of Multilateral Tariff Reductions," *American Economic Review Papers and Proceedings*, 66, no. 2 (May 1976), 142–148.

iation against our exports, which is a major argument against using tariffs for employment reasons. The jobs gained or preserved in producing import substitutes may be offset by the jobs lost or precluded in producing exports.

Second, tariffs for employment reasons use a long-run tool to deal with a short-run problem. Industries are encouraged to develop and expand under tariff protection, not because they utilize our resources more efficiently, but because we do not want workers to undergo unemployment, retraining, and relocation. Yet these are the necessary costs of a dynamic, changing, efficient market economy.[3] Ignoring or repressing market signals creates real welfare losses in terms of output foregone.

A related, partially valid argument for tariff protection is the *balance-of-payments* argument that arose under conditions of fixed exchange rates. Recall the discussion in Chapter 3 of the assumption that exports are equal to imports in value. If a country's currency is overpriced, then commodities in which one has a comparative advantage will not be priced competitively internationally and may be imported rather than exported, which is inefficient resource allocation from both a domestic and an international point of view. If there is some reason not to adjust the currency's value, a temporary tariff could be justified, perhaps a general surcharge (such as Nixon's 10 percent import tax in August–December 1971) that reflects the extent of currency overvaluation. Under flexible exchange rates, however, there is no need for such compensatory tariffs.

INVALID ARGUMENTS

Most of the popular arguments for protection are oversimplified variants on the employment or balance-of-payments theme—"keep our money at home," "don't export American jobs," and similar catch phrases. Two arguments offer variations on this theme: the mercantilist argument and the cheap foreign labor argument.

The *mercantilist argument*, which dates back at least 300 years, suggests basically that running an export surplus will increase a country's "wealth," which 300 years ago meant an inflow of gold or silver. On the surface, this argument was easily refuted. An inflow of gold or silver would expand the money supply, drive up domestic prices, and thus eliminate the export surplus (Hume's specie flow argument, which is covered more fully in Chapter 15). A country's well-being in any case consists not in its holdings of precious metals but in the standard of living its citizens enjoy, which is enhanced by encouraging trade and in obtaining as much as possible in imports in exchange for its exports.

---

[3] See Chapter 10 for a discussion of the adjustment assistance program as a response to these costs.

The famous British economist, John Maynard Keynes, found a kernel of sound reasoning within the mercantilist argument. He argued that during a time of less than full employment an export surplus could have a stimulating effect on output and employment in the same way that an increase in government spending or investment would. This reduces to the employment argument already discussed. It is difficult, however, to find any hint of this argument within the original mercantilist writings.

The *cheap foreign labor argument* is based on the fact that U.S. wages are significantly higher than in many of the countries from which we import. Advocates of protection argue that they would be able to compete in terms of physical efficiency if labor were not so much more expensive and that underselling us in goods embodying low-cost foreign labor constitutes "unfair foreign competition." Sometimes lurid verbal pictures are drawn of foreign sweatshops and starvation wages, implying that American consumers are somehow exploiting these hapless foreign workers by buying imported goods. It is easy to overlook the fact that this job is likely to be the most attractive opportunity available in a poor and often overpopulated country, and eliminating such jobs can hardly be described as an act of deliberate charity.

The more basic question, however, is to answer the charge that such competition is somehow unfair. This would seem to imply that American employers are somehow coerced into paying their workers more than they are worth. Wages have to reflect productivity; workers who add less to the value of output than they do to the firm's costs will soon be laid off.

If labor is expensive relative to capital, land, or raw materials, this is an indication that labor is relatively scarce in this country and that our comparative advantage must, therefore, lie in commodities that use relatively more of our more abundant resources. (Recall the Heckscher–Ohlin proposition in Chapter 5.) Low wages in Hong Kong, Taiwan, the Philippines, and other less developed countries are able to export to the United States only by compensating for their limited endowment of other resources by producing and exporting those goods that use relatively more of their cheap and abundant labor.

The "cheap foreign labor" argument confuses physical efficiency with economic efficiency and absolute advantage with comparative advantage. We may be equally or even more physically efficient as other countries in producing shoes, bicycles, and cotton textiles in that the number of units of capital and raw material and the number of person-hours of labor per unit of output are the same or less. The value of inputs per unit of output, however, may be higher in the United States for some products because of different relative prices of inputs. The ratio of value of inputs to value of output is a measure of economic efficiency.

Absolute advantage is allied closely to physical efficiency, whereas comparative advantage is more akin to economic efficiency. It is possible that we might produce many products with greater absolute efficiency than other countries, but we can only have a comparative advantage in a limited number. This means that countries that are supplied generously with highly productive resources will find themselves importing products in which they are physically more efficient than the supplier. The supplier is able to compete only by paying lower returns to physically less efficient inputs.

SUMMARY

Arguments for protection are generally based on income redistribution, externalities or other market imperfections, or curing domestic problems that might be dealt with more appropriately by means other than trade barriers. Any argument for protection that is valid in economic terms must somehow demonstrate that the assumptions underlying the case for free trade have been violated and, furthermore, that these violations are remedied most appropriately by a tariff. The economist's bias is in favor of free trade because of its inherent advantages in the gains from specialization along lines of comparative advantage as well as the benefits from competition and possible economies of scale. Thus, the burden of proof lies on the exceptions to the free trade case.

Infant industry and national defense are the two best known of a family of externalities arguments for tariff protection. Infant industry argues for temporary protection for industries that are presently unprofitable but that will eventually be competitive and are expected to generate positive externalities during their development period. National defense argues that certain industries generate benefits to society by being available in case of war. These benefits cannot be recouped through the private market, and the industry will not survive without protection. Both cases are vulnerable to overuse and might be served better by appropriate subsidies.

The domestic distortions argument belongs to the same family and is subject to the same criticisms; while theoretically valid, this argument lends itself to abuse. As with the infant industry and national defense cases, domestic distortions could be corrected better by appropriate domestic taxes or subsidies.

Employment and balance-of-payments arguments for protection are the most politically popular, but they are weak in terms of economic theory. There are more effective ways in which to create jobs than by forgoing the welfare benefits of specialization and trade. The balance of payments can be brought into balance by appropriate exchange rate adjustments. Tariffs are long-run policies, because they encourage investment in particular kinds of human and physical capital in producing import substitutes. Unemployment and balance-of-payments deficits are short-run rather than long-run problems.

Two popular but invalid arguments are the mercantilist argument that export surpluses create wealth and the cheap foreign labor argument. The mercantilist argument confuses money with wealth. The cheap foreign labor argument fails to distinguish between physical and economic efficiency or between absolute and comparative advantage.

KEY TERMS

balance-of-payments argument
cheap foreign labor argument
competition
domestic distortions
economies of scale
employment argument
externalities
infant industry argument
mercantilist argument
national defense argument
physical versus economic efficiency
private costs and revenues
social costs and revenues

REVIEW QUESTIONS

1. "We're just as efficient as the Taiwanese. We use the same machinery and the same methods and the same raw materials. But we can't compete because our hourly labor costs are so much higher." Criticize this argument.

2. How would you identify industries that deserve infant industry protection or national defense protection? How would you decide how high to make the tariff? Why might a subsidy be better?

3. Robert Baldwin, in a 1976 *American Economic Review* article, estimates that a 50 percent linear tariff reduction by the United States and major trading partners would increase manufactured imports by $1,717 million and manufactured exports by $1,591 million. Export-related jobs would rise by 116,400 and import-related jobs would fall by 148,100.
   a. Calculate the number of jobs gained (lost) per billion dollars of exports (imports). Try to explain the difference. (Recall the Heckscher–Ohlin proposition!)
   b. What would be the net effect on employment? On the unemployment rate?

SUGGESTED READINGS

AMACHER, RYAN C., GOTTFRIED HABERLER, and THOMAS D. WILLETT, eds., *Challenges to a Liberal Economic Order*, part 4. Washington, D.C.: American Enterprise Institute, 1979.

BALDWIN, ROBERT E., and J. DAVID RICHARDSON, *International Trade and Finance: Readings*, chaps. 7 and 8. Boston: Little, Brown, 1974.

BALASSA, BELA, ed., *Changing Patterns in Foreign Trade and Payments*, 3rd ed. New York: W. W. Norton, 1978.

Institute for Contemporary Studies, *Tariffs, Quotas, and Trade: The Politics of Protectionism*, selections 1, 3, 6, and 8. San Francisco: Institute for Contemporary Studies, 1979.

LUTTRELL, CLIFTON B., "Imports and Jobs, the Observed and the Unobserved," *Federal Reserve Bank of St. Louis Review*, 60, no. 6 (June 1978), 2–10.

YEAGER, LELAND B., and DAVID G. TUERCK, *Foreign Trade and U.S. Policy*. New York: Praeger, 1976.

APPENDIX

Petition of the Manufacturers of Candles, Wax-Lights, Lamps, Candlesticks, Street Lamps, Snuffers, Extinguishers, and of the Producers of Oil, Tallow, Resin, Alcohol, and, Generally, of Everything Connected with Lighting[1]

To Messieurs the Members of the Chamber of Deputies:

Gentlemen, You are on the right road. You reject abstract theories, and have little consideration for cheapness and plenty. Your chief care is the interest of the producer. You desire to protect him from foreign competition, and reserve the *national market* for *national industry*.

We are about to offer you an admirable opportunity of applying your— what shall we call it?—your theory? No; nothing is more deceptive than theory—your doctrine? your system? your principle? But you dislike doctrines, you abhor systems, and as for principles you deny that there are any in social economy. We shall say, then, your practice—your practice without theory and without principle.

We are suffering from the intolerable competition of a foreign rival, placed, it would seem, in a condition so far superior to ours for the production of light that he absolutely *inundates* our *national market* with it at a price fabulously reduced. The moment he shows himself our trade leaves us—all consumers apply to him; and a branch of native industry, having countless ramifications, is all at once rendered completely stagnant. This rival, who is

---

[1] From *Fallacies of Protection, Being the Sophismes Economiques of Frederick Bastiat* (5th ed.), translated by Patrick J. Stirling (New York: G.P. Putnam's Sons, 1909).

no other than the sun, wages war to the knife against us, and we suspect that he has been raised up by *perfidious Albion* (good policy as times go); inasmuch as he displays towards that haughty island a circumspection with which he dispenses in our case.

What we pray for is, that it may please you to pass a law ordering the shutting up of all windows, skylights, dormer-windows, outside and inside shutters, curtains, blinds, bull's-eyes; in a word, of all openings, holes, chinks, clefts, and fissures, by or through which the light of the sun has been in use to enter houses, to the prejudice of the meritorious manufactures with which we flatter outselves we have accommodated our country—a country which, in gratitude, ought not to abandon us now to a strife so unequal.

We trust, Gentlemen, that you will not regard this our request as a satire, or refuse it without at least previously hearing the reasons which we have to urge in its support.

And, first, if you shut up as much as possible all access to natural light, and create a demand for artificial light, which of our French manufactures will not be encouraged by it?

If more tallow is consumed, then there must be more oxen and sheep; and, consequently, we shall behold the multiplication of meadows, meat, wool, hides, and, above all, manure, which is the basis and foundation of all agricultural wealth.

If more oil is consumed, then we shall have an extended cultivation of the poppy, of the olive, and of rape. These rich and exhausting plants will come at the right time to enable us to avail ourselves of the increased fertility which the rearing of additional cattle will impart to our lands.

Our heaths will be covered with resinous trees. Numerous swarms of bees will, on the mountains, gather perfumed treasures, now wasting their fragrance on the desert air, like the flowers from which they emanate. No branch of agriculture but will then exhibit a cheering development.

The same remark applies to navigation. Thousands of vessels will proceed to the whale fishery; and, in a short time, we shall possess a navy capable of maintaining the honour of France, and gratifying the patriotic aspirations of your petitioners, the undersigned candlemakers and others.

But what shall we say of the manufacture of *articles de Paris?* Henceforth you will behold gildings, bronzes, crystals, in candlesticks, in lamps, in lustres, in candelabra, shining forth, in spacious warerooms, compared with which those of the present day can be regarded but as mere shops.

No poor *resinier* from his heights on the seacoast, no coalminer from the depth of his sable gallery, but will rejoice in higher wages and increased prosperity.

Only have the goodness to reflect, Gentlemen, and you will be convinced that there is, perhaps, no Frenchman, from the wealthy coalmaster to the humblest vendor of lucifer matches, whose lot will not be ameliorated by the success of this our petition.

We foresee your objections, Gentlemen, but we know that you can oppose to us none but such as you have picked up from the effete works of the partisans of Free Trade. We defy you to utter a single word against us which will not instantly rebound against yourselves and your entire policy.

You will tell us that, if we gain by the protection which we seek, the country will lose by it, because the consumer must bear the loss.

We answer:

You have ceased to have any right to invoke the interest of the consumer; for, whenever his interest is found opposed to that of the producer, you sacrifice the former. You have done so for the purpose of *encouraging labour and increasing employment.* For the same reason you should do so again.

You have yourselves obviated this objection. When you are told that the consumer is interested in the free importation of iron, coal, corn, textile fabrics—yes, you reply, but the producer is interested in their exclusion. Well, be it so; if consumers are interested in the free admission of natural light, the producers of artificial light are equally interested in its prohibition.

But, again, you may say that the producer and consumer are identical. If the manufacturer gain by protection, he will make the agriculturist also a gainer; and if agriculture prosper, it will open a vent to manufactures. Very well; if you confer upon us the monopoly of furnishing light during the day, first of all we shall purchase quantities of tallow, coals, oils, resinous substances, wax, alcohol—besides silver, iron, bronze, crystal—to carry on our manufactures; and then we, and those who furnish us with such commodities, having become rich will consume a great deal, and impart prosperity to all the other branches of our national industry.

If you urge that the light of the sun is a gratuitous gift of nature, and that to reject such gifts is to reject wealth itself under pretence of encouraging the means of acquiring it, we would caution you against giving a death-blow to your own policy. Remember that hitherto you have always repelled foreign products, *because* they approximate more nearly than home products to the character of gratuitous gifts. To comply with the exactions of other monopolists, you have only *half a motive;* and to repulse us simply because we stand on a stronger vantage-ground than others would be to adopt the equation $+ \times + = -$; in other words, it would be to heap *absurdity* upon *absurdity*.

Nature and human labour co-operate in various proportions (depending on countries and climates) in the production of commodities. The part which nature executes is always gratuitous; it is the part executed by human labour which constitutes value, and is paid for.

If a Lisbon orange sells for half the price of a Paris orange, it is because natural, and consequently gratuitous, heat does for the one what artificial, and therefore expensive, heat must do for the other.

When an orange comes to us from Portugal, we may conclude that it is furnished in part gratuitously, in part for an onerous consideration; in other words, it comes to us at *half-price* as compared with those of Paris.

Now, it is precisely the *gratuitous half* (pardon the word) which we contend should be excluded. You say, How can national labour sustain competition with foreign labour, when the former has all the work to do, and the latter only does one-half, the sun supplying the remainder? But if this *half*, being *gratuitous*, determines you to exclude competition, how should the *whole*, being *gratuitous*, induce you to admit competition? If you were consistent, you would, while excluding as hurtful to native industry what is half gratuitous, exclude *a fortiori* and with double zeal, that which is altogether gratuitous.

Once more, when products such as coal, iron, corn, or textile fabrics are sent us from abroad, and we can acquire them with less labour than if we made them ourselves, the difference is a free gift conferred upon us. The gift is more or less considerable in proportion as the difference is more or less great. It amounts to a quarter, a half, or three-quarters of the value of the product, when the foreigner only asks us for three-fourth, a half, or a quarter of the price we should otherwise pay. It is as perfect and complete as it can be, when the donor (like the sun in furnishing us with light) asks us for nothing. The question, and we ask it formally, is this: Do you desire for our country the benefit of gratuitous consumption, or the pretended advantages of onerous production? Make your choice, but be logical; for as long as you exclude, as you do, coal, iron, corn, foreign fabrics, *in proportion* as their price approximates to *zero*, what inconsistency it would be to admit the light of the sun, the price of which is already at *zero* during the entire day!

CHAPTER 10

Commercial Policy:
Background and Issues

Commercial policy was a product of the rise of sovereign, independent nation-states in the fifteenth through the seventeenth centuries. Tariffs provided not only revenue but also a way of separating "us" from "them," an attitude that persists in the "Buy American" (Buy British, Buy Canadian) slogans of the present day. The commercial policy that dominated Europe from the time of the Renaissance until the nineteenth century was known as mercantilism.

COMMERCIAL POLICY
IN EUROPE PRIOR TO 1800

Mercantilism involved not only tariffs but also quotas, embargoes, export subsidies, trading monopolies, colonialism, navigation laws, and (in England) the Corn Laws. All the major European nations practiced most or all of these elements of mercantilism, which was a complex commercial policy designed to generate an accumulation of precious metals through an export surplus, to build up national political and military power, and to promote industrialization. Tariffs and quotas protected fledgling industries from foreign competition; together with export subsidies, they also helped to create an export surplus. (With all the major European nations pursuing such a policy simultaneously, they obviously could not *all* develop an export surplus![1]) Embargoes (forbidding export of certain items) were used to prevent the export of raw materials, thereby increasing the likelihood that manufacturing industries for export would develop. Trading monopolies provided incentives for risky ventures (as well as rewards to royal favorites and revenues from sale of monopoly privileges), whereas colonies provided a guaranteed source of raw materials and a captive market for developing manufacturing industries. Navigation laws gave preference to goods carried in domestic (including colonial) ships, which encouraged development of shipbuilding and also naval military power. The Corn Laws restricted imports of wheat to provide protection for politically powerful landowners.

Offsetting these apparent benefits of mercantilism were costs of several kinds. Mercantilism elsewhere hampered the development of large-scale, export-oriented manufacturing industries. The gains to consumers from specialization based on comparative advantage were being lost. The buildup of military power in tightly insulated, jealously guarded sovereign nations increased the probability of military as well as economic warfare. Thus, when Adam Smith launched his famous attack on mercantilism, there were many points at which it was vulnerable to attack.

THE MOVEMENT TOWARD
FREE TRADE

England was the leading political, economic, and military power in the eighteenth and nineteenth centuries, so the British move away from mercantilism and toward free trade in the nineteenth century precipitated a similar move on the continent. The free trade movement began in the late 1700s under the combined impact of Adam Smith and John Locke, the loss of the American colonies, and the development of pottery, metalware, and cotton manufacturing industries, which had a comparative advantage and were searching for export markets. The first step in the direction of liberalization was the Anglo–French Treaty of Commerce of 1786, which was invalidated by the 1789 French Revolution and the subsequent Napoleonic Wars. Wars usually tend to create a demand for protection on the part of those industries that were established and/or that flourished under wartime conditions. War tends to isolate the domestic economy by interfering with normal trade flows, which has the same protective effect as a tariff or quota. After the war, these industries can plead for defense on the grounds that they were available in time of war when foreign supplies were cut off. This

---

[1] They could, of course, have done so by generating surpluses in extra-European trade, which was part of the motivation for seeking colonies.

happened in Britain (and elsewhere) as the war drew to a close in 1815. The Corn Laws enacted that year restricted wheat imports, and other legislation provided for taxes on coal exports, bounties (subsidies) for linen exports, colonial preference, navigation laws, prohibition of certain imports and exports, and tariffs on imported manufactures.

Under the influence of Smith and Ricardo and in response to a resurgent comparative advantage in manufactures, Britain began to move toward free trade in the 1820s. The need for cheap imports of food and raw materials as well as access to foreign markets for exports was a powerful impetus to dismantle the protective apparatus built up during the Napoleonic Wars and the War of 1812. The Corn Laws were watered down. By 1850, only 48 articles were subject to duty, and by 1882, the list was down to 12. In 1860, a new Anglo–French Treaty of Commerce was concluded with such novel features as a most favored nation clause[2] and reciprocal tariff reductions.

Other countries in Europe followed Britain's lead in tariff reductions, although few except Holland and the Scandinavian countries moved as far in the free trade direction. Protectionism revived on the continent in the 1870s with worldwide depression, resurgent nationalism, and rising revenue needs of governments. Britain, Holland, and Denmark remained on the free trade track into the twentieth century.

AMERICAN COMMERCIAL POLICY, 1789–1913

The United States never participated in the free trade movement of the nineteenth century. Even in colonial times there were tariffs of up to 5 percent for revenue purposes. One of the first acts of Congress under the Constitution was the Tariff Act of 1789, which provided for tariffs of up to $8\frac{1}{2}$ percent. This tariff represented a compromise among the need for revenue, the interest of farmers in free trade (to import manufactures for consumption and export their produce), and Alexander Hamilton's arguments for military necessity and infant industry protection.

Protectionism did not begin to escalate until the War of 1812, when the British blockade created an isolation in which new industries could flourish and "old" industries could profit from the absence of foreign competition. After the war, Congress was reminded that these industries were there when needed and should be protected to ensure that they would be available in any future conflict.

Protectionism increased after the war, culminating in the 1828 tariff nicknamed the "Tariff of Abominations." This law provided for tariffs av-

---

[2] A most favored nation clause covers tariff reductions granted to other suppliers. If A has a most favored nation agreement with B, then any tariff reductions granted by A to other suppliers will also apply to A's imports from B.

eraging 45 percent ad valorem[3] and generated serious conflict between the manufacturing oriented, protectionist North and the agricultural, free trade South. Senator John C. Calhoun propounded the "nullification doctrine" in Congress, threatening that his native South Carolina would refuse to enforce this tariff in the port of Charleston. (The nullification doctrine was an outgrowth of states' rights and basically meant that states could refuse to enforce federal laws with which they disagreed.) President Andrew Jackson responded with threats of force, and the sectional conflict between the land-intensive, export-oriented South and the capital-intensive, import-competing North was joined.

The political conflict was similar to that in England, where the landowners (scarce factor) wanted protection to maintain its high return while the more abundant factors—capital and labor—wanted cheap food imports and access to export markets for their manufactures. This conflict was destined to persist into the twentieth century.

In the interim, however, Henry Clay engineered the Compromise Tariff of 1833, which provided for gradual tariff reductions. These cuts were never implemented fully because the Panic of 1837 left the government in need of funds and the tariff was still the primary federal revenue source.

During the Civil War, higher tariffs as well as domestic excises were used to finance the war on the Union side. After the war, the locus of political power had shifted to the protectionist Northeast. The free trade forces of the land-abundant, export-oriented South had been silenced, and the result was a steady and sporadically rising level of tariffs, interrupted only by the two Democratic administrations of Grover Cleveland, up until the outbreak of World War I. The Underwood Tariff, in effect at that time, averaged 27 percent.

THE CLIMAX
OF PROTECTIONISM, 1913–1930

The effect of World War I on U.S. commercial policy was very similar to that of the War of 1812. Protected from foreign competition by German interference with shipping, manufacturers that had flourished while contributing to both defense and domestic consumption demanded protection. The first postwar recession brought the Emergency Tariff of 1921, followed by the Fordney–McCumber Tariff of 1922, which had an average duty of 38.5 percent and which included agricultural protection for the first time.

---

[3] The "average tariff" tends to understate the level of protection, since it is a weighted average, with the weights based on the relative value of imports. (Mathematically, $\bar{T} = \sum_{i=1}^{n} V_i t_i$, where V_i is the value of imports of the ith good and t_i is the tariff rate on the ith good. The higher the tariff, the more it can reduce V_i; a prohibitively high tariff would result in $V_i = 0$.)

The inevitable culmination occurred in 1930 with the Smoot–Hawley Tariff (1930) with an average tariff of 53 percent—the highest in U.S. history. In combination with foreign tariffs and the world depression, this tariff contributed to a precipitous drop in the volume of trade (down one-third) and the value of trade (down two-thirds) between 1929 and 1932. Some observers attribute much of the depth and duration of the Great Depression to worldwide protectionist policies.

SHIFTING GEARS: THE RECIPROCAL TRADE AGREEMENTS ACT

The protectionist trend was brought to a halt and put in reverse in 1934 with the passage of the Reciprocal Trade Agreements Act (RTAA). This bill represented a drastic departure from previous commercial policy in several respects:

1. The president was granted considerable authority to negotiate tariff cuts. Previously setting and changing tariffs had been a prerogative of Congress.
2. Tariff cuts were to be negotiated on a reciprocal basis embodied in formal trade agreements.
3. Trade agreements were to embody the most favored nation principle, which had been used in Europe but never by the United States.

Neither reciprocity nor the most favored principle were new, but they were new to the United States. Both were a part of the Anglo–French Treaty of Commerce of 1860. Reciprocity meant that the initial effects of our tariff cuts through increased imports on output, employment, and the balance of payments would be largely offset by expansion of exports from simultaneous foreign tariff reductions. The most favored nation principle extends the lowest tariff on any product from any other foreign supplier to the exporting nation with which we have a most favored nation agreement. This principle eliminates geographic discrimination except for particular countries with which we might wish to discourage trade (e.g., Cuba or Albania).

The bill specifically authorized tariff cuts of up to 50 percent of the 1930 tariff level. This authority was extended periodically for two- to three-year terms, with an additional grant of tariff cutting authority in 1945. By 1937, tariffs had fallen from their pre–RTAA level of 52.8 percent to 37.3 percent. By 1947, tariffs, abetted by recovery (expansion of trade in goods subject to lower average tariffs) and the further tariff cut grant of 1945, had fallen further to 20.1 percent.

The free trade momentum experienced both a gain and a setback at that point. The gain was the signing of the General Agreement on Trade and Tariffs. The setback was in Congress, which had become isolationist after the war and renewed the Reciprocal Trade Agreements Act reluctantly, for short periods and with increasing restrictions.

The General Agreement on Trade and Tariffs (GATT) was signed by 23 nations in 1947, providing for periodic multilateral trade negotiations among the signers on the most favored nation principle. The GATT agreement covered a wide range of trade restrictions and has been the "umbrella" under which negotiations have been carried out since 1947. The agreement was to have been carried out by a proposed International Trade Organization, but the ITO was stillborn when Congress refused to ratify U.S. membership. (Unlike the ITO, the GATT agreement did not require congressional assent; the president was authorized to sign under the Reciprocal Trade Agreements Act.)

Congress, in the interim, introduced some new restrictions in the 1947 and 1948 renewals of the Reciprocal Trade Agreements Act. In 1947 the *escape clause* was required to be inserted in all future agreements, providing us with the right to withdraw concessions if they threatened serious injury to domestic competitors. In 1948, the *peril point* provision was added, further restricting our scope for negotiation. The peril point is the lowest level to which the tariff can be reduced without causing injury to domestic competitors. This figure was to be determined by the Tariff Commission (now the International Trade Commission) and was binding on American negotiators.

Both the escape clause and the peril point provision reflected a reaction to events of the immediate past. In part, they both reflected the isolationism of the Eightieth Congress, which was somewhat reversed in the Eighty-first Congress, which came into being in January 1949. A deeper force at work was the recognition that there were both gainers and losers from the free trade movement that had now been underway for 13 years. Initial tariff cuts could eliminate some of the excess tariff over what was needed to protect, leaving most or all of the real protection required to sustain domestic import-competing industries. As the tariff cuts brought the level of protection closer to that at which the tariff was effective, making imports more competitive, losers surfaced—displaced workers, failed firms, and pockets of distress in New England shoe manufacturing enclaves or Southern textile mill towns.

The principle that governs the theory of policy changes in welfare economics is the notion of *Pareto optimality*. A move is desirable on welfare grounds if it makes at least one person better off and no one worse off. Once we have reached a state from which no more such moves are possible, we have arrived at a Pareto optimal position. Unfortunately, this highly restrictive "no-losers" criterion rules out a great many policy options with enormous benefits to many and modest costs to a few. Because we cannot make interpersonal utility comparisons, we have no way of weighing the gains against the losses. The pain of loss to the few may be intense and the value of the gains to the many inconsequential to each of them. To deal with this problem, the compensation principle was developed. The compensation principle states that a change from state A (in this case, protection) to state B (free trade) is desirable on welfare grounds if the gains to the gainers are sufficient to compensate the losers for their losses and still leave the gainers better off. This principle was reflected in the next major trade bill.

THE KENNEDY ROUND

Peril point and escape clause are based on the narrow "no-losers" welfare criterion of Pareto optimality, which severely restricted our ability to make any significant further progress in the free trade direction. This issue plagued U.S. trade negotiations from 1947 to 1962 when it was resolved by the Trade Expansion Act. Peril point was eliminated in the 1949 extension and restored in the 1951 extension. The 1951 act also eliminated most favored nation treatment for communist countries, most of which did not retrieve that status until the late 1970s. The Cold War added another restriction in excluding items critical to national defense.

By the time that John Kennedy was inaugurated in 1961, much of the momentum of the trade liberalization movement had been spent. The average level of duty had dropped to 12.8 percent in 1952; by 1962 further cuts brought it down to 12.3 percent, a minuscule change.

To some degree the liberalization movement was slowed by the fact that most of the "fat" had been eliminated from the tariff structure in earlier cuts. If a 10 percent tariff is sufficient to protect the domestic industry and the tariff is cut from 30 to 20 percent, it has little impact, whereas a further cut to 5 percent would evoke complaints from import-competing producers.

The impetus to new trade initiatives came from several sources, among them a mild thaw in the Cold War, a change in administration, and a sluggish growth rate and a balance-of-payments deficit that policymakers thought could both be alleviated by export expansion. The primary stimulus, however, was the formation of the European Economic Community, described more fully in Chapter 11. American exporters were concerned about loss of sales as the inner six of Europe (and the outer seven, just organizing the European Free Trade Area), began to increase trade with each other at the expense of outsiders. Organized labor was concerned about the possibility of lost jobs as exporters built plants inside the EEC to protect their sales. The best hope, many felt, was to negotiate a mutual reduction in tariffs at the same time that the EEC was putting together a common tariff wall.

The Trade Expansion Act of 1962 reflected these considerations as well as frustration with the peril point and escape clause mechanisms of the preceding 15 years. The act provided for a sweeping new grant of tariff cutting authority of up to 50 percent of the 1962 level. The negotiating period was 5 years (the longest period to date), and the peril point and escape clause provisions protecting import-competing industries were replaced by *adjustment assistance*. (A modified escape clause was retained but was never used.)

Adjustment assistance offered transitional aid to workers and firms who suffered losses as a result of tariff reductions. Extended unemployment benefits and retraining and relocation assistance were offered to displaced workers, and low-cost loans and technical assistance were to be made available to injured firms. The injury test was so stringent that no one qualified prior to 1968, but later liberalization made adjustment assistance a significant—and costly—part of the trade liberalization program in the 1970s. It was curtailed sharply in the 1981 budget cuts.

The Trade Expansion Act of 1962 contained one provision that was a specific response to the European Economic Community. The act allowed for negotiation of complete removal of tariffs on products for which the United States and the European Economic Community combined provided over 80 percent of world output. This category would prove to be significant only if Britain joined the EEC, which the United States wished to encourage. Since Britain did not join the EEC until 1972, this provision proved to be of little value.

The act also provided for complete elimination of tariffs on commodities for which the tariff was 5 percent or less. These "nuisance tariffs" provide relatively little protection but tie up resources in compliance and administration.

The resulting series of trade negotiations, called the Kennedy Round, began in 1962 and ended in 1967. The United States cut tariffs by an average of 35 percent, while the EEC cut tariffs on 87 percent of their U.S. imports, nearly half of them by 50 percent or more. Outside countries received little attention in what proved to be a confrontation of major powers, but they did receive some limited spillover benefits from the most favored nation principle.

At the end of the Kennedy Round, some unresolved issues remained that became increasingly important in the 1970s. Tariffs were low—at the end of the five-year implementation period the average U.S. tariff was down to 8.3 percent. As tariffs receded, nontariff barriers loomed relatively larger. Many nontariff barriers are expressions of domestic policy rather than primarily commercial policy and have consequently proved far more difficult to negotiate than tariffs. The less developed countries (LDCs), largely ignored in the major power confrontation of the Kennedy Round, were determined to be heard in any future negotiations. The major LDC issues were preferential treatment for their manufactured exports and basic commodity price stabilization. The first issue was addressed in the interim by the development of preferential tariff schedules (GSP, or generalized system of preference) for LDC exports to most of the major industrial countries. Efforts to organize cartels and cartellike groups for commodity price stabilization were undertaken by the LDCs themselves, with mixed results (see Chapter 9).

THE INTERIM, 1967–1974

The United States, which had played a major leadership role in the movement toward free trade since 1934, encountered domestic resistance in the post–Kennedy Round period. Vietnam had taken its toll of popular support for international involvement, while inflation had led to the dollar becoming an overvalued currency, a situation that always creates some temporarily valid pleas for protection. Adjustment assistance had not yet become an effective bandage for those injured by tariff cuts. Successive legislation to extend the Trade Expansion Act failed to pass each year, while at the same time a highly restrictive bill proposing widespread use of quotas (the Burke–Hartke bill) was not only introduced but came close to approval more than once. The only legislation during this period was the Trade Act of 1970, which liberalized the eligibility test for adjustment assistance.

By 1974, some of these conditions had changed. Two devaluations of the dollar had made exports more competitive: OPEC had put the industrial countries and the non-oil LDCs in the same bind, Vietnam was behind us, and Britain had joined the EEC. These events helped to spur the passage of the Trade Act of 1974, and the Tokyo Round was begun, to be concluded in 1979. Protectionist sentiment was still strong however, particularly among organized labor and some segments of the agricultural lobby.

The Trade Act of 1974 extended most favored nation treatment to communist countries,[4] broadened adjustment assistance, tightened the escape clause, authorized generalized tariff preferences for less developed countries, and provided for retaliatory measures against countries imposing export controls. The act had a five-year limitation and gave the president more limited discretionary authority than some earlier bills had allowed.

TOKYO ROUND, 1974–1979

While tariff cuts were a significant part of the Tokyo Round negotiations, there was much greater attention paid to nontariff barriers. The United States proposed a 60 percent tariff cut on industrial products, whereas the EEC proposed weighting tariff cuts so that higher tariffs would be cut by

---

[4] Trade with communist countries was a perennial issue for the United States since 1951 when communist countries lost their most favored nation status. Eastern Europe gradually was restored to most favored nation status, and despite the residual hostility to the Soviet Union in the wake of the U.S.–Soviet grain deal, the Soviet Union was granted most favored nation status in 1974.

a greater percentage. The result was a compromise under which tariffs were cut on a sliding scale by an average of about 35 percent. The cuts will be phased in gradually with the final reductions in 1988.

The side effect was an erosion of the generalized system of preference for less developed countries, since the differential between the general tariff rate and the preferential rate was narrowed by the tariff cuts.

Nontariff barriers were addressed by a system of codes covering five areas:[5]

1. Subsidies and countervailing measures
2. Import licensing
3. Customs valuation
4. Government procurement
5. Technical barriers to trade

Countervailing actions are permitted in GATT provisions as a response to a *subsidy* in nonprimary products. The subsidy must be an export subsidy proper rather than a more general domestic subsidy to be covered by the new code, which is an extension and interpretation of the original GATT provisions. The code provides for dispute settlement procedures and exempts less developed countries from the subsidy provisions except for demonstrable cases of injury to a highly similar product.

The *import licensing* code deals with abuses of documentation procedures for nonrestricted imports and for a fair and equitable allocation of licenses for restricted imports. This code also provides a procedure for resolution of disputes.

The *customs valuation* code is aimed primarily at the United States, which uses a valuation procedure called American Selling Price (ASP) for a few items—benzene chemicals, woolen gloves, and rubber footwear. A similar procedure is used for a few other items. Canada and New Zealand also have some marginal procedures that use fictitious, domestic, or other prices as a basis for the tariff rather than the actual purchase price. Once again, the code provides guidelines and procedures for resolution of disputes.

Government procurement policies that discriminate in favor of domestic over foreign suppliers are a common practice that has been expressly excluded from GATT regulation. In the United States, the Buy American Act gives 6 percent preference to domestic suppliers (i.e., a domestic supplier will receive the contract as long as the low domestic bid is no more than 6 percent higher than the competing foreign bid). In defense contracts, the margin of preference is 50 percent. In addition, both specifications and procedures for bidding frequently favor domestic suppliers. The code calls for more open bidding and provides for consultation in disputes.

---

[5] The section that follows draws heavily on Bela Balassa, "The Tokyo Round and the Developing Countries," *Journal of World Trade Law* 14, no. 2 (March-April 1980), 93–118.

Technical barriers have been a major and complex obstacle to trade liberalization. In some cases, the intent is frankly protectionist. In others, the regulations and standards are more difficult for foreign producers to comply with, especially LDC producers. The code urges the adoption of existing international regulations and standards whenever feasible and the adoption of national regulations that are written as performance rather than design standards.

All these codes attempt to cover a variety of local situations and are expected to be refined with practice, but taken together they represent significant progress in a very difficult area of trade negotiations. Since the LDCs felt that many of the nontariff barriers covered by the codes hampered their exports, they should benefit particularly from the codes, which should somewhat offset the erosion of the generalized system of preferences in the scheduled tariff cuts.

REMAINING ISSUES

The average level of duty at the end of the Tokyo Round implementation will largely remove tariff cutting from the commercial policy agenda. The pre-Tokyo and scheduled post-Tokyo average duty rates for the United States and Japan are

	Pre-Tokyo	Post-Tokyo[6]
United States	8.3%	4.3%
Japan	10.9	2.5

Although even low tariffs have a nuisance effect and some high tariffs remain, other issues will dominate future negotiations. Quotas and nontariff barriers have only begun to receive the attention they deserve as serious trade barriers and major negotiating issues. Capital controls dealing with cartels and restrictions on multinational corporations are major unresolved issues from the 1970s. Guaranteeing a source of supply in many commodities has suddenly loomed larger than has the more traditional search for unfettered export markets. Preferential treatment for LDCs is an issue that will not go away but rather will continue to fester. The basic conflict, which goes back to the initial negotiations, is that countries are ambivalent toward free trade. They want the output gains, the export stimulus, and the benefits to consumers, but they are reluctant to inflict on themselves the painful transition costs of modifying the output mix and letting old firms die so that new ones may be born. Workers and owners in protected and threatened industries will not hesitate to use the political process to forestall trade liberali-

[6] "Tokyo Round: A U.S. Victory," *Fortune*, May 1979, pp. 130–135.

zation. This ambivalence toward free trade softened in the United States under the impact of floating exchange rates (which greatly weakened the balance-of-payments argument for protection) and adjustment assistance, but it is still present, especially for autos and textiles. In Europe, the tariff is a unifying factor that ties the EEC member countries together; further tariff cuts may be threatening to that bond. Japan is still very conscious of her dependence on foreign sources of energy and raw materials and her resulting need to retain and expand export markets for manufactures to finance those imports.

In spite of these concerns, significant progress has been made since 1934 in lowering the level of protection, especially tariffs. U.S. tariffs have fallen from 53.8 percent in 1930 to a remarkable 4.2 percent at the end of the Tokyo Round. The issue of East–West trade has largely been resolved; the West has learned to live, however uncomfortably, with OPEC and other Third World cartels; nontariff barriers have begun to fall.

The sequence of multilateral trade negotiations that began with the Reciprocal Trade Agreements Act in 1934 will continue into the next two decades with the same basic goals—gradual, negotiated reductions in trade barriers to expand world trade and increase output, consumer choice, and competition. The unresolved issues of the post-Tokyo period are very different from those of 12 years earlier at the end of the Kennedy Round. Cartels, preferential treatment for LDCs, and the sticky issue of nontariff barriers have replaced further tariff cuts, East–West trade, and use of trade barriers to cope with balance-of-payments crises, the issues that preoccupied negotiations in 1967. But within the new set of issues, there remains the basic public policy question of whether trade policy should serve the consumer or the producer, the many or the few, and whether trade policy should permit the sacrifice of long-run efficiency to avoid short-run adjustment problems.

SUMMARY

Modern commercial policy began with mercantilism, a restrictive commercial policy focused on military power, industrialization, and an inflow of precious metals through tariffs, export subsidies, navigation laws, and embargoes. The movement toward free trade in Europe began shakily in the late eighteenth century and gained momentum in the 1820s under the influence of Smith and Ricardo, with the initiative centered in Britain.

The United States never participated in the liberalization movement of the nineteenth century. From the initial national defense-revenue-infant industry protection of the Tariff Act of 1789, U.S. tariffs escalated through the War of 1812 (national defense) to the 1828 Tariff of Abominations, a victory for the protectionist North over the free trade South. A compromise tariff in 1833 slowed the momentum of rising tariffs, but they remained the primary source of federal revenue through the Civil War. The sectional conflict between the land-intensive, free trade South and the capital-intensive, protectionist Northeast was resolved by a shift of political power to the latter for most of the period 1865–1913.

Protectionist forces had a second major victory in the period 1913–1930 when national defense and political isolationism combined to push the United States to look inward. A series of successively higher tariffs culminated in the 1930 Smoot–Hawley Tariff, the highest in U.S. history.

The escalation of tariffs was reversed by the 1934 Reciprocal Trade Agreements Act, which called for formal trade agreements negotiated by the executive branch in place of tariff schedules established unilaterally by Congress. Tariffs were to be cut by up to 50 percent of existing levels. This act was renewed periodically (with increased restrictions on the freedom to negotiate) until the last one expired in 1962. Since 1947, multilateral negotiations have taken place under the auspices of the General Agreement on Trade and Tariffs.

In 1962, a new initiative was developed in the Trade Expansion Act, which provided a longer negotiating period, a new grant of tariff cutting authority, and adjustment assistance to workers and firms injured by tariffs. The Kennedy Round of negotiations resulted in significant tariff cuts, especially by the United States and the EEC.

After an interim of protectionist sentiment, the Trade Act of 1974 and the Tokyo Round 1974–1979 put the United States back on the trade liberalization path. This round emphasized reduction of nontariff barriers to trade, specifically subsidies and countervailing actions, import licensing, customs valuation, government procurement, and technical barriers. Significant tariff cuts were also negotiated.

Issues remaining for future negotiations include the remaining tariffs, quotas, and other nontariff barriers; capital controls, cartels, and multinationals; guaranteeing supply for primary commodities; and preferential treatment for LDCs.

KEY TERMS

adjustment assistance
commercial policy
Compromise Tariff of 1833
Corn Laws
countervailing measures
customs valuation
escape clause
Fordney–McCumber Tariff of 1922

General Agreement on Trade and Tariffs of 1947
generalized system of preferences
government procurement
import licensing
Kennedy Round
mercantilism
most favored nation clause
nullification doctrine
Pareto optimality
peril point
Reciprocal Trade Agreements Act of 1934
reciprocity
Smoot–Hawley Tariff of 1930
Tariff Act of 1789
Tariff of Abominations of 1828
technical barriers to trade
Tokyo Round
Trade Act of 1974
Trade Expansion Act of 1962

REVIEW QUESTIONS

1. Identify the major trade issues at each of the following periods, the two sides, and the arguments in each case:

1789	1930
1828	1962
1865	1968
1922	1974

2. Who and what are the protectionist forces in the United States today? What specific types of policies do they support?
3. Tariff cuts are always phased in over a five- to ten-year period. What are the advantages and disadvantages in doing so?
4. Using a time line, sketch the average U.S. level of duty 1789–1981 on the basis of the information in this chapter. See if you can explain the pattern in terms of the underlying political and economic forces.
5. Advocates of protectionism during the 1967–1974 period were often accused of being "neomercantilists." In what ways were they similar to mercantilists? In what ways were they different?

SUGGESTED READINGS

BALDWIN, ROBERT E.,   "Trade and Employment Effects in the United States of Multilateral Tariff Reductions," *American Economic Review Papers and Proceedings,* 66, no. 2 (May 1976), 442–448.

Institute for Contemporary Studies,   *Tariffs, Quotas, and Trade: The Politics of Protectionism,* selections 6, 8–10. San Francisco: Institute for Contemporary Studies, 1979.

LUTTRELL, CLIFTON B.,   "Grain Export Agreements—No Gains, No Losses," *Federal Reserve Bank of St. Louis Review,* 63, no. 7 (August–September 1981), 23–29.

————, "The Voluntary Automobile Import Agreement with Japan—More Protectionism," *Federal Reserve Bank of St. Louis Review,* 63, no. 9 (November 1981), 25–30.

McCARTHY, JAMES E.,   "Contrasting Experiences with Trade Adjustment Assistance," in *Changing Patterns in Foreign Trade and Payments,* ed. Bela Balassa, 3rd ed., pp. 27–37. New York: W.W. Norton, 1978.

MEIER, GERALD M.,   *Problems of Trade Policy,* pp. 12–91, 93–183. New York: Oxford University Press, 1972.

MONROE, WILBUR F.,   *International Trade Policy in Transition.* Lexington, Mass.: Lexington Books, 1975.

ROSS, NANCY L.,   "If the Shoe Fits . . . ," in *Changing Patterns in Foreign Trade and Payments,* ed. Bela Balassa, 3rd ed., pp. 38–45. New York: W.W. Norton, 1978.

CHAPTER 11

Economic Integration: Free Trade Associations, Customs Unions, and Common Markets

One of the most significant changes in international trade relationships in the post–World War II period was the economic integration movement— the formation of multinational areas within which goods and services flowed freely without trade barriers. The best known of these is the European Economic Community (EEC). The Council for Mutual Economic Aid (CO-MECON) unites the communist nations of Eastern Europe; the European Free Trade Association (EFTA), the Latin American Free Trade Association (LAFTA), and the Central American Common Market (CACM) were the other major economic integration efforts. During the wave of formation of customs unions, other potential economic alliances were discussed—a North American free trade area, an Atlantic group, a Pacific free trade area, and unions in the Middle East, Southeast Asia, and several different regions of Africa. None of these latter groups ever developed past the discussion stage.

Economic integration constitutes a recognized exception to the most favored nation principle of the General Agreement on Trade and Tariffs. GATT has promoted partial trade liberalization (i.e., gradual lowering of tariffs and other barriers) on a near global basis. Customs unions (a generic term for all four types of integration) involve total trade liberalization on a more limited geographic scale. It is not entirely clear on the basis of economic theory that one approach is superior to the other in terms of the economic welfare of either the participating countries or the world as a whole.

LEVELS OF ECONOMIC INTEGRATION

There are four types of unions representing different levels or degrees of economic unification or surrender of national sovereignty to a multinational authority. The weakest form of integration is a *free trade area* in which trade among partners is not subject to tariffs or other restrictions but each country retains its own external tariff with respect to the rest of the world. The Latin American Free Trade Area (LAFTA) and the European Free Trade Area (EFTA) are both in this category. The difficulty lies in distinguishing between imports originating in a partner country and imports originating outside, which enter your country by way of a partner country that has a lower tariff on that particular product. If this were allowed to occur, the partners would have a de facto common external tariff structure, with the lowest tariff of any partner country on a particular good being the association tariff. If, for example, Denmark had a 10 percent tariff on bicycles and Britain's were 20 percent, bicycles would be routed to Britain through Denmark where the tariff was lower. EFTA got around this problem with *rules of origin*, which basically required that merchandise was qualified for duty-free shipment between countries only if 50 percent or more of the value originated in a member country. This unfortunately retained the "nuisance" effect of tariffs, since statements of origin had to accompany all shipments.

A more satisfactory solution occurs at the second level of integration, a *customs union*, where internal tariffs and quotas are abolished and the partners agree on a common external tariff. This requires some surrender of national sovereignty in setting tariffs, but it simplifies the flow of goods within the union and allows the union to bargain as a unit in international tariff negotiations. The unification of Germany in the nineteenth century began as a customs union (the Zollverein), and the EEC evolved from Benelux, a customs union among Belgium, Luxembourg, and the Netherlands.

Once tariffs and some nontariff barriers (such as quotas) are removed, other obstacles to the efficient allocation of resources within a union become more visible. Differences in indirect taxes, environmental regulations, monetary systems, credit policies, and so on interfere with the flow of goods and services. And, if trade in goods is to be free, why not encourage the free movement of labor and capital as well? A union that takes these additional steps is called a *common market*. The European Economic Community was designed to progress from a customs union to a common market with an eventual goal of complete economic union. A common market requires harmonization of tax systems, social insurance, unemployment compensation, and agricultural policies; fixed exchange rates with respect to each other; and development of communal labor and capital markets.

The final stage of economic integration is an *economic union*, in which member countries develop a supranational governing body to coordinate domestic and international economic policies with a common currency[1] and a single voice in international economic decisions. This was the final stage of the unification of Germany and is the ultimate goal of the European Economic Community.

At each stage, there is additional surrender of national economic sovereignty to a central governing body. Since national sovereignty is a highly prized possession that nations defend against any encroachment, there must be some anticipated benefits that are of sufficient value to offset this loss. Much of the vast body of professional literature on customs unions has focused on the static welfare effects of customs unions, that is, the increased output from reallocating production to more efficient suppliers (efficiency gains for the world as well as for the union) and the potential improvement in the terms of trade for the union. More recent literature has also examined economies of scale, changing patterns of comparative advantage (a variant of the infant industry argument) and, in underdeveloped countries, the non-quantifiable "public goods" argument for industrialization, which has a noneconomic ("status") benefit to society over and above any efficiency gains.

THEORY OF CUSTOMS UNIONS

Customs unions represent movements both toward and away from free trade. The elimination of internal barriers will shift production to the most efficient supplier within the union, but the adoption of a common external tariff may reduce trade with outside suppliers who are more efficient than any intra-union producers. In the customs union literature, the first effect of a union is called *trade creation*, and the second is called *trade diversion*. Trade creation consists of the welfare gains from free trade; trade diversion represents the same kind of welfare losses as result from a tariff. Trade creation and diversion have received more attention than have any other effects of customs unions, partly because they lend themselves more readily to measurement. The measurement of pure trade creation is illustrated in Figure 11-1.

This diagram should be familiar from Chapter 8, since this shows the welfare effects of tariff removal. It is assumed that B, the partner, has a

---

[1] The problems of a common currency were alluded to briefly in Chapter 1. These include the distribution of seignorage (profit on the production of fiat money) and control of the money supply.

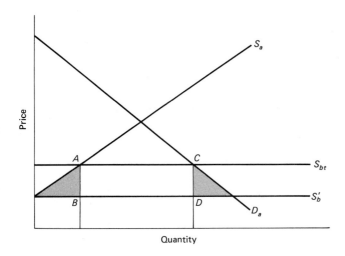

FIGURE 11-1 **Measuring Trade Creation**

perfectly elastic supply. The shaded areas represent the production effect (efficiency gains from shifting to a lower-cost producer) and the consumption effect (gain in consumers' surplus). The sum of these two represent welfare gains or trade creation. Rectangle $ABCD$ merely represents former tariff revenue now retained by A's consumers that has no net welfare effect.

Figure 11-2 represents pure trade diversion. There is no domestic supplier, at least in the relevant price range, so A imposes no tariff and buys Q_1 at price P_1 from an outside supplier C. Then A forms a union with B, which is a less efficient supplier, and adopts B's tariff, which is sufficient to raise the posttariff price from C above B's no-tariff price. Country A now buys Q_2 at price P_2 from B. There is a welfare loss in A consisting of two components: a redistribution from A's consumers to B's producers of rectangle P_1P_2HJ and a deadweight loss of triangle HJK.

Most products would probably involve elements of both trade creation and trade diversion, as is illustrated in Figure 11-3. Before the union, A was producing OE, consuming OF, and importing EF from C, the cheaper of the two foreign suppliers. After forming a union with B, the price paid by A's consumers falls to P_2, domestic production falls to OD (creating a production gain of triangle ILM), and consumption rises to OG (with a gain of consumers' surplus of triangle JNR). However, there is a loss of tariff revenue of rectangle $LNHK$. The upper rectangle $ILNJ$ represents a redistribution to consumers, but the lower rectangle $HIJK$ represents a welfare loss in shifting from low-cost supplier C to higher-cost supplier B.

Thus, there are elements of both trade creation and trade diversion. In this diagram, trade diversion effects outweigh trade creation, and there is a net welfare loss in this particular product when the low-cost supplier

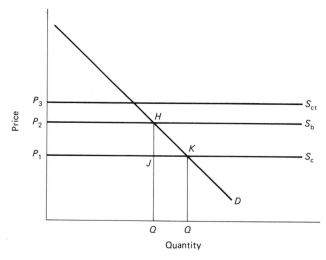

FIGURE 11-2 Measuring Trade Diversion

is outside the union. It is possible, however, that, if domestic supply and demand are quite elastic, A's initial tariff is relatively high, and the price differences between B and C are relatively small, the size of the two trade creation triangles will exceed the trade diversion rectangle and welfare will improve.

In general, if trade creation predominates over the entire range of traded products, a customs union will increase welfare, and if trade diversion dominates, welfare will be reduced. Some writers have attempted to predict

FIGURE 11-3 Trade Creation and Diversion

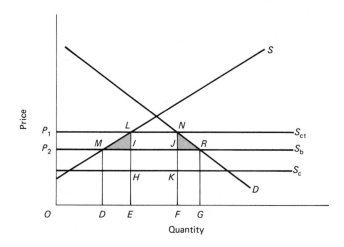

the effects of prospective customs unions on the basis of either

1. the range of products produced in the partner countries or
2. the preunion price differentials in the partner countries.

These two criteria give rise to two different definitions of the terms *competitive* and *complementary*, which are, in turn, used to determine the probable net welfare effects of a union. If the range of products produced is similar (competitive), it is likely that there will be a lower-cost producer within the union for most products and trade creation will predominate. If the range of products is different (complementary), there is a greater likelihood that the lowest-cost producer is outside the union and that partners will be switching their source of supply for goods that they do not produce from outside the union to a union partner. This reasoning suggests that competitive unions are more likely to be trade creating than unions between complementary partners.

Criterion 2 leads to a different set of definitions. Partners whose preunion prices are similar would be competitive, whereas countries with a bigger price spread would be complementary. However, in this case, the definitions predict trade creation and diversion in the opposite direction: the greater the price spread within the union (complementary partners), the greater the potential for trade creation, while a small price spread (competitive partners) not only indicates small welfare gain triangles but also a higher probability that the lowest-cost producer is outside the union.

These definitions are not as inconsistent as they might appear to be. Competitive partners are similar in their resource endowments, so they produce a similar range of products at similar prices. Complementary economies have vastly differing resource endowments, which lead to either product mixes that do not overlap or big price spreads where they do overlap. The area of overlap creates a potential for trade creation, whereas the nonoverlapping products are grounds for trade diversion. Similarly, competitive economies derive their potential for trade creation from the overlap in the product mix, whereas the narrow price spread indicates that in many cases a lower-cost supplier will be outside the union. On balance, unions between competitive economies are expected to be more trade creating.

Empirical studies of actual customs unions seem to confirm this prediction. The original six members of the EEC were more competitive than complementary, and trade creation predominated, whereas EFTA, with complementary partners, led to more trade diversion.

The other economic benefits of customs unions are more difficult to quantify or to predict. Some of the *competitive* benefits are subsumed in trade creation, in which less efficient domestic suppliers reduce output and consumers have the opportunity to purchase from more efficient foreign suppliers. Additional benefits from competition can be found under conditions of imperfect competition. In the case of monopolistic competition, the array of consumer choice is broadened by forming a customs union. In the case of oligopoly, sluggish domestic firms that had been resting comfortably behind a tariff wall are forced to modernize, innovate, and respond to both competitors and consumers. Eliminating a tariff has the same effect on oligopoly as does lowering barriers to entry.

A union that is a significant supplier or customer on world markets may be able to improve its terms of trade through a customs union. A change in terms of trade is illustrated with excess demand and supply in Figure 11-4.

Before the union, A's excess demand curve is ED; S_c and S_{ct} are excess supplies of the rest of the world (excluding B) without and with the tariff, and S_{wt} is world excess supply (including B) with the tariff. A is importing Q_1 at price P_1; net price received by C's suppliers is P_c. Now B's supply is added to A's duty free, shifting A's excess demand curve downward. Quantity imported from C falls, cum-tariff price falls to P_2, and price received by C's suppliers falls to P_f, representing an improvement in the net barter (P_x/P_m) terms of trade. The size of the improvement depends on elasticities of supply and demand.

The remaining potential benefits of customs unions are even more difficult to quantify. *Economies of scale* are frequently offered as a justification for customs unions between small countries, just as it is for trade liberalization in a global market. The argument is the same as that presented in Chapters 3 and 5. More broadly, there are certainly economies of tariff collection and political administration on a multinational scale. The elimination of duplicated functions in many small governments can offer some substantial cost savings, while the competition of ideas and methods in the

FIGURE 11-4   Improving Terms of Trade in a Customs Union

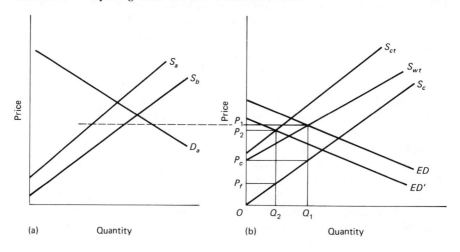

(a)   Quantity   (b)   Quantity

political arena offers an opportunity for more satisfactory solutions to social, political, and economic problems to emerge. There is, of course, a potential welfare loss for those whose desired mix of public goods is less well served by the union than by the preunion mix.

The argument for customs unions based on the dynamic nature of comparative advantage is a variant of the infant industry argument combined with the opportunity to produce and sell in a broader domestic (union) market before venturing into the chilly waters of international competition. As in the more traditional infant industry argument, it is argued that an industry could develop a comparative advantage in the shelter of a protected market, generating social benefits enroute. Furthermore, it would develop in the member of the union whose resource endowment was best suited to that product. Unlike the standard infant industry argument, this is a secondary argument for a customs union rather than a primary argument for protection.

The "public good" argument for industrialization in less developed countries is advanced for forming customs unions in those areas, especially the CACM. It is argued that there is a social benefit from industrialization over and above any expansion of GNP and that the country as a whole derives nonquantifiable social benefits from the presence of manufacturing industries.

Finally, there may be political benefits—power, influence, defense— that the partners derive from a union that add to any expected gains. These are also nonquantifiable but were certainly very important in the formation of the EEC. Jacob Viner, who wrote some of the best known of the economic literature on customs unions, argues that customs unions, like nation-states, are organized largely for noneconomic reasons.[2]

REAL WORLD EXPERIENCE

Europe

The last 100 years have provided economists with a broad array of customs unions to study. The Zollverein, Benelux, EEC, EFTA, LAFTA, COMECON, and CACM offer a spectrum of degrees of integration, sizes of countries, and stages of preunion development. The Zollverein, organized under Prussian leadership in the mid-1800s, led eventually to the unification of all except Austria among the 51 sovereign and independent German states. The other six unions are all products of the post–World War II period.

The European Economic Community developed from several smaller integration efforts, the first of which was Benelux, a customs union among

---

[2] Jacob Viner, *The Customs Union Issue* (New York: Carnegie Endowment for International Peace, 1950).

Belgium, the Netherlands, and Luxembourg organized at the end of World War II. During the same period, the European Payments Union (EPU) and the Organization for Economic Cooperation and Development (OECD) came into being in Europe. These preliminary cooperative efforts led to a movement for closer union that culminated in the Treaty of Rome in 1957 establishing the European Economic Community with six members—Belgium, Netherlands, Luxembourg, West Germany, France, and Italy. The treaty established some specific goals and timetables for increasingly closer economic and political unification, including the abolition of internal tariffs, the adoption of a common external tariff that was a weighted average of preunion tariffs, a common agricultural policy, harmonization of sales taxes, and monetary unification.

Shortly after the "inner six" were organized, the "outer seven" organized the European Free Trade Association, a more loosely knit group that later expanded to take nine members—Austria, Britain, Denmark, Iceland, Ireland, Norway, Portugal, Sweden, and Switzerland. EFTA is a free trade area whose weaker integration reflected a lesser willingness to surrender national sovereignty and, in the case of Britain, to cut special ties to the Commonwealth countries. The EEC and EFTA provide an interesting contrast. The EEC has held together after the initial momentum on the less knotty issues (common external tariff, common agricultural policy, and sales tax harmonization) was spent and tougher issues such as monetary unification had to be tackled. Empirical studies seem to indicate that the EEC was on balance a trade-creating union among economies that were largely similar in the array of products produced. Progress toward closer integration slowed in the 1970s, but this to some extent reflects the absorption of three new member states in 1972 (Britain, Denmark, and Ireland).

EFTA had more limited goals to begin with and was plagued by a number of intractable problems: a limited commitment to integration, rules of origin problems, and a dissimilar array of partner economies tending toward trade diversion. Britain was an exporter of manufactures and an importer of food and raw materials; the Scandinavian members were in the reverse situation. The resulting trade diversion was a source of friction among consumers in partner countries. In 1972, four EFTA members joined the EEC, with Britain playing the leading role in the transition. EFTA continues to function with its six surviving members.

The enlarged EEC encountered some difficulties that hampered further progress toward integration. Conflicts with Britain were particularly acute, centering around the Common Agricultural Policy, tax harmonization, and the size of the British contribution to the central governing body. The first two issues involved some fundamental changes for Britain: a shift from an income-support to a price-support system for farmers, accompanied by higher food prices for British producers, and a change in the tax system toward a value added (sales) tax in a country that had relied primarily on income taxes. These differences were ironed out, and the expanded EEC continues its slow but steady progress toward total unification.

Latin America

The 1960s witnessed two efforts toward integration in the less developed world: the Central American Common Market (CACM) and the Latin American Free Trade Area (LAFTA). The CACM treaty was signed in 1960; by 1966, the common market was in effect for most intraunion trade and with common external tariffs for 90 percent of extra-market trade. A major goal of this particular union was balanced regional economic development with centers of industrialization spread uniformly among the five small member countries. The rapid progress was brought to a halt by the 1969 war between Honduras and El Salvador, which led in 1971 to the suspension of Honduran participation in the CACM. At that point, the CACM was put on "hold," and to date no further progress has been made in restoring the CACM to its path of further integration.

The Latin American Free Trade Association was organized in 1960 with 11 member countries, spread from Argentina in the south to Mexico in the north, varying sizes and levels of development. The commitment to trade liberalization and integration on the part of members was quite weak, as the choice of a free trade area form indicates. As a consequence, very little has been achieved. Nationalism plus great differences in size, GNP, and potential gains from trade liberalization have combined to make LAFTA the weakest integration attempt to date.

COMECON

The emergence of a large group of communist nations in Eastern Europe and Asia in the post–World War II period created opportunities for mutually beneficial trade among countries that were already closely linked politically. Communist countries generally have a lower ratio of trade to GNP than do market economies, but even in controlled economies there are still some obvious benefits to trade.

COMECON (the Council for Mutual Economic Aid) was organized in 1949 to coordinate specialization and trade among the Eastern European communist countries. While it does not fit neatly into any of our four models, COMECON certainly exhibits many of the characteristics of a customs union or a common market. Appropriate patterns of specialization are more difficult to determine because of arbitrary pricing policies, including uneven indirect taxes, arbitrary factor prices, and nonmarket-determined exchange rates. World prices are used in many instances as a reference point. CO-MECON has also been plagued by bilaterialism—one-to-one exchanges closely akin to barter. The Soviet Union has dominated decisions about specialization, prices, and trade and has been accused of using its political

power in COMECON for its own economic benefit. Trade within COME-
CON has grown, but not as rapidly as planners would have wished.

SUMMARY

The economic integration movement in the postwar period spawned
a number of regional free trade areas including the EEC, EFTA, LAFTA,
CACM, and COMECON. There are four levels of integration: free trade
area (no internal tariffs), customs union (no internal tariffs and a common
external tariff), common market (a customs union with free factor movements and some harmonization of social and economic policy), and economic
union (complete political and economic unification).

The benefits of customs unions consist of the usual welfare gains of
trade liberalization and may also include improved terms of trade, economies
of scale, changed patterns of comparative advantage, benefits of competition, and the rather nebulous "public good" benefit of industrialization in
less developed countries. Because customs unions represent movements
both toward and away from free trade, the welfare-increasing and welfare-
decreasing effects need to be identified and added to determine a net welfare
effect. Trade creation increases welfare by shifting trade to lower-cost suppliers, whereas trade diversion reduces welfare by shifting trade to less
efficient suppliers. Trade creation is more likely to predominate where countries are more similar in the range of products produced and less similar in
the cost ratios for those products ("competitive"), whereas trade diversion
occurs when unions are formed between dissimilar ("complementary")
economies.

The EEC, which evolved from Benelux, the European Payments
Union, and the Organization for Economic Cooperation and Development,
is the best known and most successful of the late-twentieth-century efforts
in economic integration. The two free trade areas (EFTA and LAFTA)
remain in existence but have had little impact, and CACM's promising
beginnings in the 1960s were wrecked by internal strife in the early 1970s.
COMECON continues to function as the economic complement to the military Warsaw Pact, but its integration effects have been hampered by bi-
lateralism and the inadequate price signals endemic to centrally planned
economies.

KEY TERMS

Benelux
CACM
COMECON
common external tariff

common market
competitive
complementary
customs union
economic integration
economic union
EEC
EFTA
free trade area
harmonization
LAFTA
public good argument
rules of origin
terms of trade effect
trade creation
trade diversion
Zollverein

REVIEW QUESTIONS

1. Choose a pair of countries (e.g., Mexico and Cuba, Japan and Canada) and see what information you can gather to determine whether they are competitive or complementary. On the basis of that information, predict the welfare effects of a customs union between them.
2. What factors contributed to the success of the EEC?
3. How is the competitive effect different from the normal static welfare gains of trade liberalization?
4. "A customs union involves elements of both protection and free trade. Consequently, some customs unions may increase welfare while others will decrease welfare." Explain this statement.
5. Identify all the economic benefits of customs unions and explain what each means.
6. Redraw Figure 11-3 in such a way that the area of the two welfare gain triangles exceeds the area of the welfare loss rectangle (i.e., so that you have a trade-diverting customs union that increases welfare). How did you have to modify supply, demand, and the relationship of S_c, S_b, and S_{ct} to bring this about? Under what conditions is a trade-diverting customs union able to raise welfare?

SUGGESTED READINGS

BENOIT, EMILE, *Europe at Sixes and Sevens: The Common Market, the Free Trade Association, and the United States*. New York: Columbia University Press, 1961.

COHEN ORANTES, ISAAC, *Regional Integration in Central America*. Lexington, Mass.: Lexington Books, 1972.

KRAUSS, MELVYN B., "Recent Development in Customs Union Theory: An Interpretive Survey," *Journal of Economic Literature*, 10, no. 2 (June 1972), 413–436.

LIPSEY, RICHARD, "The Theory of Customs Unions: A General Survey," *Economic Journal*, 70 (1960), 496–513; reprinted in several books of readings.

MEIER, GERALD B., *Problems of Trade Policy*, pp. 184–285. New York: Oxford University Press, 1972.

PART 3

International Monetary Relations

While trade theory and policy have undergone few changes in the last decade, international monetary economics is in the midst of a major upheaval in both theory and institutions. The monetarist approach to the foreign exchange market to the balance of payments, to open economy macroeconomic models, and especially to the integration of world markets for goods, money, and financial assets have given economists a different way of looking at international finance. Often, the monetarist models lead to diametrically opposite policy conclusions from those of the traditional models. Empirical testing lends some limited support to many of the monetarists' contentions. Much of the debate must be resolved at the level of assessing the degree of market responsiveness to change, the extent of unification of world markets, and the significance of barriers to the free movement of goods, money, and financial assets. Both traditional and monetarist views are considered in the chapters that follow.

At the same time, institutions have changed drastically. The 1970s saw the demise of the existing international monetary system, based on the Bretton Woods agreement, and the gradual evolution of a new set of arrangements that is still far from settled. There is still a considerable body of sentiment from all points on the philosophical spectrum that supports return to a fixed rate system, either under gold or on some different standard. These developments are reflected particularly in Chapters 16–19.

CHAPTER 12

The Foreign Exchange Market

INTRODUCTION

What is so special about the foreign exchange market that makes it different from all other markets? In this and subsequent chapters, we consider this question in great detail. In many respects, buying and selling national currencies is just like buying and selling other goods. There are supply curves and demand curves, equilibrium prices, and measurable elasticities of supply and demand. The demand and supply curves shift in response to changes in underlying conditions and circumstances. But, as is true in the labor market, the loanable funds market, and the commodities futures markets—all of which share these characteristics—the foreign exchange market is treated separately from the markets for more ordinary goods and services. Each of these markets has some special circumstances that differentiate it from the typical markets for more mundane goods and services.

There are at least five such unusual characteristics in the case of markets for national currencies:

1. There is a highly developed futures market, involving both hedging and interest arbitrage.

2. There has historically been significantly greater government intervention in the market than in the market for most other traded commodities; such intervention continues to a lesser extent today.

3. Money appears on both axes of the supply and demand curve diagram, so that we may view the market from either of two perspectives: the demand and supply of one's own currency or the demand and supply of foreign exchange.

4. Persistent disequilibrium has historically been permitted, sometimes even encouraged, giving rise to methods of dealing with disequilibrium other than adjusting the price.

5. Unlike the markets for apples, skateboards, and used textbooks, the foreign exchange market is a macroeconomic market; that is, the totality of transactions in this market has significant effects on and is significantly affected by national income, employment, price level changes, and interest rate changes. While these macroeconomic variables have some interaction with all markets, the relationship with foreign exchange is likely to be particularly important, especially for a small economy.

Let us examine each of the properties in turn.

HEDGING, ORDERLY CROSS RATES, AND ARBITRAGE

You have probably heard about individuals, banks, and multinational corporations—especially oil corporations—that have made large sums of money on foreign exchange dealings. Where do the profits come from? The profits are earned in dealing in currency futures, which are contracts for future delivery of foreign currencies at an agreed-on price, which usually includes an interest premium and a risk premium (sometimes a discount in either or both cases). Futures contracts are best known to most of us in agricultural commodities, which are sold for future delivery on the Chicago Board of Trade.

For example, a potato farmer may have planted a crop that he expects to harvest in May. He has many risks—the cost of farm labor, the weather, the price of gasoline, and the price of potatoes at the time of sale, among others. The last is known as market risk. The farmer can reduce this last risk by shifting it to a speculator who will guarantee a price for his potatoes, say, $5 a bushel. If potatoes rise to $7 a bushel because of a poor harvest or an unexpected new passion for french fries, the speculator makes the profit. But, if the bottom drops out of the potato market because of a bumper crop or because most of the country goes on a low-starch diet, the speculator may see potatoes drop to $3 a bushel and lose a small fortune. The farmer,

in the meantime, has been relieved of one worry—market risk—and is free
to focus on the more basic matter of growing potatoes.

The same is true of foreign exchange. Many of the foreign exchange
buyers need delivery, not today, but at some future date—most commonly
30 days to a year ahead. This is because most international trade is carried
out at the wholesale level and on short-term credit to allow the wholesaler
to make some sales before the bill comes due. The foreign car dealer or the
wholesaler of imported wines is faced by the same kind of market risk as
our hypothetical potato farmer.

Consider the case of an American wine importer. At the time that 1,000
cases of fine French wines are imported, the cost in francs is 3,000 francs
and the exchange rate between the dollar and the franc is $1 = 5 francs.
(The price of currency for immediate delivery is called the *spot rate*). Thus,
at a cost of $600 a case, the total bill is $600,000. Suppose that there is a
change in the exchange rate, say, to $1 = 4 francs. The bill in francs is
unchanged at 3 million francs—1,000 cases at 3,000 francs a case. But it
will now cost more dollars to buy the same number of francs. Instead of
$600,000, the cost is now $750,000. There goes all the profit! (Swings of this
magnitude in exchange rates have not been uncommon in recent years under
a managed floating exchange rate system.)

As is true for the potato farmer, the importer has other problems—
wine sales, property taxes, competition, labor problems, and other matters
more familiar than foreign exchange rates. Importers know that there is also
a possibility of profit in foreign exchange by waiting 90 days and then purchasing the needed 3 million francs, but they are not sufficiently familiar
with the market to assess the risk. Professional foreign exchange dealers not
only are in a better position to estimate the probable direction of change in
the value of a currency, but they also have opportunities to cover their
position (called *hedging*) by making a forward contract with someone else
who wants to trade francs for dollars in the near future. (The typical foreign
exchange dealer is not a gnome in Zurich, as former Prime Minister Harold
Wilson of Britain once derisively called them, but rather a large commercial
bank with an international department.)

Consequently, the wine importer will go to a foreign exchange dealer
and ask for a contract for future delivery of 3 million francs at a price to be
agreed on now. The price for this *forward contract* will probably differ
slightly from the current spot rate of 5 francs = $1. (The spot rate is the
current selling price for immediate delivery.) There are two determinants
of this difference: one is the expected change in the spot rate and the other
is the market rate of interest.

If the price of the franc is expected to rise in the near future, then a
forward contract will sell at a premium (i.e., the price of a franc will be

greater than 20 cents). The dealer has three options. Francs can be purchased on the spot market sometime between now and the 90-day delivery date. The dealer can wait, gamble, and buy just before delivery, knowing that there is some probability that he will have to pay a higher price. Or, as suggested earlier, a dealer can cover the risk by finding a futures contract at about the same time in the opposite direction—delivery of dollars to someone selling francs. The third option, hedging, is the most common, and it is this two-way activity that keeps the risk premium relatively low most of the time.

To the extent that such a contract in the opposite direction is not available—that is, to the extent that the short-term future demand for francs exceeds the short-term future demand for dollars—then dealers fall back on one of the first two options. The excess demand for francs must be met through spot purchases or at higher prices if the dealer waits until delivery time to cover the forward contract. If the dealer purchases spot, financial capital is tied up, and interest earnings are forgone. Hence the interest rate is an important component of the difference between the price of spot and the price of forward foreign exchange contracts. If the dealer gambles, waiting to purchase foreign exchange at delivery time, there is going to be a risk premium reflected in the difference between spot and forward. The premium reflects both risk and interest rates.

Foreign exchange for future delivery may cost less than spot if the price of the currency is expected to fall in the interim. In this case, the probable profit to the dealer from waiting and buying spot at a lower price just before delivery offsets any other costs that might be incurred. There is no interest cost because there is no incentive to tie up capital if the spot rate is expected to fall before delivery date.

Spot and forward rates for major foreign currencies are published in many newspapers. The example in Table 12-1 is from *The Wall Street Journal.* Note the forward quotations for major currencies such as the French franc, the British pound, and the West German Deutsche mark. When all of them are selling at a premium, it would appear that the value of the American dollar (in which these prices are expressed) is expected to fall.

The term *hedging* refers to the kind of action taken by our wine dealer. If the price of francs is expected to rise in the near future, the importer will protect his financial investment against a loss by purchasing francs at a present price for future delivery. Those who sell for future delivery are called *speculators.*

A related type of foreign exchange activity is called *arbitrage.* Simple arbitrage refers to taking advantage of different prices in different regions by buying currency (or anything else) where it is cheap and selling where it is expensive. The arbitrageur makes a profit on the price differential, but

TABLE 12-1 Foreign Exchange Quotations

Foreign Exchange

Friday, January 8, 1982

The New York foreign exchange selling rates below apply to trading among banks in amounts of $1 million and more, as quoted at 3 p.m. Eastern time by Bankers Trust Co. Retail transactions provide fewer units of foreign currency per dollar.

Country	U.S. $ equiv. Fri.	Thurs.	Currency per U.S. $ Fri.	Thurs.
Argentina (Peso)				
Financial	.000095	.000095	10500.0	10500.0
Australia (Dollar)	1.1240	1.1250	.8897	.8889
Austria (Schilling)	.0633	.0631	15.81	15.84
Belgium (Franc)				
Commercial rate	.0260	.026008	38.445	38.45
Financial rate	.02341	.023529	42.725	42.50
Brazil (Cruzeiro)	.0077	.00816	129.50	122.59
Britain (Pound)	1.9170	1.9205	.5216	.5207
30-Day Forward	1.9141	1.9180	.5224	.5214
90-Day Forward	1.9102	1.9140	.5235	.5225
180-Day Forward	1.9096	1.9132	.5236	.5227
Canada (Dollar)	.8431	.8422	1.1861	1.1873
30-Day Forward	.8412	.8407	1.1887	1.1895
90-Day Forward	.8393	.8389	1.1915	1.1921
180-Day Forward	.8392	.8365	1.1916	1.1955
China (Yuan)	.5749	.5750	1.7393	1.7390
Colombia (Peso)	.0169	.0179	59.13	55.56
Denmark (Krone)	.1357	.1354	7.3674	7.3870
Ecuador (Sucre)	.0352	.0352	28.425	28.425
Finland (Markka)	.2297	.2293	4.3536	4.3610
France (Franc)	.1747	.1741	5.7255	5.7440
30-Day Forward	.1744	.1738	5.7345	5.7535
90-Day Forward	.1735	.1730	5.7645	5.7820
180-Day Forward	.1721	.1716	5.8105	5.8290
Greece (Drachma)	.0173	.0174	57.71	57.37
Hong Kong (Dollar)	.1749	.1744	5.7160	5.7350
India (Rupee)	.1100	.1103	9.09	9.07
Indonesia (Rupiah)	.00159	.00158	630.00	630.00
Ireland (Pound)	1.5755	1.5645	.6347	.6392
Israel (Shekel)	.0640	.0644	15.63	15.522
Italy (Lira)	.000827	.0008264	1209.00	1200.00
Japan (Yen)	.004519	.004509	221.25	221.80
30-Day Forward	.004553	.004562	219.60	219.18
90-Day Forward	.004605	.004684	217.15	213.50
180-Day Forward	.004698	.004857	212.85	205.90
Lebanon (Pound)	.2160	.2172	4.6300	4.6025
Malaysia (Ringgit)	.4470	.4465	2.2370	2.2395
Mexico (Peso)	.0379	.03800	26.36	26.31
Netherlands (Guilder)	.4042	.4032	2.4742	2.4800
New Zealand (Dollar)	.8236	.8230	1.2142	1.2151
Norway (Krone)	.1719	.1718	5.8175	5.8220
Pakistan (Rupee)	.1016	.1016	9.84	9.84
Peru (Sol)	.001964	.00203	509.03	493.49
Phillippines (Peso)	.1219	.1232	8.20	8.118
Portugal (Escudo)	.0153	.0153	65.40	65.17
Saudi Arabia (Rival)	.2924	.2924	3.4200	3.4200
Singapore (Dollar)	.4896	.4896	2.0425	2.0475
South Africa (Rand)	1.0435	1.0450	.9583	.9569
South Korea (Won)	.00145	.00145	690.40	690.40
Spain (Peseta)	.01028	.010251	97.23	97.55
Sweden (Krona)	.1802	.1799	5.5480	5.56
Switzerland (Franc)	.5479	.5473	1.8250	1.8270
30-Day Forward	.5507	.5500	1.8158	1.8183
90-Day Forward	.5547	.5543	1.8027	1.8042
180-Day Forward	.5633	.5634	1.7750	1.7750
Taiwan (Dollar)	.0264	.0264	37.91	37.91
Thailand (Baht)	.0435	.0435	23.00	23.00
Uruguay (New Peso)				
Financial	.0864	.0871	11.58	11.48
Venezuela (Bolivar)	.2331	.2325	4.2900	4.3000
West German (Mark)	.4429	.4424	2.2575	2.2605
30-Day Forward	.4442	.4436	2.2510	2.2543
90-Day Forward	.4467	.4463	2.2385	2.2405
180-Day Forward	.4517	.4528	2.2140	2.2085
SDR	1.16174	1.16173	.860781	.860786

Special Drawing rights are based on exchange rates for the U.S., West German, British, French, and Japanese currencies. Source: International Monetary Fund.

Source: *The Wall Street Journal*, January 11, 1982, p. 52. Used by permission.

in the process the differential is eliminated. Those who buy lettuce in California where it is cheap and sell it in Montana where fresh lettuce would otherwise be scarce and expensive are engaging in a form of arbitrage. In the process, the differential between lettuce prices in the two areas is reduced, although transport costs, shipping losses, and risk mean that the differential will never be eliminated completely.

Suppose that the exchange rate between the dollar and the mark were $1 = 3 DM in New York, and the dollar-franc exchange rate were $1 = 6 francs in Paris. Then, in Bonn, the mark should sell for 2 francs. Suppose, further, that a temporary surge in French demand for German products drove the exchange rate in Bonn to 1DM = 3 francs. This situation is one of *disorderly cross rates*, because the appropriate exchange rate between the franc and the mark was already determined by the two exchange rates with the dollar. Speculative activity would quickly eliminate this differential and restore orderly cross rates.

How would this occur? If you had $1,000 to work with, you could buy marks (3,000 of them) in New York, ship them to Bonn to exchange them for francs (9,000 francs), and return them to Paris to receive $1,500—an attractive profit. As this process is repeated by many arbitrageurs, the demand for francs in Bonn rises relative to the supply, driving the price back up toward the equilibrium price. Arbitrage is the basis for the *law of one price*, about which more will be said later.[1]

Interest arbitrage is a little more complex, since it involves not only the exchange rate but the interest rates in two countries. Suppose that the exchange rate between the dollar and the mark were $1 = 4 DM and that the interest rate in Germany were 5 percent while the U.S. interest rate were 10 percent. Suppose, further, that there were no reason to expect either currency to change in value in one particular direction, so that the sole influence on the spot-forward differential is the interest rate. What would be the forward rate between dollars and marks in one year?

One dollar one year hence is worth $1.10, whereas one mark one year hence is worth 1.05 DM. Thus, in one year, each currency invested at its domestic interest rate will yield an equivalence of $1.10 = 4.20 DM or $1.00 = 3.82 DM. Forward dollars will sell at a discount, not because of an expected depreciation, but because of an interest rate differential.

If we put this in general terms, let RS = the spot rate, RF = the

---

[1] The law of one price states that the same commodity will tend to sell for the same price everywhere; price differentials are due to transport costs, imperfect information, and deliberate barriers to flows of goods and assets.

forward rate, and IU = U.S. interest rate, while IG = the German interest rate. Then

$$\$1(1 + IU) = RS(1 + IG)$$

or

$$RF = \frac{RS(1 + IG)}{1 + IU}$$

The depreciation of the forward dollar will tend to discourage the capital inflow that would otherwise occur because of the interest rate differential. To the extent that capital does flow from Germany to the United States, interest rates will tend to fall in the United States and rise in Germany, which will then reduce the spot-forward differential arising from the difference in interest rates.

GOVERNMENT INTERVENTION

Historically, the government has been involved more heavily in setting prices and in maintaining them in opposition to market forces in foreign exchange than has been true of almost any other market. Currencies are linked more closely with the sovereign powers of government than are almost any other forms of expression of sovereignty except perhaps the flag and the armed services. The reasons for government involvement encompass a broad range, including national pride, encouraging (or discouraging) trade and capital flows, concern about the terms of trade, stubborn independence in monetary and fiscal policy in the face of contrary influences from abroad, preservation of the asset value of foreign currency reserves, and myriad other reasons that we encounter in future chapters.

Under the gold standard, the government bought and sold gold and/or its own currency to maintain the price of its currency in terms of gold. The money supply was tied to gold, and thus the fluctuations in currency prices were confined to very narrow limits. Under the Bretton Woods system (1945–1973),[2] the government was again actively involved in foreign exchange markets, directly buying and selling currencies to maintain the price

---

[2] The gold standard is explained in greater detail in Chapter 16, and the Bretton Woods System is discussed in Chapter 19.

of its own currency and periodically changing the official price under pressures of persistent surpluses and deficits. Under exchange control, the government acts as a monopsony buyer and monopoly seller of foreign exchange, sets the official price, engages in price discrimination in currency markets, and allocates available exchange to specific uses. Even under the present floating rate system, governments intervene to narrow the range of fluctuations. All these government actions in foreign exchange markets are discussed later, when we examine the various alternative international monetary arrangements that are possible in a world where corporations, banks, and money supplies stray well beyond the boundaries set by supposedly sovereign national governments.

SUPPLY, DEMAND, AND ELASTICITY

Most people discover in the principles of economics course that supply and demand curves are two ways of expressing the same idea. A supply of apples is a demand for dollars or income, while a demand for apples means that one is supplying dollars. Dollars represent all the other goods and services that are being exchanged for apples. We sometimes lose sight of the fact that what is really going on is a sophisticated form of barter, that goods and services are really being traded for each other and that money is merely a convenient intermediary.[3] This point comes home more strongly when we examine the foreign exchange market. We can look at "our" demand for foreign exchange and "their" supply of foreign exchange—in the examples that follow, American and German, respectively. (Germany is being used here to represent the rest of the world.) Alternatively, we can look at the demand and supply of the dollar on international markets. There should be a one-to-one correspondence between the two markets, with the same conclusions emerging from each view on price, quantity, and measure of disequilibrium. This correspondence is developed more precisely in the pages that follow.

The foreign exchange view of the market is represented in Figure 12-1, where the Deutsche mark is taken to stand for foreign exchange in general.

---

[3] This view is sometimes referred to as the neutrality of money. This statement is certainly an oversimplification, since it not only ignores markets in financial assets but it also assumes that currencies are totally unsatisfactory substitutes for one another. It does, however, help us to focus initially on the real variables on both sides of the market. For now, we ignore the demand for dollars and foreign exchange as an asset (e.g., Americans wanting to hold Swiss franc or British pound bank deposits as part of a portfolio of assets). We return to this point later, because it represents a relatively recent development in both theory and practice that complicates analysis of the foreign exchange market. We also assume initially that exports and imports of goods and services are the only sources of demand and supply of foreign exchange. This assumption is relaxed shortly.

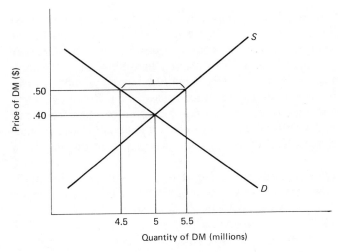

FIGURE 12-1 The Market for Foreign Exchange

The dollar view is represented in Figure 12-2. The demand for foreign exchange is a demand for foreign goods and services (imports) and also a demand to invest abroad. The supply of foreign exchange, similarly, is really a demand for American exports and also a demand for dollars to invest in the United States. For the present, we are ignoring the market for financial assets to focus on the demand for goods and services, known more commonly as the trade balance.

These curves are really both demand and supply curves at the same time, in that either can be shifted by changes in the underlying factors

FIGURE 12-2 The Market for Dollars

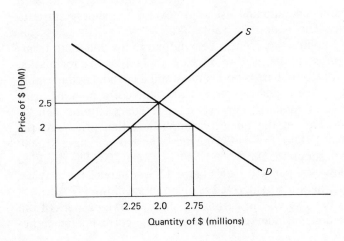

associated with both demand and supply. The demand for foreign exchange can shift in response to changes in relative domestic prices for imported goods and import substitutes, domestic income, tastes, population, and other demand variables. But the demand for foreign exchange also depends upon what is available in the way of domestic substitute goods, which, in turn, is a function of resource availability, resource prices, and technology. Some of the demand for foreign exchange is to purchase foreign resources or to transfer domestic capital abroad, which again is a function of both demand- and supply-side variables. The same considerations apply to the supply of foreign exchange.

In Figure 12-1, the equilibrium price of foreign exchange (the mark) is $0.40 and the equilibrium quantity is 5 million DM. If the price were set higher, say, at $0.50, the quantity supplied would exceed the quantity demanded by 1 million DM. This would be equivalent to a balance-of-payments surplus for the United States of 1 million DM or $0.5 million.

Figure 12-2 looks at the same situation from the vantage point of the market for dollars. Note that the price of the dollar is measured in marks and that the corresponding equilibrium quantity is $2.0 million. The supply curve of dollars has a direct correspondence to the demand curve in Figure 12-1, since the dollars are supplied to purchase foreign exchange. Similarly, the demand for dollars is a supply of foreign exchange. The disequilibrium we examined at a price of $.50/DM is now a disequilibrium at a price of 2.5 DM/$. The quantity of dollars demanded at that price exceeds the quantity supplied, which again is a balance-of-payments surplus of $0.5 million. The identification of surpluses and deficits depends upon which market you are looking at—the "own-currency" market or the market for foreign exchange. A shortage of foreign exchange at the current price or a surplus of own currency is a balance-of-payments deficit; a surplus of foreign exchange or a shortage of own currency corresponds to a balance-of-payments surplus.

The one-to-one correspondence can be brought into sharper focus if we examine a demand schedule and use it to develop the supply curve to which it corresponds. This is done in Table 12-2.

The first two columns represent a demand curve for dollars in terms of marks. These figures can be used to develop a supply curve for marks, since the offer of marks for dollars is both supply and demand. On the supply curve for marks, the price is just the reciprocal of the corresponding price on the demand curve for dollars. For example, 12 DM/$ is equivalent to $0.085/DM. How do we get the quantity supplied at that price? At the corresponding price of 12 DM, those offering marks wish to purchase $1,800, which means they will supply 12 DM/$ × $1,800, or 21,600 DM. The resulting supply curve is shown in panel (b) of Figure 12-3, whereas the original demand curve from which it was derived is given in panel (a).

Not only does this exercise in deriving a supply curve of marks from a demand curve for dollars underscore the one-to-one correspondence be-

TABLE 12-2 Converting a Demand Curve to a Supply Curve

Price	Quantity	$P' = 1/P$	$Q' = P \times Q$
20	1000	.05	20,000
19	1100	.053	20,900
18	1200	.056	21,600
17	1300	.059	22,100
16	1400	.063	22,400
15	1500	.067	22,500
14	1600	.071	22,400
13	1700	.077	22,100
12	1800	.085	21,600
11	1900	.091	20,900
10	2000	.10	20,000
9	2100	.111	18,900

tween supply and demand, but it also raises a question about elasticity. If we plot the supply curve from Table 12-2, which is derived from a linear demand curve, we find that it bends backward. This should not be surprising since it is essentially a total revenue curve, and, as you have learned elsewhere, total revenue increases, remains constant, and then decreases as a linear demand curve passes through its elastic, unitary elastic, and inelastic ranges.

For a long time, there was concern on the part of national governments that not only was the supply curve backward bending but also the demand curve could be highly inelastic. This could lead to a situation of multiple equilibria, some stable and others unstable. Such a situation is depicted in Figure 12-4.

FIGURE 12-3 Deriving a Supply Curve from a Demand Curve

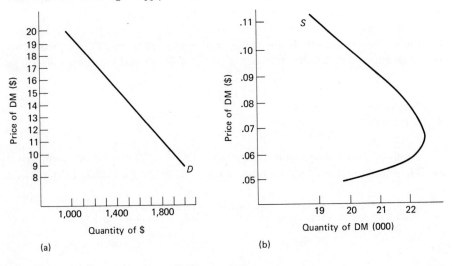

(a)

(b)

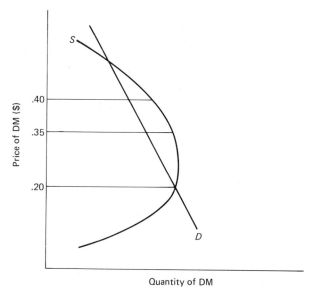

FIGURE 12-4 Unstable Equilibrium in the Foreign Exchange Market

Note that the upper equilibrium is unstable, because, if the price rises above equilibrium, quantity demanded will exceed quantity supplied, putting further upward pressure on prices and leading farther from equilibrium. Similarly, at a price below equilibrium, quantity supplied will exceed quantity demanded, putting downward pressure on prices. Left to itself, the price of the mark would sink toward the lower equilibrium at $0.20. This concern—that a currency that was floated might sink—is called *elasticity pessimism*. Elasticity pessimism refers to the concern that a devaluation[4] may worsen rather than improve an existing deficit because of inelastic demand on both sides—the demand for the mark and the demand by mark holders for the dollar, from which the supply curve was derived. This happens on the diagram, for example, between a price of $0.40 and a price of $0.35.

THE MARSHALL–LERNER CONDITION

The demand elasticities required for devaluation or depreciation to improve rather than worsen a trade balance are given by the Marshall–Lerner con-

---

[4] A market-directed fall (rise) in a currency price is called *depreciation* (*appreciation*). A deliberate change by the government in the official price is called a *devaluation* (decrease) or a *revaluation* (increase).

TABLE 12-3 Effects of Devaluation on the Trade Balance

(1) Export Demand Elasticity	(2) Change in Export Earnings (millions)	(3) Import Demand Elasticity	(4) Change in Import Outlays (millions)	(5) = (2) − (4) Change in Trade Balance (millions)
0	0	0	+ .5	− .5
.2	+ .05	.2	+ .5	
			− .132	− .318
.4	+ .1	.4	+ .5	
			− .264	− .136
.6	+ .15	.6	+ .5	
			− .396	+ .046
.8	+ .2	.8	+ .5	
			− .528	+ .228
1.0	+ .25	1	+ .5	
			− .66	+ .41

dition:[5]

$$|\epsilon_x| + |\epsilon_m| > 1$$

where ϵ_x is foreign demand elasticity for our currency (= export demand elasticity) and ϵ_m is domestic demand elasticity for foreign currency (= import demand elasticity). This condition merely states that the sum of the quantity changes in both exports and imports must be sufficient to offset the decline in the exchange rate to improve total revenue on the trade balance, a point that is intuitively plausible but complex to demonstrate mathematically.

It is clear from the polar cases of zero elasticities and infinite elasticities that in the former case a trade balance would deteriorate and in the latter it would improve. Table 12-3 gives some results of different elasticities for a hypothetical case of a country whose exchange rate is changed from $1 = 4 DM to $1 = 3 DM. The initial exports are $1 million and imports are $1.5 million; both are measured in home currency (dollars); and in the case of import outlay, the income effect is measured before the substitution effect.

The first component under change in import outlay is the increase in dollars needed to purchase the same quantity of marks, which is an income effect. The second component reflects the decrease in purchases due to the

[5] This condition is named for Alfred Marshall, who first suggested it, and Abba Lerner, who developed its implications more fully. For a mathematical derivation of the expression, see Peter Lindert and Charles Kindleberger, *International Economics* (Homewood, Ill.: Irwin, 1982), pp. 523–529. Note that supplies of export and import goods are assumed to be perfectly elastic and that the Marshall–Lerner condition measures the deficit or surplus in own currency.

rise in the dollar price of foreign goods. Export earnings reflect only a substitution effect since they are measured in own currency.

The question of elasticities was believed to be of crucial importance in the choice between a fixed and a flexible exchange rate regime. The period prior to the 1960s was one of pessimism about the values of elasticities. Empirical studies in the 1960s provided mixed evidence, but generally the Marshall–Lerner condition tended not to be fulfilled (i.e., the sum of the two demand elasticities was less than unity). Criticisms of biases in the statistical methods employed, however, combined with more encouraging although less precise observations of real world experiences, produced a shift to elasticity optimism that dominated the dialogue of the 1970s. Differences in expected elasticities to a large extent reflect differences in the belief about the efficiency of markets and the speed of market adjustment processes.

While estimates of elasticities differ and are subject to identifiable downward biases, it is true that elasticities in the short run may be so low that devaluation will worsen a trade balance, but over a period of a year or more the trade balance generally improves—indirect evidence of adequate elasticities.

In any case, the emphasis on the trade balance obscures the fact that the adjustment also takes place in the other two markets—the market for money (overall balance of payments) and the market for financial assets (capital account). A somewhat more general approach developed in the 1960s that emphasized income and macroeconomic adjustment effects was known as the absorption approach.

THE ABSORPTION APPROACH

The basic relationship for the absorption approach is

$$BOP = Y - E$$

where BOP = balance-of-payments surplus or deficit, Y = domestic money income or output, and E = domestic expenditures (absorption). Both domestic policies and foreign exchange actions of government will have an impact on income (= aggregate supply) and on absorption (= aggregate demand), but to the extent that these impacts are unequal, the balance-of-payments surplus or deficit will be changed. This model, again, emphasizes the trade balance, with the addition of some direct investment, but it still neglects the market in existing financial assets. It is of some help in analyzing the differential impact of policies where aggregate income effects are more important than relative price effects, a defect of the elasticities approach just discussed. For example, the impact of a tax cut on the balance of payments would depend on its impact on aggregate supply relative to aggregate demand; if the tax cut raised aggregate supply relative to aggregate demand, the balance of payments would improve, and vice versa. In some ways, the absorption approach represented an intermediate development between the elasticities approach of the 1950s and early 1960s and the monetarist approach developed in the early 1970s.

THE MONETARIST VIEW OF THE FOREIGN EXCHANGE MARKET

The monetarist view of the balance of payments is developed more fully in the next few chapters. At this point, it is sufficient to note that it differs from the preceding views in that it looks at the foreign exchange market overall as representing excess demand and supply of money. The excess demand or supply for money can arise from relative rates of real or monetary growth or other factors, but it is expressed in either or both of the two components: excess demand for or supply of goods (the trade balance) and excess supply of or demand for bonds and other financial instruments (the capital market). The division of the excess demand for money into the two components of goods and bonds depends upon the relative elasticities mentioned earlier—the extent to which an excess supply of money drives up prices versus interest rates and the relative responsiveness of the goods and bond markets to these two sets of prices. It may also depend on the choice of a fixed or a flexible exchange rate regime.

This may on the surface not appear to be fundamentally different, but it is. The excess demand or supply of currency that we consider as a disequilibrium phenomenon in the next section would be regarded as a part of an equilibrating process by monetarists, as markets attempt to adjust domestic money supplies to domestic money demands throughout the world. The adjustment process may incorporate exchange rate changes as well as world price level and interest rate changes, but the law of one price and the existence of unified (or at least integrated) and efficient world markets will tend to push prices and interest rates into equality. This puts much of the burden of adjustment on the quantities of exports, imports, and bonds changing hands.

The evidence for the monetarist position is equivocal, but there is some empirical support for their contention that such phenomena as one-time increases in the money stock or one-time changes in exchange rates (under the old Bretton Woods regime) work their effects fairly quickly, leading to appropriate transfers of money supplies and in the long run leaving very little change in the real underlying variables. The monetarist view may also be "catching up" with real world developments: the expansion of the Eurodollar market (described in the appendix to Chapter 19), the extensive multicurrency operations of multinational corporations, the sharp increase in two-way multinational investment between the United States and the rest of the world in the wake of OPEC, and general improvements in financial technology and sophistication have in fact tied international financial markets much more closely together than used to be the case. One particular outcome of these developments is currency substitution, which means that those who wish to hold cash balances no longer necessarily wish to hold all of them in their own national currencies. Some may, in fact, prefer a mixture of currencies with varying exchange risk, convertibility, and other attributes. To the extent that this is true of individuals, banks, multinationals, and others, world markets will be indeed more integrated and efficient than in the more traditional isolated and separate view of national monies.

In the light of these considerations, it may be true that the elasticities and absorption approaches will soon be classed as short-term or transitional descriptions, whereas the monetarist view describes the ultimate equilibrium toward which the system is headed. This still begs the question of how long is the long run and how short is the short run, a fundamental area of disagreement between monetarists and more traditional economists that extends well beyond the bounds of international monetary economics into virtually all questions of aggregate economic policy.

PERSISTENT DISEQUILIBRIUM

One of the peculiar characteristics of foreign exchange markets is that disequilibria are allowed to persist and are even supported in their persistence. In other markets, it is generally assumed that a disequilibrium will be corrected by adjusting the price, although price regulations and other forms of intervention sometimes prevent this from occurring. Historically, price regulation has been the norm rather than the exception in foreign exchange markets. This has led to a search for other ways of dealing with disequilibrium. There are basically only four ways of dealing with a persistent surplus or deficit:

1. Change the price.
2. Shift the supply and/or demand curve back into equilibrium at the old price.
3. Draw on or accumulate reserves.
4. Ration foreign exchange (deficit only).

Most of us react automatically to a surplus or shortage in any market by suggesting that the price be used to adjust the quantities supplied and demanded. While this solution is not ruled out in the foreign exchange market, until recently it was regarded as a last resort. Some of the reasons for preferring alternative solutions are developed in later chapters when we explore the various types of international monetary systems. At least one has already been suggested—a concern that a price adjustment will have the immediate effect of worsening rather than improving a deficit (or surplus) because of low short-run elasticities of supply and demand. One reason for not relying primarily on price adjustments that has relevance to all international monetary systems derives from the question of what is the appropriate function of the exchange rate. Is its primary role to balance the foreign exchange accounts, or is it to reflect comparative advantage correctly? Can the same exchange rate accomplish both goals? And if the two goals are in conflict, which should dominate?

THE ROLE OF THE EXCHANGE RATE

An exchange rate whose primary purpose was to equate the supply and demand for foreign exchange for all purposes could be highly unstable, depending on the frequency and extent of shifts in the supply and demand curves. Every source of shifts—export sales, import demand, short-term capital flows, interest rate changes, foreign aid, private foreign investment— could change the price. Nevertheless, the balance-of-payments problem would be resolved. What would be sacrificed?

The exchange rate that translates comparative cost in one country correctly into relative prices in the other country is not the same as the one that balances the balance of payments or the foreign exchange market unless exports and imports of goods and services are the only components of supply and demand for foreign exchange. This problem is illustrated in Figure 12-5.

In the diagram, D_1 and S represent the demand and supply for foreign exchange (represented here by marks) for purposes of importing and exporting goods and services only. There are no capital flows or other sources of demand and supply for foreign exchange. The exchange rate that balances exports and imports of goods and services is $0.25 in this diagram. This exchange rate should reflect comparative advantage correctly. You may recall from Chapter 3 that one of the assumptions of the classical model that we identified and examined was that exports equal imports, or that the exchange rate lies inside the limits within which country A will import the good that is relatively cheaper abroad and export the good that is relatively more expensive abroad. The exchange rate serves as a "translator" of both relative and absolute prices from one currency and one country to another. If it translates information accurately, such an exchange rate promotes the allocation of production on the basis of comparative advantage.

What happens to this function when we introduce another source of

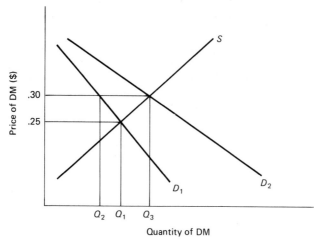

FIGURE 12-5   Effect of Capital Flows on the Exchange Rate

demand, in this case, capital outflows? The capital flows are incorporated into D_2, which lies to the right since more foreign exchange is now demanded at every possible price. The increase in demand raises the price of foreign exchange (marks) to $0.30. Note that at this price the quantity of foreign exchange supplied rises from Q_1 to Q_3 and the quantity demanded for the original (D_1) purposes of importing goods and services falls to Q_2. The gap between Q_2 and Q_3 represents the amount of capital outflow at that price. To make a capital transfer possible, the United States had to generate a surplus of exports over imports. But, in the process, there was a sacrifice of comparative advantage. American exporters are now able to undersell foreign competitors over whom they may not truly have a comparative advantage—just a temporary price advantage derives from the fact that they live in a capital-exporting country.

Obviously, we do not want to eliminate capital flows for the sake of comparative advantage. It is quite possible that many capital transfers do more to improve the efficiency of world resource allocation than does any equivalent trade in final goods and services. Nevertheless, once capital flows enter the determination of exchange rates, we have deviated significantly from the model in Chapter 3, where we indicated that the exchange rate assumption was nearly indispensable. Once we extend the "privilege" of influencing the exchange rate to long-term, production-enhancing capital flows, there are a number of other candidates waiting at the door. Short-term capital flows, unilateral transfers (public and private), government expenditures abroad, and even smuggling could affect the exchange rate!

The argument that the sole function of the exchange rate is to equate the supply and demand for foreign exchange is called the balance-of-payments theory of exchange rate determination. The polar alternative, an ex-

218

change rate that equates only trade in goods and services and thus correctly reflects comparative advantage, is not feasible because capital flows would create persistent balance-of-payments deficits and surpluses that have to be resolved in some way.

A compromise approach would be an exchange rate that provided "basic balance" and was changed infrequently, because relative certainty in exchange rates promotes trade and encourages investment in export industries when exporters can be reasonably sure that their comparative advantage will not be wiped out suddenly by an unexpected change in the exchange rate. Basic balance is defined as

$$X = M \pm \text{long-term capital flows}$$

Exports (X), imports (M), and long-term capital flows are considered to be the regular, persistent balance-of-payments items that must be balanced over the long run. For a net capital exporter such as the United States, this means that exports must be sufficient to pay for both imports and capital outflows. For a net capital importer, export proceeds plus capital inflow must be sufficient to finance imports. Under the basic balance approach, the exchange rate would be set so as to balance this equation, not necessarily annually, but over a period of time.

Would the exchange rate ever be adjusted under such a system? One of the most popular approaches to answering this question is called *purchasing power parity*. This view of exchange rates calls for periodic adjustments of exchange rates for one reason and one reason only—changes in relative domestic price levels. If France had 10 percent inflation and Germany had 20 percent inflation over the same time period, France's exports to Germany would increase and her imports would decline under a fixed exchange rate. This decline would represent a distortion of comparative advantage, which under this approach is a primary function of the exchange rate. Periodically, therefore, exchange rates would be adjusted in response to the change in purchasing power. For example, let the initial exchange rate between the mark and the franc be 1 DM = 2 francs. With 20 percent inflation, it now requires 1.2 DM to purchase what used to cost 1 DM, while it takes 1.1 francs to purchase the equivalent of 1 preinflation franc. Therefore, the new equivalence is given by

$$1.2 \text{ DM} = 2.2 \text{ francs}$$

or

$$1 \text{ DM} = 1.833 \text{ francs}$$

The mark has depreciated by 8.35 percent relative to the franc. In general, if the initial exchange rate is R, the two currencies are denoted C_1 and C_2, and the rates of inflation are P_1 and P_2, respectively, then the purchasing power parity adjustment is given by

$$C_1 = R \cdot \frac{P_2}{P_1} \cdot C_2$$

This discussion should sound familiar to anyone who has ever considered the question of farm price supports. The farmer is asking for the same kind of adjustment in his price in response to changes in the prices of the goods and services he is purchasing, and the term parity is used in exactly the same sense.

Purchasing power parity is not only a prescription for when and how much to change exchange rates under a fixed rate regime. It is also a theory of exchange rate determination that regained popularity in the 1970s with the simultaneous emergence of monetarist international economics and floating exchange rates. The latter called for good forecasts; the former thought that they had a forecasting tool in purchasing power parity.

Monetarists generally expect some form of purchasing power parity to result from unfettered markets in foreign exchange, because of the linkages of national money supplies through the balance of payments. The fundamental relationships that are seen by monetarists as governing domestic prices and exchange rates are the following:

$$MS_1 = MD_1 = P_1 \times f(Y_1, i_1)$$
$$MS_2 = MD_2 = P_2 \times f(Y_2, i_2)$$
$$P_1 = r \times P_2$$

where MS = the money supply, MD = money demand, Y = income, i = the interest rate, P = the price level, and r = the exchange rate. The subscripts 1 and 2 denote the two countries, or more likely, the country under observation and the rest of the world. The first two equations are the familiar money market equilibrium conditions; the third equation represents the law of one price. At a simple level, this would imply that the exchange rate is a function of the two price levels. We return to a somewhat more complex interpretation shortly.

The notion of purchasing power parity goes back to Gustav Cassell,[6] writing in the interwar period, who proposed the notion in absolute terms. That is, if country A's prices rose relative to country B's, country A's currency should depreciate sufficiently to offset the price rise. There are several difficulties with this notion, but the most obvious is the measurement

[6] Gustav Cassell, *Post-War Monetary Stabilization* (New York: Columbia University Press, 1928).

of absolute price levels in the face of all the difficulties encountered in different measures of output, different bases for price indexes, and similar problems.

A more tolerable version reduces the absolute to relative terms, comparing relative rates of inflation based on initial price indexes that are not comparable. This is the hypothesis tested frequently in the 1970s and largely found lacking, especially in the short run. Longer-term relationships between currency prices and relative rates of inflation are more consistent with the notion of purchasing power parity.

A number of explanations have been offered for the failure of purchasing power parity to adequately explain exchange rate movements. As with elasticities, it is perhaps too narrow. Real income and productivity changes, anticipated changes (expectations and speculative activity), and similar factors enter into the short-run exchange rate movements. The better fit in the longer term is somewhat encouraging. It is also possible that the poor predictive power of purchasing power parity for exchange rate movements reflects a lesser degree of unification and efficiency in world money markets than monetarists envision.

A broader interpretation of purchasing power parity is to go back to the system of three equations describing money market equilibrium and the exchange rate, solve the first two for P_1 and P_2, and insert them into the exchange rate determination. If we do this, we wind up with a relationship

$$r = \frac{P_1}{P_2} = \frac{MS_1 \times f(Y2, i2)}{MS_2 \times f(Y1, i1)}$$

In this case, the exchange rate depends not only on relative rates of monetary growth but also on relative rates of real growth and on relative interest rates changes. To the extent that monetary growth is dissipated in real output increases and interest rate changes, less of it will show up in relative price changes. This is a better explanation of purchasing power parity, but it still fails to account for the relatively unsatisfactory empirical results in testing in the 1970s, since the tests were performed directly on price levels rather than indirectly on monetary growth.

MACROECONOMIC ASPECTS

As the preceding discussion implies, the foreign exchange market is a highly aggregative market, much like the stock market, the commodities exchange, "the" labor market, and other broad markets that are distinguished from more familiar microeconomic markets by their volume, scope, number of participants, and interaction with macroeconomic influences. We can safely ignore most changes in national income, interest rates, unemployment rates, and so on in forecasting the demand for haircuts at Joe's Barber Shop in downtown Milwaukee. Although these variables do impact Joe's business over time, he is more responsive to particular local conditions, including population, competition, tastes in haircuts, and local wages.

The foreign exchange market is highly sensitive to macroeconomic variables, particularly in a relative sense. Increases in our national income will shift our demand for foreign exchange to the right; increases in national incomes in the rest of the world will shift supplies of foreign exchange to the right. If the two shifts are proportional, the quantities exchanged will increase, but the exchange rate will remain about the same. The same is true of rates of inflation and interest rates. The interaction of the macroeconomy and the foreign exchange market is considered in greater detail in Chapters 14 and 15. Before we can turn to that question, however, we need to examine the balance-of-payments accounts, which is the subject of Chapter 13. We might just note at this point that changes in exchange rates are often changes in the terms of trade—the rates at which our wheat, airplanes, and other exports are converted into oil, coffee, and shoes. Changes in the terms of trade affect our economic welfare and the distribution of income. The impact of changes in exchange rates on the amount of goods and services we receive in trade for what we sell is yet another element in the perpetual and unresolved controversy over fixed versus floating exchange rates.

SUMMARY

This chapter is a broad overview of the operation of markets in national currencies. The market is different from other markets in several respects, although all the unusual characteristics are shared to some extent by some other markets. There is a highly developed futures market that transfers risk of exchange rate changes from the importer, exporter, or investor to a professional foreign exchange dealer, which charges a premium reflecting perceived risk. The premium can be negative if the currency being purchased is expected to decline in price before the delivery date. Hedging is the term for shifting the risk to a dealer. Arbitrage refers to the process of making a profit on differences in price for currencies in different markets. Interest arbitrage tends to be reflected in the forward market and to reduce differences in interest rates between different countries.

The government has historically been involved more heavily in setting prices and in keeping them within narrow limits in this market than it has been in most other markets, under all the various kinds of international monetary systems we have experienced.

The foreign exchange market can be examined from either the perspective of the supply and demand for one's own currency or from the viewpoint of the market for foreign exchange. There is a one-to-one correspondence between the supply of one's own currency and the demand for foreign exchange and also between the demand for one's own currency and the supply of foreign exchange. The demand curve for one's own currency can be used to derive a corresponding supply curve of foreign exchange. When this is done, it can be observed that the derived supply curve bends backward, which raises the question of elasticities and stability of equilibrium. The concern that the elasticities of supply and demand are so low that a devaluation (reduction in own currency price) may worsen rather than improve a balance-of-payments deficit is called elasticity pessimism. This view, popular in the 1940s and 1950s, has been increasingly called into question in recent years.

Foreign exchange markets, which are managed markets, are prone to persistent disequilibrium, which can be dealt with by adjusting the price, shifting the supply and demand curves, rationing, or drawing on or accumulating foreign exchange reserves. The reasons for not always using price adjustments to clear the market include elasticity pessimism, concern over preserving comparative advantage, and a desire to maintain the existing terms of trade, among others. There is no general agreement as to whether the primary function of the exchange rate should be to balance the supply and demand for foreign exchange (the balance of payments function) or whether its primary role is to correctly reflect comparative advantage. The purchasing power parity approach to exchange rate determination comes down more heavily on the latter role. Purchasing power parity advocates would set the exchange rate so as to balance exports, imports, and long-term capital flows with periodic adjustments primarily for different relative rates of inflation.

Finally, foreign exchange markets are macroeconomic markets, which are highly sensitive to changes in macroeconomic variables such as output, income, interest rates, and inflation rates. This aspect is considered in Chapters 14 and 15.

KEY TERMS

appreciation
arbitrage
balance-of-payments theory of exchange rate determination
basic balance
comparative advantage function of exchange rate
determination
deficit
depreciation
devaluation

disequilibrium
disorderly cross rates
elasticity pessimism
exchange rate
forward rate
hedging
interest arbitrage
Marshall–Lerner condition
multiple equilibria
orderly cross rates
purchasing power parity
revaluation
risk premium
spot rate
surplus

REVIEW QUESTIONS

1. Follow the spot and forward rates of exchange for one of the major currencies for a period of a month. Plot the changes. From newspapers and other sources, try to identify the forces that changed the exchange rate.
2. If the spot rate for marks is 10 DM = $1, and U.S. interest rates are 12 percent while the foreign interest rate is 8 percent, what forward rate (one year) would interest arbitrage dictate? What do you think the six-month forward rate should be?
3. Suppose that the spot rate is the same as in question 2 and that over a five-year period the dollar experiences 30 percent inflation while the foreign inflation rate is 50 percent. According to purchasing power parity, what should the new spot rate be at the end of five years?
4. See if you can identify some of the factors that might make demand and supply for foreign exchange inelastic in the short run.
5. What other forward markets are there besides the foreign exchange market? Why do they exist? In what ways are these markets similar to the foreign exchange market?
6. Why might we want exchange rates to be stable?

SUGGESTED READINGS

ALIBER, ROBERT Z., *The International Money Game*, 2nd ed. New York: Basic Books, 1976.
BILSON, JOHN F.O., "The Current Experience with Floating Exchange Rates: An Appraisal of the Monetary Approach," *American Economic Review Papers and Proceedings*, 68, no. 2 (May 1978), 392–397.

CHACHOLIADES, MILTIADES,   *Principles of International Economics*, chap. 12. New York: McGraw-Hill, 1981. See also pp. 386–388 (mathematical) and pp. 381–384 (empirical).

FRENKEL, JACOB,   "The Collapse of Purchasing Power Parities During the 1970s," *European Economic Review*, 16 (1981), 145–165.

FRENKEL, JACOB, and HARRY JOHNSON, eds.,   *The Monetary Approach to the Balance of Payments*, chaps. 1–3. Toronto: University of Toronto Press, 1976.

FRENKEL, JACOB, and HARRY JOHNSON, eds.,   *The Economics of Exchange Rates*, pp. 1–25. Reading, Mass.: Addison-Wesley, 1978.

KREININ, MORDECHAI,   *International Economics: A Policy Approach*, 3rd ed., chap. 5. New York: Harcourt Brace, 1979.

LAFFER, ARTHUR B., and MARC A. MILES,   *International Economics in an Integrated World*, chaps. 9, 11–13. Glenview, Ill.: Scott, Foresman, 1982.

LEVICH, RICHARD,   "On the Efficiency of Markets in Foreign Exchange," in *International Economic Policy: Theory and Evidence*, eds. Rudiger Dornbusch and Jacob Frenkel, chap. 8. Baltimore, Md.: Johns Hopkins University Press, 1979.

LINDERT, PETER, and CHARLES KINDLEBERGER,   *International Economics*, 7th ed., pp. 317–325. Homewood, Ill.: Irwin, 1982.

ROOT, FRANKLIN D.,   *International Trade and Investment*, 4th ed., chaps. 9, 11–12. Cincinnati, Ohio: Southwestern, 1978.

VERNON, RAYMOND, and LOUIS T. WELLS, Jr., *Manager in the International Economy*, 4th ed., chaps. 4, 9–10. Englewood Cliffs, N.J.: Prentice-Hall, 1981.

YEAGER, LELAND B.,   *International Monetary Relations: Theory, History, and Policy*, 2nd ed., chaps 2 and 8. New York: Harper & Row, 1976.

CHAPTER 13

The Balance of Payments

INTRODUCTION

The concept of surplus or deficit in the balance of payments appeared in Chapter 12 as an alternative description of the excess demand or supply in the market for foreign exchange. In this chapter, we put this surplus or deficit concept on a somewhat firmer statistical basis by examining the nature, format, and uses of the balance of payments, as well as the cumulative effect of surpluses and deficits on the balance of international indebtedness accounts.

Concern for the surplus or deficit in the balance of payments goes back to the era of mercantilism that preceded Adam Smith—the seventeenth and eighteenth centuries. At that time, the emphasis in commercial policy was on accumulating gold and silver (the equivalent of foreign exchange reserves today) as a measure of national wealth and a reserve to finance future wars should the latter occur. The language of the mercantilists survives today, so that a favorable movement in the balance of payments is one in the direction of surplus.

The focus of balance-of-payments accounting has taken several turns since then. Between 1944 and 1973, under the Bretton Woods system, the stress was on the measurement of surplus or deficit, because those would determine the amount of pressure on a country to revalue or devalue its currency. Surpluses and deficits relative to available foreign exchange reserves were of particular interest because in most cases they helped in forecasting not only the direction of change in the currency price but also how soon it was likely to occur.[1]

Since 1973, the size of the surplus or deficit in the balance-of-payments accounts, especially for the United States, has been downplayed for two reasons. First, under floating exchange rates there is less emphasis on the role of the government in managing surpluses and deficits as some of that function has been shifted to market forces. Changes in the exchange rate in response to shifts in supply and demand for currencies now play a major role in eliminating what would otherwise have been imbalances in the balance-of-payments accounts. Second, there has been some shift in the economics profession toward a monetarist approach to the balance of payments that regards deficits and surpluses as transitory. We consider this argument later in this chapter. These developments do not mean that there is no longer any need to keep balance-of-payments accounts, however.

USES OF BALANCE-OF-PAYMENTS DATA

There are several important remaining uses for the balance of payments. First, even under a floating rate system, the accounts do not balance instantaneously, and the direction of imbalance (such as, surplus or deficit) is useful in forecasting the direction of change in a currency's price. Since we are under a managed float rather than a totally free float (which will be discussed further in Chapter 17), governments are interested in such indications because it is their responsibility to keep their exchange rate fluctuations within acceptable limits.

The other two uses for the balance of payments have to do with some of the component accounts. Current account corresponds largely to the item of net exports in the national income accounts, and the rise and fall in this balance has an impact on the level of output, employment, and prices domestically. We explore this more fully in Chapters 14 and 15. Also, the capital account is a measure of the amount, direction, and maturity structure of international capital flows. This is of interest to the American investment community, to the recipient countries, to competing industrial countries, and to multinational agencies such as the World Bank and the International Monetary Fund, which are concerned with economic development and redistribution of income-producing resources.

---

[1] This was not necessarily true of reserve currencies, such as the U.S. dollar. Particularly in the 1950s and early 1960s, U.S. deficits at least partly reflected excess foreign demand for dollars as an asset. We return to this point later.

BASIC CONCEPTS

There are several formats for the balance-of-payments accounts, each emphasizing different aspects or functions of the accounts. The three that we present are those of the U.S. Department of Commerce, the United Nations, and the Federal Reserve Bank of St. Louis. The first is fairly traditional, the second stresses capital flows, and the third stresses broad aggregates and the monetary base effect without much attention to the overall surplus or deficit.

Before we can look at the accounts, we need some basic definitions. The *balance of payments* is a statistical account of the transactions between residents of one country and residents of the rest of the world for a period of one year or a fraction thereof. That may look like a pretty straightforward definition, but there are some words in the explanation that can create some unanticipated problems.

Transaction means that something—goods, services, credit instruments, cash, or anything of value—actually changed hands. Placing orders does not count. If, for example, I ordered a Honda in July 1981, and I finally took delivery in June 1982, and the American Honda dealer did not pay for it until January 1983, this transaction would show up in the balance of payments in two of the three years. The year 1981 does not count because nothing actually changed hands. In 1982, there was an import of merchandise—the Honda arrived. Since this is double-entry bookkeeping, we have to find an offsetting entry to make it balance—in this case the IOU of the American Honda dealer, which shows up as "short-term commercial credit" or some similar entry in most balance-of-payments accounts. In 1983, the short-term credit instrument is exported and paid off in dollars or yen, again yielding two offsetting entries.

The second problem term in this is "resident." Most of us live, work, earn income, vote, collect our mail, and perform all the other activities that define residence in a single country. But what about people who dwell in Michigan and work in Canada or who "jet set" around the world to their homes in five countries and derive income from investments all over the world? Who claims the Elizabeth Taylors and Jackie Onassises of the world as residents?

The question is important because it affects many transactions on the balance of payments. If, for example, jetsetting Jane Doe is a New York resident who just happens to also have a Paris apartment, then her transactions in the United States are domestic and her purchases in Paris are imports. If we reclassify her as a French resident, her New York purchases suddenly become exports and her French expenditures are purely domestic and do not enter the balance of payments of either the United States or France. Not only purchases of goods and services but also labor income, investment income, and many capital transactions are in question when we deal with multicountry residents.

When the various criteria for residence give different answers, physical residence—the place in which you actually maintain your physical self for the greatest part of the year—usually dominates. One exception to that rule is military and diplomatic personnel stationed abroad, who continue to be treated as residents of the country that sent them. Private overseas assignments of a clearly temporary nature would be treated the same way.

Finally, there is the matter of a year. Balance-of-payments statistics are available on an annual, quarterly, or monthly basis. The last two are likely to be "at annual rates, seasonally adjusted." This means that the monthly or quarterly figures are adjusted for the fact that certain months are always greater than others in imports or exports or both. Harvest season always increases U.S. exports, for example, since 25 percent of U.S. exports are agricultural. The adjusted figure is then multiplied by 12 (monthly) or 4 (quarterly) to project the annual balance-of-payments figures.

If you have taken any accounting courses, you have probably recognized that the balance of payments is not, as its name implies, a balance sheet, but rather an income statement. The balance sheet for one country vis-à-vis the rest of the world is called the balance of international indebtedness, described at the end of this chapter.

A GENERAL ACCOUNTING FORMAT

A very simple format for a hypothetical balance of payments is presented in Table 13-1. Note that the use of the terms credit and debit is somewhat different from traditional business accounting. In the balance-of-payments accounts, a credit is any payment to you or anything that give rise to a claim to payment to you. Thus, exports are credits; income on foreign investments is a credit (equal to an export or sale of financial instruments such as stocks, bonds, or commercial paper); unilateral transfers to us are credits. As we see later on for reasons that are slightly more complex, a sale of foreign exchange or gold is also a credit.

Since a debit is defined symmetrically, it is any payment by you or anything that gives rise to a payment by you. Imports of goods and services, interest and dividends paid for foreign stock- and bondholders, capital outflow, and unilateral transfers abroad are all debits.

Even the simple format in Table 13-1 enables us to identify some of the information that we indicated we wanted from the balance of payments at the beginning of the chapter. This country is a net exporter of goods and services, which enables it to finance an outflow of capital on both private

TABLE 13-1 A Simplified Balance-of-Payments Format (millions of U.S. dollars)

Credits		Debits	
Merchandise exports	200	Merchandise imports	140
Service exports	65	Service imports	50
Investment income	40	Interest, dividends	15
Unilateral transfers	(net)		20
Capital, private, long term	50	Capital, private, long term	85
Capital, government	0	Capital, government	35
Capital, short term	15	Capital, short term	25

and government account. There are four types of "current" income and outgo, the sum of which can finance a capital transfer: exports less imports of goods, exports less imports of services, net unilateral transfers, and net investment income. In our simplified example, these total 305 minus 225, or a surplus on current account of $80 million. If we assume that the government capital flows are all long term, then the long-term capital outflow is 120 minus 50, or $70 million. The other $10 million is accounted for by the balance in a catch-all category, short-term capital, which at this point includes both normal commercial credits and transactions undertaken to make the balance of payments balance, such as purchase or sale of foreign exchange.

The distinction between current and capital transactions is an important one, somewhat analogous to the difference between income and wealth or flows and stocks. Any purchase of goods and services is treated as a current expenditure, regardless of whether it is air fare or purchase of a DC-10 aircraft. Capital transactions are exchanges of financial instruments, and no distinction is made between 30-day commercial credit and a 30-year bond. The difference, then, is whether the transaction creates immediate or deferred income. Many transactions involve both a current account entry and a capital account entry. Exporting an aircraft, for example, would result in a current account export of merchandise, whereas the financing transaction is likely to appear in capital account.

The general format for a balance-of-payments account has four major categories with many subcategories. These categories are:

1. Current account
2. Capital account
3. Statistical discrepancy (formerly known as errors and omissions)
---
4. Settlement account[2]

Entry 4, settlement account, should be equal in magnitude and opposite

[2] The U.S. Department of Commerce presentation no longer distinguishes between capital account and settlement account.

in sign to the sum of the first three accounts. The line between the third and fourth accounts reflects a distinction between "autonomous" and "compensatory" transactions, the former being undertaken for their own sakes and the latter to bring the balance of payments into balance. Settlement account includes gold sales and purchases, foreign exchange sales and purchases, use of borrowing rights at the International Monetary Fund (explained in detail in Chapter 19), and foreign acquisition or redemption of one's own currency. All these are financing or compensatory transactions. There has been some disagreement about additional entries in this category, which we consider a little later.

CURRENT ACCOUNT
AND CAPITAL ACCOUNT

We have already encountered current account and capital account—the normal day-to-day transactions in goods, services, and financial instruments. These are just a few of the items that may require additional explanation.

Investment income—interest and dividends on stocks and bonds and profits on wholly owned foreign subsidiaries—is entered on current account because it is payment for the current use of capital. The capital itself is entered on capital account at the time the investment is made and again when the stock or plant is sold or the bond is redeemed. But the regular flow of payments for the services is a current transaction.

Also, unilateral transfers (sometimes known as unrequited receipts or unrequited payments) are entered on current account. This category includes private gifts as well as government foreign aid grants (foreign aid loans are entered in capital account). There are two reasons for entering unilateral transfers on current account rather than on capital account even though they are more analogous to financing transactions than to the other items on current account.

First, unilateral transfers generate no claim to future income and no change in the net asset position of the country, two important pieces of information that we will derive subsequently from the capital account. Second, many foreign aid transactions, both by government and by private voluntary organizations such as CARE, involve a direct flow of merchandise. For example, suppose that the government were to donate $1 million in disaster relief to Pakistan in the form of a shipment of food and medical supplies. The food and medical supplies would appear as an export of goods. We need a second entry to make the accounts balance. A fictitious entry in unilateral transfers solves the problem. We treat this action as if we gave Pakistan a gift of $1 million that it, in turn, used to purchase food and medical supplies from the United States.

The value of putting the fictitious financing entry for unilateral transfers in current account rather than in capital account is now apparent. The net effect of this transaction on the current account balance is zero. We counted all our exports, but we must realistically accept that a donation of exports is not exactly the same as a sale of export goods, which would have increased the current account balance. We want to count all our exports, but we do not wish to overstate our competitive position. This method of treating unilateral transfers (which at one time were treated as a separate, fifth category) is a good resolution of the dilemma.

STATISTICAL DISCREPANCY

The third major category is statistical discrepancy. Although it is third, it is computed last as a residual. The sum of the current and capital accounts is compared with the settlement account balance. If there are no errors or omissions, the two should be equal in value and opposite in sign. Such is rarely the case.

There are many unreported transactions in the balance of payments, including smuggling and unrecorded short-term capital flows. The individuals of indeterminate residence whom we encountered earlier give rise to some errors in the balance-of-payments accounts. There may be deliberate misrepresentation of the value of imports to reduce the amount of tariff paid. All these will keep the three major accounts from being in balance. If, for example, you brought in $10,000 of marijuana from Mexico (failing to check in with customs officers in the process) and you paid in cash, eventually $10,000 of U.S. dollars would find their way into the hands of the Mexican banking system and be duly entered in settlement account. But the other piece of the transaction is missing. The government may suspect marijuana, but it cannot record the transaction without some firmer evidence.

SETTLEMENT ACCOUNT

The last category is settlement account, an account that records stock changes rather than flows. At the end of the year, we inventory gold holdings, foreign exchange holdings, loans due to the I.M.F., and foreign holdings of American dollars and compare them with the figure at the end of the previous year (or quarter, if we are doing a quarterly estimate). The net change in each of these items is recorded in settlement account.

This category presents the greatest conceptual difficulty in remembering the sign. A sale of foreign exchange, for example, is an export of something we were holding in "inventory" and is therefore recorded as a plus entry; the same is true of gold sales. Dollars, likewise, are "exported" when they are acquired by foreigners, so a dollar outflow is a plus entry and a dollar repatriation is a minus entry in settlement account. Another way of remembering the signs in this account is to consider what they are offsetting above the line to make the total account come out to zero. Any transaction that finances a deficit above the line should be entered as a plus and any transaction that finances a surplus above the line should be entered as a minus.

Alternate definitions of how to measure surpluses or deficits give rise to different allocations of certain items between settlement account and capital account. After we have looked at the accounting process more closely, we consider the different measures.

SOME SAMPLE TRANSACTIONS

At this point, it might be helpful to "practice" some balance-of-payments accounts. Additional exercises are given in the questions at the end of the chapter.

Suppose that you get a haircut in Paris, paying with 100 francs that you are carrying in your wallet. How would that appear in the balance-of-payments accounts? The haircut is a service import, and the 100 francs are U.S. holdings of foreign exchange, which is entered in settlement account. The two entries are as follows:

Current Account Merchandise Imports	Settlement Account Foreign Exchange
− 100 francs	+ 100 francs

The net effect of this transaction is − 100 francs as far as the sum of the three "above-the-line" accounts is concerned.

Let us try another transaction. Suppose that the United States ships $100 million of grain to the Soviet Union, on the basis of six months commercial credit. How would this appear in the balance of payments?

Current Account Exports, Merchandise	Capital Account Short-Term Capital
+ $100 million	− $100 million

At some later date, the Russians repay the loan, presumably in dollars, and the repayment transaction looks like this:

Capital Account Short-Term Capital	Settlement Account Foreign Dollar Holdings
+ $100 million	− $100 million

Note that the first transaction had no net effect on the above-the-line balance but that the payment did; as we shall see shortly, it added $100 million to our measured balance-of-payments surplus.

MEASURING THE SURPLUS
OR DEFICIT

In the preceding examples, reference was made to the measurement of surplus or deficit. The operational definition of the surplus or deficit is the sum of the "above-the-line" transactions, that is, current account plus capital account plus statistical discrepancy, or alternately, the value of settlement account with the sign reversed. The above-the-line transactions are those undertaken for their own sakes and represent the normal demand for one's own currency or the normal supply of foreign exchange. The settlement account transaction fills in the gap. In the case of a U.S. deficit, settlement account would represent the supply of foreign exchange to the market by official agencies to clear the deficit or the excess supply of dollars taken off the market for the same purpose.

For most countries, the definition of the surplus or deficit is simple. The deficit is financed by sale of gold and foreign exchange, by drawing on rights at the I.M.F., or by the acquisition of one's own currency by foreign central banks. The only question that might arise is the treatment of private holdings of foreign exchange on both sides. Again, in most cases this is a small item. Few private citizens of other countries hold Italian lira, Mexican pesos, or Indian rupees. If they receive them, the foreign currency will be exchanged quickly for one's own currency at the commercial bank, which, in turn, exchanges them at the central bank, at which point the transaction shows up in settlement account.

The exception is a reserve currency, particularly the American dollar, that is widely held by private foreigners—individuals, corporations, and commercial banks—for future transactions, not only with the United States but also with third countries. These dollar outflows do not immediately turn up in foreign central banks and would normally be recorded as short-term capital flows under capital account. For example, I could buy a shipment of German automobiles and pay in dollars. Instead of turning the dollars in for marks, the German exporter might deposit the proceeds in a short-term account at an American bank. How should this be treated? Is this a financing transaction, undertaken to resolve a deficit, or is it just a normal, commercial transaction that goes above the line? Or is it even, as monetarists might argue, a reflection of excess demand for money in Germany?

This question became very important in the 1960s when it was recognized that the usual way of measuring the surplus or deficit was adequate for currencies not widely held by private foreigners but not satisfactory for

TABLE 13-2   Alternate Measures of Surplus and Deficit[1]

Official Settlements—Settlement Account

1. Changes in gold holdings
2. Changes in central bank holdings of foreign exchange
3. Changes in foreign central bank holdings of own currency
4. Changes in borrowings at the I.M.F.

Gross Liquidity—Settlement Account

All the items listed above plus

5. Changes in private foreign holdings of own currency

Net Liquidity—Settlement Account

All the items listed above plus

6. Changes in our private citizens' holdings of foreign currency

[1] Some minor items are omitted to focus on the significant differences.

a reserve currency. Dollars were being held by private foreigners not only for transactions with the United States or even third countries (since the dollar was the most widely accepted form of international currency); they were also being held as an asset in a portfolio of assets. The dollar was a convenient medium for holding part of one's wealth because it was stable— the currency considered least likely to be devalued. It was the currency representing the most developed, diverse, and sophisticated markets for financial instruments, so that it could be invested in a variety of short-term assets and shifted conveniently from one to another. It appeared that this demand for dollars was a normal demand (above the line) rather than a financing transaction. The problem lay in the fact that, if the confidence in the dollar were ever shaken, there would likely be a mass exodus from dollars to other assets. The dollars would then find their way into the central bank, which was generally obligated to redeem them for their own currencies. These dollars would show up as a part of the deficit, not the year they entered foreign hands, but the year that they were turned into the central banks. Thus, we were likely to understate our deficits for many years, followed by a massive overstatement when enthusiasm for the dollar suddenly waned.[3] This prospect was recognized in the early 1960s, and three alternate measures of the surplus or deficit were created at that time. For convenience, these three measures are summarized in Table 13-2.

[3] Still a third interpretation of deficits is offered by the monetarist view, which is considered in a separate section since it was developed largely after the dispute over measuring deficits in the 1960s.

236 International Monetary Relations

The first measure has the advantage of being symmetric with the measurement of surplus or deficit used by the rest of the world, but it probably understates the extent of the U.S. deficit because of the widespread private use of the dollar as a multinational currency. The gross liquidity definition (sometimes known simply as the liquidity definition) is equally likely to err in the other direction and overstate the deficit, since some of the dollar holdings acquired by foreigners may be of a somewhat permanent nature.

The third definition, net liquidity, was never widely adopted. This one took into account American acquisition of private holdings of foreign currencies and would in most years give a deficit figure that was higher than official settlements and lower than (gross) liquidity. Needless to say, if there were a sudden disenchantment with the dollar and massive amounts of private dollar holdings suddenly poured into the coffers of foreign central banks, the official settlements definition would show a greater deficit than would either of the other two. But, in the situation that was regarded as "normal" from 1944 until the late 1960s, official settlements tended to create the smallest measured deficit or the largest measured surplus.

It might be helpful at this point to take a hypothetical set of balance-of-payments data and compute the three measures of surplus or deficit. For simplicity, the normal entries in capital account and current account are given as net rather than as gross figures (Table 13-3).

TABLE 13-3   A Hypothetical Balance of Payments: Measuring the
Deficit (millions of dollars)

Net export of goods and services	+210
Net unilateral transfers	−30
Net investment income	+40
Net direct investment	−130
Net other long-term investment	−120
Net government loans	−50
Statistical discrepancy	−10
Short-term capital outflows[1]	−20
Short-term capital inflows[1]	+70
Changes in U.S. gold holdings[2]	+10
Changes in U.S. official holdings of foreign currency[2]	+25
Changes in foreign official holdings of U.S. dollars[2]	+5

[1] The minus sign is to be interpreted as an "import" of a short-term capital investment instrument by an American for example, a deposit of francs in a French bank, and the plus sign refers to an "export" of dollars to foreign private holders. For simplicity, we are ignoring the great variety of possible short-term transactions to focus on those that could be in either capital account or settlement account. In reality, even under the gross liquidity definition there would be some categories of short-term capital flows that are entered in capital account rather than in settlement account.

[2] The plus sign in each case does not indicate an acquisition but rather a deficit-financing transaction that is, an "export" of gold, foreign currency, or dollars. Only in the case of foreign dollar acquisition can the " + " sign also be interpreted as an increase in the stock.

The current account balance is the sum of the first three items, or + $220 million. The balance on capital account depends on which items we choose to put in that account as normal commercial transactions rather than as financing transactions. If we use the official settlements definition, the short-term capital transactions are entered in capital account, which then contains six entries—two short term, four long term—and has a balance of − $250 million. Current account plus capital account plus statistical discrepancy gives an above-the-line deficit of $40 million. This is financed by the three entries in settlement account of changes in holdings of gold and foreign exchange by our central bank and changes in foreign central bank dollar holdings. These total + $40 million, financing the measured deficit.

The gross liquidity would remove the $70 million in short-term capital outflow from the capital account and place it in settlement account. This would increase the deficit above the line to $110 million and also increase settlement account to + $110 million, once again financing the deficit. Net liquidity would do the same with the − $20 million entry in U.S. acquisition of short-term foreign assets (currency, foreign bank deposits, etc.), which will reduce the deficit to $90 million and change the settlement account figure to + $90 million.

SOME ACTUAL BALANCE-OF-PAYMENTS ACCOUNTS

At this point, we need to take a look at the kinds of balance-of-payments accounts one would encounter if one went looking for actual statistics. While there are many formats, we concentrate on only three widely available ones. The first is the Commerce Department format, which is reprinted here from the Federal Reserve Bulletin as Table 13-4.

The current account is the most recognizable part of this accounting format. Lines 1–10 constitute current account with some additional details we had omitted—separate entry for military transactions and an additional line item for noninvestment current income called remittances, pensions, and other transfers. The item we had called unilateral transfers is partly line 9, all of line 10, and probably includes some military transactions as well.

Lines 12–16 (reprinted as line 38) are clearly settlement account items, although this listing is not complete even for the narrow official settlements definition of this account. If we add lines 38, 39, and 40 (changes in foreign official assets in the United States), which incorporate parts of lines 12–16 and 22–27, we should have a reasonable approximation to the official settlements definition of the surplus in excess of $9,000 million for 1979. This needs to be corrected by subtracting the allocation of SDRs (special drawing rights), which was a creation of new reserve assets added to our balance and not a surplus or deficit financing transaction. In 1979, this change would reduce our measured surplus to $8,074 million.

TABLE 13-4   U.S. Balance of Payments: Commerce Department Format,[1] 1978–1980 (millions of U.S. dollars)

Item Credits or Debits	1978	1979	1980
1 Balance on current account	−14,075	1,414	3,723
2 Not seasonally adjusted			
3 Merchandise trade balance[2]	−33,759	−27,346	−25,342
4 Merchandise exports	142,054	184,473	223,966
5 Merchandise imports	−175,813	−211,819	−249,308
6 Military transactions, net	738	−1,947	−2,515
7 Investment income, net[3]	21,400	33,462	32,762
8 Other service transactions, net	2,613	2,839	5,874
9 Remittances, pensions, and other transfers	−1,884	−2,057	−2,397
10 U.S. government grants (excluding military)	−3,183	−3,536	−4,659
11 Change in U.S. government assets, other than official reserve assets, net (increase −)	−4,644	−3,767	−5,165
12 Change in U.S. official reserve assets (increase, −)	732	−1,132	−8,155
13 Gold	−65	−65	0
14 Special drawing rights (SDRs)	1,249	−1,136	−16
15 Reserve position in International Monetary Fund	4,231	−189	−1,667
16 Foreign currencies	−4,683	257	−6,472
17 Change in U.S. private assets abroad (increase, −)[3]	−57,158	−57,739	−71,456
18 Bank-reported claims	−33,667	−26,213	−46,947
19 Nonbank-reported claims	−3,853	−3,026	−2,653
20 U.S. purchase of foreign securities, net	−3,582	−4,552	−3,310
21 U.S. direct investments abroad, net[3]	−16,056	−23,948	−18,546
22 Change in foreign official assets in the United States (increase, +)	33,561	−13,757	15,492
23 U.S. Treasury securities	23,555	−22,435	9,683
24 Other U.S. government obligations	666	463	2,187
25 Other U.S. government liabilities[4]	2,359	−133	636
26 Other U.S. liabilities reported by U.S. banks	5,551	7,213	−159
27 Other foreign official assets[5]	1,453	1,135	3,145
28 Change in foreign private assets in the United States (increase, +)[3]	30,187	52,703	34,769
29 U.S. bank-reported liabilities	16,141	32,607	10,743
30 U.S. nonbank-reported liabilities	1,717	2,065	5,109
31 Foreign private purchases of U.S. Treasury securities, net	2,178	4,820	2,679
32 Foreign purchases of other U.S. securities, net	2,254	1,334	5,384
33 Foreign direct investments in the United States[3]	7,896	11,877	10,853
34 Allocation of SDRs	0	1,139	1,152
35 Discrepancy	11,398	21,140	29,640
36 Owing to seasonal adjustments			
37 Statistical discrepancy in recorded data before seasonal adjustments	11,398	21,140	29,640
MEMO			
Changes in official assets			

TABLE 13-4 *(Continued)*

Item Credits or Debits	1978	1979	1980
38 U.S. official reserve assets (increase, −)	732	−1,132	−8,155
39 Foreign official assets in the United States (increase, +)	31,202	−13,624	14,856
40 Change in Organization of Petroleum Exporting Countries official assets in the United States (part of line 22 above)	−1,137	5,543	12,744
41 Transfers under military grant programs (excluded from lines 4, 6, and 10 above)	236	305	635

[1] Seasonal factors are no longer calculated for lines 12 through 41.
[2] Data are on an international accounts (1A) basis. Differs from the census basis data, shown in Table 3.11, for reasons of coverage and timing, military exports are excluded from merchandise data and are included in line 6.
[3] Includes reinvested earnings of incorporated affiliates.
[4] Primarily associated with military sales contracts and other transactions arranged with or through foreign official agencies.
[5] Consists of investments in U.S. corporate stocks and in debt securities of private corporations and state and local governments.

Source: *Federal Reserve Bulletin*, December 1981, p. A-54.

There is some question as to how much of line 41 actually belongs in settlement account and how much in capital account, since this is a mixture of short-term dollar holdings and longer-term investments. Nevertheless, 1979 was clearly a surplus year, whereas 1978 and 1980, totaling the same items, experienced deficits of $30,797 million and $20,597 million, respectively. In all years there was a rather large statistical discrepancy (line 35) that was positive in sign—over $11,000 million in 1978, $21,000 million in 1979, and $29,000 million in 1980. A positive sign in this category is usually attributed to an unrecorded inflow of short-term capital.

What about capital account? Items 17–33 would go in capital account under the official settlements definition. However, lines 22–27 included some of the transactions identified in lines 39–40 as settlement account items. If we subtract lines 39 and 40 from the sum of lines 23–27 (= line 22), we have a net entry in capital account of changes in officially held assets for 1979 (mostly foreign aid loans) of −$13,757 million + $13,624 million − $5,543 million = −$5,676 million. Adding this to the sum of private asset transactions—lines 11, 17, and 28—gives a balance on capital account of −$14,479 million.

Table 13-5 summarizes the major categories for 1979 and 1980 from the balance-of-payments data in Table 13-4.

If we wanted to recast these balances in the liquidity format, we would have to identify those items in capital account that properly should be transferred to settlement account. The most likely candidate is line 29 (U.S. bank-reported liabilities) for gross liquidity and lines 29 and 18 (bank-reported changes in U.S. private assets) for net liquidity. If we transfer line 29 to settlement account, the 1979 surplus changes to a deficit of $24,533 million under the gross liquidity definition, and the 1980 deficit rises to $31,340 million. If we also incorporate line 18 into settlement account under the net liquidity definition, then the 1979 surplus reappears as $1,680 million, while the 1980 deficit becomes a surplus of $15,600 million. There are probably other short-term claims buried in other entries, but the bank liabilities on both sides are the most plausible candidates for financing items, although some part of these are probably long-term claims that should remain in capital account.

The second format we look at is much more abbreviated and, therefore, easier to interpret. This is the one developed by the Federal Reserve Bank of St. Louis and published monthly in its *International Economic Conditions Bulletin,* reproduced here as Table 13-6.

If we look again at 1980, we find the same results as we did in the Commerce Department format. This presentation is broken down into three broad categories of trade flows (goods and services, incorporating the other current account items) with a balance of $3723 million, capital flows (incorporating the other three accounts), and a new item, monetary base effect. It is not possible to pick out from this format the items that go into settlement account and measure the surplus or deficit. This is intentional, because the developers of this format did not think that balance was particularly important under a system of floating exchange rates. The monetary base effect measures the impact of the foreign sector on the U.S. monetary base, which consists of U.S. bank reserves at the Federal Reserve System (including vault cash) and currency in banks. When foreign exchange comes into the country and finds its way to the Fed, it increases the monetary base and can have a multiple expansionary effect on the money supply unless it is "sterilized" by the Fed—offset by open market operations in the opposite direction. This has become a serious problem for monetary management in the United States and is even more significant in small countries where the flows of foreign exchange are even larger relative to the sizes of their mon-

TABLE 13-5   Summary of the U.S. Balance of Payments, 1979–1980 (millions of U.S. dollars)

Account	1979[a]	1980
Current account	$ 1,414	$ 3,723
Capital account	− 14,479	− 53,960
Statistical discrepancy	21,140	29,640
Above-the-line balance	+ 8,075	− 20,597
Settlement account	− 8,074	+ 20,597

[a] There is a $1 million rounding error in 1979, which accounts for the discrepancy between above-the-line balance and settlement account.

TABLE 13-6 Balance of Payments, Federal Reserve Bank of St. Louis Format, 1960–1980 (millions of dollars)

ANNUAL SERIES
U.S. INTERNATIONAL TRANSACTIONS[1]

	Trade Flows					Capital Flows								
Year	Merchandise Exports	Merchandise Imports	Service Exports	Service Imports	Current Account Balance	Direct Investment Abroad	Direct Investment in U.S.	Security Purchases Abroad	Security Purchases in U.S.	Bank Claims on Foreigners	Bank Liabilities to Foreigners	U.S. Government Assets Abroad	Foreign Official Assets in U.S.	Monetary Base Effect[2]
1960	$ 19,650	$ 14,758	$ 9,211	$ 8,971	$ 2,824	$ 2,940	$ 315	$ 663	$ -82	$ 1,148	$ 678	$ -1,045	$ 1,473	$ -2,128
1961	20,108	14,537	9,829	9,054	3,822	2,653	311	762	475	1,261	928	303	765	-1,061
1962	20,781	16,260	11,022	9,518	3,387	2,851	346	969	68	450	336	-450	1,270	-1,012
1963	22,272	17,048	11,942	9,999	4,414	3,483	231	1,105	138	1,556	898	1,284	1,986	-539
1964	25,501	18,700	13,325	10,522	6,823	3,760	322	677	-231	2,505	1,818	1,509	1,660	-114
1965	26,461	21,510	14,626	11,291	5,432	5,011	415	759	-489	-93	503	380	134	-1,378
1966	29,310	25,493	15,252	13,106	3,031	5,418	425	720	550	-233	2,882	973	-672	-879
1967	30,666	26,866	16,648	14,740	2,583	4,805	698	1,308	550	495	1,765	2,370	3,451	1,748
1968	33,626	32,991	18,737	15,809	611	5,295	807	1,569	881	-233	3,871	3,144	-774	-1,540
1969	36,414	35,807	21,108	18,322	339	5,690	1,263	1,459	4,550	570	8,886	3,379	-1,301	-72
1970	42,469	39,866	23,205	20,184	2,331	7,590	1,464	1,076	3,062	967	-6,298	-892	6,908	-355
1971	43,319	45,579	25,519	20,990	-1,433	7,618	367	1,113	2,270	2,980	-6,911	-465	26,879	-922
1972	49,381	55,797	28,114	23,638	-5,795	7,747	949	618	2,265	3,506	4,754	1,572	10,475	-39
1973	71,410	70,499	38,831	28,720	7,140	11,353	2,800	671	4,468	5,980	4,702	2,486	6,026	-328
1974	98,306	103,649	48,360	33,708	2,124	9,052	4,760	1,854	3,825	19,516	16,017	1,101	10,546	-34
1975	107,088	98,041	48,641	34,795	18,280	14,244	2,603	6,247	1,075	13,532	628	4,323	7,027	469
1976	114,745	124,051	56,885	38,197	4,384	11,949	4,347	8,885	5,093	21,368	10,990	6,772	17,693	759
1977	120,186	151,689	63,479	42,099	-14,110	11,890	3,728	5,460	4,067	11,427	6,719	4,068	36,816	-414
1978	142,054	175,813	78,967	54,217	-14,075	16,056	7,897	3,582	2,971	33,667	16,141	3,912	33,561	693
1979	184,473	211,819	104,452	70,098	1,414	23,949	11,877	4,552	4,432	26,213	32,607	4,900	-13,757	2,039
1980	223,966	249,308	120,701	84,580	3,723	18,546	10,854	3,310	8,063	46,947	10,743	13,320	15,492	2,947

[1] Signs reflect asset stock adjustments.
[2] Not seasonally adjusted. Since July 1980, includes changes in U.S. official holdings of Swiss franc denominated assets.

Source: Federal Reserve Bank of St. Louis, *International Economic Conditions*, January 22, 1982. p. 7.

TABLE 13-7   U.S. Balance of Payments: International Monetary Fund Format, 1965–1979 (billions of U.S. dollars)

	1965	1966	1967	1968	1969	1970	1971	1972
Trade balance	4.95	3.82	3.80	.64	.60	2.59	−2.27	−6.41
Merchandise, exports	26.46	29.31	30.67	33.63	36.41	42.45	43.31	49.37
Merchandise, imports	−21.51	−25.49	−26.87	−32.99	−35.81	−39.88	−45.58	−55.78
Other goods services, and income, net	3.41	2.27	2.05	3.07	2.95	3.18	4.64	4.67
Private unrequited transfers	−.68	−.65	−.88	−.84	−.94	−1.10	−1.11	−1.12
Official unrequited transfers	−2.27	−2.41	−2.38	−2.24	3.85	−2.35	−2.74	−2.94
Capital other than reserves	−6.27	−3.42	−5.80	.61	3.76	−12.86	−19.27	−3.32
Net errors and omissions	−.43	.64	−.22	.43	−1.52	−.24	−9.82	−1.98
Counterpart items	—	—	—	.01	.06	.87	.88	.76
Liab. Const. Fgn Author. Reserves	.07	−.81	3.33	−.79	−1.55	7.36	27.46	10.30
Total change in reserves	1.22	.57	.05	−.89	−1.25	2.47	2.19	−.01

	1973	1974	1975	1976	1977	1978	1979
Trade balance	.94	−5.33	9.07	−9.29	−30.89	−33.79	−29.45
Merchandise, exports	71.42	98.31	107.13	114.76	120.82	142.05	182.05
Merchandise, imports	−70.47	−103.64	−98.06	−124.04	−151.71	−175.83	−211.50
Other goods services, and income, net	10.20	14.87	14.09	18.96	21.76	25.02	34.94
Private unrequited transfers	−1.28	−1.00	−.91	−.92	−.84	−.80	−.96
Official unrequited transfers	−2.87	−6.40	−3.97	−4.41	−4.15	−4.72	−5.17
Capital other than reserves	−9.70	−9.26	−28.63	−25.26	−20.27	−28.92	−9.48
Net errors and omissions	−2.54	−1.66	5.68	10.43	−.69	11.44	23.66
Counterpart items	.21	.02	−.50	−.04	.22	−.71	−2.45
Liab. Const. Fgn Author. Reserves	5.10	10.24	5.51	13.05	35.43	31.06	−13.56
Total change in reserves	−.07	−1.49	−.35	−2.52	−.52	1.35	2.47

Source: International Monetary Fund, *International Financial Statistics Yearbook, 1980*, Washington, D.C., p. 433.

etary bases and their money supplies. The monetary base effect is the item most emphasized by monetarists.

The last and simplest format is that of the International Monetary Fund. This one is presented in Table 13-7. The main attraction of this format is that U.S. balance-of-payments data and that for numerous other countries is available in comparable form. This would be a fairly easy format to recast into current account, capital account, statistical discrepancy (errors and omissions), and settlement account, an exercise that is left for the reader.

THE MONETARIST APPROACH
TO THE BALANCE
OF PAYMENTS

In recent years, along with the growing influence of monetarism on domestic macroeconomic policy, there has been developed a monetarist approach to the balance-of-payments accounts that was reflected in the format from the Federal Reserve Bank of St. Louis. The monetarist model was developed under a system of fixed exchange rates, but it can be adapted to a system of flexible rates. It assumes that the world, rather than the nation, is a single closed economy and that the surplus or deficit in the balance of payments is a monetary phenomenon resulting from an excess demand for or supply of (respectively) the domestic money stock.

When the money supply increases more rapidly domestically than abroad, people find themselves with excess money balances relative to the amount that they wish to hold. People will increase their expenditures both at home and abroad, and the country will run a balance-of-payments deficit, leading to an outflow of the national currency until the monetary stock is adjusted to the desired level. (This explains the emphasis on the monetary base effect in the Federal Reserve Bank of St. Louis presentation.) When the monetary authority attempts to offset the reduction in the monetary base from a balance-of-payments deficit (sterilization), they are frustrating the automatic adjustment process and putting more of the adjustment burden on domestic prices. As those prices rise, the deficit is worsened.

Interest rate adjustments from monetary expansion will affect the level and direction of capital flows. Monetary expansion will initially lower but ultimately raise nominal interest rates. Under a fixed rate regime, deterioration of current account will be offset by rising capital inflows. Falling exports, rising imports, capital inflows, and a net outflow of money will eventually combine to restore equilibrium as prices and interest rates tend toward equality worldwide. Under a floating rate system, the quantity adjustments for both goods and financial instruments are dampened as rising prices and interest rates are offset by exchange depreciation, while the net money outflow brings about the appropriate reduction in the domestic money supply.

The policy implications of this approach are clear. The focus is on control of the domestic money supply and particularly with not frustrating built-in corrective processes. If we allow the surplus or deficit to be reflected in the monetary base and thus in the money supply, the surplus or deficit will tend to be transitory—a money stock adjustment—and self-correcting. An earlier and simpler version of this policy was embodied in the international gold standard, which is discussed in Chapter 17. Under floating exchange rates, the self-correcting process is one of prices, but more of the burden of adjustment falls on domestic prices as rising domestic prices and interest rates are offset by a falling exchange rate.

THE BALANCE
OF INTERNATIONAL
INDEBTEDNESS

The final account to be considered is the balance of international indebtedness, which actually is a balance sheet. The balance of international indebtedness for the United States for selected years is given in Table 13-8.

TABLE 13-8 Balance of International Indebtedness, Selected Years 1950–1979 (billions of U.S. dollars)

Type of Investment	1950	1955	1960	1965	1970	1971	1972
1. U.S. net international investment position	$ 36.7	$ 37.2	$ 44.7	$ 61.6	$ 58.6	$ 56.1	$ 49.6
2. U.S. assets abroad	54.4	65.1	85.6	120.4	105.5	179.5	199.5
a. U.S. official reserve assets	24.3	22.8	19.4	15.5	14.5	12.2	13.2
b. U.S. govt. assets, other	11.1	13.1	17.0	23.5	32.1	34.2	36.1
c. U.S. private assets	19.0	29.1	49.2	81.4	118.8	133.1	150.3
3. Foreign official assets in the United States	17.6	27.8	40.9	58.8	106.8	123.3	159.9
a. Foreign official assets	NA	NA	12.4	16.8	26.1	52.5	63.2
b. Other foreign assets	NA	NA	28.5	42.0	80.7	70.9	86.7

Type of Investment	1973	1974	1975	1976	1977	1978	1979
1. U.S. net international investment position	47.6	58.3	74.6	82.5	72.3	75.3	95.0
2. U.S. assets abroad	222.5	255.7	295.1	347.2	383.0	450.9	513.2
a. U.S. official reserve assets	14.4	15.9	16.2	18.7	19.3	18.7	18.9
b. U.S. govt. assets, other	38.8	38.4	41.8	46.0	49.6	54.2	58.5
Long term	36.2	36.3	39.8	44.1	47.8	52.3	56.5
Short term	2.6	2.1	2.0	1.9	1.8	1.9	1.9
c. U.S. private assets	169.3	201.5	237.1	282.4	314.1	378.0	435.8
Direct investment	101.3	110.1	124.1	136.8	149.8	167.8	192.6
Portfolio investment	27.5	28.2	34.9	44.2	49.4	53.4	56.7
Other long term	11.1	12.6	15.5	17.8	18.8 }		
Short term	29.4	50.6	62.6	83.6	96.1	156.8	186.5
3. Foreign assets in the United States	174.9	197.4	220.5	264.7	310.6	375.5	418.2
a. Foreign official claims	69.6	80.3	86.9	105.6	141.9	174.8	160.3
U.S. govt. securities	53.8	57.7	63.6	74.0	106.8	130.9	118.3
Other (mostly short term)	15.4	21.9	20.5	26.0	27.9	25.5	42.0
b. Other foreign assets in United States	105.3	117.1	133.6	159.1	168.7	200.7	257.9
Direct investment	20.6	25.1	27.7	30.8	34.6	42.5	53.3
Portfolio investment	46.1	34.9	45.3	54.8	52.9	55.4	61.9
Other long term	2.2	2.9	5.1	8.1	9.1 }		
Short term	36.5	54.3	55.5	65.4	72.1	102.9	143.7

Source: Adapted from *Statistical Abstract of the United States, 1981* (Washington, D.C.: Government Printing Office, 1981), p. 863.
NA – Not available.

This statement is a balance sheet for the foreign sector. The net total of transactions in financial instruments (currency, securities, direct investments, bank deposits, etc.) shows up on the balance of international indebtedness in the various accounts and also in the line called "U.S. net international investment position," which is sometimes called net creditor or net debtor position. This balance sheet is analogous to the balance sheet of a household or a firm. The statement tells us what would be left over if we liquidated all our assets and paid off all our liabilities. The United States is clearly solvent by this test—that is, the market value of our assets exceeds the market value of our liabilities, in 1979 by $95 billion.

The other piece of information that is usually derived from a balance sheet is liquidity; that is, how does the maturity structure of our assets compare with the maturity structure of our liabilities? If our assets are mainly long term and our liabilities are short term, we may have a liquidity problem—we cannot liquidate enough assets soon enough to pay off liabilities that are coming due quickly. If the value of our personal assets exceeds the value of our liabilities, but if most of our assets are tied up in a house, land, and other hard-to-liquidate assets and most of our liabilities are bills due in the next six months, we are solvent but not liquid. The information we can glean from the balance of international indebtedness seems to indicate that this is true of the United States.

It is difficult to separate short-term assets and liabilities clearly from long term in the format given, but we can make an estimate for 1977, the last year for which some of the data are separated into those categories. Under assets, items 2a, 2b (short term), and 2c (short term) are short term, totaling $116.7 billion in 1977. Under liabilities (euphemistically called "foreign assets in the United States"), items 3a (short term) and 3b (short term) fit in this category and came to $100 billion in that year. Long-term assets are items 2b (long term) and the first three items under 2c. These totaled $265.8 billion. Long-term liabilities consisted of 3a (government securities) and the first three items under 3b. These came to $203.4 billion. Thus, the United States was both liquid and solvent in 1977. Note the change from 1973, however, which was more typical of the period from 1960 on. Short-term assets totaled $46.4 billion in 1973, and short-term liabilities came to $51.9 billion, so that our short-term liabilities exceeded our short-term assets. The data from earlier periods do not permit a breakdown by maturity, but in the 1960s the U.S. liquidity position was even less favorable than it was in 1973.

The reason for this change was that the United States was functioning as a commercial banker to the world in the 1960s, creating reserves (short-term U.S. liabilities) and using the proceeds to make long-term investments abroad, just as domestic commercial bankers borrow short (demand deposits) and lend long (consumer and business loans of up to five years). When the dollar was devalued, the United States ceased to play this role to the extent that it had been, and our international asset position changed to reflect this development. We look at the international liquidity position again later, when we discuss the Bretton Woods system.

SUMMARY

This chapter introduces two very important international accounting statements: the balance of payments and the balance of international indebtedness. The balance of payments is useful in forecasting the direction of change in currency prices as well as in measuring the impact of international transactions on domestic economic activity. There are difficulties in measuring precisely the flow of transactions, giving rise to a relatively larger statistical discrepancy here than in the national income accounts.

The general format consists of four major accounts: current account, capital account, statistical discrepancy, and settlement account. The first three are autonomous or "above-the-line" categories of transactions undertaken for their own sake without reference to the balance of payments. These correspond to the demand and supply curves for foreign exchange in the previous chapter.

Settlement account consists of financing transactions in gold, foreign exchange, or one's own currency to finance the deficit or surplus. The size of the surplus or deficit is the value of this account with the sign reversed.

Current account consists of exports and imports of goods and services, income on foreign investments (net), unilateral transfers, and government grants. Capital account includes transactions in financial instruments—stocks, bonds, bank deposits—foreign aid loans, and also direct investment. Statistical discrepancy is computed as a residual to bring the other three accounts into balance. Statistical discrepancy is the result of smuggling, unrecorded short-term capital flows, and other unreported or misreported transactions.

Any payment to us or claim for payment to us is a credit (+); any payment by us or claim to payment by us is a debit (−). Each transaction gives rise to two entries. If both entries are above the line, there is no net effect on the balance-of-payments surplus or deficit.

There are three measures of the surplus or deficit, depending on the treatment of short-term capital transactions. The narrowest definition is official settlements, which treats only changes in foreign exchange holdings, changes in gold and IMF drawing rights, and acquisition of one's currency by foreign central banks as financing items. Gross liquidity considers private acquisition of short-term claims (including currency and demand deposits) as financing transactions. Net liquidity would also incorporate changes in short-term claims against foreigners by one's own citizens in settlement account. For most countries, these would all be about the same, but for a reserve currency, the measure of surplus or deficit can vary significantly among the three definitions.

The balance of international indebtedness is a statement of claims against foreigners, both public and private, and liabilities to foreigners. It is a balance sheet with respect to the rest of the world. This statement indicates a country's net creditor position (solvency) and can also be used to measure liquidity. The most recent figures for the United States indicate that the United States is, as it has been for many years, a net creditor and also that its liquidity position has improved significantly since the early 1970s.

KEY TERMS

autonomous transaction
balance of international indebtedness
balance of payments
capital account
credit
current account
debit
deficit
financing transaction
gross liquidity surplus or deficit
liquidity
net creditor position
net liquidity surplus or deficit
official settlements surplus or deficit
resident
settlement account
solvency
statistical discrepancy
sterilization
surplus
unilateral transfers

REVIEW QUESTIONS

1. Identify the two entries on the balance-of-payments accounts for each of the following transactions, as well as the net effect on the surplus or deficit.
    a. General Motors builds a $500 million plant in Canada, drawing on its holdings of Canadian dollars in a Toronto bank.

b. John Jones smuggles in $10,000 worth of marijuana from Mexico. He is not caught. He pays cash; the cash shows up in the Mexican Central Bank. (You might also want to consider how the accounts would differ if he were subsequently caught and confessed that he had brought the marijuana from abroad.)

c. Your aunt in England sends you a £ 5 note for your birthday. You cash it in for dollars (about $9) at your bank. Your bank forwards it to the U.S. Central Bank.

d. A private voluntary organization donates two tractors (cash value $160,000) to poor farmers in Africa.

e. You receive a dividend of $200 on your Underwood-Olivetti stock. (This is an Italian corporation.) The company pays you by drawing on the dollar holdings of the Italian Central Bank.

f. You buy 10 shares of Nestlé, a Swiss corporation, valued at $1,200. The payment is not due until after the end of the calendar year for which the balance of payments is being computed.

2. Try making up your own transactions similar to those in question 1.

3. Find some other balance-of-payments formats and try to convert them into the general format used in this chapter.

4. Trace the U.S. balance-of-payments deficit or surplus on current account, capital account, and overall from 1960 until the 1971 devaluation. Why do you think the deficit increased? (You may have to wait until a later chapter for a complete answer.)

5. Identify the kinds of information you could glean about a particular country from a series of balance of payments.

6. Choose a country other than the United States and trace the history of its balance of payments for the last ten years. Observe the relationship between its surplus or deficit and subsequent changes in the exchange rate. (A good source is the International Monetary Fund's *International Financial Statistics* and *Balance of Payments Yearbook.*)

7. Explain why most countries can manage with one definition of surplus or deficit, but the United States, until recently, needed three.

SUGGESTED READINGS

KREININ, MORDECHAI,   *International Economics: A Policy Approach,* 3rd ed., chap. 7. New York: Harcourt Brace, 1979.

LAFFER, ARTHUR B., and MARC A. MILES,   *International Economics in an Integrated World,* chap. 10. Glenview, Ill.: Scott, Foresman, 1982.

PIPPENGER, JOHN,   "Balance of Payments Deficits: Measurement and Interpretation," *Federal Reserve Bank of St. Louis Review,* 55, no. 11 (November 1973), 6–14.

"Report of the Advisory Committee on the Presentation of Balance of Payments Statistics," *Survey of Current Business,* June 1978, pp. 18–27.

STERN, ROBERT, et al.,   *The Presentation of the U.S. Balance of Payments: A Symposium,* Essays in International Finance, no. 123. Princeton, N.J.: Princeton University Press, 1977.

CHAPTER 14

The Macroeconomic Context I: Income and Interest Rates

INTRODUCTION

The last two chapters have introduced you to the basic components of the international financial system—the foreign exchange market and the balance-of-payments accounts. We would like to use these tools to analyze and evaluate alternative international financial arrangements, but before we can do that, we need to consider the process of adjustment to disequilibrium in the balance of payments and the foreign exchange market.

Much of the literature of international finance for the last 200 years has been concerned with the process by which a payments imbalance[1] can be resolved. The first step is to examine the causes of disequilibrium, which means the sources of shifts in the demand and supply of foreign exchange. The second step is to distinguish imbalances that are temporary and can be ignored from those that are of a more long-term nature and call for some kind of policy response. This leads us into a discussion of the ideas of basic balance and fundamental disequilibrium.

[1] The terms imbalance and disequilibrium are being used interchangeably as if all excess demand or supply of foreign exchange constituted compensatory or financing transactions. As was noted in Chapters 12 and 13, some of the perceived deficit for a reserve currency country may consist of normal private demand for transactions purposes.

The choice of adjustment mechanisms cannot be made without reference to the interaction of such policies with domestic policies and goals, so we must next examine the relationship between internal balance—a target level of national income, defined as full-employment income (Y^*)—and external balance.

Only a very small country can ignore the multinational repercussions of its domestic fluctuations and/or policies. It is logical, therefore, to shift at this point to a large-country context and examine the interrelationships among fluctuations in income, interest rates, exports, imports, and capital flows of one country and those of its major trading partners.

Price adjustments and aggregate supply are considered in Chapter 15.

SOURCES OF SHIFTS
IN DEMAND AND SUPPLY

In the short run, the demand for a country's currency can shift for many of the reasons that any demand or supply curve can shift. (Recall from Chapter 12 that the demand curve for a currency incorporates both supply and demand variables, and so does the supply curve.) The price of substitutes (other monetary assets) may change. Income may have risen in the rest of the world, increasing their demand for all kinds of goods and services, including those that your country exports. The underlying price of particular export commodities or their foreign substitutes may have changed. (For example, a rise in the price of wheat—a major American export—because of bad weather, increased world demand, or crop failures in other grains would affect the demand for the U.S. dollar.) Tastes and preferences, resource depletion, technological change, and relative rates of interest are among the many familiar influences on demand and supply we expect to see at work in the short run. Droughts, earthquakes, floods, dock strikes, and other unpredictable short-run events also have an impact on a country's ability to supply exports and its "need" for imported goods and services.

Any of these factors can create a short-term balance-of-payments surplus or deficit, reviving a question that was raised in Chapter 12. Do we want the exchange rate to fluctuate in response to every one of these short run shifts? This could introduce a great deal of volatility and uncertainty into exchange rates. Or do we want the exchange rate to be relatively stable, changing only in response to long-run shifts in underlying conditions? In the latter case, who will be the expert who differentiates between temporary, short-run shifts and long-run, persistent problems? Is it not better to let the market correct than to let the "authorities" try to second-guess market forces? This question is central to any discussion of alternative international monetary arrangements. It reduces in part to a question of how short is the long run, or how long is the short run; that is, how long do we attempt to "ride out" an imbalance before we decide to do something about it?

Long-run changes are similar to short-run changes, but there are some additional sources of shifts as well as a requirement of persistence or permanence. For example, a country that experienced a one-year surge in its price level in excess of the rest of the world's annual inflation rate can expect that the supply of its currency will rise relative to the demand. But if the differential rate of inflation is only temporary, the balance-of-payments problem will be temporary also. In contrast, a country that persistently experiences inflation well above the average of its major trading partners will find that, other things being equal, it will also have a persistent balance-of-payments problem. The country whose rate of inflation consistently runs below that of the rest of the world can expect a payments surplus (i.e., currency demand exceeds supply). Similarly, a country whose real income growth rate is well above (below) the world average can expect this to lead to a payments deficit (surplus).[2] If interest rates can be maintained well above (below) the world average, a capital inflow (outflow) can be expected, tending toward surplus (deficit) in the balance of payments.

The items in the preceding paragraph are a part of the balance-of-payments adjustment process and will be considered in greater detail later in this chapter. In addition to persistent trends in prices, income, and interest rates, however, there are some other sources of long-run shifts.

One of these is the creation of preferential arrangements, such as the customs unions and common markets discussed in Chapter 11. Similarly, other institutional changes with wide impact on "who trades what with whom at what price" can create persistent payments imbalances. OPEC is one example; the formation of an Eastern European trading bloc with a Russian orientation in the 1950s was another. The tariff cuts and other commercial policies negotiated in settings such as the Kennedy Round and the Tokyo Round had a significant impact on the balance of payments of the participating countries.

Changes in technology can be another important source of shifts in the supply and demand for foreign exchange, especially changes in transportation, communications, and banking, which are services of particular importance to international trade. Improvements in technology and communications are likely to increase the volume of trade, but there is no reason to assume that it will be increased uniformly among all participants. The patterns and sizes of surpluses and deficits will usually exhibit some long-term shift as a result of such changes. Changes in banking, for example, new services, innovations such as electronic funds transfer, and regulatory change, will shift the volume and direction of the flow of funds among countries.

Technological change in the form of development of new products or changes in the relative costs of production of products is another source of

---

[2] Monetarists would argue that, if real growth above the world average is unaccompanied by monetary expansion, the resulting excess demand for money would lead to a payments surplus, most of it in the form of capital inflow.

fairly long-term shifts in the demand and supply of foreign exchange. The developer of the product or process will be the initial exporter. During the period before it becomes feasible to produce the product or introduce the process elsewhere, the result should be a balance-of-payments surplus, whose size depends on the sales volume of this product relative to other exports.

Resource discovery and/or depletion is a long-term process with long-term balance-of-payments implications. Charles Kindleberger suggested that each country is in a race between discovery of new raw materials resources and depletion of existing, known supplies.[3] The United States, for example, was a major exporter of raw materials in the nineteenth century, but has shifted to a significant net importer in the twentieth. A worldwide shift to coal in the future could reverse this pattern. Discoveries of resources have certainly been an important influence on the balance of payments for many developing countries in the last half of the twentieth century, particularly discoveries of oil in such countries as Libya and Nigeria.

Finally, divergent national monetary and fiscal policies can create either short-run or long-run imbalances in the demand and supply of foreign exchange. A country that consistently pursues a monetary and/or fiscal policy that is more expansionary or inflationary than that of the rest of the world can expect a persistent deficit in the balance of payments, whereas a country that pursues a more conservative, restrictive policy can expect a resulting payments surplus. Brazil at the inflationary extreme and Switzerland at the stable end of the spectrum are two examples from recent decades.

BASIC BALANCE
AND FUNDAMENTAL
DISEQUILIBRIUM

In Chapter 12, we introduced a simple model of the foreign exchange market that consisted of the supply generated by export demand and the demand generated by imports and capital flows.[4] If we qualify capital flows further to consist only of regular, "normal," persistent, long-term capital flows in both directions and broaden exports and imports to include all regular current account entries, we have the elements of what is called basic balance. The major exclusion here is short-term capital flows; these are usually considered transient, temporary, reversible, and often speculative and, therefore, not

---

[3] Charles Kindleberger, *Foreign Trade and the National Economy* (New Haven, Conn.: Yale University Press, 1962), chap. 3.

[4] Again, in this section, we are ignoring the possibility of a normal, transactions-related excess demand for a country's currency so that imbalances can be assumed to be equivalent to disequilibria.

a normal, regular component of supply or demand. If a country is in basic balance, this means that its regular, normal demand for foreign exchange is being met by regular, normal sources of supply. The expression for basic balance is written

$$X = M \pm \text{net long-term capital flows} \qquad (14.1)$$

which can be rewritten for a capital exporter as

$$X = M + \text{net long-term capital outflows} \qquad (14.2)$$

and for a capital importer as

$$X + \text{net long-term capital inflows} = M \qquad (14.3)$$

Equation 14.2 states that a capital-exporting country must be earning enough from exports (including not only goods and services but also investment income and other current account inflows) to finance both imports and capital outflows. Equation 14.3 indicates that a capital importer must generate enough receipts from exports plus capital inflow to finance its imports. If the relevant equation does not hold, and if, moreover, the imbalance is a significant percentage of the total balance of payments and continues for a period of several years, then a country is said to be in fundamental disequilibrium. Fundamental disequilibrium means that the balance-of-payments deficit (or surplus) cannot be expected to clear up without some policy response, which could consist of an adjustment in the exchange rate, controls, restrictive macroeconomic policies, or other deliberate action to eliminate at least part of the imbalance.

Fundamental disequilibrium is a theoretical and somewhat elusive concept, and an effort to describe a situation in which an international monetary policy response is called for. Basic balance is an attempt to make that concept operational by identifying specific items in the balance of payments that can be aggregated to measure the size and direction of the fundamental disequilibrium. The resulting number must be considered in relation to the overall volume of currency flows and to the balance in the preceding few years before determining whether or not a fundamental disequilibrium actually does exist.

INTERNAL AND EXTERNAL BALANCE

As we suggested in Chapter 2, policies to correct the balance-of-payments deficit or surplus cannot be considered in isolation from the domestic economy. These policies have repercussion on output, employment, prices, and

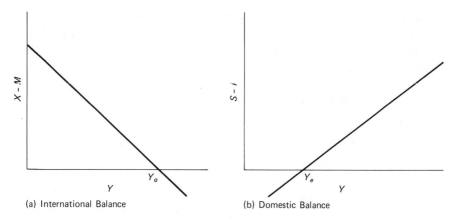

FIGURE 14-1   Effects of Income Changes on International Balance and Domestic Equilibrium

interest rates, while at the same time policies undertaken to affect domestic output, employment, prices, and interest rates affect the balance-of-payments surplus or deficit.

Figure 14-1 illustrates the concepts of external and internal balance. Panel (a) depicts the relationship between the balance of payments and the level of real national income, Y. The balance of payments surplus or deficit is measured by $X - M$, where both terms can incorporate not only the flow of goods and services but also foreign source income and capital flows.[5] Exports thus defined are largely independent of the level of domestic income but, rather, depend on the level of income in the rest of the world, which we are treating as given. Imports, however, are related positively to the level of national income. (This relationship is usually written as $M = mY$, where m = marginal propensity to import.) The less income we have, the fewer goods and services we can import and the less we have available to invest abroad. The term $X - M$, therefore, will be negatively related to the level of national income, and the balance of payments will be in balance at one and only one level of national income, Y_o, at which the value of $M(Y)$ is equal to the exogenously determined X_o. At income levels above Y_o, the balance of payments will be in deficit.

Panel (b) of Figure 14-1 shows the determination of the equilibrium level of national income in a simple Keynesian framework. As you should recall from Chapter 2, the equilibrium level of national income occurs where saving is equal to investment. Saving, like imports, is positively related to the level of national income (Y), while investment is autonomous (i.e., determined by factors outside the simple model we are using here). At an

---

[5] Capital flows may be related to income, interest rates, and other variables. This initial model ignores interest rates and assumes that net capital flows are exogenous with respect to income. The monetarist model would suggest that net capital inflows are positively related to real income, which would at least considerably flatten $X - M$.

income level of Y_o, the level of saving, $S(Y)$, is equal to the autonomous investment, I_o. At incomes below Y_o, investment exceeds saving, putting upward pressure on income until it reaches equilibrium. At incomes above Y_o, saving exceeds investment, putting downward pressure on output until equilibrium is again restored. Given our saving and investment functions, Y_o is the only level of income and output that can be sustained.

Saving can incorporate taxes and imports as additional leakages out of the income stream, while investment can include government spending and exports as additional injections into the income flow. The addition of taxes and government spending opens up the possibility of shifting the $S - I$ curve through fiscal policy actions.

Figure 14-2 combines the two panels into a single diagram to demonstrate that the level of income that is determined by S and I need not be the one that gives us balance-of-payments equilibrium and also that neither of these levels of national income may correspond to full employment. $S - I$ is in balance at the relatively low income level of Y_1, at which we have a balance-of-payments surplus of OA. If we could shift $S - I$ to $(S - I)'$, we would have a higher level of national income and also eliminate the balance-of-payments surplus. If full-employment income is defined as Y^*, then shifting from Y_1 to Y_o moves us in the right direction both from the viewpoint of the balance of payments and also from the standpoint of fiscal policy for full employment. If, however, we attempt to move all the way to Y^* (shifting $S - I$ until it intersects the horizontal axis at Y^*), we will create a balance-of-payments deficit in the amount of OD. From Y_o on, we have a conflict

FIGURE 14-2   Using Fiscal Policy to Bring About Balance-of-Payments Equilibrium

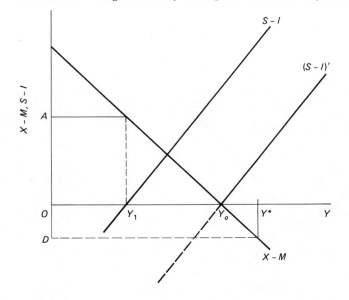

of internal (full employment) and external (balance-of-payments equilibrium) goals.

POLICY OPTIONS

How is the shift in $S - I$ brought about? The usual expansionary fiscal policy tools of tax cuts and government spending increases will shift S (which now is $S + T$ or even $S + T + M$) plus I (now $I + G$ or even $I + G + X$) to the right. A tax cut will mean that $S + T + M$ is smaller at every level of income; a government spending increase means that $I + G + X$ is now larger at every possible level of income.

You can identify other possible policy choices by shifting the location of $S - I$ relative to $X - M$ and/or by moving Y^* to various points on the horizontal axis. For example, Y^* could have been to the left of Y_1, so that the current equilibrium level represented overfull employment; inflationary pressures now are coupled with a balance-of-payments surplus. A restrictive fiscal policy to shift $S - I$ to the left (raise taxes or cut government spending) would have increased the balance-of-payments surplus—another policy conflict. Or Y^* could have fallen between $S - I$ and $X - M$, which would represent no conflict.

Even in this simple model, fiscal policy is not the only option. It is possible to shift $X - M$ by adjusting the exchange rate and through other methods as well. This possibility is illustrated in Figure 14-3.

FIGURE 14-3   Conflict of Policy Goals: Resolution Through Exchange Rate Adjustments

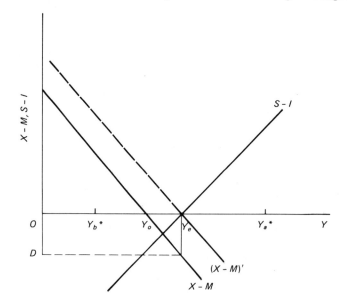

The initial situation in this diagram indicates that the equilibrium level of national income occurs at Y_e, while the balance of payments is in balance at Y_o and in deficit in the amount OD at Y_e. If full employment is at Y_a^*, an attempt to shift $S - I$ in the desired direction will make the balance of payments even worse. This was the situation confronting the Kennedy administration in the early 1960s. One way of dealing with this problem is to shift $X - M$ to the right. We have shifted it only to Y_e, eliminating the balance-of-payments deficit at the current level of income, but it would be appropriate to attempt to shift both $X - M$ and $S - I$ to the right until they intersect each other and the horizontal axis at Y_a^*.

We already know how to shift the $S - I$ schedule through fiscal policy. (Monetary policy could also be effective, as we see in our next model.) The $X - M$ schedule can be shifted in several ways. One way is to change the exchange rate. A devaluation of the currency will make exports cheaper and imports more expensive, so that there will be more exports and fewer imports (if elasticities are not too low) at every possible level of national income. Thus a devaluation will shift $X - M$ to the right. Similarly, a revaluation will shift $X - M$ to the left.

Tariffs or quotas on imports or controls on capital flows, changes in relative interest rates, and changes in tastes and preferences, such as President Lyndon Johnson's "See America First" advertising campaign in the late 1960s, are other possible ways in which to shift $X - M$. This list should sound familiar. Early in the chapter we discussed the factors that could shift the supply and demand for currency as a function of price. Now we are dealing with an $X - M$ function that represents excess supply (supply minus demand) for currency as a function of income. Any influence other than income or price that can shift one curve will also shift the other. Income changes can shift the price demand and supply curves, and price changes can shift the income excess supply curve.

If demand management (monetary and fiscal) policies were the only tools for obtaining both internal balance (full employment at stable prices) and external balance, then we would not have enough tools. External policy tools such as those mentioned in the preceding paragraph offer additional options for dealing with situations in which the policy required for domestic goals is inconsistent with the policy required for balance-of-payments equilibrium.

Returning to Figure 14-3, we have an alternate full-employment level of income at Y_b^*. If this is the full-employment level of income, then the equilibrium level of income needs to be reduced by shifting $S - I$ to the left. This will improve the balance-of-payments picture, but the deficit will be overcorrected and will turn to surplus at Y_b^*. A revaluation, import promotion, or encouragement of capital outflow might be in order as a corrective measure if the country feels pressured to correct the surplus.

If the preceding policy discussion indicates that countries in surplus are as concerned about their balance of payments as countries in deficit, you have been misled. The main policy problem created by a payments surplus is for the central bank to "sterilize" (offset) the effect of the foreign exchange inflow on the monetary base to prevent unwanted monetary expansion. Surplus countries may also be under external pressure from deficit countries to make the adjustment, but the internal pressure is fairly weak.

A deficit country is under much greater pressure because it can run out of reserves to finance the deficit. This was one of the drawbacks of both the gold standard and the Bretton Woods system, addressed in later chapters.

MONETARY POLICY
AND INTEREST RATES:
A MODIFIED IS-LM MODEL

Thus far we have ignored the role of interest rates in both domestic policy and balance-of-payments policy. In order to introduce interest rates, we need to borrow some concepts from macroeconomic theory, in particular the notion of an IS curve and an LM curve.[6] The IS curve is a summation of goods market equilibrium on the assumption that the level of investment is a negative function of the rate of interest and the level of saving is a positive function of the level of income. (Again, it is possible to incorporate G and X into investment, especially since state and local government spending is quite interest sensitive, and to include taxes and imports in saving, since both are positively related to income.) An equilibrium level of income and interest rates is one that makes saving equal to investment, as we discussed in Chapter 2. Since

$$I = I(i) \tag{14.4}$$

and

$$S = S(Y) \tag{14.5}$$

there are a number of combinations of Y and i that will satisfy

$$I(i) = S(Y) \tag{14.6}$$

These combinations are represented in Figure 14-4 as the IS curve. Higher interest rates discourage investment and would be compatible with lower levels of income, which would discourage saving. Similarly, low levels of interest rates are associated with high levels of investment, which will be

---

[6] These are derived in the appendix to this chapter.

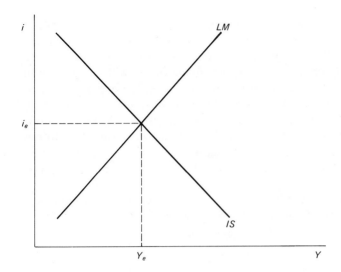

FIGURE 14-4 *IS-LM*: **Equilibrium Combinations of Income and Interest Rates**

equal to high levels of saving only at higher incomes. For this reason, the *IS* curve slopes downward from left to right.

The *LM* curve represents those combinations of income and interest rates that will clear the market for money, that is, for which the supply of money is equal to the demand for money. The supply of money is assumed to be determined by the monetary authority and is independent of income and interest rates. There are two major sources of demand for money: transactions demand, which is positively related to the level of income, and speculative demand, which is negatively related to the rate of interest.

Transactions demand is the money people choose to hold to meet their day-to-day expenditures, since they make transactions more frequently than they receive income. As income rises, so does the total dollar value of transactions, and larger money balances are needed to meet the larger volume of transactions.

Speculative demand is demand for money as an asset in a spectrum or portfolio of assets. Money earns no interest, unlike most other financial assets, but it has the advantages of being perfectly liquid and low in risk (other than inflation risk). For this reason, most people will choose to hold some of their portfolio of financial assets in the form of money—currency and demand deposits. The opportunity cost of holding money is the interest forgone by not investing it in interest-bearing financial assets.

When interest rates are low, demand for money will be higher, not only because of lower opportunity cost of holding money but also because of the greater capital risk associated with interest-bearing assets. If current interest rates are so low that there is no way to go but up, then buying bonds at current interest rates is risky. When yields go up on newly issued bonds in the future, the bonds currently being issued will be less attractive and will decline in price. Our speculator will want to hold cash when interest rates are low rather than invest it in low-yielding bonds with a high risk of capital loss. Conversely, when interest rates are high, the opportunity cost of holding money is higher; there is also a possibility of capital gain from rising bond prices if interest rates decline in the future. At high interest rates, speculative balances will be cut to a bare minimum and asset portfolios will be shifted toward bonds, stocks, certificates of deposit, and other financial assets. Thus, the speculative demand for money is negatively related to the rate of interest.

If MS = the money supply, L_1 = transactions demand for money, and L_2 = speculative demand for money, then the money market is in equilibrium where money supplied = money demanded, or

$$MS = L_1(Y) + L_2(i) \tag{14.7}$$

A number of values of Y and i will satisfy this equation. They are given by the LM curve. Note that the LM curve slopes upward from left to right. Higher income levels call for higher levels of transactions balances, L_1. Given a fixed money supply, this is possible only if speculative balances are reduced, which will occur at higher rates of interest. Thus, higher income levels are associated with higher interest rates in clearing the money market.

There is a unique equilibrium combination of Y and i that will clear both the goods market, IS, and the money market, LM. In Figure 14-4, this combination is Y_e and i_e.

Monetary policy tools work primarily by shifting the LM curve, and fiscal policy tools operate mainly through the IS curve, although monetary policy has repercussions in the goods market and fiscal policy has an impact on the money market. A simple version of monetary and fiscal policy in an *IS-LM* framework is given in Figure 14-5.

Panel (a) represents an expansionary fiscal policy, cutting taxes and/or increasing government spending. The simple Keynesian model in Chapter 2 ignored interest rates. In that model, you learned that these actions would increase income. It is now apparent that they will also increase interest rates because of the feedback through the money market, if the money supply does not expand to accommodate the fiscal policy action. The higher level of income created by fiscal expansion will generate increased demand for transactions balances, cutting back on speculative balances, which drives up interest rates and discourages some investment.

The new equilibrium is at Y_2, i_2, which represents not only a higher interest rate and higher national income but also more saving (including taxes, which are an involuntary form of saving) and more investment (which

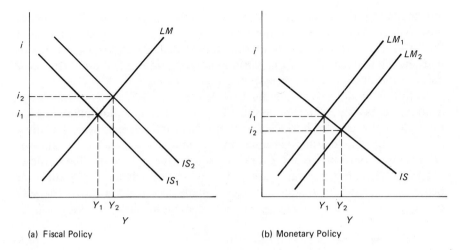

(a) Fiscal Policy   (b) Monetary Policy

FIGURE 14-5   Monetary and Fiscal Policy in an *IS-LM* Framework

can include government spending in this model.)[7] The higher income level and interest rates result in larger transactions balances and smaller speculative balances.

The same analysis applies to monetary policy, which consists of changes in the money supply. Panel (b) of Figure 14-5 illustrates an expansionary monetary policy. The increased money supply means that people have excess money balances. Some of the new money will be spent, driving up income; some will be saved (invested in financial instruments), driving down interest rates. Eventually, Y will rise enough and i will fall enough so that people are satisfied with larger transactions and speculative balances. Rising Y increases savings, and falling i encourages investment, so once again $S = I$ but at a higher level of both variables. The new equilibrium is shown as Y_2, i_2 in panel (b).

FOREIGN EXCHANGE EQUILIBRIUM

The preceding model is the general macroeconomic framework of a closed economy, or at least an economy that is ignoring the question of balance-of-payments equilibrium. That model should be familiar to anyone who has taken a course in intermediate macroeconomics. If you feel uncomfortable with the *IS-LM* model at this point, you might want to consult a good

---

[7] The additional G (government spending) may partially displace some private I (investment) by driving up interest rates—the familiar "crowding out" situation.

intermediate macroeconomic theory text before proceeding.[8] We proceed now to develop a schedule for the balance of payments, BB, that is analogous to the IS curve for the goods market and to the LM curve for the money market. That is, it shows the various combinations of Y and i that will balance the demand and supply for foreign exchange.

In this model, we define the $X - M$ quadrant as consisting of current account items only, which are assumed to depend on income and not interest rates. (Other variables besides these may have influence as well, but these are the only explanatory variables in our model.) Another quadrant will relate capital outflows to interest rates in a negative fashion, so that outflows are high when interest rates are low and outflows become low or even negative when interest rates are high. Finally, since we want the balance of payments in basic balance, we impose the equilibrium condition

$$X - M \pm \text{net capital flows} = 0 \qquad (14.8)$$

These three quadrants can be used to generate a combination of interest rates and income levels that will balance the balance of payments, as is illustrated in Figure 14-6. Quadrant I shows the familiar $X - M$ relationship, now limited to current account. Quadrant II is a 45° line, imposing the equilibrium condition that $X - M$ be equal to capital outflows. (If $X - M$ is negative, capital outflows must be also; that is, there must be a capital inflow. This possibility accounts for the extension of the 45° line into the negative quadrant.) Quadrant III shows the relationship between capital outflow and the interest rate. Quadrant IV is derived from the other three.

To derive BB, the set of interest rate and income combinations that will balance the foreign exchange market, choose any income level such as Y_1. Corresponding to Y_1 is some unique value of $X - M$ in the first quadrant. According to the basic balance equation, $X - M$ must be equal to the dollar value of capital outflows, K_1. In the third quadrant, we find that this value, K_1, occurs at an interest rate i_1. Thus, i_1 and Y_1 is one combination that lies on the BB curve. Other points are derived in similar fashion. (The reader familiar with intermediate macroeconomics will recognize that this derivation parallels the derivation of the IS curve.)

We now have an overdetermined system, as can be seen clearly when we add the $IS\text{-}LM$ diagram to the BB four-quadrant model. This is done in Figure 14-7.

The equilibrium combination for the domestic economy is Y_o, i_o, which lies on both the IS curve (clearing the market for goods) and the LM curve (giving us money market equilibrium). However, this combination does not lie on the BB curve in Figure 14-7, so the balance of payments does not

---

[8] A brief derivation of $IS\text{-}LM$ is in the appendix. Suitable macroeconomics texts are listed in the suggested readings at the end of Chapter 15.

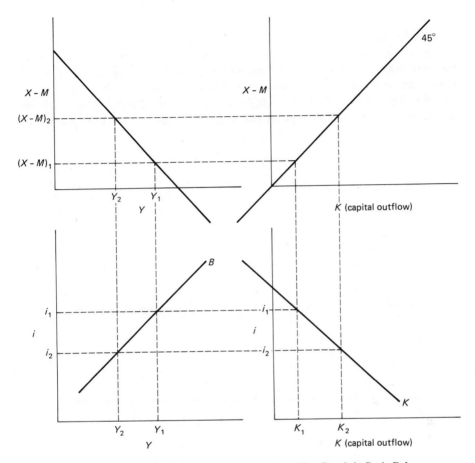

FIGURE 14-6 Combinations of Interest Rates and Income That Result in Basic Balance

balance. Y_o generates a current account surplus of OM, while interest rates are so high that capital outflow is only ON, giving a balance-of-payments surplus of MN. Other sets of IS and LM curves would generate different combinations of interest rates and income levels, but it would only be coincidence if the particular combination where IS intersects LM should also lie on the BB curve.[9]

Policy, however, can shift any one of the three curves. Fiscal policy shifts the IS curve; monetary policy shifts the LM curve; and exchange rate policy or commercial policy can shift the BB curve. We illustrate only one of these possibilities, fiscal policy, in Figure 14-8. The other possibilities are left as exercises for the reader.

[9] This inconsistency is due partly to the absence of prices and price level changes in our model, which is remedied in Chapter 15.

In that figure, the initial *IS-LM-BB* combination generates an income level of Y_o, an interest rate of i_o, and a balance-of-payments surplus of *MN*. The authorities wish to stimulate the level of economic activity (presumably, the economy is at less than full employment) but also are under pressure from abroad to correct the balance-of-payments surplus. They have three options. They can shift *IS* to the right by expansionary fiscal policy, driving up income and interest rates; they can shift *LM* to the right through monetary

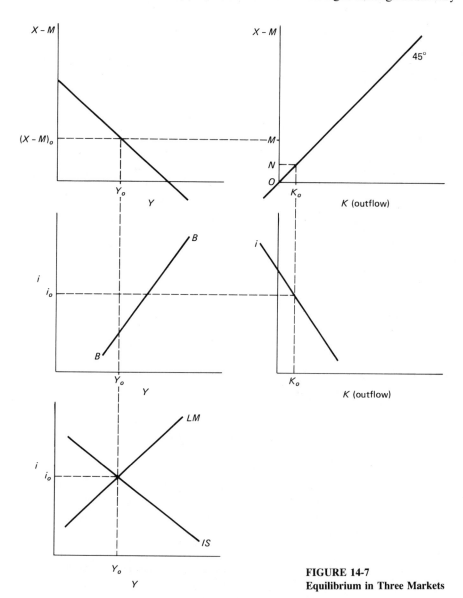

FIGURE 14-7
Equilibrium in Three Markets

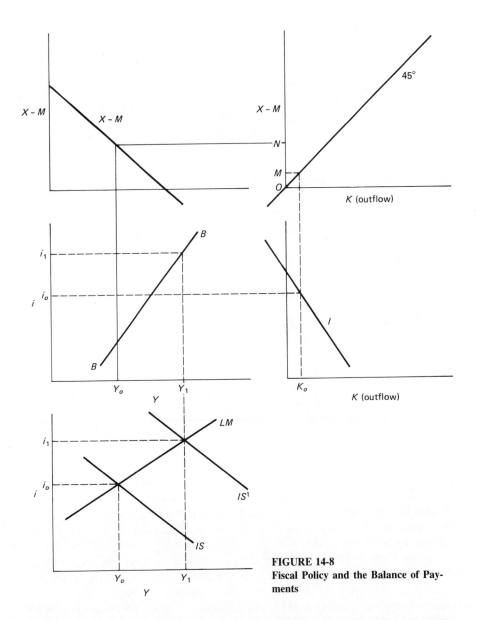

FIGURE 14-8
Fiscal Policy and the Balance of Payments

policy, driving down interest rates and raising the level of income; or they can shift *BB* by raising the price of the currency (or other methods suggested earlier), having no significant effect on interest rates or income levels but eliminating the payments surplus. (Actually, there is some "feedback" from $X - M$ to the *IS* curve and from capital flows to the money market, which we consider shortly.)

In the diagram, we have chosen to illustrate fiscal policy. Shifting to

IS' raises both *Y* (to *Y'*) and *i* to (to *i'*), eliminating the balance-of-payments surplus. Note that the increase in *Y* reduced the current account surplus, whereas the increase in interest rates reduced the capital outflow. Since we have drawn the curves so that the payments balance is more sensitive to income levels than to interest rates, the former effect outweighs the latter, eliminating the balance-of-payments surplus.

POLICY OPTIONS
IN AN OPEN ECONOMY

To summarize the possible situations in the preceding section, the government can be confronted with four possible combinations:

1. Aggregate demand below the desired level (more unemployment problems than inflationary pressure) and a balance-of-payments surplus.
2. Aggregate demand below the desired level and a balance-of-payments deficit.
3. Aggregate demand above the desired level and a balance-of-payments surplus.
4. Aggregate demand above the desired level and a balance-of-payments deficit.

Situation 1 can be met with either monetary or fiscal policy, depending on the relative responsiveness of current account to income changes and capital flows to interest rates. There is no serious conflict of policy goals here, although it is important to choose the proper combination of policies. This was the policy problem depicted in Figure 14-8.

Situation 2 presents a conflict of policy goals. An expansionary domestic policy will aggravate the balance-of-payments deficit. This dilemma is illustrated in Figure 14-9, where a shift from IS_o to IS_2 along *LM*, brings us to point *C* in the *BB* diagram. It was mentioned earlier that this was the situation confronting the Kennedy administration early in the 1960s. The administration was unwilling to use any external policy tools, including exchange rate adjustment, so a novel approach was developed called "Operation Twist."

The Federal Reserve attempted to reduce long-term interest rates and increase short-term interest rates on the theory that domestic investment is more sensitive to long-term rates whereas the pool of "hot money" flowing from country to country seeking the highest yields was more responsive to short-term rates. (This is especially true of a fixed rate system, as we see in later chapters.) The Fed bought long-term bonds, raising their price and depressing their yield, and sold short-term issues with the opposite effect. This is more or less a "one-shot" policy, since it is not at all clear that the Fed can permanently alter the relationship between interest rates on financial instruments of different maturities, but it was a creative attempt to deal with the conflict between internal and external policy goals.

Situation 3 also represents a policy conflict since contractionary policies will increase the balance-of-payments surplus. In both situations 2 and 3, an appropriate monetary and fiscal policy mix can be selected that will mitigate the conflict if the elasticities of the $X - M$ and capital flow functions are known. One such possibility is illustrated in Figure 14-9 at point A,

FIGURE 14-9   Choosing the Best Policy Mix

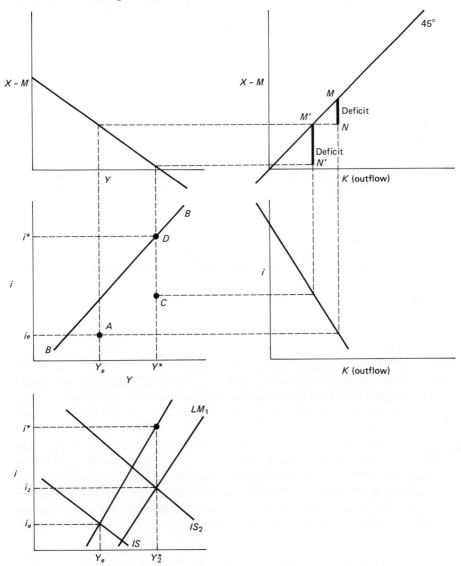

where a balance-of-payments deficit coexists with a situation of insufficient aggregate demand ($Y_e < Y^*$).

A pure fiscal policy response would move the IS_o curve to IS_1, bringing us to Y^*, i^* on the BB curve. The current account is now in deficit, but the sharp rise in interest rates has attracted a compensating capital inflow. In contrast, a monetary-fiscal policy mix (LM_1 and IS_2) that attempts to accomplish the same income goal (Y^*) while only increasing the interest rate to i_2 will aggravate the balance-of-payments deficit. Capital outflows are reduced, but current account is substantially in deficit.

Finally, situation 4 does not represent a significant conflict of policy goals. Both the balance of payments and the domestic situation call for contractionary policies.

QUALIFICATIONS
TO THE *IS-LM-BB* MODEL

One of the necessary qualifications of the *IS-LM-BB* model is the introduction of prices and aggregate supply, a qualification of sufficient importance and complexity that it is reserved for the next chapter. The modifications we address here have to do with the feedback from $X - M$ to *IS* and from capital flows to *LM* that was mentioned earlier, as well as the interest sensitivity of capital flows and its effect on monetary and fiscal policy.

The *IS* curve is a shorthand expression for

$$S(Y) + T(Y) + M(Y) = I(i) + G(i) + X_o \tag{14.9}$$

If there is a change in the exchange rate or in commercial policy that shifts the $X - M$ function, it will also affect the $S + T + M$ function and the $I + G + X$ function, shifting *IS*. It is important to note that the *IS-LM* function and the BB four-quadrant diagram are all in *real* terms, that is, independent of the level of prices. However, a change in the exchange rate will lead to substitution of our exports for domestic goods abroad and of domestic goods for imports at home, so that the real variables will respond to the exchange rate.[10]

The increase in X and decrease in M will shift the $X - M$ curve, the BB curve, and the *IS* curve to the right, as in Figure 14-10. In the initial situation, at (Y_o, i_o), the balance of payments is in deficit because i_o is far below the level i that would equate capital outflow with the current account surplus. The shift of $X - M$ to the right shifts both BB and *IS* to the right. If BB were the only function to shift, the balance-of-payments deficit would

---

[10] X is autonomous for countries that are small relative to the total incomes and trade of the sum of these trading partners. For very large countries, X may depend on Y.

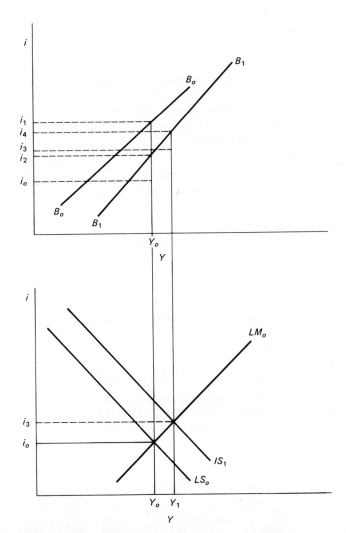

FIGURE 14-10 Effects of a Shift in $X - M$ on BB and IS

fall because the interest rate gap between i_2 and i_o is much smaller. But this ignores the repercussions on IS, which shifts to IS_1, driving income up to Y_1 and the interest rate up to i_3. The balance-of-payments deficit, whose relative (but not absolute) size is indicated by the interest rate gap, now i_4 to i_3, has been reduced further at a higher level of income and interest rates.

A shift in the K outflow function for any reason will have repercussions on the LM curve unless the central bank chooses to offset the effect on the monetary base. A shift of the capital outflow function to the right (for example, as a result of a revaluation) will reduce the monetary base and shift both LM and BB to the left; a devaluation will have the opposite effect. This is shown in Figure 14-11. If there were no *LM* repercussions, the *BB* shift would eliminate the balance-of-payments surplus since Y_o, i_o lies on the new B_1B_1 curve. However, *LM'* also shifts to the left, depressing income and raising interest rates (Y_1i_1), which puts the balance of payments back into surplus.

The models of Figure 14-10 and 14-11 represent a considerably more complex view of reality than do the simpler models of Figures 14-1, 14-2, and 14-3. The generalization that a payments deficit paired with a domestic recession, or a payments surplus at full employment, always creates a conflict of policy goals, can no longer be regarded as automatically correct. It does remain true that such situations certainly call for more careful choices of direction and mix of policies undertaken than is true of the alternative combinations.

The question of the interest sensitivity of capital flows is of considerable importance for the effectiveness of fiscal policy. The success of fiscal policy is measured by the extent to which expansionary policies expand real output rather than drive up interest rates. The *LM* curve will shift to the right in response to an increased capital inflow, so the determination of the new equilibrium is based on the new intersection between *IS* and *BB* when *IS* shifts to the right. This situation is illustrated in Figure 14-12.

Three possible slopes for *BB* are shown; BB_1, with capital flows perfectly interest inelastic; BB_2, moderately elastic; and BB_3, perfectly elastic. Compared to the original position (i_o, Y_o), the new equilibria are (i_1, Y_o), (i_2, y_2), and (i_o, y_3), respectively. When capital flows are totally unresponsive to interest rates, the outflow on current account generated by rising income leads to a monetary contraction. The smaller money supply shifts LM_o to LM_1. Rising interest rates crowd out investment, while an increase in gov-

FIGURE 14-11   Effect of a Shift in Capital Flows on *BB* and *LM*

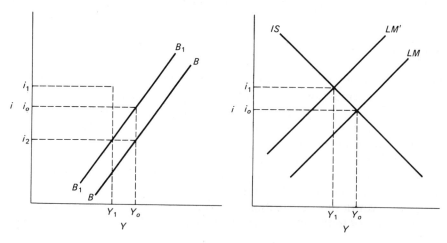

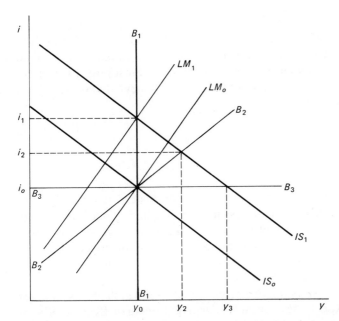

FIGURE 14-12   Fiscal Policy and the Interest Elasticity of Capital Flows

ernment spending or consumption (the original fiscal policy) offset by a deteriorating $X - M$ means that fiscal policy is totally ineffective in this situation. The opposite is true for BB_3, where the initial increase in interest rates attracts an immediate large capital inflow that continues until the interest differential is eliminated. The large capital inflow expands the money supply far more than the deterioration on current account (from rising real income) tends to contract MS. This shifts LM to the right to intersect the new IS along BB_3. In the intermediate case, both real income and interest rates rise.

It is obviously a matter of considerable interest to policymakers to have some measure of the interest sensitivity of capital flows. This sensitivity depends on the extent to which assets denominated in different currencies are considered good substitutes for one another (including substitution of one currency itself for another—holding francs instead of dollars as well as franc-denominated bonds instead of dollar-denominated bonds).

With the rise of multinational corporations, technological innovations in banking, and other events of the 1970s that made financial managers more aware of international opportunities, the degree of substitutability among currencies has undoubtedly risen. The uncertainties associated with flexible exchange rates, however, would tend to discourage currency substitution between countries or currency areas whose exchange rates are not fixed with respect to each other. (Currency areas under flexible rates are described in Chapter 17.) Monetarists, who believe in efficient and integrated markets as a general premise, would expect a considerable degree of currency substitutability even if currencies are less than perfect substitutes. Some limited evidence that cyclical fluctuations and particularly interest rates in different countries move together lend support to those who believe that capital flows are highly interest sensitive.

INTERCOUNTRY REPERCUSSIONS

Up to this point, we have assumed implicitly that this country's action had no effect on the rest of the world, unless its interest rate became high enough relative to those elsewhere to attract a capital inflow or reduce a capital outflow. We now relax the "small-country" assumption to consider the international repercussions in a two-country model, A and B, under the initial assumption of fixed exchange rates.

If A's income rises, its imports from B will rise, which are exports for B. The increased exports have a multiplier expansionary effect on B's income. As B's income rises, so do its imports from A, setting off a diminishing chain reaction that eventually peters out. In this way, expansion in one country spills over to expansion in the partner. The same is true of contraction. U.S. import demand was such an important market for many countries during the period after World War II that its impact was described by the adage, "When the United States sneezes, the rest of the world catches pneumonia."

If A's income and B's income rise together, both will increase imports with the damped repercussions just described. The result will be a larger volume of exports and imports. The net effect on surplus or deficit depends on the relative rates of income change and the relative elasticities of import demand.

If incomes move in opposite directions—for example, if the United States is enjoying a boom while Canada is experiencing a recession—then the effect of U.S. income growth on increasing its payments deficit will be magnified by the effects of Canada's recession, which tends to decrease its imports from the United States and reinforce the American deficit/Canadian surplus.

What about interest rates? Usually, interest rates in the industrial countries tend to move somewhat in unison, mitigating the effect of one country's changes in interest rates on capital flows. But they can diverge. To take an extreme case, if American interest rates were rising while Canada's were falling, capital would have a double incentive to move from Canada to the United States.

If we combine interest movements and income trends, we can usually assume that interest rates and income levels move up and down together. Thus, the rise in income will push a country in the direction of deficit, but the accompanying increase in interest rates will tend to mitigate the income effect by attracting a capital inflow or decreasing a capital outflow.

This last conclusion is one we had already reached in the *IS-LM-BB* analysis, so that we are just putting that conclusion in a large-country context to account for the spillover effects. If we now have the United States boom in both income and interest rates matched by the same circumstances in Canada, then we have a rise in the volume of imports and exports and a rise in the volume of capital flows on both sides (the substitution effect of rising interest rates is canceled because both sides have rising interest rates, but there is still an income effect attracting more investment both at home and abroad). The net effect on the balance of payments cannot be predicted, but there is no reason to assume a trend toward greater or smaller surpluses or deficits in either country.

Finally, if the United States is experiencing rising interest rates and income while Canada is seeing both fall, then we would expect the United States to be moving strongly in the direction of deficit on current account and surplus on capital account. Which of these effects dominates for the overall surplus or deficit would depend on the relative amounts of income and interest changes and the slopes of the $X - M$ and capital outflow functions in both countries.

The transmission of disturbances is weakened considerably under a system of flexible exchange rates, a point that will be developed further in Chapter 17. A rise in domestic income that stimulates imports, accompanied by a rise in domestic prices that stimulates imports and discourages exports, will put downward pressure on the exchange rate that will tend to offset the initial impact. Thus the domestic expansion will tend to be self-contained, particularly in the absence of capital flows. If interest rates rise along with real income and prices, the resulting capital inflow will dampen the downward pressure on the exchange rate, and there will be more potential for the transmission of domestic fluctuations through the current account.

There is some limited empirical evidence from both recent experience and early-twentieth-century data for the proposition that business cycles tend to move together among countries under flexible as well as fixed exchange rate regimes, although somewhat less closely in the former case. Michael Mussa[11] points out that the degree of insulation or transmission of disturbances depends not only on the exchange rate regime but also on the nature of the disturbance, namely, where it originates, whether it is fiscal, monetary, or private in origin, and so on.

---

[11] Michael Mussa, "The Exchange Rate, the Balance of Payments, and Monetary and Fiscal Policy Under a Regime of Controlled Floating," chap. 3 in Jacob Frenkel and Harry Johnson, eds., *The Economics of Exchange Rates* (Reading, Mass.: Addison Wesley Publishing Company, Inc., 1978.

SUMMARY

This is the first of two chapters that put the foreign sector in the context of current macroeconomic models to see how the foreign sector affects macroeconomic variables and how macroeconomic policy changes impact on the foreign exchange market and the balance of payments. This chapter concentrates on income and interest rate effects, along the lines of traditional macroeconomic models, integrating the current account balance and capital flows into an *IS-LM* model. Chapter 15 adds price effects and summarizes the current view of the adjustment mechanisms for the balance of payments. This will give us a complete framework for analyzing alternative international monetary arrangements.

Macroeconomic variables are among the major sources of change in the demand and supply of foreign exchange. These and other sources of short-run and long-run shifts were inventoried in the early part of the chapter. Short-run shifts in demand and supply for foreign exchange can come from income changes, interest rate changes, price level changes, tastes and preferences, technological change, natural disasters, dock strikes, and other one-time events. Long-run changes come from largely the same sources except that the income, interest rate, and price level changes (relative to the rest of the world) must be long term in nature, changes in technology and tastes and preferences must be relatively permanent, and such long-run changes as population expansion and contraction, resource discovery and depletion, and institutional change (e.g., formation of a customs union) are added to the list of influences.

The question of shifts in the supply and demand for foreign exchange leads naturally to the question of whether a policy response is called for. If the international monetary system is one that tolerates short-run deficits and surpluses and only calls for a policy response to long-run imbalances, then we need a definition that separates the two situations. The definitions are basic balance—exports equal imports plus or minus long-term capital flows—and fundamental disequilibrium—a lack of basic balance that is significant in amount and persistent over time.

If there is to be a policy response, it must be done in a way that is consistent with domestic policy objectives. This was done in the context of two models—a simple model with income as the only explanatory variable and a more complex *IS-LM-BB* model that also incorporates interest rates. The first model develops an $X - M$ curve that is negatively related to income and an $S - I$ curve that is positively related to income and identifies situations in which policy goals are harmonious and in which they are inconsistent. Where they are inconsistent, the use of international policy—commercial policy, capital controls, or changes in the exchange rate—becomes a complementary tool to domestic fiscal policy.

The more complex approach introduces the *IS-LM* macroeconomic model (which is derived in the appendix to this chapter) that makes saving dependent on income and investment on interest rates and the demand for money a function of both. This model determines an equilibrium level of output (income) and interest rates. We then developed a schedule (*BB*) of income and interest rate combinations that gave us balance-of-payments equilibrium. Combining these two models enabled us to determine the balance-of-payments surplus or deficit at the equilibrium level of income and interest rates and also to assess the effects of monetary and fiscal policy on the balance of payments. The conflicts of internal and external policy goals that appeared in the simple income-dependent model are no longer as clear cut, since the balance-of-payments effects of an expansionary policy now depend on both the income and interest rate effect and hence on the mix of monetary and fiscal policy.

   We then modified the model to take into account feedback from $X - M$ to the *IS* curve and from the capital outflow function to the *LM* curve. This feedback seems to provide for some automatic correction to the effects of domestic policy on the foreign exchange market, mitigating the initial impact toward surplus or deficit, if the feedback is not itself offset by "corrective" fiscal or monetary actions.

   Finally, we examined the multinational repercussions of income and interest rate changes in a large-country (or more simply, two-country) context. Countries moving in the same direction in income and interest rates will see a rise in the volume of flows of both goods and capital in the upswing and a fall in both in the downswing, but there is no inherent, predictable tendency toward surplus or deficit. Countries moving in opposite directions tend toward current account deficits and capital account surpluses for the expanding country and the opposite for the contracting country.

KEY TERMS

   basic balance
   BB curve
   capital flows
   conflict of policy goals
   currency substitution
   demand management policies
   equilibrium level of income
   exchange rate policy
   external balance
   feedback effects
   fiscal policy
   full-employment level of income
   fundamental disequilibrium

intercountry repercussions
internal balance
IS curve
K (outflow function)
LM curve
monetary policy
Operation Twist
real income
speculative demand for money
transactions demand for money
$X - M$ function

REVIEW QUESTIONS

1. Suppose that you were the government confronting each of the following policy situations. Explain, using appropriate diagrams, what policy or combination of policies you would select.
    a. The balance of payments is in deficit and the economy is in equilibrium at a level beyond full-employment income, creating inflationary pressures.
    b. The balance of payments is in surplus and the other conditions in situation a hold.
    c. The balance of payments is in deficit, the economy is below full-employment income, and the banking and housing industries do not want to see interest rates rise.
    d. The balance of payments is in surplus and the rest of conditions are the same as in situation c.
2. How would you distinguish between a short-run, temporary deficit and a long-term, fundamental disequilibrium?
3. Draw a diagram such as those shown in Figures 14-2 or 14-3 but with $X - M$ intersecting the horizontal axis to the left of the $S - M$ intersection with the axis. Pick various points on the line to designate as full-employment income and consider the policy choices and the possible conflict of policy goals.
4. Redraw Figure 14-8 with your own set of functions, which may be different in slope (but not direction) and/or position from those in the text. Trace the effects of a change in the money supply; of a contractionary fiscal policy. Be sure to measure the change in the balance-of-payments surplus or deficit.
5. In August 1971 President Nixon announced several policy changes at once. The one of interest to us at the moment is that he imposed a temporary 10 percent tariff (in addition to any other tariffs) on imports. How did this affect the *IS-LM-BB* diagram?

SUGGESTED READINGS

Suggestions for further reading are given for both Chapters 14 and 15 at the end of Chapter 15, p. 299.

APPENDIX

Derivation of *IS* and *LM* Curves

The *IS* and *LM* curves used in this chapter are derived from underlying functions in exactly the same way that we derived the *BB* function for the balance of payments. Figure 14A-1 shows the derivation of the *IS* curve. *S*

FIGURE 14A-1   Derivation of an *IS* Curve

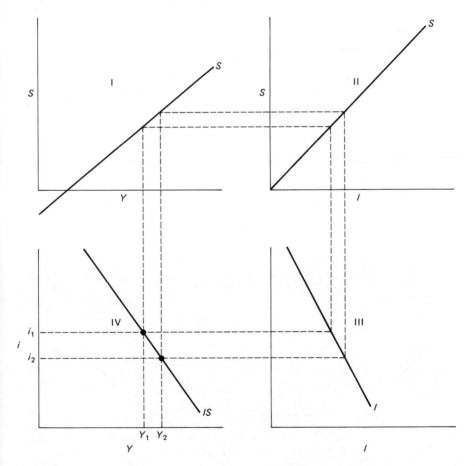

$+ T + M$ is sketched in the first quadrant as a positive function of the level of income. The negative intercept indicates that, at very low levels of income, taxes become transfer payments and consumption exceeds income. Thus, saving is also negative at very low income levels. The slope is a function of the marginal propensities to save and to import and the marginal tax rate.

In the third quadrant, $I + G + X$ is plotted as a negative function of the real rate of interest. Exports are not a function of the interest rate, so they are a constant in the function, capable shifting the whole function to the right or left as they change. Investment and state and local government spending are negatively related to interest rates. Federal government spending is also relatively independent of interest rates. Like exports, it determines the position of the curve and can shift it to the right or left.

The first quadrant contains all the "leakages" out of the income stream in the form of income received that does not return to the flow as a demand for goods and services. The third quadrant contains all the injections into

FIGURE 14A-2   Derivation of an *LM* Curve

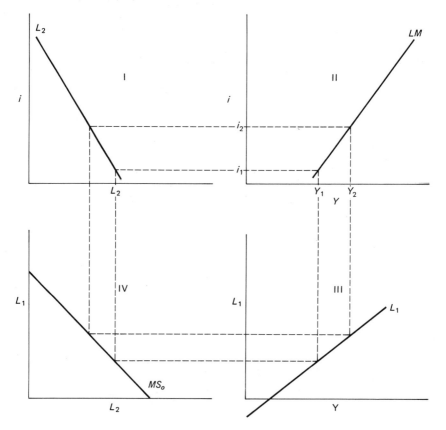

the income stream—demand for goods and services not financed out of current income but financed out of the leakages or other sources. In equilibrium, as you should recall from Chapter 2, leakages must equal injections. This condition is imposed in quadrant II in the form of a 45° line along which $S + T + M = I + G + X$. Quadrant IV is then derived from the other three as follows.

Select an income level such as Y_1 and determine in quadrant I what level of $S + T + M$ is associated with that income level. In quadrant II, this $S + T + M$ must be equal (along the 45° line) to $I + G + X$. Carrying that level of $I + G + X$ down to quadrant III, we find the interest rate, i_1, that will make this occur. This (Y, i) combination is one point on the *IS* curve in quadrant IV. Other points are derived in similar fashion. The *IS* curve can then be shifted by a change in the S function, the T function, the M function, the I function, the G function, or the X function. When T and/or G shifts, these are fiscal policy actions. You might want to experiment with shifting these functions to see the effect on *IS*.

The *LM* function is derived in the same way in Figure 14A-2. The speculative demand for money, described briefly in this chapter, is plotted as a negative function of the interest rate in quadrant I, while the transaction demand for money is shown as a positive function of the income level in quadrant III. Quadrant IV shows the given money supply that is available to be divided among transactions and speculative balances. Given *MS*, higher transactions balances require dollar-for-dollar reductions in speculative balances, and vice versa.

Select an income level and determine the level of L_1 balances associated with it. This L_1 is then carried to quadrant IV, which determines the amount of money left for L_2 balances, and in quadrant I we find what interest level will make people satisfied with that amount of L_2 balances. This (Y, i) combination is then plotted in quadrant II as one point on the *LM* curve. Other points are derived in the same manner. The *LM* curve can be shifted by a shift in any other underlying functions, but the most likely is in quadrant IV, where monetary policy shifts the money supply to the left or right and shifts *LM* in the same direction.

CHAPTER 15

The Macroeconomic Context II: Money and Prices

In Chapter 14, we examined the relationship among output, employment, and interest rates and the balance of payments. In this chapter, we incorporate the domestic price level in those international macroeconomic models. This will give us all the macroeconomic background necessary to examine alternative international monetary systems, which are introduced in this chapter and examined individually in the chapters that follow.

THE SPECIE FLOW
MECHANISM

The relationship between the flow of money and the domestic money supply and price level was described by David Hume in 1732 as the *specie flow mechanism,* an automatic correcting force in the presence of balance-of-payments surpluses and deficits. When a country loses specie (gold or silver, the monetary base at that time), as a result of a balance-of-payments deficit, the money supply will shrink. Domestic prices will fall, leading to a substitution of domestic goods for foreign goods—domestic import substitutes for imports at home, exports for foreign goods abroad. This tends to correct the deficit. This correction is reinforced by the effect of the specie inflow abroad, which increases the money supply, raising the prices, increasing the imports, and decreasing the exports. The effect is diagrammed for the foreign exchange market in Figure 15-1.

S_1 and D_1 are the supply and demand curves, which at an officially maintained exchange rate of P_1 show a balance-of-payments deficit of AB. The gap is filled in by the sale of specie (gold or silver), which then contracts the domestic money supply. The contraction of the money supply leads to a decline in domestic prices, which shifts demand for foreign exchange to the left and supply of foreign exchange to the right (S_2 and D_2). The expansion of the foreign money supply and the resulting rise in foreign prices further shifts the demand to the left and the supply to the right (S_3 and D_3). As long as a deficit exists, this process will continue until the deficit is eliminated. This was the basic corrective mechanism of the gold standard, as we shall see in Chapter 16. (The reader might try diagramming the correction process for a surplus as an exercise.)

There are two qualifications that need to be added to this model. First, monetary expansion and contraction have not only price but also income (= real output) and interest rate effects. The income effect would reinforce the corrective process just described but would also cause some domestic dislocation—recession and unemployment. The interest rate effect would lead to a change in capital flows opposite to the current account effect, thus reducing the deficit.

Second, it is possible for the monetary authority to offset the effects

FIGURE 15-1   The Specie Flow Mechanism

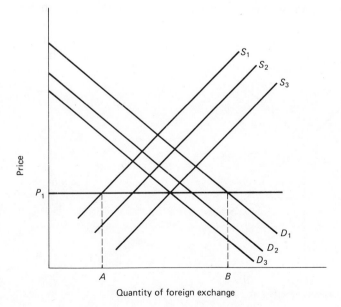

Quantity of foreign exchange

of the inflows and outflows of specie, thus frustrating the automatic correction process. Emphasis on domestic macroeconomic problems, as well as development of new techniques to frustrate the automatic adjustment process in the short run, have combined to reduce the likelihood of automatic correction at present in comparison with earlier time periods. In earlier periods governments were involved less actively in demand management policy and had less discretion about the relationship between the gold stock and the money supply.

CORRECTION THROUGH CHANGING THE EXCHANGE RATE

The other price correction mechanism is to change the exchange rate, which changes external prices as at least a partial substitute for changing domestic prices. If we return to the situation of deficit just described, then in Figure 15-2 we have a shortage of foreign exchange of AB. The exchange rate, or price of foreign exchange, is allowed to adjust upward from P_1 to P_2, leading to a reduction in the quantity demanded of BC and an increase in the quantity supplied of AB. Again, foreign goods have become more expensive than our domestic goods for both our own citizens and foreigners, leading to a substitution of our domestic goods for foreign goods both at home (import substitutes for imports) and abroad (our exports for foreign

FIGURE 15-2 Exchange Rate Adjustments

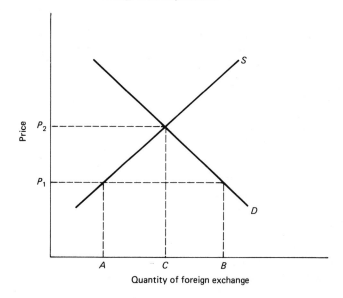

Quantity of foreign exchange

produced domestic goods) until prices are again equalized. This mechanism should be familiar from Chapter 12.

However, there is some interaction between the exchange rate change and the income and interest rate effects described in Chapter 14. Devaluation or depreciation increases demand for exports and decreases demand for imports, shifting $X - M$ to the right and thus also shifting IS to the right. The $X - M$ shift tends to correct the balance of payments, but the IS shift puts upward pressure on output that partly (through $M = mY$) offsets the price effect and restores part of the deficit. When we add prices to our macroeconomic model, we find that part of the increased demand shows up in additional output and part in higher prices, the division depending on aggregate supply conditions. If we are close to capacity output when the exchange rate adjustment is made, much of the effect will be felt in domestic prices rather than in output. The rise in domestic prices will tend to offset the balance-of-payments improvement from the devaluation.

These two mechanisms are the basis for the relationship between domestic prices and the balance of payments. In the models that follow, we elaborate on these two types of changes—balance-of-payments-induced changes in the money supply and price level and exchange-rate-induced changes in demand and prices. This modification of the Chapter 14 model will also enable us to examine the price effects of monetary and fiscal policy and the balance-of-payments implications of such policy changes.

PRICES AND THE *IS-LM-BB* MODEL: FIXED EXCHANGE RATES

One peculiar feature of the model in Chapter 14 was that prices were ignored; that is, the price level was assumed to be constant. There is one slight modification of the *IS-LM* diagram (a family of *LM* diagrams corresponding to different price levels) and one additional diagram (the aggregate supply-aggregate demand curves) that, taken together, will enable us to incorporate prices into our model. This is necessarily a sketchy treatment of some topics covered more thoroughly in intermediate macroeconomic theory, but usually only in the context of a closed economy. The reader who is confused or who is curious about details is referred to any good intermediate macroeconomics textbook.[1]

Prices are incorporated into the *IS-LM* model through the *LM* curve. You may recall from Chapter 14 that the *IS-LM* model is all in real terms. This means that the money supply is the real money supply, which is defined as MS/P (money supply divided by the price level). Thus, a change in prices

---

[1] Several texts are listed in the suggested readings at the end of this chapter.

would change the real money supply and give us a new *LM* curve. We have a whole family of *LM* curves, each corresponding to a different price level. If we want to focus on the price-income relationship, we can plot these points in *P, Y* space instead of *Y, i* space. This is done in Figure 15-3.

A higher price level with the same nominal money supply will mean

FIGURE 15-3   Deriving an Aggregate Demand Curve

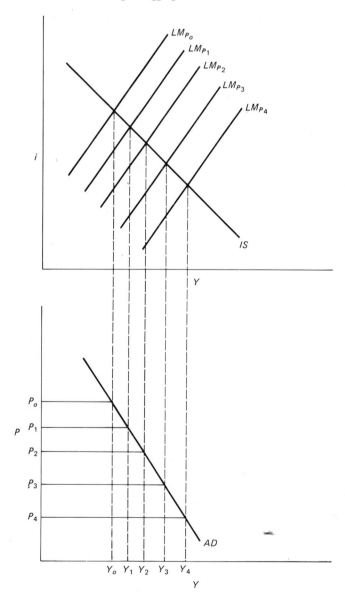

a smaller real money supply, shifting LM to the left. A price level of P_o, for example, will locate LM (given nominal MS, L_1, and L_2) far to the left, intersecting the IS curve at Y_o. This gives us one price and income level combination that generates equilibrium in both goods and money markets. Other combinations are found in similar fashion. The resulting line or curve is called an aggregate demand curve, showing the amounts of real output that people are willing to purchase at various alternative price levels. Aggregate demand can be shifted by a shift in any of the underlying functions— $I + G + X$, $S + T + M$, MS, L_1, or L_2—although the first three are the most likely to shift.

If we combine the aggregate demand curve with the aggregate supply curve, they should determine an equilibrium level of prices and output. Taking this back to the IS-LM diagram will determine which LM curve we are on, since that depends on the price level. The aggregate supply function depends on the usual supply variables at an aggregate level—capital stock, labor supply, technology, cost and availability of natural resources, and so on. It is sometimes drawn as vertical, especially in the long run, but in the short run it is usually possible to vary output somewhat, especially if rising prices create short-run profit opportunities. We have drawn aggregate supply in Figure 15-4 as steeply sloped but not vertical.

How do prices affect the four quadrants of the BB diagram? Under a system of fixed exchange rates, a change in the domestic price level will shift $X - M$, and, if it affects nominal interest rates, it will also shift capital flows. (The interest rate in the IS-LM diagram and in the BB diagram is a real interest rate, which does not include an inflation premium. Thus, any variable that is plotted as a function of real interest rates but is also responsive to nominal interest rates will shift in response to inflation.) The reason that the foreign sector is responsive to prices as well as to changes in real variables is that, under fixed exchange rates, these represent real changes in the terms of trade or relative price changes—changes in our prices relative to theirs are real changes to them. Floating exchange rates would tend to offset such relative price changes internationally, leaving real flows of goods, services, and capital unchanged. The extent to which this actually occurs under floating rates is a matter of great debate at this time.

Figure 15-5 combines the domestic aggregate supply and demand curve with the foreign sector, with one modification of the former. Since prices affect X and M, there will be a less than proportional shift in the IS curve to the left when the price level rises. The size of the shift depends on the size of the foreign sector relative to the domestic economy and the elasticity of demand for exports, imports, and import substitutes.

The initial equilibrium values are given as Y_o, P_o, i_o, $(X - M)_o$, and K_o. The balance of payments is initially in balance. Then there is a shift— for example, an expansionary fiscal policy that shifts IS to the right. What are the repercussions in this more complex model?

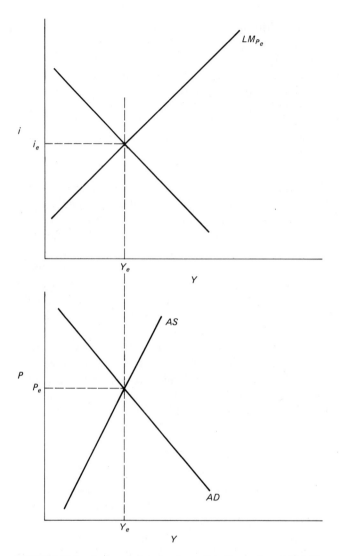

FIGURE 15-4   Aggregate Supply, Aggregate Demand, and *IS-LM*

In Chapter 14, we would have identified an increase in *Y* (lowering the current account balance) and in interest rates (reducing capital outflow or attracting capital inflow). Now, however, there are price repercussions. A shift in *IS* to the right will initially drive up interest rates, but it will also put upward pressure on prices as the increased demand runs into a limited supply. The next step is up to the monetary authority. If the expansion is ratified by expanding the money supply, the real money supply and real interest rates will remain unchanged, while *Y, P,* and nominal interest rate

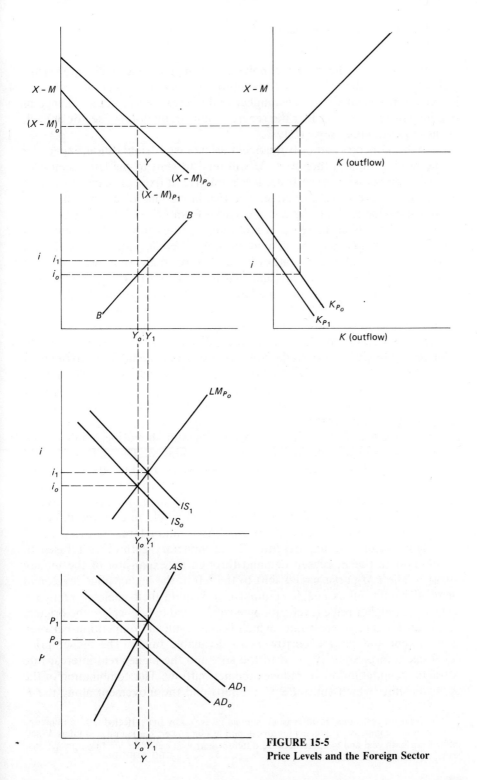

FIGURE 15-5
Price Levels and the Foreign Sector

i_n, will all rise.[2] If the money supply is unchanged while prices are rising, LM will shift to the left, so that real output is unchanged and interest rates just rise further—higher prices, higher real interest rates, and no change in real income. Let us consider the repercussions in the foreign sector of each of these possibilities separately.

If the monetary authority finances the increased demand by an expansion of the money supply, then $X - M$ will tend to shift to the left because of the rising prices—our exports are less attractive at fixed exchange rates and foreign goods are more attractive. The rise in income, of course, just calls forth a movement along the $X - M$ curve from $(X - M)_o$ to $(X - M)_1$. Similarly, there is an increase in real interest rates from i_o to i_1 that calls forth a movement along the capital outflow schedule; but there is also an increase in nominal interest rates over and above that rise in real rates that is not reflected in the diagram and that is the result of rising prices. (Remember, nominal interest rates include an inflation premium.) Under fixed exchange rates, this rise in nominal rates will attract additional capital inflow (or reduce the net outflow), shifting the K curve to the left. The net effect of these two shifts on BB is hard to predict, because it depends on the relative responsiveness of trade flows to prices and capital flows to nominal interest rates. It is possible that BB will not shift at all, so we will just see a smaller current account surplus and a smaller capital account deficit (or a larger current account deficit and a larger capital account surplus, in the case of a capital importer).

The feedback effects to the IS-LM diagram should be familiar from Chapter 14, even though they are now price induced. The shift of $X - M$ to the left will also shift IS to the left, which would tend to offset the initial fiscal expansion. The shift of the K outflow curve to the left will tend to expand the monetary base if it is not sterilized by the monetary authorities. This would shift LM to the right. Both effects would tend in the direction of restoring the original level of prices, output, and interest rates.

How would the impact differ if the monetary authorities refused to accommodate the increased demand through an expansion of the money supply? The LM curve would shift to the left at the higher price level, and demand would fall as people scrambled to rebuild their depleted real cash balances at higher price levels. Income would tend to fall back to the original levels at a higher interest rate, which is the result of competition between government and private borrowers for available funds. The higher price level, as before, shifts $X - M$ to the left, and the higher real interest rate attracts a capital inflow or reduces the net outflow. The combination of the $X - M$ shift (which shifts BB to the left) and the movement along the K

---

[2] Real interest rates (i) differ from nominal rates (i_n) by the expected rate of inflation. The difference compensates lenders for loss of purchasing power. Market rates of interest may differ from both real and nominal because different borrowers involve differing transactions, costs, and degrees of risk.

curve in response to higher real interest rates should leave the balance of payments approximately in balance.

THE VARIABLE PRICE LEVEL
MODEL WITH FLOATING
EXCHANGE RATES

The model we have been using can be adapted to floating exchange rates. A rising price level from increased aggregate demand will put downward pressure on the exchange rate. The decline in the exchange rate will shift $X - M$ to the right, because imports have become more expensive while our exports have become cheaper to foreigners. Since nominal as well as real interest rates rise, K may shift to the left. This will tend to correct the balance-of-payments deficit, shifting BB to the right.

What about the feedback effects? The shift in the $X - M$ curve to the right will also shift IS to the right and put further upward pressure on prices and output. The capital inflow will expand the monetary base and the money supply if it is not offset by the action of the monetary authorities. These two feedback effects will tend to exacerbate the inflationary pressures created by the initial expansionary policy. Thus, under floating rates, it is generally believed that inflationary pressures will be more "self-contained" and less likely to be transmitted via the balance of payments to the rest of the world. The empirical evidence on this point is not yet well established, as was indicated at the end of Chapter 14.[3]

A diagrammatic interpretation of this sequence of events is given in Figure 15-6. Note that we have assumed that the monetary authority "ratifies" the demand shift by allowing the money supply to expand in proportion to the increase in prices, so that the real money supply is unchanged. Prices and income rise; interest rates are unchanged. $X - M$ falls from $(X - M)_o$ to $(X - M)_1$. This creates a balance-of-payments deficit since, initially, K is unchanged (no change in interest rates). The deficit leads to a fall in the currency price that shifts the $X - M$ curve to $(X - M)'$ and the K curve to K'. The feedback effects on IS, LM, and AD are shown as IS_3, LM_3, and AD_3. As the feedback mitigates inflationary pressure, the currency will tend to appreciate back in the direction of the original level. The LM shift in response to the capital inflow (or reduced capital outflow) is critical in determining the final effect. Once again, the response of the monetary authority to events elsewhere that affect the monetary base or the real money supply plays an important role in determining the final values of all the relevant variables.

[3] See, for example, the Michael Mussa article cited in footnote 11 of Chapter 14.

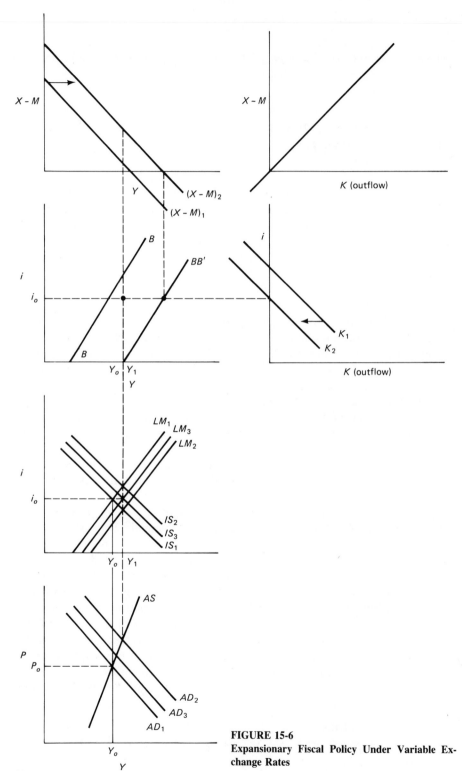

FIGURE 15-6
Expansionary Fiscal Policy Under Variable Exchange Rates

A SYSTEMS FRAMEWORK

The models in this chapter do not exhaust the exploration of the relationship between the balance of payments and domestic macroeconomic activity and policy, but they are sufficient to understand the differences between the various kinds of international monetary arrangements and the difficulties encountered in finding an international monetary system that is both durable and widely acceptable. The choice of a system depends on the goals it is intended to serve. Some of the policy goals that might be served have become evident in the last two chapters, although these largely reflect the aims of the major industrial countries. They can be sorted out into four categories of goals that the ideal international monetary system might serve:

1. Stable exchange rates.
2. Freedom of trade and capital movements.
3. Independence of monetary and fiscal policy.
4. Balance-of-payments equilibrium.

The potential for conflict among these goals is obvious, and the ranking would vary greatly from one country on one set of circumstances to another.

Stable Exchange Rates

As we discussed in the first part of the book and also in Chapter 12, stable exchange rates have the potential to be closer to the comparative advantage function than do floating rates. They also provide more certainty, stability, and predictability in international trade, which encourages a larger volume of trade and greater efficiency in world resource allocation. While it is not true that exchange rates are necessarily more stable under a fixed rather than under a floating rate regime, the former tends to offer periods of temporarily greater certainty.

Freedom of Trade and Capital Movements

This goal, again, flows from the earlier chapters of the book. Efficient allocation of production, consumption, and trade to obtain the highest level of well-being possible out of available resources is a goal that emerges from Part 2 of this book. This implies among other conclusions, that allocational decisions should be as independent as possible of national boundaries.

Independence of Monetary and Fiscal Policy

Most countries would like to be able to pursue a monetary and fiscal policy that is aimed at its particular national goals in terms of price stability, employment, and economic growth. No country wants these policies dic-

TABLE 15-1 Systems, Methods, and Goals in International Finance

System	Adjustment Mechanism	Goal Sacrificed
Floating rates	Change the price	Stable (certain) exchange rates
Gold standard	Shift the curves	Independent monetary and fiscal policy
Exchange	Rationing	Freedom of trade and capital movements
Bretton Woods	Draw on reserves	Balance-of-payments equilibrium

tated by the rest of the world through the foreign sector. Large countries with small foreign sectors, such as the United States, are particularly prone to assert their right to tailor their monetary and fiscal policy to purely domestic objectives. There is considerable disagreement over the ability of any country to pursue an independent macroeconomic policy under any exchange rate regime.

Balance-of-Payments Equilibrium

This is less a goal than a constraint. If the system does not provide for something reasonably close to balance over time, the demand for reserves to "tide one over" interminable deficits becomes unmanageably large, a point we return to in a later chapter.

Goals, Systems, Methods

We indicated in Chapter 12 that there are four ways of dealing with a disequilibrium in the foreign exchange market: change the price (exchange rate), shift the curves, ration foreign exchange, or draw on or accumulate reserves. Corresponding to each of these as a primary adjustment mechanism is an actual, historical, international monetary system that has been tried and has worked for some group of countries for some period of time. Each of these four systems will achieve, more or less, three of the goals set forth, at the expense of the fourth. The four systems are floating rates, the gold standard, exchange control, and the Bretton Woods system. For convenience the goals, methods, and systems are summarized in Table 15-1. This table is to be interpreted broadly; the adjustment mechanism is to be viewed as primary rather than exclusive, the sacrificed goal is never totally abandoned and the other three are never perfectly achieved.

The discussion of these four systems, with their adjustment mechanisms, strengths and weaknesses, and historical experience, will occupy the next four chapters. Before we proceed to examining systems, however, we need to summarize the nature of balance-of-payments adjustment mechanisms common to all systems.

ADJUSTMENT MECHANISMS

There are three automatic balance-of-payments adjustment mechanisms: price, income, and interest rates. Other adjustments come through deliberate policies designed to change tastes and preferences or to impose controls on the individual's freedom to make particular economic decisions.

The price adjustment mechanism is the specie flow process described earlier in this chapter, with all the modifications we have added in the aggregate demand and aggregate supply model. There is a definite linkage between domestic and foreign prices through the exchange rate, and when overall domestic prices rise relative to foreign price levels, there will be a response that tends to be self-correcting. Either the money supply will shrink through the specie flow process or its modern equivalent, the monetary base, or the exchange rate will depreciate. Either of these responses will move the balance of payments back in the direction of equilibrium. However, there will be some feedback to the domestic price level from the balance-of-payments response; in an aggregate demand-aggregate supply model, the increased exports and decreased imports will shift *AD* and *IS* to the right and thereby put more upward pressure on prices, partly undoing the beneficial effects of the money supply response and/or the devaluation. This is especially true under a floating rate system, because the money supply shrinkage under a fixed rate system limits the ability of aggregate demand to expand.

There will also be a response of capital flows to the price mechanism, although it is not clear which way it will go. Under a fixed rate system, a deficit in the balance of payments will put downward pressure on prices in the deficit country. This makes it cheaper for foreigners to invest, but it also means that the same investment can be made for fewer units of foreign currency, so the net effect on the total inflow of foreign exchange is uncertain. A country in the throes of deflation and presumably also falling income and employment may not be a very attractive place to invest. Under a variable rate system, the first two effects are present, but the deflation and unemployment are less likely to occur, so capital flows may show a more positive response to a depreciation.

To the extent that the monetary authorities offset the monetary base effects of a deficit in the balance of payments under a fixed rate system, the price adjustment mechanism will be greatly weakened. This was a major criticism of the Bretton Woods system.

The real income adjustment mechanism also follows logically from our earlier models. A balance-of-payments surplus will have a multiplier expansionary effect on the domestic economy. As imports expand in response to rising income, the current account surplus shrinks. A deficit, similarly, has a deflationary effect. Thus, the income effect also is an automatic correcting mechanism. Capital flows, however, are likely to be perverse, since capital is attracted to countries that are growing and expanding—the same ones that are experiencing export-led growth through a current account surplus. The income adjustment mechanism is largely a twentieth-century discovery and the income elasticities of import and export demand, discussed in the following paragraphs, are large enough for this mechanism to have considerable impact. Again, however, it can be frustrated by offsetting actions of the monetary and/or fiscal authorities, a frequent occurrence under the Bretton Woods system.

The interest adjustment mechanism is the most uncertain of the three in terms of direction and magnitude of its impact. A country experiencing a deficit can expect a fall in its relative price level and/or its exchange rate as well as a decline in its income level in the absence of intervention by the government. But what can it expect to happen to interest rates?

Interest rates in our previous models were a result of *IS-LM* interaction. A balance-of-payments deficit will shift *IS* to the left, lowering real interest rates. (Check Figure 15-3 if you have forgotten how this works.) However, the shrinkage of the money supply resulting from the payments deficit will shift *LM* to the left, restoring real interest rates. If interest rates are unchanged, there is no interest effect. So the impact of interest rate changes really depends on which shift (*IS* or *LM*) dominates, on whether the monetary authorities offset part or all of the monetary base effect of the balance-of-payments deficit, and on how the changes in income and prices affect nominal as well as real interest rates. When prices fall, nominal interest rates fall; under fixed exchange rates this will lead to a capital outflow, partly offsetting the corrective effect of the price adjustment mechanism. (Nominal interest rates will also fall under a variable exchange rate system, but the impact will be offset by the decline in the exchange rate.) Similarly, when income falls, real as well as nominal interest rates fall, with the same effects just described. Thus, the interest rate effect tends somewhat to frustrate the workings of the price and income mechanisms, but it is generally believed to be less powerful and also more transitory.

ELASTICITIES: EMPIRICAL EVIDENCE

How powerful are these effects—the income elasticities of import and export demand, the price elasticities, the feedback to the domestic price and income levels, and the responses of capital flow to interest rates? It is very difficult to give a precise answer to any of these questions, but approximate numbers are available as a composite of the empirical results of a number of different researchers using different methods and time periods.

The income elasticities of import demand (domestic income) and export demand (rest of world income) are mostly in excess of 1. The United States, for example, has an income elasticity of demand for imports in the neighborhood of 1.5.[4] The value of the multiplier is also estimated to be about

---

[4] Hendrik S. Houtthakker, and Stephen P. Magee, "Income and Price Elasticities in World Trade," *Review of Economics and Statistics,* vol. 51, no. 2 (May 1969) 111–125.

1.5 for the United States. This means that, if our initial imports were $100 billion and we experienced a $10 billion increase in domestic demand, the multiplier process would convert that to a $15 billion increase in income and ouput, and imports would rise by 1.5 × $15 billion = $22.5 billion. Such an increase is likely to have repercussions on the demand, income, and output in other countries, since they too have income elasticities of demand for imports in excess of 1, so there will be feedback to our exports. Nevertheless, with such a high income elasticity of import demand, policymakers are forced to consider the balance-of-payments impact of any expansionary fiscal policy.

Price elasticities are somewhat lower; as was pointed out in Chapter 12, with some exceptions they tend to cluster around the .5 level.[5] (These are short-run elasticities; long-run elasticities are probably higher.) The Marshall–Lerner condition for exchange market stability requires that the sum of import and export demand elasticity be greater than 1. Most current observers expect that this condition would normally be fulfilled, so that devaluation or depreciation tend to improve the balance of payments.

Finally, the feedback from the foreign sector to the domestic economy can be fairly substantial. We have already observed an income multiplier of about 1.5, which responds to changes in imports and exports. There is also a feedback to the price level from changes in the prices of internationally traded goods. This change is most likely to be observed in response to a devaluation or a revaluation, although it can also be found in response to changes in foreign prices. For the United States, the feedback to the domestic price level is variously estimated with a range from 10 percent to 40 percent. This means that a 10 percent devaluation of the dollar, making U.S. goods cheaper and imports more costly, will tend to increase the domestic price index by two percentage points.

No elasticity estimates are available for the response of capital flows to income changes, price level changes, interest rate differentials, or devaluations, but they are believed to respond to all four of these influences and particularly the last two. Capital flows undergo major adjustments following a devaluation for several reasons.

1.   Investors who had fled that currency in anticipation of its devaluation will now return, restoring their normal portfolio balance and obtaining the capital gain that they had "set up" by abandoning the currency initially. If, for example, I had owned pounds sterling in 1967, and had sold them before the November devaluation for $2.80 and repurchased them afterward for $2.40, I would have made a profit of $0.40, or 14 percent on each pound transferred and repurchased. This adjustment makes it very difficult to measure other influences on capital flows in the wake of a revaluation.

2.   A devaluation under a fixed rate system gives some assurance of future stability, since such actions are supposed to be relatively infrequent. This makes

[5] Ibid.

the recently devalued currency an attractive haven relative to some others that are due for devaluation soon.

3.   The devaluation makes it immediately cheaper to invest in that country, since it takes fewer units of foreign currency to purchase one of theirs, although the return on investment should be similarly affected.

4.   The devaluation itself will put upward pressure on prices and interest rates in the devaluing country, improving short-run profit prospects for direct investors (because of increased external and domestic demand for internationally tradable products in the devaluing country) and also attracting lenders with the higher nominal interest rates if further short-term devaluations are not expected.

There is, however, one offsetting influence. The devaluation imposes a capital loss on foreign holders of the devalued currency. This gives them less capital to invest in the devaluing country or elsewhere and may also make them more reluctant to invest abroad in any case.

SUMMARY

Chapter 15 completes our survey of the macroeconomic interactions between the domestic economy and the foreign sector. This chapter is concerned with prices and the monetary base in their relationship to the balance of payments as well as a survey of types of international monetary systems and a survey of the nature and empirical significance of automatic balance-of-payments adjustment mechanisms.

The specie flow mechanism is the classical view of the automatically self-correcting nature of the link among the balance of payments, the money supply, and the price level. Outflows of gold and silver contract the money supply, lowering prices and stimulating exports while discouraging imports. Inflows have the opposite effect. This process will tend to eliminate any deficits or surpluses that occur, unless the money supply change is frustrated by the monetary authorities.

The alternative price adjustment mechanism is a change in the exchange rate, which will also correct a deficit or surplus. The process is not quite so simple as adjusting the price of widgets to clear the market, because of the feedback effects on income, interest rates, and domestic price levels.

These two types of price adjustments were incorporated into the IS-LM model through the addition of an aggregate demand and aggregate supply schedule, which puts prices into what had been a fixed price model. Price changes shift the LM curve and also shift $X - M$ and possibly the K outflow curve (depending on whether exchange rates are fixed or variable). An increase in income in Chapter 14 created a current account deficit (or reduced the surplus). Now we find that it is associated with a rise in prices, which reinforces the tendency toward current account deficit.

This more complete model enabled us to observe the price-induced feedback effects from *IS-LM* shifts to domestic prices to $X - M$ and back to *IS*, partly offsetting the initial rise in aggregate demand. We also observed the impact of the monetary authority refusing to accommodate the shift in *IS* through expanding the money supply, which mitigates the impact on prices but drives up real interest rates and attracts a capital inflow.

The impact of shifts in *IS* and *LM*, including feedback effects from the balance of payments, depends on whether we are operating under a fixed or a variable exchange rate system. A variable rate system will tend to correct the balance of payments directly, but a depreciation will create inflationary pressures on the domestic economy that the government may choose to offset by fiscal and/or monetary actions.

All these considerations affect the choice of an international monetary system, since different systems will create different interactions between the foreign sector and the domestic economy. The four systems that have been used are floating rates, the gold standard, exchange control, and Bretton Woods. Each has a primary adjustment mechanism. The respective adjustment mechanisms are exchange rate changes, shifting supply and demand back into equilibrium through money supply changes, rationing, and drawing on or accumulating reserves. Each of the four accomplishes three major goals at the expense of the fourth. These goals (corresponding to each system as the respective goal sacrificed) are stable exchange rates, independence of monetary and fiscal policy, freedom of trade and capital movements, and balance-of-payments equilibrium.

The discussion of Chapters 14 and 15 enables us to identify some automatic correcting forces that are known as adjustment mechanisms and that function to some degree under all four systems. These are the income mechanism, the price mechanism, and the interest rate mechanism. All of them tend to operate (in the absence of deliberate intervention) so as to correct deficits. The price mechanism refers to either the adjustment of exchange rates or the adjustment of the domestic price level in response to a deficit or surplus, which tends to move exports and imports in the corrective direction. The income mechanism refers to the effects of a current account surplus or deficit on income and output, which also tends to react on imports in a corrective direction. For example, a current account deficit will depress income (through the multiplier process), which will tend to reduce imports.

The interest rate adjustment mechanism is the hardest to interpret, but a balance-of-payments deficit will tend to shrink the monetary base, raising real interest rates and correcting a capital outflow. The empirical effects of these corrective mechanisms appear to be substantial: income elasticities of import demand in excess of 1 in most cases and price elasticities in the range of .5 to 1 for both imports and exports. Interest elasticities are not available because of measurement problems.

Chapters 14 and 15 provide a reasonably complete macroeconomic framework for examining the working, advantages, disadvantages, and historical experience with the four alternative types of international monetary arrangements, which will occupy the next four chapters.

KEY TERMS

adjustment mechanisms
aggregate demand
aggregate supply
feedback effects
fixed exchange rates
flexible exchange rates
income elasticity of import demand
independent macroeconomic policy
international monetary systems
monetary base
nominal money supply
price elasticity of import and export demand
price level
real money supply
real versus nominal interest rates
specie flow mechanism
variable exchange rates

REVIEW QUESTIONS

1. All the models in this chapter were worked on a "one-way" basis, namely, an increase in aggregate demand or a devaluation. Go through the examples and rework them with alternate assumptions, for example, a decline in aggregate demand or a revaluation.
2. Suppose that Inlandia were running a balance-of-payments deficit. Identify the adjustment mechanisms and the effect on domestic prices, income, and interest rates if
    a. Inlandia has a variable exchange rate and the monetary authorities do not let the balance of payments affect the monetary base.
    b. Inlandia has a variable exchange rate and the monetary authorities do let the balance of payments affect the monetary base.
    c. Inlandia has a fixed exchange rate and the monetary authorities do not let the balance of payments affect the monetary base.
    d. Inlandia has a fixed exchange rate and the monetary authorities do let the balance of payments affect the monetary base.

3. Why are the values of the income and price elasticities so important to macroeconomic policy and to balance-of-payments policy?
4. Explain the relationship you would expect between nominal interest rates and the *K* curve under a fixed rate system; under a variable rate system.
5. Consider the four possible mixes of fixed versus variable exchange rates and cooperative versus offsetting monetary response. Under which combination do you expect the balance-of-payments adjustment mechanisms to be most effective? Least effective? Why?

SUGGESTED READINGS

DORNBUSCH, RUDIGER, *Open Economy Macroeconomics*. New York: Basic Books, 1980.

DORNBUSH, RUDIGER, and STANLEY FISCHER, *Macroeconomics*, 2nd ed., chap. 4. New York: McGraw-Hill, 1981.

DORNBUSH, RUDIGER, and JACOB A. FRENKEL, eds., *International Economic Policy: Theory and Evidence*. Baltimore, Md.: Johns Hopkins University Press, 1979. See the articles by Michael Mussa, Richard Levich, and Koichi Hamada.

FRENKEL, JACOB, and HARRY G. JOHNSON, *The Monetary Approach to the Balance of Payments*. Toronto: University of Toronto Press, 1976.

FRENKEL, JACOB A., and HARRY G. JOHNSON, *The Economics of Exchange Rates*, chaps. 2, 3, and 11. Reading, Mass.: Addison-Wesley, 1978.

GORDON, ROBERT J., *Macroeconomics*, 2nd ed., chaps. 3–4. Boston, Mass.: Little, Brown, 1981.

YEAGER, LELAND B., *International Monetary Relations*, 2nd ed., chaps. 4–6. New York: Harper & Row, 1976.

CHAPTER 16

Automatic Systems I:
The Gold Standard

INTRODUCTION

If it is possible to be nostalgic and sentimental about anything as unromantic as an international monetary system, then those words accurately describe the feelings many people still have about the international gold standard. This system evolved in the nineteenth century, was in full operation for only about 35 or 40 years, died in 1914, and was buried belatedly in 1935. Remnants of the gold standard held on until the late 1960s, but the likelihood of a significant number of the major industrial nations ever returning to gold or any other commodity-based international financial system in the immediate future is slim indeed.[1]

Why this romance with the gold standard? In part, it derives from its simplicity of operation and, in part, from the constraints it supposedly imposes on governments. As you recall from Chapter 15, each international monetary arrangement sacrifices one of the four goals we have postulated and achieves (more or less) the other three. The gold standard sacrifices independence of monetary and fiscal policy. Among those who not only

---

[1] There is, however, a strong and persuasive faction in the Reagan administration, as well as numerous conservative economists (including Arthur Laffer), who favor a return to the gold standard. See the section on the "gold buff" later in this chapter.

place little value on that independence, but even feel that it is undesirable for the government to pursue any kind of activist monetary or fiscal policy, this drawback of the gold standard turns into an advantage.

OPERATION OF THE GOLD STANDARD

To participate in the international gold standard, there were three simple rules a nation had to follow. These rules were never drawn up formally; rather, they evolved out of the practice instituted in England, the first nation to be on what was later called the gold standard.

First, the currency had to be defined in terms of its gold content. When the United States was on the gold standard in the late nineteenth and early twentieth centuries, the dollar was defined as 23.22 grains of pure gold (25.8 grains 11/12 fine), whereas the British pound was defined as 113 grains of pure gold (123.274 grains 11/12 fine). This was equivalent to $20.67 and £4.25 per ounce of gold. These ratios automatically established an exchange rate between the dollar and the pound sterling of $4.8665 (123.274/25.8). The same was true of any pair of countries that were both on the international gold standard.

Second, the money supply had to consist of gold or be tied to gold in some fixed (maximum) ratio. For the United States during that period, the ratio was 4:1—$1 worth of gold for every $4 of paper money in circulation. The ratio could fall below 4:1, but was not allowed to exceed that. (A true gold or commodity standard would call for a 1:1 ratio, that is, all paper money in circulation fully backed by gold. This, however, was not practical in the absence of substantial downward price flexibility because there was not enough gold to meet the normal currency needs for everyday transactions.)

Third, the government must stand willing to buy gold from anyone and to sell gold to anyone at that fixed price. This ensured that the price of gold set by the government would, in fact, be the actual price at which transactions in gold took place and would, therefore, also guarantee the fixed exchange rate between this currency and all other gold standard currencies.

If a country followed these rules, any deficits or surpluses in the balance of payments would be automatically self-correcting through the specie flow mechanism without any adjustment of exchange rates. The only variations in exchange rates should occur as the result of changes in the cost of shipping gold from one country to another. Figure 16-1 illustrates the exchange market under the gold standard, where for simplicity we have assumed that the dollar price of the pound (determined by the gold content of each) is $5 and that it costs $0.15 to ship £1 worth or $5 worth of gold between the United States and England.

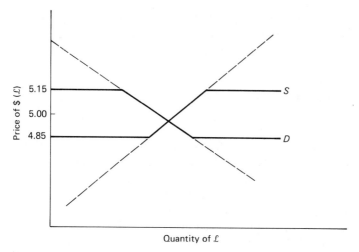

FIGURE 16-1   The Foreign Exchange Market Under the Gold Standard

The exchange market is initially in equilibrium and looks deceptively like the foreign exchange markets in Chapter 12. However, a large part of both the supply curve and demand curve is irrelevant. If either curve were to shift, so that equilibrium price were above $5.15 or below $4.85, the price would no longer be allowed to clear the market. Instead, gold would flow from one country to another to ensure that the price remained between $4.85 and $5.15 (the *gold points*). The "irrelevant" portions of the supply curve and demand curve are shown as dashed lines in Figure 16-1, and solid black lines at $4.85 and $5.15 mark the boundaries of possible exchange rates.[2]

How are the gold flows brought about? Suppose there were a shift in the demand curve to D_2, as is illustrated in Figure 16-2. The shift in demand for pounds represents an increase in the demand for British goods for any of the reasons suggested in Chapter 12. The equilibrium price rises to $5.30. At the old equilibrium price of $5.00, there is now a gap of *AB* between quantity supplied and quantity demanded, putting upward pressure on the price. The price rises to $5.15 as Americans, attempting to buy more British goods, bid the pound up. But $5.15 is the upper limit, because no sensible American will pay more than he or she has to for a British pound. If the asking price rose to, say, $5.20, it would be cheaper for the American to purchase $5.00 worth of gold from the government, ship it to England at a cost of $0.15, and redeem it at the bank of England for a British pound. Thus, as the currency price reaches its upper limit, gold flows into the country. This upper limit is thus known as the gold import point.

Similarly, a shift in supply or demand that would push the price of the

[2] The government could charge more to sellers and less to buyers than the official price to cover its transactions cost. We ignore this possibility in this discussion.

pound below $4.85 would lead to an outflow of gold once the price of the pound reached the lower limit, known as the gold export point. No intelligent Englishman would sell his pound for less than $4.85 when he could exchange it for an ounce of gold, ship it to the United States for $0.15, and redeem it there for $5.00.

What has happened to the supply and demand gap of *AB?* A small part of it (*AC* plus *DB*) was eliminated by the rise in the price of the pound from $5.00 to $5.15. The remainder was accounted for by the inflow of gold from the United States in the amount (measured in British pounds) of *CD*.

Clearly, we have not yet encountered the automatic correcting mechanism, because at this rate, the United States is going to run out of gold while Britain is swimming in American gold. We need to invoke rule 2 (having already used rule 1 to determine exchange rates and rule 3 to keep the exchange rate within limits) of the international gold standard to explain how equilibrium is restored. The gold flows are a short-run solution, but rule 2 provides a longer-term solution.

When gold flows into England, according to rule 2, the British money supply should expand, driving up prices. The supply and demand curves for foreign exchange are drawn on the assumption that domestic prices (as well as many other variables) are given, so that along each of these curves the only price that is allowed to vary is the exchange rate. When domestic prices rise in Britain, British exports become less attractive to Americans and they switch to domestic substitutes. American goods become cheaper relative to higher-priced British goods in Britain, and the British increase their import

FIGURE 16-2   Gold Flows Under the Gold Standard

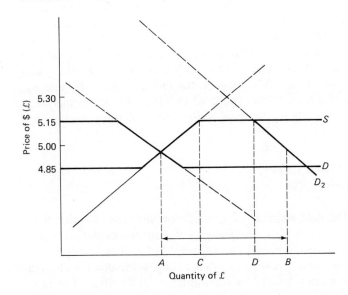

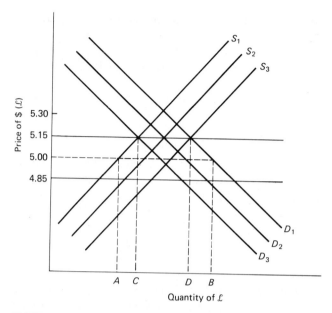

FIGURE 16-3   The Specie Flow Mechanism in Operation

demand. The first effect shifts the demand for pounds back to the left. The second shifts the supply of pounds out to the right.

The effects of gold flows in England are reinforced by events in the United States, where gold is flowing out and the money supply is shrinking. American prices are falling, so that Americans are further encouraged to substitute domestic for foreign goods while the British are even more inclined to substitute imports for their domestic goods. This leads to an additional leftward shift in demand and rightward shift in supply. In Figure 16-3, the demand and supply curves in the initial disequilibrium situation are labeled D_1 and S_1; when the British money supply expands, they shift to D_2 and S_2; when the U.S. money supply contracts, the curves shift to D_3 and S_3. Lo and behold, we are back within the gold points; equilibrium has been restored simply by adhering to the three simple rules of the gold standard game.

A MONETARIST PERSPECTIVE
ON THE GOLD STANDARD

This description of the gold standard would call for some qualification from a monetarist perspective. A balance-of-payments surplus or deficit would be interpreted as an excess demand for or supply of money, arising from newly mined gold, economic growth, or other changes, including an expansion of the domestic money supply by the monetary authorities. The price changes resulting from specie flow would induce an appropriate quantity response in exports and imports; for example, a deficit creates an outflow of specie, lowering the money supply and prices, expanding exports and contracting imports until the money supply and prices are restored to the original level. Thus, not only deficits and surpluses but also price level changes are self-correcting. This would be reinforced by temporary interest rate changes inducing capital flows to assist in what is a short-term adjustment process.

One qualification to this view stems from the size of countries relative to the rest of the world. A small country is tied to the world price level; its monetary expansion, deficit, price adjustments, and so on will ultimately wind up with no discernible change in volume of exports and imports, prices, or money supply. A large country, however, may be "home" to a significant fraction of the world's money supply, and its money supply and price level changes can change the size of the world money supply and the level of world prices as its "new money" flows out via the balance of payments.

As we discussed in earlier chapters, this view rests heavily on the law of one price; the absence of barriers to flows of goods, capital, and information; and in general, a high degree of integration and responsiveness in all markets. The more traditional view is based on some degree of market segmentation and thus envisions persistent price differentials as a possible outcome.

A PRELIMINARY EVALUATION

The gold standard has both advantages and disadvantages, which will become even clearer as we examine alternative systems. First, it provides stability of exchange rates, which encourages trade by removing a major source of uncertainty in contracts where there may be a fairly long lapse between contract and delivery and also between delivery and payment. Exchange rates should not normally wander outside the very narrow confines set by the gold points, which, in turn, are determined by the costs of shipping gold between countries.

Second, and closely related, it promotes freedom of trade and capital movements, both because of stable exchange rates and because governments do not need to impose restrictions for balance-of-payments reasons.

Third, the gold standard provides an automatic balance-of-payments adjustment mechanism through the specie flow process, so that large and persistent deficits should not normally occur.[3] These first three advantages correspond to three of the four goals in Chapter 15.

---

[3] Newly discovered gold or excess demand for money will create deficits and surpluses, respectively, until, once again, money supply is adjusted to money demand.

In addition, there are some other advantages. For those who place a high value on the use of the market and minimize the role of government in the marketplace, this system does much to accomplish that end. Furthermore, when changes occur, they tend to be incremental rather than massive (such as imposing controls or a one-shot devaluation), giving the economy a chance to adjust on a marginal basis rather than responding to a "shock."

This system provides balance-of-payments discipline on inflation-prone governments. The ability of government to run deficits by inflating the money supply and thus debasing the currency is severely restricted by the automatic gold outflows and monetary restraint that inflation creates. In the first place, the capacity to expand the money supply is restricted by the gold available. In the second place, the inflation that results shifts the supply of the currency outward and the demand for the currency inward in response to rising domestic prices. This creates a balance-of-payments deficit, a gold outflow, and a monetary contraction, restoring the original price level and money supply.

Finally, a system that links money supplies closely among countries provides a cushion for localized recessions, as the contraction spills over into imports, sharing some of the contraction with the rest of the world and reducing the localized impact. (The rest of the world might not regard this transmission of fluctuations quite so benevolently, however!)

What about the drawbacks? Some of the drawbacks are advantages viewed from a different perspective; most of the others arise from problems with the gold base. The stability of exchange rates, for example, can also be viewed as complete inflexibility. The exchange rate becomes a "Procrustes' bed"[4] to which the economy must be fitted by stretching or lopping. Regardless of how much deflation is required, or how long it takes, or how much pain and suffering in lost employment and output occurs in the interim, the gold standard calls for returning to the original parity when some disturbance shifts the economy out of equilibrium. Yet that parity itself is largely arbitrary, a number that was picked out of nowhere and that reflects neither the cost of production of gold (since existing stocks dwarf new production) nor the value of gold in its nonmonetary uses. (Commodity demands for gold tended to be very small relative to monetary uses during the heyday of the gold standard).

Second, the twentieth century saw the rise of the major opposition force to the gold standard—Keynesian and neo-Keynesian economics—which called for an activist role for government in determining output, employment, prices, and interest rates that would be impossible under the gold standard. Those who believe in significant government involvement in de-

---

[4] Procrustes, according to Greek legend, was hospitable to visitors, but insisted that they exactly fit the bed, by either stretching the body to fit the bed or by lopping off the excess person at the feet or head.

termining the aggregate level of output through monetary and fiscal policy would have to reject the gold standard, under which the money supply is determined by gold flows. An activist, expansionary fiscal or monetary policy would be frustrated by balance-of-payments deficits leading to monetary contraction.

Essentially, both objections imply that the domestic economy should be allowed to pursue its own course without domination by the foreign sector or the rest of the world. Classical gold standard advocates as well as some contemporary monetarists would argue that this is not possible under fixed exchange rates, where there is essentially a world money supply flowing from country to country in response to differentials in inflation rates and real interest rates. Modern gold standard advocates and some of the more conservative contemporary monetarists would argue that isolation of the domestic economy is not only impossible but also undesirable—the "balance-of-payments-discipline-on-inflationary-governments" argument.

Certainly for major upheavals—wars, revolutions, widespread natural disasters—the gold standard had no built-in device for adjusting payments imbalances; rather, it relied on the tried and true specie flow mechanism when other responses might have been more appropriate. In reality, countries often responded to such catastrophes by suspending the gold standard, and later restoration of the gold standard at an altered parity was not uncommon.

A closely related objection again is one of the advantages viewed from a different perspective—the transmission of fluctuations from one country to another through gold and the money supply. While we suggested that this was an advantage by providing a cushion for the country where the fluctuation originated, it can also be regarded as allowing one country to impose either inflation or recession on the rest of the world. The expression "when the United States sneezes, the rest of the world catches pneumonia" dates from a later period, but it captures the idea behind this criticism of the gold standard. Many individuals prefer a system that contains fluctuations within the originating country, both allowing and requiring that country to deal with its business cycle in its own way.

Many of the flaws in the gold standard are related to its base. There is a finite stock of gold available already mined or still underground. In the absence of new gold discoveries or improvements in mining, obtaining the gold in the ground is subject to increasing marginal costs. As the marginal cost of gold mining rises, while the price of gold remains fixed, the incentive to mine diminishes and the gold stock ceases to grow. As with the inevitable logic of Malthus on population, the day of reckoning can be postponed by new discoveries and/or by improvements in gold mining technology. The former was the salvation of the gold standard in the nineteenth century with new discoveries in California, Colorado, Alaska, Russia, South Africa, and Canada. If the monetary base fails to grow, while both the parities and money supply-gold ratio are fixed and unvarying, then the result of growth in population, income, and output is deflation, which is usually painful, often accompanied by bank failures, monetary crises, and unemployment. (Conversely, new gold discoveries can set off worldwide inflation, as was true not only of some of the nineteenth-century discoveries, but also of Spain's influx of gold from the New World in the fifteenth and sixteenth centuries.)

The problems created by the eventual slowdown in the growth of the monetary base are compounded by the demand for gold for other uses, principally jewelry, dentistry, industrial uses, and private hoarding. By the late 1960s in the United States, the first three of these four uses were demanding more than the total annual new production, with nothing left for either public holdings or private hoards. If inflation were possible, the fixed price of gold would make it increasingly attractive in private uses as a substitute for other metals whose prices were rising. Even without inflation (which should not persist under the gold standard), the demand for gold is still fairly income elastic and sensitive to population increases. Also, if the metals used as substitutes for gold are subject to increasing marginal extraction costs, and as a result their prices rise relative to the fixed price of gold, demand will shift to gold, putting upward pressure on the market price and depleting the monetary base.

A final drawback, which we shall see is shared by the Bretton Woods system, is that the gold standard puts greater corrective pressure on deficit than on surplus countries if the money supply-gold ratio is greater than 1. A gold outflow will force a multiple contraction of the money supply, especially if the money supply is already at its upper limit (in the case of the United States, at four times the value of the monetary gold stock), but a gold inflow merely permits a multiple expansion of the money supply. The money supply need not expand by the full amount permitted.

INTEREST AND INCOME
EFFECTS

The models of our preceding chapters suggest that there would have been some additional forces at work under the gold standard besides the price effects of the specie flow mechanism. In particular, there would have been income and interest rate effects.

The income effects of gold flows would have reinforced the price effects, so that prices would not have to rise or fall as much as our model indicated to restore balance-of-payments equilibrium. The monetary expansion in the surplus country would have increased income and output, and since import demand is highly income elastic, imports would have risen sharply, shifting currency supply to the right and currency demand to the left. In the deficit country, the opposite would occur. With both price and income effects at work, the adjustment mechanism would have been fairly strong when it was permitted to operate (i.e., when the money supply was permitted to expand or contract in response to gold flows).

The interest rate effect works in the opposite direction and accounts for the fact that actual gold flows were relatively modest under the gold standard. As the money supply contracts, interest rates tend to rise, attracting an inflow of capital (and gold) from abroad. This restores the balance-of-payments equilibrium with a relatively small change in the gold stock in the deficit country and a relatively modest change in the money supply. For relatively small shifts in supply and demand, these three adjustment mechanisms worked fairly well. It was the large shifts caused by major upheavals and the long-run slow growth of the monetary base that were the downfall of the gold standard.

It might appear that interest rates acted to frustrate the adjustment mechanism, when, in fact, they both mitigated and reinforced the effects of the price and income adjustment mechanisms. In the short run, capital inflows slowed the contraction of the money supply. Higher interest rates, however, had a dampening effect on demand, and this meant falling income and prices, so that the adjustment mechanism was still operative. The adjustment mechanisms of the gold standard had the potential to deal effectively with moderate shifts in supply and demand. It was not uncommon, however, for monetary authorities to sterilize the effects of gold flows on the money supply, particularly in the upward direction.

THE GOLD STANDARD
IN PRACTICE

One myth about the gold standard is the widely held belief that it dates back to antiquity, or at least to the late Middle Ages. It is true that a monetary system in which the money supply consisted of gold and/or silver or which included paper money that was redeemable in gold or silver has a long history, but this is not equivalent to an international gold standard that requires adhering to all three rules of the game. Britain was the first country to go on a full gold standard in 1821, with adequate gold reserves to redeem its currency both domestically and internationally in gold on demand and a legal commitment to do so. Most of the rest of the countries of the developed world at that time, including the United States, were on either a bimetallic standard or an inconvertible paper standard. Some, including India, were on a silver standard.

The impetus toward establishing an international gold standard came from the major gold discoveries of the midnineteenth century, with gold finds in California, Colorado, Alaska, Australia, Canada, South Africa, and Russia. This expansion of the gold stock made it possible for countries to acquire enough reserves to go on and stay on a gold standard without undue deflationary pressures.

By 1870, England was fully on gold, and several other countries that were nominally bimetallic were, in fact, on gold, because the price of gold had fallen relative to the price of silver. Countries that had recently experienced wars and revolutions—Russia, Austria-Hungary, Italy, and the United States—were on inconvertible paper standards. The United States had been moving in the direction of a gold standard when her progress was interrupted by the Civil War. The United States finally went on the gold standard at the pre–Civil War parity of the dollar in 1879. Thus, the heyday of the gold standard was the relatively brief period 1879–1914, a mere 35 years. (As we note later, this is precisely the period for which the Bretton Woods system functioned—1946–1971, or 35 years.)

London functioned as the financial center of the gold standard, with the pound sterling used to settle third-party transactions and much international banking being centered in London. The British bank rate (the rate at which the Bank of England lent to commercial banks, which, in turn, influenced the whole structure of interest rates) dominated interest rates around the world. When Britain suffered a recession, it was transmitted to the rest of the world through the international financial system.

The gold standard did not function in the precise fashion suggested by textbooks. Checking account money developed in a number of countries in the late nineteenth century, including Britain and the United States, loosening the established ratio between gold and the money supply. Various devices were available to discourage gold outflows, such as interest-free loans by the central bank or redemption of British notes offered by foreigners in sovereigns (British gold coins) instead of gold bars or foreign gold coins, which was an inconvenience. Worn sovereigns were even offered at some times, which when melted would yield less than their supposed gold content. Other countries followed similar practices to discourage gold outflows.

Yeager[5] also points out that some of the undesirable features of later systems were present from time to time in the gold standard prior to World War I. These include destabilizing speculation, hot-money movements, attacks on currency forcing departure from the gold standard, concern about short-term debt and reserve adequacy, and calls for better international cooperation among national monetary authorities.

The gold standard functioned relatively well during this period because of several circumstances: the expansion of the gold stock from newly discovered gold, the absence of any major disturbances (wars, revolutions, or prolonged depressions), a somewhat greater tolerance of governments for

---

[5] Leland Yeager, *International Monetary Relations*, 2nd ed. (New York: Harper & Row, 1976). Chapters 15–17 contain an excellent discussion of the history of the gold standard.

letting the balance of payments influence the money supply, and (perhaps) a greater downward flexibility of prices, so that deflation fell more heavily on prices and less on output and employment. In terms of the aggregate supply and demand model of Chapter 15, this means that the aggregate supply curve would be more nearly vertical.

The immediate effect of the outbreak of World War I on the gold standard was that the risk of shipping gold across the Atlantic rose sharply, so that gold flows were not feasible. This was followed shortly by a gradual disintegration of the gold standard in Europe as monetary expansion became necessary to finance the war. In England, the obligation to buy and sell gold remained legally in force until 1939 but did not function in practice. Only the United States was in a position to continue to observe the rules of the game in a literal sense, and even there restrictions were imposed on both redemption of paper currency domestically and outflows of gold.

By the end of the war, there was a significant realignment of equilibrium currency values, even on a simple purchasing power parity basis. Inflation over the four-year period had expanded money supplies among major European nations from 70 to 400 percent and prices had risen by 200 to 300 percent. There were two alternatives to deal with this problem. The gold standard rules would suggest that each country reduce its money supply sufficiently to restore the price level and, therefore, the equilibrium price of its currency to the prewar level, and then return to the full gold standard. This required a willingness to tolerate deflation and unemployment, which a war-weary populace and the weak governments of the time were not willing to accept. The alternative was a major currency realignment.

The United States, which had suffered least, was able to return to a full gold standard in 1919. However, the early 1920s saw hyperinflation in Germany, Poland, Russia, Austria, and Hungary, further distorting currency relationships. Most countries attempted to restore the gold standard at a new par value, several of which eventually appeared to be undervalued. Britain insisted on returning to the prewar parity of the pound in 1925, which was preceded by several years of deflation. Even that deflation was not sufficient, especially in the light of the adjustment of other currency prices downward, and Britain suffered through an extended period of stagnation and unemployment in the 1920s because of the overvalued pound.

The final demise of the gold standard was precipitated by the worldwide depression of the 1930s. Countries responded to the sharp fall in income and employment in three ways: tariffs to replace imports with domestic production (including the Smoot–Hawley Tariff of 1930 in the United States), suspension of gold convertibility both domestically and abroad, and devaluation. The suspension of gold convertibility was not only to stop the erosion of the monetary base and the resulting shrinkage of the money supply, but also was a prelude to devaluation. The government rather than private gold holders thus profited from the devaluation, which meant a rise in the official price of gold. The devaluation complemented tariffs as a way to promote exports and discourage imports for employment reasons.

While the depression finished off the remnants of the gold standard, it had been deteriorating in the 1920s. Increasingly, governments were offsetting the effects of gold flows on the money supply rather than permitting them to work their effects through deflation. The linkage between the money supply and gold had never been as clear cut as the rules of the game implied, particularly since the evolution of checking accounts. The Federal Reserve Act, for example, required a 40 percent ratio of gold to Federal Reserve notes (reduced to 25 percent in 1945 and eliminated entirely in 1967), but the actual ratio of M_1 (money supply = currency + demand deposits) to gold was generally much higher than the implied 2.5:1. As the adjustment mechanism was weakened, balance-of-payments deficits and surpluses persisted for longer periods, weakening enthusiasm for the gold standard and prompting a search for alternatives. This culminated in the establishment of the Bretton Woods system in 1946. The United States experienced gold inflows in the 1920s, but the Federal Reserve did not allow these inflows to lead to proportionate expansion of the money supply. Other countries responded similarly to gold outflows, particularly after the onset of the depression.

The United States was the last country to leave the gold standard. As other countries departed from gold, the United States remained the only country redeeming its currency for gold. Those who reacted to the international crisis by hoarding gold found the United States to be the only available supplier, and the United States began to experience a gold outflow. In 1933, the United States suspended the gold convertibility of the dollar, prohibited private ownership of gold in the United States, and revalued gold from $20.67 to $35.00 an ounce. The United States did, however, continue to redeem dollars for gold internationally after 1935.

THE ROLE OF MONETARY GOLD SINCE 1935

Gold has continued to play an important international monetary role and, in some countries, a domestic role as well. Once the devaluation was accomplished, the United States resumed the redemption of dollars from foreigners, public and private, in gold. American citizens were still not permitted to hold gold, a regulation not changed until 1975, after the second dollar devaluation. The United States retained the gold cover behind the principal form of U.S. currency, Federal Reserve notes. (The other form of currency, silver certificates, was backed by silver until the 1960s.) The

40 percent gold ratio was reduced to 25 percent in 1945. The ratio also applied to deposits at the Federal Reserve, which meant that the effective ratio of gold to M_1 was on the order of 10 percent. (Currency is roughly 25 percent of the money supply and demand deposits about 75 percent. The 25 percent reserve gold cover behind currency and a 25 percent gold backing behind reserves, which, in turn, were about one-sixth of deposits, gives a total gold-to-M_1 ratio of $.25 \times .25 + .75 \times .25 \times .17 = .0938$.) This gold cover was finally eliminated entirely in the 1960s when it was felt necessary to free the gold to settle international payments.

A second role for gold in the postwar period was as a major component of international reserves in the newly created International Monetary Fund. This reserve pool, which we discuss in detail in Chapter 19, consisted of gold and currencies on which members could draw to settle a balance-of-payments deficit. Gold and dollars quickly became the two media of exchange in widespread use.

At the end of World War II, the world monetary gold stock was about $35 billion, or 1 billion ounces at $35 an ounce. This was nearly 70 percent of total international financial reserves available to meet balance-of-payments deficits, the rest consisting of holdings of other countries' currencies and drawing rights at the International Monetary Fund. The monetary gold stock grew very slowly thereafter, as purchases by private hoarders and industrial/commercial users absorbed most of the limited supply of newly mined gold. Increases in reserves were provided by dollars and by expansion of the I.M.F. resources in the form of national currencies.

The role of monetary gold was even more important than the 70 percent figure might indicate, because much of the rest of foreign exchange reserves consisted of U.S. dollars, the only major currency still redeemable to foreigners on demand for gold. It was possible for the United States to maintain gold convertibility because at the end of the war two-thirds of the world's monetary gold stock had found its way into the coffers of the American central bank. The dollar was thus the basis of the gold exchange standard. Rather than hold reserves in gold, many countries held reserves in dollars as direct claims to gold, which enabled the American gold to be "counted" twice—once as U.S. exchange reserves and once as reserves behind the reserves of other countries that were held in dollars.

The same problems that had surfaced under the gold standard proper persisted. The gold supply could not grow fast enough at a fixed price to keep up with the growing volume of trade that resulted from growth in world income and population, as well as inflation in many instances. Using gold alongside dollars really just disguised the problem, because willingness to hold dollars depended on the size of the U.S. gold stock relative to the number of dollars outstanding. Thus, gold was still indirectly limiting the growth of reserves. Raising the price of gold was suggested as a possible solution, but that too had several drawbacks:

1. It eliminated the stability and predictability of the price of the most basic asset, gold, which was the foundation of both the gold standard and the Bretton Woods system.
2. It distributed capital gains to those who had chosen to stick with gold as an asset rather than cooperate with the new system and hold a portfolio of assets that was weighted heavily with other currencies, especially dollars.
3. Anticipation of revaluation of gold will lead to private, speculative hoarding, increasing the scarcity of official gold that the system is trying to escape.
4. A large part of the gains would have accrued to South Africa and the Soviet Union, which would have been politically unpopular.

The partially gold-based system hit serious difficulties in the 1960s. The first sign was in 1960, when the price of gold rose temporarily above its official price in the London gold market, from $35 to $43 an ounce. As the United States found it increasingly difficult to hold down the price of gold by sales, the London Gold Pool, a group of six countries organized to maintain the official price of gold, was formed in 1961–1962. In the interim, the United States eliminated its gold cover behind the domestic money supply, freeing its shrinking gold reserves for international use.

In anticipation of the British devaluation in late 1967, the level of activity on the London gold market hit an all-time high, and gold disappeared rapidly from official coffers into private hoards. In 1968, the participants in the London Gold Pool announced that they would no longer attempt to maintain the official price of gold in private markets. Gold would continue to be traded internationally among central banks at $35 an ounce, but no longer would central banks (through the London Gold Pool) attempt to maintain the private market price of gold at $35 or any other official price. They would neither buy nor sell from private gold traders. This caused momentary—and as it developed, unfounded—panic in South Africa, the major new gold producer, which feared that the elimination of monetary uses of gold would depress the market price below $35 an ounce. This development was known as the "two-tiered gold market"—one price for official transactions and another (market determined) for private sales and purchases.

The private price of gold has undergone significant fluctuations since that time, with a high of over $1,000 an ounce. As might be expected, rising prices have called forth an increase in supply, moderating the rise in price. Some of the demand is for industrial-commercial uses, but much is speculative, anticipating a restoration of the gold standard, a collapse of present international monetary arrangements, or just sufficient "bandwagon" demand by other speculators to keep the price high, although it has fallen considerably from its mid-1970s peak.

The United States took the final step in demonetization of gold by permitting U.S. citizens to hold gold again in 1975 for the first time in 40 years. The U.S. Treasury, as well as the International Monetary Fund, have sold off some of their monetary gold stock on an auction basis, largely as a symbolic gesture to underscore the "dethronement" of gold. The devaluation of the U.S. dollar in 1971 was preceded by a four-month suspension of gold convertibility with other central banks. Since 1973, that obligation has been waived permanently.

What is the present role of monetary gold? The official view is that gold is but one in a spectrum of international assets including foreign exchange, short-term claims of various kinds, and regular and special drawing rights at the International Monetary Fund that may be used to support the price of one's currency. Under floating exchange rates, the need for reserves is less pressing, although the managed floating rules that govern present operations do create some need for reserves. But the attempt to dethrone gold has met with considerable resistance. As late as the mid-1960s, one major nation—France under de Gaulle—was calling for a return to the international gold standard. In the United States, there is a powerful political minority still advocating the same goal, largely to put constraints on activist and deficit-prone governments.

The speculation that eliminating the monetary role for gold would depress its price proved false. Gold has had a long history of being money in the mind of mankind, and that view will not be changed easily, despite the obvious production cost advantages of paper money. Private speculative demand has more than taken up the slack left by official monetary demand, so that, while gold has receded considerably from its high of over $1,000 an ounce, it still commands a significantly higher price than it did in its official monetary days.

THE GOLD BUFFS

There are numerous organized groups in the United States who advocate a return to the international gold standard, ranging from the far right fringe to some thoughtful academics, politicians, and business people. These are individuals who are disillusioned with the past 45 years of activist fiscal and monetary policy, mistrustful of the excesses of democratic government. They would like to impose some external constraints on what they regard as a rather freewheeling political system. These are also people who value long-term price stability more highly than short-run full employment. Some of the advocates of a return to gold argue that price stability is necessary to encourage capital formation and that capital formation is necessary for economic growth. Economic growth, in turn, creates both employment and income for the poor who are the supposed beneficiaries of short-run, inflationary full-employment policies. (This venerable viewpoint, academically respectable in most circles although not universally agreed to, has recently been rechristened supply-side economics.)

Most of the new gold standard advocates would revalue gold before returning to the gold standard, providing ample reserves for the new system. They do not deal with the problem of future reserve growth or the difficulties of a unilateral gold standard in a world that is prone to inflationary policies. They do represent a valid alternative viewpoint to the interventionist policies of the last several decades, although there are other opponents of such government intervention who do not advocate a return to gold.

SUMMARY

The first of the four types of international monetary systems to be considered is the international gold standard, which evolved in the nineteenth century, held sway from 1879 to 1914, and died a lingering death between 1914 and 1935. The gold standard has a great deal of intuitive appeal because it is simple and automatic and has a built-in corrective mechanism for balance-of-payments deficits and surpluses.

Nations on the gold standard must define their currency in terms of gold content, tie their money supplies to gold in some fixed ratio, and be willing to buy and sell their currency for gold and vice versa to anyone on demand. If these rules are followed, then balance-of-payments deficits and surpluses will be self-correcting; a deficit will lead to a gold outflow and a surplus to a gold inflow, which will change the monetary base, the money supply, and the price level. A deficit, gold outflow, monetary contraction, and fall in the price level will stimulate exports and contract imports; a surplus has the opposite effect. The result of the gold flow price mechanism is to shift the supply and demand curves back into equilibrium at the old parity price.

The price mechanism is reinforced by the income effects, with an expanding money supply raising income and imports and a shrinking money supply reducing income and imports. The initial shrinkage (expansion) of the money supply will also raise (lower) interest rates, leading to a corrective capital inflow (outflow). The capital flow will also have an effect on income and prices, which reinforces the initial effect of the gold outflow or inflow.

The gold standard provides stable exchange rates, freedom of trade and capital movements, and balance-of-payments equilibrium at the expense of independence of monetary and fiscal policy. It minimizes the role of government in international finance, leads to incremental rather than to massive adjustments, and provides some discipline for otherwise inflation-prone governments. Finally, it provides a cushion for local recessions and inflations by transmitting them through gold flows to the rest of the world.

Most of the drawbacks are advantages from a different viewpoint—

invest in gold. Outline the considerations that would enter into your decision.

SUGGESTED READINGS

ALIBER, ROBERT Z., *The International Money Game,* 2nd ed., chap. 5. New York: Basic Books, 1976.

FRENKEL, JACOB, and HARRY JOHNSON, *The Monetary Approach to the Balance of Payments,* chap. 16. Toronto: University of Toronto Press, 1976.

MACHLUP, FRITZ, *International Payments, Debts, and Gold,* part 3. New York: Scribner, 1964.

TRIFFIN, ROBERT, *Our International Monetary System: Yesterday, Today, and Tomorrow,* chap. 1. New Haven, Conn.: Yale University Press, 1968.

YEAGER, LELAND B., *International Monetary Relations: Theory, History, and Policy,* 2nd ed., chaps. 15–17. New York: Harper & Row, 1976.

CHAPTER 17

Automatic Systems II:
Floating Exchange Rates

INTRODUCTION

This chapter is devoted to the system that prevails presently and its close relatives—free float, managed float, partial float, dirty float, and other variants on a primarily market-determined exchange rate. As yet, our limited experience with floating exchange rates makes it difficult to judge the real world effectiveness of such a system, which was advocated by a significant number of academic economists long before its widespread adoption in 1973. Prior experience was limited: some floating was used as a temporary device in the serach for a new parity in earlier periods, especially during the Great Depression, and Canada had floated unilaterally from 1952 to 1963. But a widespread, managed float such as the major industrial countries have supported since 1973 is a new phenomenon. It has taught us much about how the textbook model of floating exchange rates operates in the real world.

OPERATION OF FLOATING
RATES

The floating rate system is the easiest of the four to understand, because it is a simple supply and demand model that puts the entire adjustment burden on one price—the exchange rate. In a pure float, any force that shifts the supply or demand curve—inflation, economic growth, drought, earthquake, dock strike, speculation, interest rate changes—will shift the exchange rate in response. There is no distinction between basic balance and overall balance. If a shift creates a disequilibrium, market forces are allowed to correct the disequilibrium by adjusting the currency price.

In practice, particularly recent practice, governments are unwilling to tolerate quite that much volatility in exchange rates and will quietly intervene to buy and sell foreign exchange in attempts to stabilize the price. The I.M.F. has, in fact, developed guidelines for appropriate intervention that specify that such interventions should be directed toward moving the currency in the direction of what is perceived as the equilibrium price. Such a system is called a managed float. A dirty float is an apparent free float with under-the-counter intervention by the government not openly acknowledged and not necessarily in the direction that the market might indicate to be appropriate. A partial float is a single country or a minority of the I.M.F. member countries floating while the majority adhere to fixed rates. Finally, there is the system under which a small number of major country currencies are under a managed float and a larger number of other countries tie the price of their currencies to one of the floating major country currencies, most commonly the dollar. This is the present system, which, for lack of a better name, we designate as the "modified float."

Figure 17-1 illustrates the effects of exchange rate depreciation on the balance of payments and on prices, employment, interest rates, output and prices. The depreciation of the currency shifts the $X - M$ curve to the right to $(X - M)'$, since the change in the exchange rate stimulates exports and discourages imports. The $X - M$ shift also shifts the BB curve to the right to BB', so that for the same interest rate the balance of payments will now be in balance at a higher income level. At the same time the $X - M$ shift has a smaller shift effect on the IS curve, since $(X - M)$ is a component of aggregate demand. IS also shifts to the right to IS', and aggregate demand shifts to AD', driving up output, employment, interest rates, and the price level.

The higher domestic price level will have a feedback effect on the $X - M$ curve, shifting it back to the left. The backward shift will never be enough to offset the initial shift, because the foreign sector is usually small relative to the total economy and the impact of the exchange rate change is diffused. Note that at the higher interest rate the capital account balance also improves.

Thus we can conclude that the depreciation of the exchange rate will move the balance of payments in the correct direction, but because of feedback effects through the domestic economy, the exchange rate cannot instantaneously and continuously guarantee balance-of-payments equilibrium.

The diagram, in fact, illustrates an overcorrection—at the initial levels

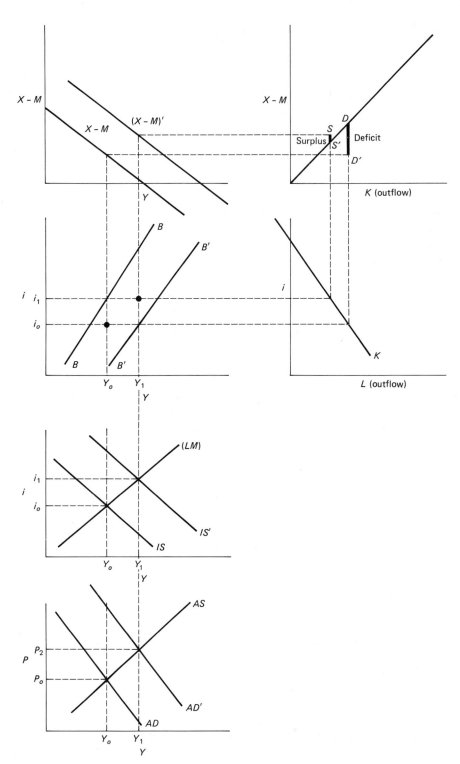

FIGURE 17-1 Impact of Exchange Rate Depreciation

of Y and i, the balance of payments was in deficit, but at the new combination Y_1, i_1, the balance of payments is in surplus. (Check through the diagram to measure the surplus or deficit along the 45° line if this is not apparent to you.) The domestic price rise, however, will tend to correct this by shifting $X - M$ back to an intermediate location not shown in the diagram. Thus the balance of payments will move in the direction of equilibrium.

A monetarist viewpoint would express these insights differently but would arrive at the same conclusion. The monetarist view of a balance-of-payments deficit is an excess supply of domestic money. A depreciation reduces the excess supply in part by stimulating foreign demand and in part by diverting some of the excess supply into domestic uses. This is reinforced by the effect of depreciation on domestic prices; depreciation drives up first the prices of exportables (unless supply is perfectly elastic) and import substitutes, then spreads to substitutes for those two categories. The rising price level reduces the value of money holdings, which means that a larger nominal money stock is demanded for the same real money stock. This will absorb more of the excess supply. This process of depreciation, import-export adjustment, and domestic price level adjustment will continue until the excess supply of money disappears, that is, until the balance of payments is once again in balance. Exchange depreciation must be sufficient to offset the domestic price rise so that the law of one price holds in the new equilibrium position.

ADVANTAGES
AND DRAWBACKS

There are several obvious advantages associated with floating rates, some that are apparent in contrast with the gold standard and others that will become more evident as we examine the remaining two managed systems. First, floating rates, like gold, minimize the role of government. Other than occasional intervention under the present modified float system, the government is more an observer than an active participant in the system.

Second, the system achieves three of the four goals set forth in Chapter 15, more or less. A modified float (or any other type of float) will give us something close to balance-of-payments equilibrium, freedom of trade and capital movements, and independence of monetary and fiscal policy. The balance-of-payments equilibrium is neither continuous nor exact, but the system does normally tend in that direction. As with gold, floating rates is a system that offers an alternative adjustment mechanism—the exchange rate in this case—to direct controls, so it is less likely than exchange control to lead to reliance on tariffs, quotas, and capital controls to deal with a deficit in the balance of payments. Finally, the burden of adjustment falls on the exchange rate rather than on the domestic price level (as well as income and interest rates), which means that domestic monetary and fiscal policy is more free to pursue domestic goals than it would be under the gold standard.

Another advantage of floating rates is that such a system does not call for large reserves of foreign exchange, which is a major drawback of both the Bretton Woods system and the gold standard. When the exchange rate is available as an adjustment device, deficits and surpluses should be smaller in size and shorter in duration. A free float, ideally, would require no reserves; a managed float requires some, but not nearly as much as other international financial arrangements.

Advocates of floating rates have long pointed to the fact that it is the simplest of the four systems to understand and to implement. This system also shares with gold the advantage that changes are usually incremental rather than massive—depreciation or appreciation as opposed to devaluation or revaluation. The former represents marginal shifts brought about by market forces; the latter, deliberate and usually large (5 to 20 percent) changes in official currency prices decreed by government.

Unlike both gold and Bretton Woods, this system enjoys the unique advantage of putting equal pressure on both surplus and deficit countries. The same corrective forces we diagrammed in Figure 17-1 for a deficit country will be working in reverse for a surplus country, at least under a free float. Under a managed float, surplus countries can attempt to offset the upward pressure on their currency's price by selling their currency and purchasing foreign exchange. The modified I.M.F. rules governing surveillance discourage doing this, however.

Finally, it is logical to expect that this system is more likely to contain inflation or recession within the country than to export it through the international financial system, and there is some limited empirical evidence to support this contention. If a country expands demand and/or the domestic money supply, domestic prices will rise, discouraging exports, prompting imports, and putting downward pressure on the exchange rate. The effects of the exchange rate decline offset the effect of rising domestic prices with very little, if any, net effect on trade, the balance of payments, or demand experienced by foreign countries, so there should be no substantial transmission of excess demand. The same is true of recession. How effective this "containment mechanism" is remains a bone of contention, but there is some evidence of greater divergence in domestic rates of inflation under floating rates than under fixed rates. This would seem to imply that there is some containment effect.

What about the drawbacks? There are some obvious complaints and some less clearly evident ones, some backed by experience and others still speculative. It is widely argued that floating rates introduce much uncertainty and instability into international trade, which will discourage both trade and capital flows and thus reduce the efficiency of world resource allocation. When contracts are made calling for forward payment, and an exchange risk is added to the normal risks of commerce, it may discourage trade at the margin, or it may lead the trader to hedge—to cover his or her risk in the forward market by the procedure described in Chapter 12. There is a cost associated with hedging, made up of a risk premium and/or an interest cost. This hedging premium can discourage marginal import-export trades or foreign investments. The uncertainty is compounded by the instability—wide fluctuations in exchange rates that continuously shift relative prices and confuse the price signals on which trading decisions are based.

The evidence at this point is mixed. It is true that there have been wide swings in exchange rates—as much as 10 to 20 percent in a brief three- to four-month period. However, the volume of trade has grown faster than the rate of output growth under floating exchange rates in the 1970s (consistent with the high income elasticities cited earlier).

Bernstein[1] suggests that exchange rate volatility may have distorted the pattern rather than the volume of trade. The banking system has shown remarkable resiliency in being able to provide a forward market in which hedging premiums are not excessively high. Capital flows have continued unabated. It has, in fact, been argued that a fixed rate system in which an exchange rate persists at an overvalued or undervalued level for a long period leads to a skewed ratio of offshore production—foreign direct investment—to exports. This ratio would be too high for such countries as the United States and Britain whose currencies were long overvalued and too low for such countries as West Germany and Japan, whose currencies were priced too low throughout the 1960s. If this criticism of fixed rates is valid—and the evidence is inconclusive at this point—then a more appropriate mix of export industries and direct foreign investment may be added to the list of advantages of floating rates.

Another concern that was raised both in advance of and during the current floating rate regime was that of destabilizing speculative activity. Currencies that are sinking from fundamental supply and demand forces may experience additional downward pressure from speculators "jumping ship," thus overcorrecting, while rising currencies may experience a similar "bandwagon effect" upward, raising the currency price above the level justified by nonspeculative transactions. Although no one argues against the proposition that currency prices will return to equilibrium over time, doubts have been raised about how helpful speculative activity is to that process and how much distortion of trade and capital flows is created in the short run by speculative activity.

Yeager[2] points out that the analogies to commodity speculation and

[1] Edward Bernstein, "The Economics of Fluctuating Exchange Rates, in *Exchange Rate Flexibility*, eds. Jacob Dreyer, Gottfried Haberler, and Thomas Willett (Washington, D.C.: American Enterprise Institute, 1978), pp. 9–24.

[2] Leland B. Yeager, *International Monetary Relations: Theory, History, and Policy*, 2nd ed. (New York: Harper & Row, 1976), chap. 12.

to the stock market are weak. In the case of commodities, there is a finite limit to supply and demand in the short run; monies have no such restriction because the short-run cost of creating additional units of national currency is almost zero. Ownership shares in corporations have no clearly defined "normal," underlying price and should therefore be subject to wider speculative swings than currencies. Destabilizing speculators are guessing wrong, and it is often argued that the market will ultimately select out the wrong guessers and leave the successful ones, who will push the currency toward rather than away from its equilibrium price. There is no clear evidence that the observed volatility in exchange rates is due more to speculative activity than to volatility of underlying supply and demand forces. It should be noted, however, that at least a floating rate plays off one speculator against another (making speculation a zero-sum game for speculators in the aggregate), whereas a fixed rate system can play off speculators against the central bank, with a net gain to speculators and a net loss to the central bank. This point will be expanded in Chapter 19.

Another concern that was expressed in advance of the widespread adoption of floating rates was elasticity pessimism, a subject we discussed in Chapter 12. There was much concern expressed in the late 1960s and early 1970s that short-run elasticities of supply and demand might be so low that the system would grossly overcorrect a surplus or deficit in the search for a new equilibrium. The result would be a distortion of trade patterns, investment flows, and the terms of trade (see the following discussion on this last point). While the exchange rate would eventually converge on equilibrium as the long-run with greater elasticities came into play, there were serious reservations expressed about the length of the short run and the size of the short-run elasticities.

Experience has neither borne out nor completely refuted this pessimism. Exchange rates have been rather volatile, as was indicated earlier, and would have fluctuated even more in the absence of periodic government intervention to stabilize fluctuations. The exchange rate has not brought about continuous and instantaneous or even approximate and occasional balance-of-payments equilibrium, nor has the new system significantly alleviated the demand for and use of international reserves. On the other hand, measured elasticities seem to indicate a strong response to exchange rates over time. The combined income and price effects of depreciation and appreciation do seem to impel the balance of payments in the correct direction over time. Much of the volatility was observed in the first few years of the system, which had to cope not only with correcting the cumulative currency misalignments of the preceding 27 years but also with the drastic alteration in the pattern of trade and capital flows brought about by the quadrupling of the price of OPEC oil.

Another criticism of floating rates should be familiar from the discussion in Chapter 12 of the function of the exchange rate, with a choice between a comparative advantage function and a "balance-of-payments balancing" role. Floating rates opt totally for the latter function, and as a result, the frequent changes in rates confuse the price signals that direct resource allocation efficiently. One partial response to this criticism is found in Murphy,[3] who indicates that the movements in exchange rates from 1973 to 1977 did largely reflect movements in relative unit labor costs, a proxy for relative price movements and, therefore, for purchasing power parity. Similar results were found in a 1976 I.M.F. study using GNP price deflators to measure relative price movements. Thus, the floating rate system may be doing what a fixed rate system with occasional exchange rate adjustments based on some variant of purchasing power parity (Bretton Woods) failed to do— correctly reflect comparative advantage to the extent compatible with a steady flow of capital between nations.

Murphy[4] does point out that the direction of causality in the price level-exchange rate studies is not entirely clear and probably two way, since a rising price level forces the exchange rate downward whereas falling price levels fuel demand and thus put upward pressure on exchange rates. However, the same criticism could be made of a fixed rate system that provides for periodic adjustment of exchange rates based on relative rates of inflation.

Still another criticism of floating rates is that this system eliminates all balance-of-payments discipline on inflation-prone governments and thus has contributed not only to local inflations but to the worldwide inflation of the 1970s. This argument is particularly popular among those urging a return to gold. This criticism is the "flip-side" of the argument for (or against!) floating rates that they reduce the transmission of inflation from one country to another. Independence in monetary and fiscal policy, self-contained fluctuations, and no balance-of-payments discipline (or very little) are a package deal of benefits and costs. There is probably some truth in the argument that reduction in the importance of the balance-of-payments constraint may have touched off some degree of inflation in some countries. However, for the first time those countries are largely bearing the consequences of those inflationary policies rather than exporting part of the problem through trade as they have been able to do in the past.

Some countries have found that their terms of trade have deteriorated under floating rates, since the terms of trade are reflected in the exchange rate. This imposes a welfare loss on consumers of trade-related goods (exportables, imports, and import substitutes) but also creates some compensating welfare gain for the factors of production used in those products,

---

[3] J. Carter Murphy, *The International Monetary System: Beyond the First Stage of Reform* (Washington, D.C.: American Enterprise Institute, 1979).

[4] Ibid.

which experience an increase in demand for their productive services. This is less a criticism than an observation, but it should be noted that less developed countries frequently avoid floating rates and choose exchange control over devaluation because of their concern over the effects of a falling exchange rate on the amount of imports they can buy with their export earnings. (Note that this argument is keyed into elasticity pessimism, but it is valid even if the elasticities are favorable. When the exchange rate for the dollar falls, 1 ton of American wheat will buy less French wine regardless of the elasticities. If the elasticity of demand for wheat is low, the net wheat earnings will fall even farther and the terms of trade will deteriorate even more.)

None of these arguments is overwhelming, yet there remains a strong constituency in the United States, Western Europe, and elsewhere for a return to some kind of fixed exchange rate system. Why? Some of the arguments, particularly the inflation versus balance-of-payments-discipline argument, are at the root of this philosophy. But the more general basis for this preference lies in the national experience, where different parts of a single country are linked by a common currency and local "balance-of-payments" problems are resolved almost unnoticed by capital flows, factor mobility, and localized recessions and inflations. Some would like to return to gold or Bretton Woods and extend this common currency model, which simplifies and encourages trade, to a multinational scale. They like the predictability, the certainty, and the linkage of national currencies that is provided by (ideally) a multinational currency or (more likely) a fixed relationship between existing national currencies.[5]

ESTABLISHMENT
OF THE NEW SYSTEM

The new system was ratified belatedly by the International Monetary Fund with the Jamaica Agreement in January 1976. This agreement abolished the official price of gold and recognized the freedom of I.M.F. member countries to choose the type of exchange rate system that best met their needs. Guidelines were developed for currency surveillance by those countries that were on a floating system, implying that a managed float was to be chosen over a clear float by those countries that opted to float. In particular, they are obligated to stabilize wide swings in currency values and to intervene in a stabilizing rather than in a destabilizing direction (i.e., to attempt to move the currency in the direction of what is perceived as market equilibrium).

[5] The lengthy interruption of the momentum of trade liberalization negotiations in 1967–1974, the period of breakdown of the Bretton Woods regime, raises some doubts about whether trade really would fare better under fixed rates.

CURRENCY AREAS
AND OTHER MODIFICATIONS

One compromise that has evolved between fixed and floating rates is the development of currency areas. A currency area consists of a group of countries whose exchange rates are keyed to each other, usually defined in terms of one currency of the group. They float as a group with respect to the rest of the world. A variant on this scheme is the "snake in the tunnel" or just "the snake" in the European Economic Community. The snake in the tunnel operated toward the end of the Bretton Woods and provides for limited bands of fluctuation ($\pm 1\frac{1}{4}$ percent of parity) among the participating countries and a broader band of fluctuation ($2\frac{1}{4}$ percent of parity) with outside countries. Thus, for example, if 1.0 mark was established as 1.5 francs and .25 U.S. dollars, it was allowed to vary in value up to 1.51875 francs and down to 1.48125 francs. Both would fluctuate together with respect to the dollar with a range of $0.24375 to $0.25625 per mark or $0.365625 to $0.384375 per franc. Since the Smithsonian Agreement in 1971, which marked the beginning of the end of Bretton Woods, the margins have been widened and changed, and countries have periodically withdrawn from participation in the snake. The simple snake would involve a fixed relationship among the currencies of the member European countries and a float with respect to the rest of the world, which is one variant of a currency area. Under either arrangement, countries participating in a currency area are required to sell and purchase foreign exchange as needed to keep the fluctuations within limits. This system has some similarity to the gold standard, but it is closer to the Bretton Woods system, which we discuss in greater detail in Chapter 19.

Other regions have developed a variety of arrangements to establish a compromise between floating and fixed rates. These include payments unions and clearing arrangements, both of which clear balances of foreign exchange bilaterally or among several countries periodically. The former also includes some credit facilities. Such arrangements are most common among groups of developing countries, which are least enthusiastic about floating rates.

A number of currencies are tied in value to the U.S. dollar and rise and fall with it. The choice of the dollar is due to the fact the U.S. trade and capital flows continue to dominate world trade. The United States is the principal trading partner for most of these countries.

While more countries are tied to the dollar than to any other single currency, there are also countries pegged to the French franc, the pound sterling, the SDR (special drawing rights; see Chapter 19), or a market basket of several major currencies.

The advantages of floating rates that appeal most to developed countries—greater independence of monetary and fiscal policy, reduced need for reserves—are secondary to the less developed countries. They are more concerned about the potential impact of floating on their terms of trade when they deal in primary commodities for which fluctuations in supply are unpredictable and both income and price elasticities of demand are very low. (Recall the immiserizing growth model discussed earlier.) Either system is likely to tie fluctuations in demand at home to the trade sector. The workings of floating exchange rates depend to a large extent on the responsiveness of domestic prices and resource allocation to the exchange rate signal. If that responsiveness is weak in less developed countries, the principal effect of depreciation and appreciation may simply be redistribution of income and wealth. Finally, there is more risk involved in floating rates. Sophisticated financial markets handle such risk more efficiently and at lower cost, so this drawback is not as significant to developed as to less developed countries.

UNRESOLVED QUESTIONS

A number of questions about floating rates are yet to be resolved. The experience of the last ten years offers some information, alleviates some fears, and raises new questions about the effects of floating rates on such matters as trade volume, capital flows, income distribution and the terms of trade, cost of hedging, volatility of exchange rates, elasticities of supply and demand for currency, need for reserves, transmission of inflation and recession, and other pertinent issues. However, the evidence, much of which we have cited already, needs to be considered in the light of several special circumstances.

First, floating rates were adopted in a period of cumulative misalignment of exchange rates, also known as "dollar overhang." That is, private foreigners were holding a great many dollars as assets because they were "guaranteed" in price, which made dollars attractive relative to other forms of assets. Once that advantage disappeared, a stock adjustment took place as foreigners (including foreign central banks) readjusted their portfolio mix to fewer dollars and more assets denominated in gold or other currencies. This stock adjustment accounts for much of the sharp drop in the value of the dollar in the early years (1971–1976). The dollar subsequently recovered from most of that decline.

Second, of course, was OPEC, whose price hikes drastically altered the flow of currency, the terms of trade, and the composition of the balance of payments of the entire noncommunist world. Any data from 1974–1977 at least must be viewed in the light of that tremendous shock to the international financial system.

Third, the float was not "clean": the initial dirty float (undercover government intervention) was subsequently replaced by a "managed float," with governments intervening in accordance with guidelines established by the International Monetary Fund. Thus data on exchange rate fluctuations—both the volume and the relationship to domestic price level differentials—are distorted by such intervention.

Bearing all this in mind, what is the initial consensus? As we indicated earlier, the volume of trade has performed well, increasing more than in proportion to increases in income. This relieves a major fear expressed in advance about floating. Capital flows have held up well although there appears to have been an increase in the volume of speculative short-term capital flows. The rapid rise in interest rates and the volatility of interest rates is bound to confuse the evidence on this point. Capital flows to less developed countries have put some banks in a shaky position, but much of this is a result of OPEC actions and questionable lending practices rather than floating rates per se.

Different researchers arrive at different conclusions about the transmission of inflation under floating rates in comparison with the fixed rate system. Here the effects of intervention, dollar overhang, and OPEC particularly seem to distort the data, and additional experience may be needed before a conclusion can be reached.

Demand for currencies of major industrial nations appears to be sufficiently elastic. Too few developing countries are floating to provide much evidence, largely due to a fear of unfavorable elasticities of supply and demand for the underlying commodities.

The volume of international reserves has more than tripled between 1969 and 1978, but much of this was due to inflation. Nevertheless, it appears that the reduced demand for reserves expected under a floating system has not materialized. Much of this demand exists because of the managed float and the fact that some 70 countries have pegged their currencies to some other major currency of SDRs and are thus not really floating.

While there are still advocates of returning to a fixed rate system, and while the present system has some drawbacks, it appears that a floating rate system will continue to meet the needs of a number of major industrial countries for the near future.

SUMMARY

This chapter jumps from the gold standard of the late nineteenth and early twentieth centuries to the present modified floating system because the two systems share the characteristic of being somewhat automatic in operation rather than being heavily managed by governments, a characteristic of the two remaining systems. While floating rates have been tried on an occasional and/or unilateral basis before, the 1970s marked the first widespread use of floating exchange rates. In their simplest form, floating rates are purely market-determined. The depreciation of the exchange rate stimulates exports and discourages imports, which in turn puts upward pressure on domestic prices and income, somewhat offsetting the effect of depreciation. The converse is true of appreciation. Effects on capital flows are not clear, since the price and income effects must be added to interest rate effects.

Advantages claimed for the system include its automatic adjustment of deficits and surpluses (balance-of-payments equilibrium), greater independence of monetary and fiscal policy, freedom of trade and capital movements, less need for reserves, simplicity, a minimal role for government, incremental rather than massive changes, equal pressure on deficit and surplus countries, and less transmission of inflation and recession from country to country.

Critics complain that such a system increases instability and uncertainty, raising the transactions cost and/or risks associated with trade and thus reducing the efficiency of world resource allocation. Other concerns center on elasticity pessimism, the loss of the comparative advantage function of the exchange rate, the removal of balance-of-payments discipline on inflation-prone governments, and deteriorating terms of trade.

The evidence on these points is unclear because of the limited experience with floating rates and because of the effects of dollar overhang, OPEC, and managed floating on the data available for study. Mixed evidence appears on transmission of inflation and recession. The elasticities appear to be favorable, at least for those countries that have chosen to float. The volume of trade has held up well, but the pattern has been distorted by periods of great volatility in exchange rates. International reserves have continued to grow.

The actual system is considerably more complex than is the simple floating model. Major countries are on a managed float, sanctified by the Jamaica Agreement of 1976 that modified the I.M.F. articles of agreement. Other countries have pegged their currencies to some other major currency, and the EEC has a joint float known as the snake. In general, the system has functioned better than its *ex ante* critics predicted and less satisfactorily than its advocates had expected, but it appears to have met the needs of the countries involved in the first ten years. Much additional research is needed when a longer period of experience is available to provide the data.

KEY TERMS

appreciation
clearing arrangement
containment effect
currency area
depreciation

dirty float
dollar overhang
elasticity pessimism
floating exchange rates
hedging
Jamaica Agreement
managed float
modified float
payments union
Smithsonian Agreement

REVIEW QUESTIONS

1. What are the advantages and drawbacks of a floating rate system? What empirical evidence is there to back up some of the claimed advantages and disadvantages?
2. What kinds of values and preferences would make a country choose a free float? A managed float? An exchange rate pegged to other currencies? Why do not all nations make the same choice?
3. What is the transmission mechanism versus the containment effect argument all about? What is the relationship among the exchange rate, the rate of inflation, and the balance of payments?
4. Figure 17-1 was drawn to illustrate depreciation. Redraw the diagram to show the effects of currency appreciation.

SUGGESTED READINGS

BALASSA, BELA, ed., *Changing Patterns in Foreign Trade and Payments,* 3rd ed., part 4. New York: W. W. Norton, 1978. See especially essays by Tom DeVries and John Williamson.

DREYER, JACOB, GOTTFRIED HABERLER, and THOMAS WILLETT, eds., *Exchange Rate Flexibility,* conference proceedings. Washington, D.C.: American Enterprise Institute, 1978. Wide range of topics relating to the development and operation of the current floating rate system.

FRIEDMAN, MILTON, "The Case for Flexible Exchange Rates," in *Essays in Positive Economics,* pp. 157–203. Chicago: University of Chicago Press, 1953.

MEIER, GERALD, *Problems of a World Monetary Order,* pp. 212–295. New York: Oxford University Press, 1974. Background on the development of the present system.

MUNDELL, ROBERT, and JACQUES POLAK, eds., *The New International Monetary System.* New York: Columbia University Press, 1976. Conference on the modified I.M.F.-floating system.

CHAPTER 18

Managed Systems I: Exchange Control

INTRODUCTION

Exchange control is a catch-all category of practices that basically involve the government acting as a monopoly buyer and seller of foreign exchange, usually to maintain an overvalued exchange rate. In terms of the systems framework developed in Chapter 15, exchange control relies on nonprice rationing as an adjustment mechanism. All incoming foreign exchange accrues to the government and all outgoing foreign exchange must be purchased from the government. Because of this, monopoly role for government, exchange control tends to lead to black markets and/or corruption.

As with the two systems already studied, exchange control rarely exists in a pure form. Just as there are dirty floats and managed floats under floating rates, and just as bimetallism, sterilization, and limitations on convertibility coexisted with the gold standard, variations and modifications exist under exchange control. This system, in fact, exhibits greater variety than does any other system. Single rates and multiple rates, capital controls only, auction markets, coexistence of regulated and free markets, and balance-of-trade restrictions for foreign exchange market reasons are just some of the numerous variations in exchange control.

Exchange control sacrifices freedom of trade and capital movements to permit stable exchange rates, to enable independence of monetary and fiscal policy, and to create a balance-of-payments "equilibrium" of a sort by suppressing disequilibrium. Countries practicing exchange control are not characterized by exceptionally stable rates but rather by frequent devaluations, crawling pegs,[1] and/or exchange rates that fluctuate in harmony with some floating currency to which they are pegged. Independence of monetary and fiscal policy is somewhat illusory since countries practicing exchange control are still vulnerable to some transmission of inflation via fixed rates, particularly from the country to whose currency its own currency may be pegged. If the foreign sector is large relative to the domestic economy, importation of disturbances from abroad is almost inevitable. Thus, it is necessary to look elsewhere to find the major objectives of exchange control.

GOALS

The adoption of a system of exchange control is usually to maintain an overvalued currency price (underpricing foreign exchange) in a situation where reserves are inadequate to sustain the deficit. The usual reason given for maintaining the price is a concern about unfavorable elasticities and/or the terms of trade. Countries that are exporters of primary products (especially agricultural) and importers of manufactures argue that they find themselves as suppliers facing a market demand that is both price and income inelastic, especially if they are the major supplier, while the products they purchase tend to be characterized by inelastic import demand and (for a small country) highly elastic supply. A devaluation may, therefore, reduce their foreign exchange earnings from exports while having little impact on import expenditures. The following example may clarify this point.

Bananas are selling in world markets for $50 a stalk, and the peso-dollar exchange rate is 10 to 1. Country A is exporting 1000 stalks of bananas at that price. Now the peso is devalued to 20 to 1. Demand is inelastic: banana sales rise to only 1,200 stalks even though the price to foreigners has fallen to $25 a stalk as a result of devaluation.

Foreign Exchange Earnings

Before   1,000 stalks @ 50/stalk $50,000
After   1,200 stalks @ 25/stalk $37,500

Demand for widget imports is also price inelastic, however, and foreign

---

[1] A "crawling peg" is a fixed rate that is adjusted upward or downward at regular intervals by a percentage determined by the monetary authorities, usually related to output growth or inflation.

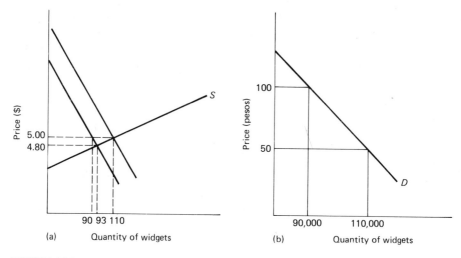

FIGURE 18-1   **Imports After Devaluation with Unfavorable Elasticities**

supply is highly price elastic, especially to a small country. This situation is depicted in Figure 18-1.

The inelastic domestic (peso) demand curve for widgets is shown in panel (b); the devaluation reduces quantity demanded from 110,000 to 90,000 widgets at a price of $5.00, which appears in the dollar-widget panel (a) as a shift in the demand curve from D_1 to D_2. Foreign supply price falls slightly from $5.00 to $4.75, at which price 93,000 widgets is the equilibrium quantity. The result is

Before devaluation	110,000 widgets × $5.00	$55,000
After devaluation	93,000 widgets × $4.80	$44,640

The dollar expenditure on imports will always fall, or at worst remain the same, but the fall in export earnings will exceed the fall in import outlay, and the result will be a larger deficit. In this case, the deficit has risen from $5,000 to $7,140 measured in foreign exchange. Measured in local currency, the deficit of 50,000 pesos became a surplus of 142,800 pesos. However, it is the foreign exchange imbalance that is the primary concern, since that is the medium in which deficits are usually financed.

What about the terms of trade? Before devaluation, the rate of exchange was 11,000 widgets = 1,000 bananas or 11 widgets = 1 banana. After devaluation 9,300 widgets trade for 1,200 bananas, or 7.75 widgets = 1 banana—almost a 30 percent deterioration in the terms of trade. The more inelastic the foreign demand, the worse the deterioration.

In addition to the inelasticity and terms of trade arguments, there are other reasons put forth for exchange control. Less developed countries use controls for infant industry protection, prevention of capital flight, and revenue for the government and to allocate a scarce resource in accordance with some socially determined set of priorities. All these are based on externalities arguments of the type encountered in Chapter 8. Infant industry is the same argument already described. Prevention of capital flight implies that the foreign private rate of return may be higher than the domestic private rate of return, but the domestic social rate of return is perceived to be higher than both. Government revenue may be generated by price discrimination in the purchase and sale of foreign exchange, as is explained in the next section. Finally, the priorities argument implies, again, that there is a divergence between the private and the socially optimal allocation of foreign exchange. After we have examined the operation of the system in greater detail, we examine and criticize each of these arguments.

OPERATION

A system of exchange control is very simple in theoretical terms and very complex in operational terms. The foreign exchange market model of chapter 12 is presented in Figure 18-2. Note that exchange control is usually adopted in response to a balance-of-payments deficit and overvalued exchange rate, although theoretically it could also be used to perpetuate a surplus and an undevalued exchange rate.

The equilibrium price of foreign exchange is P_e. The actual (official) price is P_a. Foreign exchange is too cheap, or domestic currency is too expensive. The balance-of-payments deficit is AB. OA of foreign exchange

FIGURE 18-2   The Foreign Exchange Market Under Exchange Control

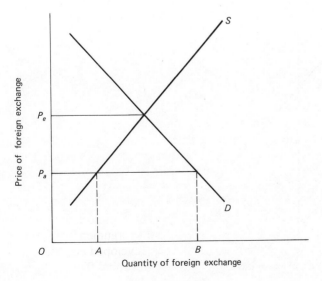

is received and allocated in some fashion among competing users to prevent the deficit of *AB* from occurring, which would require financing a deficit that this country lacks the resources to underwrite.

The unanswered question is the method of allocating foreign exchange among competing users. A number of methods suggest themselves from other kinds of rationing experiences or from actual exchange control practices, such as

1. First come, first served
2. Auction import licenses
3. Establishment of priorities for use of foreign exchange
4. Discretionary allocation by a designated public official
5. Allocation of some by priorities and selling the balance at auction

All these methods involve some distortions of efficiency and/or questions of equity, and all tend to lead to black markets, especially the third and fourth.

A system of first come, first served will measure the intensity of preferences in terms of willingness to wait in line, although it might function more efficiently if the initial holders were allowed to resell their rights or foreign exchange on a private market. This allocation, as is true for any nonmarket allocation scheme, creates windfall gains to favorite recipients

FIGURE 18-3   Multiple Exchange Rates

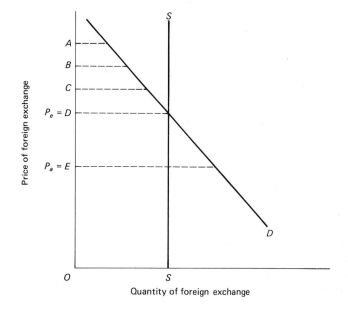

by making foreign exchange artifically scarce and conveying ownership rights to the scarce commodity to a small number of fortunate individuals.

Auctioning import licenses ensures that the property rights created by artifically underpricing a scarce resource (foreign exchange) accrue to the government rather than to private individuals. This would have some advantages from the government's viewpoint over a free market system, as is illustrated in Figure 18-3. If the supply of foreign exchange is treated as a given quantity, OS, the equilibrium price which the market would support is P_e. The price P_a represents some sort of official price that is below equilibrium, the normal situation for a system of exchange control. The solution to this problem is to let P_e be the "average" price, charging some users higher prices and others lower prices. It is even possible to have the majority of transactions take place at P_a and still clear the market while making a profit for the government—particularly if there are multiple buying as well as selling rates. Suppose, for example, that the foreign exchange inflow is $800,000, of which 500,000 was purchased at the official rate of 5 pesos and $300,000 at the equilibrium rate of 10 pesos, for a total cost of 5.5 million pesos. The government faces a demand schedule as follows:

	Price	Quantity of $
A	25	200,000
B	20	400,000
C	15	600,000
D	10	800,000
E	5	1,000,000

If the government acts as a perfectly discriminating monopolist, it will sell

1st	200,000 @ 25 pesos =	5,000,000
2nd	200,000 @ 20 pesos =	4,000,000
3rd	200,000 @ 15 pesos =	3,000,000
4th	200,000 @ 10 pesos =	2,000,000
5th	200,000 @ 5 pesos =	1,000,000
		15,000,000 pesos!

Even if the government wished to maintain the official rate for the bulk of transactions by selling $600,000 at 5 pesos, the remainder could be sold at rates sufficiently attractive to still make a profit of up to 6.5 million pesos. The government makes this profit by capturing some, or all, of the consumers' surplus (triangle ADP_e at the equilibrium price) through price discrimination.

Those who obtain foreign exchange at the lower rate may or may not have an opportunity for private profit. If foreign exchange is auctioned, the government extracts any surplus created by the artificial scarcity. But, if some nonauction allocation scheme is used, the possibility develops of private profit from favorably priced allocations of foreign exchange. The simplest way to profit is to resell the foreign exchange at a higher price to someone farther up the demand curve. A more complex source of profit arises if the supply of goods and services from abroad is at all elastic. The effect of the exchange controls on price and quantity of a representative imported good is shown in Figure 18-4.

Suppose that the amount of foreign exchange allocated to good A (ignoring, for a moment, the details of the allocation scheme) is restricted to OP_1BQ_1, which means that foreigners will supply Q_1 at price P_1. Domestic consumers are willing to pay P_f, a signal to expand quantity that goes unheeded. The price differential of $P_f - P_2$ will accrue as monopoly profits (shaded area) to the favored importer who received an import license or an allocation of foreign exchange earmarked for good A. This defect can be remedied by auctioning foreign exchange or by auctioning import licenses. The other allocation methods all tend to create monopoly profits.

A priority system involves a significant government role in resource allocation. The government can use a priority system to protect infant industries, encourage the inflow or discourage outflow of raw materials (the latter as an incentive to process at home), discourage luxury imports and/ or capital outflow, encourage capital inflow, redistribute income among groups of consumers, and raise revenue for the government. The hypothetical example of buying and selling rates shown in Table 18-1 incorporates

FIGURE 18-4   Exchange Control and Monopoly Profit

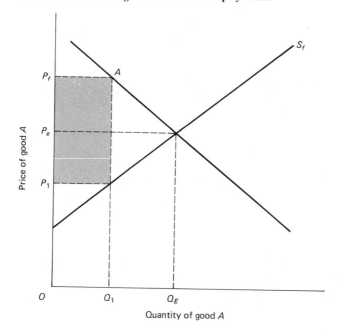

Quantity of good A

TABLE 18-1   Hypothetical Buying and Selling Rates (pesos/U.S. $)[1]

Selling		Buying	
A. Food, raw materials	4 pesos	F. Capital inflow	8 pesos
B. Basic consumer goods and capital equipment	5 pesos	G. Raw materials	3 pesos
		H. All other exports	5 pesos
C. Competing manufactures	8 pesos		
D. Luxury goods	10 pesos		
E. Capital outflow	auction rate		

[1] Official rate: 5 pesos/U.S. $; estimated equilibrium rate: 8 pesos/U.S. $.

all these goals. Suppose that the government purchased $100 million of foreign exchange inflow from the following sources:

H.	$60 million (other exports)	300 million pesos
G.	$20 million (raw materials)	60 million pesos
F.	$20 million (capital inflow)	160 million pesos
	Total outlay	520 million pesos

This foreign exchange is then allocated in order of priority.

A.	$15 million (food, raw materials)	60 million pesos
B.	$55 million (consumer goods, capital equipment)	275 million pesos
C.	$10 million (competing manufactures)	80 million pesos
D.	$10 million (luxury imports)	100 million pesos
E.	$10 million (capital outflow @ auction rate = 12 pesos)	120 million pesos
	Total revenue	635 million pesos

What has been achieved? Capital inflow has been encouraged by a favorable rate, whereas raw materials exports have been either discouraged or generated revenue if foreign demand is inelastic. Imports have been concentrated (70 percent) in the two priority categories, A and B, benefiting low-income consumers and encouraging development at the expense of competing manufactures and luxury goods. Capital outflow has been discouraged, since the auction rate is 50 percent above equilibrium and 140 percent above the official rate. The majority of transactions have taken place at the official rate of 5 pesos (55 percent of selling and 60 percent of buying is at that rate). And, finally, the government has made a profit from monopoly price discrimination of 115 million pesos, or 22 percent. This example illustrates all the goals that a government might attempt to achieve through exchange control.

The fourth and fifth allocation schemes mentioned are really just combinations and variations of the first three. All the goals that we identified can be served with varying degrees of effectiveness under any of these allocation schemes. It is apparent from the hypothetical example why the idea of exchange control has been so attractive to less developed countries. What about its drawbacks?

EVALUATION

There are three major drawbacks to exchange control, all of which might be labeled "inefficiency." As with any price controls, exchange controls distort market signals and reduce the efficiency of resource allocation. The controls themselves are generally ineffective, leading to the development of black markets in foreign exchange. Finally, capital markets suffer distortions and inefficiencies.

The first type of inefficiency distorts the international pattern of comparative advantage. Exports are overpriced and imports are underpriced at the official rate of exchange, discouraging the development of export industries that might be competitive and creating a frustrated demand for cheap imports that, in turn, strengthens incentives for the development of black markets. The actual prices for imports will not necessarily reflect the "cheap" foreign exchange, however, since the foreign exchange may have to be acquired by standing in line, dealing in black markets, bidding for import licenses, or bribing public officials. For many imports, the actual price may be considerably above rather than below equilibrium, leading to the development of inefficient import-substitute industries. As the country artificially restricts the size of the foreign sector, the gains from specialization and trade are reduced. This may be a high price to pay in the long run.

The altered set of relative prices derived from a system of multiple exchange rates contains further difficulties. Supposedly, these prices reflect correction of positive and negative externalities associated with the import, export, production, and consumption of certain types of goods and services, encouraging some and discouraging others through appropriate exchange rate subsidies and premiums. Unfortunately, while it is easy to identify the existence and sign of an externality, it is very difficult to measure its size. Overcorrection and undercorrection are likely to be the norm rather than the exception. The appropriate amount of correction for externalities is difficult to determine even in a sophisticated, developed market economy. It is much more difficult in the less developed economies most prone to using multiple exchange rates.

Black markets (or "gray markets"—unofficial but tolerated private markets) are an inevitable consequence of exchange control. If the government is offering 3 pesos to purchase dollars while there are private buyers eager to purchase at 10 pesos, the profit potential will overcome the risk of being caught and penalized for at least some individuals. The techniques of evasion are endless. Exports can be understated to save some foreign exchange for the illegal market; imports can be overstated and the surplus foreign exchange sold on the private market. Tourists are a popular source of private transactions. Smuggling can generate foreign exchange. The greater the divergence between the official price and the private market equilibrium, the larger the diversion of funds from the official to the private market.

Capital flows will also be distorted, particularly since it is difficult to determine the exchange rate that will correctly reflect the divergence between the private and social rates of return. A favorable exchange rate on capital inflow and a penalty rate on capital outflow is usually intended to offset a greater perceived risk in investing in less developed countries, which is the primary source of divergence between the two rates of return. The secondary source of divergence is the same as the social revenues and infant industry arguments for protection—that there are benefits to society from the development of certain types of industrial development over and above the private return that will not enter into the calculations of the private investor. The favorable exchange rate on capital inflow constitutes a subsidy for investors. To the extent that the capital inflow buying rate does not distinguish by type of investment, it constitutes an indiscriminate subsidy to all investments, which will exhibit a great variety of social rates of return. Direct subsidy of selected industries would undoubtedly be more efficient.

In general, an extensive system of controls is difficult and costly to manage. The administrative costs and difficulties of an extensive system of controls with considerable diversion of resources into the private illegal market can easily offset the expected benefits set forth earlier.

CURRENT EXPERIENCE

The use of controls has been widespread in the period since World War II. Virtually all countries—including those in Western Europe—practiced extensive exchange control in the decade following the war, but controls were gradually relaxed by the developed countries during the 1950s and used only intermittently thereafter during short-run balance-of-payments difficulties. If controls are defined broadly to include quotas and nontariff barriers, no countries are free of controls. If they are defined more narrowly to include only the items listed in Table 18-2, then only 14 of the 140 countries surveyed by the International Monetary Fund do not practice some form of exchange control. If exchange control is defined as requiring surrender of export proceeds to the government, then 112 of the 140, or 80 percent, practice exchange control.

Capital restrictions are the most popular form of exchange control, but at least 24 countries practice some form of currency control. Since the fixed

TABLE 18-2   Forms of Exchange Control, 1979

Type of Control	Number of Countries
Different exchange rate for imports and exports	24
More than one rate for imports	18
More than one rate for exports	17
Restrictions on current account items	68
Restrictions on capital transactions	105
Bilateral arrangements[1]	42
Import surcharges	60
Advance deposits[2]	25
Prescription of currency[3]	81
Surrender of export proceeds required	112

Source: International Monetary Fund, *Annual Report of Exchange Restrictions and Exchange Rate Practices, 1980* (Washington, D.C.: International Monetary Fund, 1980), p 2–7.

[1] Bilateral arrangements are clearing procedures for periodically settling balance-of-payments deficits and surpluses between pairs of countries.

[2] Advance deposit requires the importer to deposit funds well in advance of importation of goods in amounts ranging from a small percentage to several thousand percent of the value. The interest forgone and the purchasing power risk serve as a significant deterrent to imports.

[3] Proscription of currency forbids the removal of currency (bank notes) and coins from the country. This is a fairly common restriction even among countries that do not practice exchange control.

rate regime of Bretton Woods disintegrated, most countries practicing exchange control (108 countries in all, but including some that do not practice currency control) have pegged their currencies to some other major currency or currencies, representing a major trading partner or group of trading partners. The U.S. dollar is the most popular of these currency standards. With the advent of floating rates, there has been some perceptible reduction in controls, particularly among developed countries, but exchange control continues to dominate the international monetary relations of the less developed world.

SUMMARY

Exchange control is an international monetary system in which the exchange rate is pegged and resulting disequilibriums are suppressed by rationing. The government acts as a monopoly buyer and seller of foreign exchange.

Exchange controls not only suppress a deficit but also generate revenues, protect infant industries, encourage capital inflows, discourage capital flight, and allocate foreign exchange in accordance with social priorities. All but the first of these involve externalities arguments. This system is also often adopted because of concern about unfavorable elasticities and the terms of trade.

Foreign exchange can be allocated on the basis of first come, first served; auction foreign exchange and/or import licenses; establishment of priorities; discretionary allocation by a designated public official; or various combinations of these methods. All but auctioning create the potential for monopoly profits for the recipients; auctioning captures part or all of the monopoly profits for the government.

The major drawbacks of exchange control are the distortion of market signals, the administrative costs, the development of black markets and corruption, and the inability to measure the size of the externalities to generate an appropriate correction.

Controls are currently in widespread use, particularly among less developed countries. Multiple exchange rates, capital controls, current account restrictions, import surcharges, advance deposits, proscription of currency, and mandatory surrender of export proceeds to the government are the primary forms of exchange control.

KEY TERMS

advance deposit
allocation methods
bilateral arrangements
black market
exchange control
externalities argument
gray market
inefficiency
monopoly profits
multiple exchange rates
proscription of currency
price discrimination
priority system
rationing
unfavorable elasticities

REVIEW QUESTIONS

1. Why do countries adopt exchange control? Why might another system be preferable?
2. Where do the monopoly profits from exchange control come from? How can they be captured by government?

3. Using the multiple exchange rate schedule in Table 18-2, identify the gainers and losers from this system.

4. Why are exchange controls more popular in less developed countries than in the industrial world?

5. Recompute the example of devaluation in the chapter with more elastic demand for imports and exports. Try Q_2 of bananas $= 1,400$, P_2 of widgets $= \$4.50$, Q_2 of widgets $= 100$. Try some other combinations until you can see clearly the effect of devaluation on the deficit in both pesos and dollars.

SUGGESTED READINGS

BHAGWATI, JAGDISH H., and SUKHAMOY CHAKRAVARTY, "Contributions to Indian Economic Analysis: A Survey. Part III. Foreign Trade," *American Economic Review,* Vol 59, No 4, Part 2 (September 1969), 60–66. Description of exchange control in India.

CHACHOLIADES, MILTIADES, *Principles of International Economics.* New York: McGraw-Hill, 1981. Chapter 19 is a survey of all the varieties of direct control.

CHENERY, HOLLIS, "Restructuring the World Economy," in *Changing Patterns in Foreign Trade and Payments,* ed. Bela Balassa, 3rd ed., pp. 55–77. New York: W. W. Norton, 1978.

HALEVI, NADAV, "Economic Policy Discussion and Research in Israel. Part III. Foreign Exchange Rates," *American Economic Review,* Vol 59, No 4, Part 2 (September 1969), 99–94. Description of exchange control in Israel.

INTERNATIONAL MONETARY FUND, *Annual Report of Exchange Restrictions and Practices,* Washington, D.C.: International Monetary Fund, 1980.

YEAGER, LELAND B., *International Monetary Relations: Theory, History, and Policy,* 2nd ed., chap. 7. New York: Harper & Row, 1976.

CHAPTER 19

Managed Systems II: Bretton Woods

INTRODUCTION

The last of the four prototypes of international monetary arrangements relies on reserves to settle deficits. This was the most distinctive characteristic of the international monetary system that was adopted by a large group of countries in 1944, went into operation in 1946, and came to an end in 1973. This system is most commonly known as the Bretton Woods system, named for the New Hampshire town in which the articles of agreement were drawn up. Of the four systems, this was the only one to be deliberately constructed by a group of representatives of the major nations. It was designed to deal with the problems observed during the interwar period, 1918–1940. Had those problems repeated themselves, the system might have functioned well. In fact, it can be argued, the problems of inadequate reserves, trade barriers, controls, competitive devaluations, and declining volume of trade were resolved with the help of the Bretton Woods system, but in the process new problems were created that were at least partly the fault of the new system—worldwide inflation and insufficient reserves in particular.

OPERATION

The operation of the Bretton Woods system combines some of the characteristics of the gold standard with certain properties of floating rates. In fact, some of its advocates argued that it gave us the best of both—the certainty and predictability of the gold standard, which encourages trade and capital flows, with the flexibility and capacity to adjust to major change, which is the hallmark of the floating rate system. Critics argue that in attempting to give us both certainty and flexibility it gave us neither, or rather the worst of both—the rigidity of gold and the instability of floating rates.

The Bretton Woods system requires the participating country to establish an official price for its currency in terms of gold or dollars—the par value or parity. This price should be set as close to what is believed to be the market equilibrium price as possible. The country is then obligated to maintain the value of its currency within 1 percent of par either way by buying and selling foreign exchange. If the deficit or surplus is substantial in amount, and if it persists over time, then the country is said to be suffering from a fundamental disequilibrium and should adjust the price of its currency—set a new par value to be maintained within 1 percent either way. To keep this from occurring too frequently, the International Monetary Fund (the supervising agency of the Bretton Woods system) required consultation for any devaluation that represented a cumulative change of 10 percent or more over a three-year period. Thus, when the British pound was devalued from $2.80 to $2.40 in 1967, the 14 percent decline in parity required I.M.F. consultation and approval. This requirement was designed to hold down the number of devaluations and, in particular, to avoid what were perceived as competitive, "beggar-thy-neighbor" devaluations of the 1930s.

The operation of the system is illustrated in Figure 19-1. The par value for the German mark is $0.25 (which it was for quite some time). D_o and S_o show the mark in equilibrium at that price. The mark must be maintained within 1 percent, so its price cannot rise above $0.2525 or fall below $0.2475. Suppose that demand for the mark increases to D_1, raising the equilibrium price to $0.30. The price of the mark rises to its ceiling of $0.2525. At that price Germany will find itself experiencing a surplus in its balance of payments of 5,000 marks, which is also a surplus of dollars (foreign exchange) and a shortage of marks. Germany will resolve this problem by supplying the market with 5,000 marks and taking $1,262.50 off the market.

If the problem persists over time, Germany will be under some pressure to revalue or raise the price of the mark so as to eliminate the surplus. Generally, surplus countries are under less pressure than are deficit countries, because it is possible for a surplus country to accumulate foreign exchange indefinitely, while a deficit country must draw on reserves that will eventually be exhausted. The surplus country will frequently sterilize (offset) the effect of the inflow of foreign exchange on the monetary base and the money supply to avoid inflation. The central bank will sell bonds in sufficient quantity to neutralize the effect of the foreign exchange inflow on the money supply. (This is by no means a requirement, just the usual pattern. In fact, from the standpoint of correcting payments imbalances,

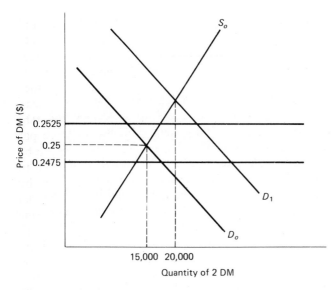

FIGURE 19-1   The Market for Marks Under Bretton Woods

sterilization of foreign exchange inflows is undesirable, because an unsterilized inflow or outflow should lead to inflation in the surplus country or deflation in the deficit country, which would tend to correct the balance-of-payments surplus or deficit.) Scarce currency provisions of the Articles of Agreement of the fund do provide for pressures to be put on persistent surplus countries, but these provisions have never been invoked.

You may have noted two critical elements in this process that were largely or entirely missing in the two previous systems. One was the International Monetary Fund. The other was the mention of reserves. These represent two key features of this system. The International Monetary Fund is discussed in greater detail later in this chapter, but it should be noted that the I.M.F. acts as a "supervisor" for the system, overseeing changes in official exchange rates, and also provides reserves to deficit countries. Originally conceived as an international central bank, lending to national central banks, it was established in somewhat weaker form—more like an international savings and loan association. Nevertheless, it did provide additional reserves and a source of emergency loans to meet balance-of-payments crises. Reserves were also crucial under the gold standard, although the only form for reserves was gold, and later (between World War I and 1971) gold-based currencies. Under the Bretton Woods system, reserves consisted of gold, key currencies (especially the U.S. dollar), I.M.F. drawing rights, and toward the end, I.M.F. special drawing rights (SDRs). The problem of providing adequate reserves in satisfactory form plagued the International

Monetary Fund from the beginning. We also return to a discussion of the reserve problem later in the chapter.

EVALUATION

The goals of the Bretton Woods system were defined in negative fashion. Its creators wanted to resolve the difficulties of the interwar period, characterized by high tariff walls and declining trade volume, deflation and unemployment, capital controls, competitive devaluation, and isolationism. In other words, they wanted stable exchange rates and freedom of trade and capital movements—two of the four goals identified in Chapter 15. Unfortunately, they also wanted independence of monetary and fiscal policy. In 1944, policymakers were enamored with the power of the new Keynesian macroeconomics, which they felt would enable countries to pursue full employment, stable prices, and economic growth independently of one another if only they could resolve this nuisance from abroad—the balance-of-payments surplus or deficit. The United States, with only 5 percent of its GNP entering into international trade at that time, was particularly prone to this viewpoint. Thus, independence of monetary and fiscal policy was added to the list of goals. This left balance-of-payments equilibrium as the only goal available to be sacrificed.

The system functioned very well in many respects. An orderly procedure for exchange rate changes was provided, an improvement over both the inflexibility of gold and the chaotic devaluations of the 1930s. A central source of reserves was available to countries in short-term difficulties, relieving them of pressure for a hasty devaluation, a resort to controls, or the need to deflate to correct a deficit. The gradual dismantling of controls and the continuing reduction in tariff barriers during the Bretton Woods era can be attributed in large measure to the fact that the system relieved countries of excessive concern about the balance of payments, at least in the short run.

Trade liberalization and fewer controls, in turn, helped to promote the period of spectacular economic growth of the 1950s and 1960s. The central role of gold was gradually reduced, resolving a built-in constraint on system growth from the short and uncontrollable supply of what had been the key reserve element. The existence of such a multinational institution, along with its companions—the International Bank for Reconstruction and Development (World Bank, a multinational development loan agency), the General Agreement on Trade and Tariffs (GATT), and the United Nations— promoted a degree of international cooperation that certainly enhanced trade and capital flows as well as international harmony in other areas.

The weaknesses of the Bretton Woods system can be grouped for convenience under three headings: microeconomic problems, macroeconomic problems, and reserve problems. The first two are similar to the problems discussed in connection with the other two systems. The third is shared in part only by the gold standard.

Microeconomic problems of the system have to do with the appropriateness of the exchange rate being maintained. The exchange rate is intended to either balance the balance of payments or correctly reflect comparative advantage. Under the Bretton Woods system, it is supposedly set so as to provide "fundamental equilibrium." (Actually, it is supposed to be changed only to correct a fundamental disequilibrium, which amounts to the same thing.) This means (recall Chapter 12, $X = M \pm$ long-term capital flows) that the exchange rate under Bretton Woods does neither of these. An incorrect exchange rate can promote an export surplus or generate an undeserved balance-of-trade deficit. The U.S. dollar, for example, was overvalued in the late 1960s, giving rise to legitimate demands for protection among certain import-competing industries that would have been competitive with the correct rate of exchange.

On the other hand, this system does provide fairly long periods of certainty about exchange rates, which should promote a greater volume of trade by reducing the risk premium. This is analogous to reducing transport costs, as was pointed out in Chapter 4.

A final microeconomic effect points out an inequity in the system. When the exchange rate is fixed, and remains fixed until an official devaluation or revaluation takes place, this provides a bonanza for private speculators at the expense of the central bank and thus ultimately at the expense of the taxpayer. It will be clear long in advance when a devaluation is due to occur. There may be doubts about the precise timing or size of the devaluation but not about its inevitability. A speculator who held British pounds in 1967 sold them to the Bank of England for marks, francs, or U.S. dollars, repurchasing his pounds after the devaluation. The pounds were sold to the central bank at $2.80 and were repurchased at $2.40, a nice 14 percent profit on a short-term and virtually riskless transaction. The loss was borne by the taxpayer. This one-way risk was a basic flaw in the Bretton Woods system that does not occur in other systems.

The fact that devaluations could be anticipated does not necessarily mean that speculation was more stabilizing under this system than under floating rates. The size of the devaluation could not be forecast clearly by the market, so speculative activity could overcorrect or undercorrect. The difference from floating rates is that speculative activity changed the size of the surplus or deficit at a fixed rate rather than the rate itself and could send incorrect signals to policymakers attempting to estimate the desired change in the rate. For example, a currency in need of devaluation would be overdevalued if the anticipatory speculation, "bailing out" of that currency, were mistakenly interpreted as normal market activity. After the fact, speculators returning to the currency to collect their profits would again send misleading signals about the effect of the devaluation of the balance of payments, making it appear to have overcorrected. Thus, speculative activity under this system tended to cloud the already unclear signals about the correct price being received from the marketplace. Much of the attention given to the measurement of deficits or surpluses in the 1960s was an effort to clarify those market signals by filtering out speculative activity.

A drawback that overlaps the micro-macro categories is that the changes that occur under this system are a shock—large, one-shot changes to which all kinds of prices and market participants must make a sudden adjustment. This is in contrast to both gold and floating rates, where changes tend to be incremental. The massive nature of adjustment can be overstated, however, since devaluations were usually anticipated and some of the adjustments were made in contracts and decisions in the period immediately preceding the devaluation or revaluation.

The macroeconomic effects are still in great dispute. Does this system transmit inflation more readily or less so than do floating rates? Is it inflationary? What are the effects of the reserve system on the world money supply? Certainly theory would suggest that this system transmits inflation from one country to another as excess demand spills over through a fixed exchange rate. Inflation in country A sends its citizens searching for bargains abroad while its exports suffer reduced sales at fixed rates. The excess demand then transmits inflation from country to country. A similar experience under gold in the sixteenth century is often cited as the classic example. Spain brought back Indian gold from the New World, experienced inflation, began purchasing cheaper goods from the rest of Europe (at fixed exchange rates), and spread inflation throughout Europe.

Inflation will, of course, also drive up nominal interest rates in the inflating country, which under fixed rates will attract a capital inflow and partly offset the balance-of-trade deficit. Consider the following example.

The United States is experiencing 10 percent inflation and France 5 percent. U.S. interest rates are 12 percent, and those in France are 7 percent; thus, real interest rates are roughly equivalent. The rate of exchange is 5 francs to a dollar. The Frenchman can invest 1,000 francs at home, earning 7 percent (70 francs). Or, he can invest in the United States—$200 at the current exchange rate, which will earn $24. At the end of the year, if no exchange rate change has occurred, the $244 will convert at 5 francs/dollar to 1,120 francs, earning a true 12 percent. As long as the Frenchman can get into and out of dollars before a devaluation, it is possible to convert the higher nominal return into a higher real return. This will, of course, not occur as readily under floating rates, where the higher rate of inflation in the United States would put downward pressure on the price of the dollar.

This aspect of the Bretton Woods system can be viewed in either a positive or a negative light. On the one hand, it does provide one of the few automatic balance-of-payments corrective devices or adjustment mechanisms that exist under the Bretton Woods system. On the other hand, it encourages a speculative flow of "hot money" (short-term liquid assets) from country to country seeking the highest nominal rate of return, which does not in any way reflect real return or efficient allocation of capital.

The model presented in Chapter 15 would certainly suggest that transmission of cyclical fluctuations would be greater under a fixed rate system than under a floating rate system. The evidence to date is unclear, largely because (as was noted in Chapter 17) we have only eight years of experience of floating rates on which to draw, and the early years were characterized by special circumstances such as dollar overhang, OPEC, and worldwide recession.

What about interest rates? To the extent that the effects of foreign exchange flows on the money supply are sterilized, interest rates will be affected. If a country experiencing a deficit refused to allow the deficit to reduce the money supply, the initial result is lower real interest rates and the ultimate effect is higher prices and high nominal interest rates. (You might, as an exercise, check that statement out using the macroeconomic models of Chapters 14 and 15). If the surplus country similarly sterilizes foreign exchange inflows, the result there will be higher real interest rates than would otherwise have occurred, attracting a capital flow from the deficit country to the surplus country and thus worsening the balance-of-payments imbalances already existing.

The rest of the macroeconomic effects of this system can be determined readily from the fixed rate model of Chapters 14 and 15.

It has been argued that the Bretton Woods system was inflationary because the expansion of reserves that it engendered (for reasons to be set forth shortly) expanded the world's monetary base and, therefore, inflated the world money supply. This is an additional argument beyond the simple contention that the system tends to transmit inflation as well as other fluctuations through the linkage created by a fixed rate system. Certainly, there were many countries for which the burden of offsetting the effects of foreign exchange flows on the money supply was excessive in terms of interest rates or in terms of the size of the flows relative to the volume of open market assets at the disposal of the central bank. To the extent that the monetary authorities found it difficult to sterilize foreign exchange flows, especially in surplus countries, there may be some truth in the contention that the Bretton Woods system had an inherent inflationary bias.

As was suggested, a major defect of the Bretton Woods system was the ineffectiveness of adjustment mechanisms. The usual corrective forces for balance-of-payments deficits and surpluses arise from changes in the exchange rate, the domestic price level, the domestic and world income levels, changing interest differentials, or the resort to controls. Most of these mechanisms operate weakly if at all under the Bretton Woods system. Sterilization of foreign exchange flows (especially inflows) weakens the price effects that were the mainstay of the gold standard as well as the income effects.[1] (However, a balance-of-trade deficit will still exert a depressing effect on income in a deficit country and a stimulus in surplus countries; but with monetary sterilization the effect is much weaker.) Interest rates tend to work in the corrective direction if the monetary authorities do not intervene to the contrary. Controls are not considered desirable and are used only as a last resort. A system with such weak adjustment mechanisms can expect deficits to be larger and more persistent than under a system with more effective adjustment devices. This defect leads to an excessive demand for reserves, a subject that was at the top of the agenda for the International Monetary Fund from the beginning to the end of the Bretton Woods system.

RESERVES

There were basically only three possible sources of international monetary reserves under the Bretton Woods system. Gold was always possible, and for most of the 27 years of the system it was a significant component of total reserves. Strong national currencies acceptable in third-party transactions were the second source of reserves. A key currency needed a fairly substantial gold reserve of its own, a sufficient volume of its currency outstanding to provide some reserves for others, and acceptability for third-party transactions (e.g., using dollars to settle accounts between Switzerland and Turkey). It also needed to be far less likely to devalue than other currencies. The American dollar was really the only major currency that fit that description at the end of World War II. It quickly became the secondary source of reserves, with other currencies playing a lesser role as "vehicle currencies" (currencies used in third-party transactions and in foreign exchange sales and purchases by central banks).

The third potential source of reserves is newly created reserves issued by the central bank, in this case the International Monetary Fund. The I.M.F. originally had no such credit-creating power but was granted a limited amount of reserve-creating authority in 1969 when it began to issue special drawing rights. Until that time, the two sources of reserves were gold and key currencies. The usefulness of reserves was "stretched" by pooling reserves in the I.M.F. from which countries could draw from time to time to meet deficits, repaying when the deficit was eliminated by either shifting market forces or devaluation.

At the end of World War II, the United States was enjoying a balance-of-payments surplus and owned two-thirds of the world's monetary gold stock. Major devaluations (17 countries) in 1949 realigned other countries' exchange rates with respect to the United States and precipitated U.S. deficits for the next 20 years. At first, the deficits were small and were

---

[1] Sterilization of outflows only weakens the income effect if there is little downward price flexibility.

welcomed as a source of international liquidity. The United States was lending heavily abroad, both in the form of private investment and in public aid (foreign military aid and economic assistance). Paying for this capital outflow with dollars made the balance sheet of the United States look much like that of a commercial banker for the world, borrowing short and lending long.

As the U.S. deficits persisted into the 1960s, unanticipated problems began to develop. As long as the number of dollars outstanding abroad was less than the massive U.S. gold stock, there was no concern about the value of the dollar holdings. But ten years of growing deficits increased the dollars outstanding relative to gold, and some countries elected to redeem part of their dollar holdings in gold, as they were entitled to do. As the dollars abroad continued to grow, and the U.S. official monetary gold stock began to shrink, a crisis of confidence developed with two key elements. First, holders of dollars began to be concerned about the ability of the United States to continue to redeem dollars for gold, a critical component in the acceptability of the dollar as an international medium of exchange. Second, and probably more important, they began to worry about the possibility of devaluation of the U.S. dollar, which would impose a capital loss on holders of dollars and create a capital gain for gold holders. These concerns were escalating in the mid-1960s and reached crisis point toward the end of the decade, a time to which we return shortly.

The important point about what occurred was that it would have happened to any key currency. With weak adjustment mechanisms, the demand for liquidity (international reserves) is very large, putting pressure for expansion on the key currency as the major source of new reserves. If the key currency country obliges this demand by running deficits to generate international liquidity, there will develop a crisis of confidence in the key currency. The fact that such an inherently unstable situation was able to persist for as long as it did was the result of the unusual size, strength, and international assets of the United States at the end of World War II. This three-part problem is referred to as confidence, liquidity, and adjustment. If the adjustment mechanisms are strong, the demand for liquidity is less and the system is less likely to develop problems of confidence. In the late 1960s, the I.M.F. attempted to address this problem by developing an alternative form for international reserves in special drawing rights, which are international fiat money issued in limited quantities by the I.M.F.

THE INTERNATIONAL MONETARY FUND

The International Monetary Fund and its sister institution, the World Bank, were set up in 1944 at Bretton Woods, New Hampshire, at a conference among the Allied powers still fighting World War II. The International

Monetary Fund was charged with supervision of foreign exchange activities, maintaining a schedule of par values, consulting on devaluations, and providing a pool of international monetary reserves on which member countries could draw from time to time to finance a balance-of-payments deficit.

The rules were very simple. Each country was to register a par value, defined in gold or dollars, with the fund, which it agreed to maintain within 1 percent of par by appropriate purchases and sales. Devaluations of more than 10 percent over three years required prior consultation with the I.M.F.; smaller devaluations merely required *ex post* notification. Participating countries were assigned quotas in the fund based on their populations and gross national products. Each country paid in 25 percent of its quota in gold and/or U.S. dollars and the balance in its own currency. In exchange, the country received automatic drawing rights of 125 percent of its quota in the fund.

For example, a country with a $10 million quota would pay in $2.5 million in gold or dollars (i.e., out of its own foreign exchange reserves) and $7.5 million in its own currency, which was much easier to come by. In exchange, it could borrow up to $12.5 million in any combination of currencies to use to finance a balance-of-payments deficit. (More borrowing than that was also possible, but the right to do so was not automatic.) This multiplied its foreign exchange contribution by five times, expanding world reserves and economizing on them by making the same reserves available to several countries. Since someone must be running a surplus if someone else is running a deficit, not everyone would be drawing on the pool at the same time.

The International Monetary Fund setup represents the viewpoint of the United States as expressed in the White Plan, authored by Harry Dexter White. The alternative plan was offered by England and called the Keynes Plan after its famous author. Keynes proposed a true international central bank with credit-creating powers that would create international reserves (variously known as "bancors" or "unitas") that were neither gold nor national currencies. This, however, represented a substantial surrender of one of the most basic components of national sovereignty, the power to coin money. The United States was not willing to make such a concession. In retrospect, Keynes' plan had several advantages. Proposed regulation on accumulation of bancors would put some pressure on surplus countries, a defect of the White Plan. Lack of dependence on particular national currencies and gold was a major advantage. The system did probably have more inflationary potential than did the White Plan, in that it would require the International Central Bank to exert a degree of self-restraint in monetary expansion rarely observed among national central bankers.

The International Monetary Fund began to encounter some difficulties in the mid-1950s that were probably to have been expected. The Fund had insufficient resources for several reasons. First, the quotas were based on 1937 data—a depression year; in the intervening 20 years, prices in world trade had risen 140 percent and volume 160 percent. Thus, both deficits and surpluses were larger. Second, simultaneous crises in several countries at once were more common than had been anticipated. Third, the dismantling of all capital controls and some trade controls in Europe expanded deficits and surpluses. Finally, the newly emerging nations (former colonies) of Africa and Asia were pursuing inflationary development strategies with the inevitable result of large and persistent balance-of-payments deficits. Devaluations were more frequent than expected (88 devaluations between 1949 and 1967), but the demand for reserves persisted. In response to a 1958 speech by Per Jacobssen, managing director of the fund, the 1959 meeting of the I.M.F. authorized a 60 percent expansion of quotas, increasing resources from $9 billion to $15 billion.

The International Monetary System hit its first major difficulties in the 1960s, as the beginnings of worldwide inflation coincided with the deterioration of the position of the dollar and the loss of gold from central banks to private hoarders. The early 1960s spawned many proposals for reform. Basically, they came down to several broad alternatives:

1. Revalue gold and restore it to a central place as a monetary reserve asset.
2. Find other key currencies besides the U.S. dollar.
3. Allow a greater degree of flexibility in currency prices than 1 percent of par.
4. Create international assets by the I.M.F. along the lines of the Keynes proposal.

This last was advocated by economist Robert Triffin of Yale, who differed from Keynes mainly by advocating limited rather than unlimited credit-creating power for the I.M.F. This proposal and variants thereof became known as the Keynes–Triffin Plan in the early 1960s and eventually resulted in the creation of SDRs in 1969.

Other developments in the 1960s also tended to undermine the International Monetary System and/or to put additional pressures on it. The formation of the inward looking European Economic Community, the isolation of the United states resulting from the war in Vietnam, the further impetus to trade from the Kennedy Round negotiations, and the beginning of worldwide inflation in the mid-1960s shook confidence in the system in general and the American dollar in particular. As reform proposals were aired, the prospect for devaluation of the dollar and the British pound and/or a general rise in the price of gold became more likely. At this point, a group of ten countries were maintaining the official price of gold at $35 an ounce, the price on which I.M.F. parities were based, by buying and selling (mostly selling) gold at that price in the London gold market to private purchasers. In 1968, a massive outflow of gold led to suspension of private gold sales and establishment of the two-tier gold market—an official price of $35 an ounce for central bank transaction and a market-determined private price. This was the prelude to the end of the Bretton Woods system.

The September 1969 meeting of the International Monetary Fund authorized the creation of special drawing rights as a supplementary source of international reserves. Only $3 billion worth of SDRs were authorized for an initial three-year period. Quotas were again expanded as had been done in 1959 and 1964. It was agreed that SDRs would only be created at times and in amounts to be approved by directors representing nations with 85 percent or more of the fund's quota, providing veto power to both the United States and the then six members of the European Economic Community.

During this period, the dollar was under considerable pressure. U.S. balance-of-payments deficits were large and growing—larger than could be justified by demand for additional international reserves. Rather than piling up dollars eagerly, foreign central banks were reluctantly accepting dollars to reduce the pressure for dollar devaluation. Some were turning in their dollars for gold in anticipation of devaluation. Private foreigners who had held dollars for transaction purposes were turning them in to their central banks for their own currency in expectation that the dollar would shortly be devalued. The United States was in a difficult situation. Devaluation would reward those who had turned dollars in for gold and penalize those allies who had been willing to accept and hold U.S. dollars. Domestic deflation (or even disinflation) was politically impossible in the midst of an unpopular war and an extensive social welfare program (The Great Society). Limited use of controls—mostly moral suasion ("See America First," "Buy American"), an interest equalization tax, and a proposed tourist tax that never made it through Congress—was a significant part of the U.S. response to the persistent deficit. The other options available to the United States were very limited. Any other country would have devalued under those circumstances, but the United States dollar was the kingpin of the Bretton Woods system, and it was widely feared that a dollar devaluation would take Bretton Woods down with it.

THE END OF BRETTON
WOODS: 1971 AND BEYOND

The United States was finally forced to respond to the huge deficits and the rapid repatriation of dollars from abroad and the piling up of unwanted dollars in foreign central banks. In August 1971, President Nixon announced a suspension of the gold convertibility of the dollar and a temporary 10 percent surcharge on imports (along with a wage-price freeze, part of a disinflationary package aimed at both home and abroad). This was widely and correctly viewed as a prelude to U.S. devaluation, which occurred in December 1971 in the Smithsonian Agreement. The dollar was devalued by 8 percent, raising the official price of gold to over $38.00, and the bands around parity were widened to $2\frac{1}{4}$ percent. It was hoped that these steps would be sufficient to give the system a breather. The higher price for gold increased the value of both U.S. and part of the I.M.F. reserves; the wider bands reduced the amount of balance-of-payments pressure on both deficit and surplus countries. Several countries began to float shortly after the Smithsonian Agreement, and the downward pressure on the dollar continued. (Floating was technically in violation of the I.M.F. articles of agreement, although Canada had floated its currency from 1952 to 1963 with the knowledge and reluctant consent of the I.M.F. The charter was not changed to permit floating and establish appropriate guidelines until the Jamaica Agreement in 1976.)

Prior to devaluation, the dollar had a unique attraction in a portfolio of assets. Its value was fixed, and it could be held in interest-bearing form. Once it, too, was vulnerable to capital loss, the asset demand for the dollar dropped substantially, and dollars began to return home to roost. This portfolio adjustment put further downward pressure on the dollar, which was devalued again just 14 months later, in February 1973. This devaluation raised the price of gold to $42 an ounce. Shortly thereafter, the U.S. dollar and a number of other major currencies began to float, and many of the nonfloating currencies were pegged to one that was, usually that of a major trading partner. February 1973 marked the end of Bretton Woods, although the International Monetary Fund continues to function in a number of important capacities.

BRETTON WOODS
IN RETROSPECT

The Bretton Woods system, like most man-made systems, was designed to solve the problems of the past rather than to anticipate and forestall the problems of the future. It did provide for orderly devaluations, reduce dependence on controls, provide resources for dealing with temporary deficits, promote free trade, and link the countries of the world together through somewhat stable exchange rates while providing some flexibility that the gold standard did not. Its drawbacks were numerous, but two in particular stand out: it had very little in the way of effective adjustment mechanisms, and it was unable to provide an adequate supply of international monetary reserves in a widely acceptable form. It may well be that no system could have done what the world asked of Bretton Woods. In a world where foreign exchange flows are sterilized, fundamental disequilibria ignored, and national sovereignty in the creation of money and the control of monetary and fiscal policy are safeguarded jealously, while at the same time lip service is paid to the notion of free trade and capital movements and efficient resource allocation, it is very likely that no system would have accomplished all these objectives.

In addition to the reserve and adjustment problem, the Bretton Woods system provided a golden opportunity for speculators at the expense of taxpayers; transmitted inflation and recession from country to country; misdirected capital flows by encouraging response to nominal rather than real interest differentials; and probably played some role, still not fully clear, in the acceleration of worldwide inflation in the late 1960s and early 1970s.

VESTIGES OF BRETTON WOODS IN THE LATE 1970S

The demise of Bretton Woods left some remains of the system that continue to function. A number of currencies are pegged to something—dollars, francs, pounds, SDRs, or a composite basket of currencies. (The SDR was defined originally as equivalent in value to one U.S. dollar. Since the dollar was twice devalued and then floated, the SDR is now defined as one pre-devaluation U.S. dollar. A currency tied to a floating currency will float with it, but a currency tied to SDRs is fixed in value.) International reserves continue to be important not only for those countries that peg their currencies—more than half the member countries—but also for those countries that are on a dirty float or managed float, which is the majority of the remaining I.M.F. member countries. The I.M.F., in fact, developed guidelines for currency surveillance in 1976, recognizing floating as a normal procedure and obligating members to keep the markets orderly and to intervene as necessary, always in a stabilizing direction.

Other events of the 1970s reduced the likelihood of an immediate return to a fixed rate regime. The massive shifting of assets and income flow patterns resulting from the oil price hike, the slow adjustment to the newly diminished asset role of the dollar, and the worldwide inflation that accelerated in the late 1970s were just a few of the factors that led to continuous readjustment of currency prices and thus discouraged return to a Bretton Woods–type system. Unless some way can be found out of the reserve asset bind, developing an internationally controlled asset that is universally acceptable in settlement of deficits and surpluses, it is unlikely that the world will return to a fixed rate system in the near future.

SUMMARY

The last of the four systems is the Bretton Woods system, established in 1944 and operated from 1946 to 1973. The system was designed to deal with the problems of the interwar period and was slow to respond to the very different situations of the postwar period. This system relies on reserves to settle balance-of-payments disequilibria and thus purports to accomplish three of the four goals—stable exchange rates, independence of monetary and fiscal policy, and absence of controls—at the expense of balance-of-payments equilibrium. Reserves are the first line of defense, with devaluation or revaluation a fallback in the case of a fundamental or persistent disequilibrium.

Participating countries establish a par value and intervene in the foreign exchange market to keep that par value within 1 percent either way, drawing on their own reserves or the pooled reserves at the I.M.F. as needed. The International Monetary Fund is an institution that maintains surveillance over exchange markets and provides loans of reserves to meet temporary deficits out of a pool of foreign exchange contributed by member countries. The I.M.F. is also consulted prior to major devaluations and notified after minor ones. Reserves consist of gold, key currencies (most commonly the U.S. dollar), I.M.F. drawing rights, and special drawing rights. The regular drawing rights are from the pool contributed by members, 25 percent in gold and/or dollars and 75 percent in their own currency. Special drawing rights are created by the I.M.F. and are international fiat money.

The advantages of this system are that it provides for relatively stable exchange rates with independent monetary and fiscal policy and limited resort to controls. The drawbacks are the problem of confidence in the major reserve asset, lack of satisfactory substitute reserve assets, speculative capital flows, gains to speculators from anticipated devaluation at the expense of taxpayers, massive rather than incremental changes, inadequate adjustment mechanisms, and transmission of cyclical fluctuations. There is some limited evidence that the expansion of reserves played a role in worldwide inflation, but the evidence is inconclusive.

Reserves expanded through the 1950s and 1960s by means of U.S. deficits, which created a crisis of confidence; the number of dollars outstanding began to outstrip the value of the U.S.-held gold stock for which they were supposed to be redeemable, raising the possibility of inconvertibility and/or devaluation of the dollar. Massive repatriation of dollars in the period 1969–1971 ultimately forced the devaluation of the dollar. Attempts to patch up the system with currency price adjustments and wider bands were not successful, and the Bretton Woods system finally collapsed in 1973. Vestiges of the system remain, with some currencies pegged, with rules for surveillance of currency prices, and with the lending role of the I.M.F. intact, but the nations of the world today are on a hodgepodge of systems dominated by modified floating.

KEY TERMS

adjustment mechanism
Bretton Woods

confidence
devaluation
Eurodollar
fundamental disequilibrium
International Monetary Fund
key currency
Keynes Plan
Keynes–Triffin Plan
liquidity
parity
quota (I.M.F.)
regular drawing rights
reserves
revaluation
scarce currency
SDRs
Smithsonian Agreement
speculation
transmission of inflation
White Plan

REVIEW QUESTIONS

1. What was the I.M.F. designed to accomplish? Why did the system break down?
2. Explain the difference between the Keynes Plan and the White Plan. What do you think would have happened if the Keynes Plan had been adopted?
3. Explain the relationship among confidence, liquidity, and adjustment under Bretton Woods; under the gold standard. Describe the differences.
4. In what sense is the Bretton Woods system a compromise between the gold standard and floating rates? What features of each does it preserve? What advantages and disadvantages of each does it carry over?
5. Using I.M.F. data, plot the relationship between international monetary reserves and the volume of world trade (either exports or imports); between both and the world price level. See if you can identify any current or lagged relationship. If you have the facilities and skills, try a regression, lagging the data for various amounts of time.

SUGGESTED READINGS

ALIBER, ROBERT Z., *The International Money Game,* 2nd ed., chaps. 1–7, 10. New York: Basic Books, 1976.

MEIER, GERALD,   *Problem of a World Monetary Order,* pp. 3–92 and pp. 97–210. New York: Oxford University Press, 1974.
STERN, CARL, JOHN MAKIN, and DENNIS LOGUE,   *Eurocurrencies and the International Monetary System.* Washington, D.C.: American Enterprise Institute, 1976.
YEAGER, LELAND B.,   *International Monetary Relations: Theory, History, and Policy,* 2nd ed., chaps. 19–32. New York: Harper & Row, 1976.

APPENDIX

The Eurodollar/Eurocurrency Market

One of the more striking developments of the Bretton Woods era was the development of what Robert Aliber calls "offshore money."[2] The more usual name is the Eurodollar or Eurocurrency market, and its development was a response to several factors: regulation of American banking, widespread private holdings of dollars, and an increased volume of transactions denominated in vehicle currencies, especially dollars. Although the market is often referred to as the Eurodollar market, there are also Europounds, Euromarks, Eurofrancs, and so on. Furthermore, the market extends well beyond Europe; one of the major centers of the so-called "Eurocurrency market" is Hong Kong!

The Eurocurrency market consists of deposits and loans that are denominated in a currency other than that of the country in which the bank is located—a deposit of dollars in a French bank of pounds sterling in a German bank would qualify. The deposit is repayable in that currency and the value of the deposit rises and falls with the value of that currency. Most often, the depositor is not of the same nationality as the currency being deposited either, although that is perfectly possible. A large part of the Eurodollar deposits in the 1970s were recycled petrodollars—payments for newly expensive oil imports.

Why would a German exporter deposit dollars in an account redeemable in dollars when it seems more logical to trade in the dollars for marks? You may recall the difficulties we encountered in Chapter 13 with classifying changes in foreign private dollar holdings for balance-of-payments purposes. Virtually all of that entry became Eurodollars. A number of reasons suggest themselves. The German exporter may anticipate a need for dollars for another transaction in the near future, and this deposit saves him the inconvience of dealing in the forward market while still earning interest. Currency speculation is another reason. Multinational corporations are active in both speculation and normal transactions demand for many currencies.

[2] Robert Aliber, *The International Money Game,* 2nd ed. (New York: Basic Books, 1976), chap. 7.

Bank regulation and interest differentials, however, probably account for the largest share of these deposits. American banking has until recently been strictly regulated with respect to interest payable, reserve requirements, and types of loans and investments permitted. European banks are generally less strictly controlled. If dollar deposits are attractive because the dollar is a strong currency and the forward demand is strong, and because inflation in the United States is relatively low and interest rates on dollar deposits fairly high, then there will be a demand for dollar deposits. But, if dollar deposits are available in European banks with a more favorable yield because of lower regulatory costs, then the dollar deposits will not show up in American banks but in European banks. This, in a nutshell, was the genesis of the Eurodollar market. These original dollar deposits then provided a base for expansion through loans and loan-originated deposits.

If American banks and European banks were subject to the same regulation, many of these deposits would have wound up in American banks, owned by foreigners, payable in dollars. This would have been recorded on the balance of payments as a short-term capital inflow, a normal financing transaction for a balance-of-payments deficit. The alternative for the foreigner would have been to convert the dollars to the home currency, in which case the dollars would have found their way to the foreign central bank, recorded in settlement account as changes in foreign official dollar holdings. The sudden development of the Eurodollar market between 1966 and the mid-1970s caught the balance-of-payments accountants without an adequate framework.

Concern has been expressed about the effect of the Eurodollar market on bank safety (Eurocurrency dealings were involved in the failure of the Franklin National Bank in the 1970s) and on world inflation, since looser reserve requirements allow the same monetary base to accommodate a larger money supply.

The growth of the Eurodollar market has been truly spectacular, from $9 billion in 1966 to over $250 billion just ten years later. The growth of this market depends on interest rates on Eurodollars being higher than yields on either American bank deposits or home currency deposits. This means that the differential regulation—on yields, reserves, and riskiness of loans—is the major source of the growth of the Eurocurrency market. A harmonization of regulations would probably reduce the demand for this type of deposit significantly, although in a world of floating exchange rates and a significant volume of transactions in vehicle currencies, the Eurodollar market is undoubtedly here to stay. The service it provides to currency speculators and to regular participants in international transactions has a value of its own that transcends its origins in regulatory differences.

The currency substitution alluded to in earlier chapters has undoubtedly been enhanced by the existence of Eurodollar markets, which simplify the process of realigning portfolios to adjust the mix of currencies represented. Thus, one effect of the growth of Eurodollars has been to increase currency substitutability and short-term capital mobility. This move in the direction of more integrated financial and capital markets has done much to increase the plausibility of the still-developing monetarist view of international monetary economics.

CHAPTER 20

Epilogue

The developments in international economics in the 37 years since the end of World War II have rewritten all the textbooks into almost unrecognizable forms. The institutions have changed. The International Monetary Fund, the World Bank, the General Agreement on Trade and Tariffs, the agencies of the United Nations, and all the various economic integration experiments—EEC, EFTA, COMECON, LAFTA, CACM—are new since World War II. The Bretton Woods experiment has come and gone, leaving vestiges of fixed rates and putting much of the world for the first time on a system of floating rates. The number of countries has exploded with the independence of former colonies, secessions, and reorganizations. The geography learned in elementary school in the late 1940s is totally irrelevant today; only the shapes of the continents remain the same. Trade barriers have been dismantled to all-time lows, and negotiations continue. The dollar acquired, enjoyed, and lost a position of dominance much as the pound sterling had done before, although the dollar remains a strong and popular currency. Multinational corporations entered the language, while cartels, an old institution, acquired a new lease on life with the startling success of OPEC.

Paralleling these institutional developments have been theoretical and empirical developments extending our knowledge of how the system of international trade and finance operates in a variety of institutional frameworks. The Leontief study of the Heckscher–Ohlin proposition in 1957 spawned a whole new literature, both theoretical and empirical, examining the determination of the patterns of trade. The rise of real world customs unions of various types led to theoretical and empirical extensions of the customs unions literature. The development of multinationals, similarly, gave rise to a considerable literature on why they go abroad, what their effects are, what policy implications they give rise to, and an extensive management literature on the practical side of running a multinational. The revival of cartels in OPEC not only generated experimental copies but considerable revision of our understanding of how cartels work and under what conditions they can be expected to succeed. The great waves of migration that followed World War II, followed by substantial flows of capital among countries, renewed interest in the study of factor mobility and the substitutability among factor movements of goods and services.

On the monetary side, the expansion in our understanding has similarly paralleled the revolution in institutional developments. The Keynesian revolution has been overtaken by a monetarist counterrevolution that is in the process of developing a synthesis of our understanding of how income, prices, employment, and interest rates are determined. The model in Chapters 14 and 15 is an imperfect description of this yet incomplete synthesis. International economists have been aware since the time of David Hume and specie flow of the importance of feedback mechanisms. That awareness is penetrating macroeconomics, so that a literature of open economy macroeconomics is beginning to develop and have an impact on undergraduate students. No longer will intermediate macroeconomics be able to focus on the closed economy, nor can international economics take a simple Keynesian income determination model without prices and graft the foreign sector onto it, as we used to do. Monetarists have also forced us to rethink the balance-of-payments accounts, while external developments—floating rates— have altered our emphasis on overall balance. Floating rates have also given us a chance to test some of the theoretical propositions about the effects of floating rates on capital flows, transmission of inflation, volume of trade, and other important variables. The Bretton Woods experiment itself provided a wealth of experience on which to draw to better understand and design international monetary arrangements.

This brief summary does not begin to exhaust the theoretical, empirical, and institutional developments that have revolutionized internationl economics in recent years, but it does indicate where we have been and, perhaps, where we are going. The 1980s are no more immune to turbulent change than were the previous three decades. What might we anticipate in the next two decades?

While theoretical developments are hard to anticipate, most economists are at least looking forward to a better synthesis of open economy macroeconomics—the area with which we wrestled in Chapters 14 and 15.

Much progress has been made in our understanding of the interrelationship between the foreign sector and the domestic economy, but much remains to be done.

On the empirical side, more experience with floating rates should enable economists to better evaluate the impact of this system on interest rates, capital flows, inflation, transmission of business cycles, and exchange rate volatility. At the same time, there will probably be renewed pressure for the restoration of some type of fixed rate system. If it occurs, the lesson of Bretton Woods is that only a system based on an international medium of exchange can long survive, which means either gold or international flat money issued in sufficient quantities by the International Monetary Fund. A return to gold is unlikely because of the severe constraints it places on independent monetary policy. An international money will run into a refusal to surrender that much sovereignty. So restoration of fixed rates must await a greater degree of international community than can be observed at present.

Concern about worldwide inflation, however, may lead to a greater harmonization of domestic monetary and fiscal policies than exists at present; that, in turn, may provide the basis for a return to a modified fixed rate system in the more distant future. There is still a strong and frustrated constituency for fixed rates, although their voices have been somewhat muted since floating rates have not proved as disastrous as anticipated.

The economic integration movement has probably peaked, with the EEC being the major survivor. Other forms of integration based on narrower common interests have somewhat displaced customs unions. Cartels and multinationals serve some of the same functions. Lower tariff barriers in the industrial world as a result of the Kennedy and Tokyo Rounds have reduced the "us-them" distinction, which once held customs unions together. In a world of low tariffs, the raison-d'etre of customs unions is much weaker.

We can expect continued efforts to reduced tariffs and nontariff barriers, but the marginal cost of doing so is rising while the marginal benefit is diminishing; therefore, further tariff NTB negotiations will be more difficult. The losers at home are becoming more vocal and suffering greater losses while the marginal gains are shrinking. Thus, the momentum of the trade liberalization movement is diminishing.

The problems of the less developed countries have been continuously pushed to the background while "more important" issues were being resolved—first European recovery and the Cold War, then Vietnam, the crisis of the international monetary system, the American response to the EEC, and finally OPEC. The Tokyo Round was the first major confrontation between the developed and the less developed countries. Cartels or price supports for primary products, tariff preferences for simple manufactures, and economic aid are on the agenda for the 1980s.

In addition to these forecasts, there are likely to be developments we have not anticipated. Certainly, no one foresaw OPEC, the demise of Bretton

Woods, the formation of the EEC, or other startling developments long in advance, although hindsight indicated that the germs were there long before the actual development took place. There is no telling what the next two decades will bring, but if they are as hectic as the last three, international economists will have no difficulty in finding grist for their intellectual mills. International economics has been, is, and will continue to be an exciting area in which to think, work, and study. It is my hope that this introduction to the subject has merely whetted your appetite and that you will continue to be interested, curious, and involved in this field of study in some way for many years to come.

Index